COMBAT AV

Flight Path 1

COMBAT AVIATION

Flight Path 1968-2018

Kishore Kumar Khera

KNOWLEDGE WORLD
KW Publishers Pvt Ltd
New Delhi

MANOHAR PARRIKAR
idsa
MANOHAR PARRIKAR INSTITUTE FOR DEFENCE STUDIES AND ANALYSES
मनोहर पर्रिकर रक्षा अध्ययन एवं विश्लेषण संस्थान

Manohar Parrikar Institute for Defence Studies and Analyses
No. 1, Development Enclave, Delhi Cantt.
New Delhi-110 010
Phone: +91-11-26717983
Website: www.idsa.in

ISBN 978-93-89137-44-6 Hardback

Published in India by Kalpana Shukla

KW Publishers Pvt Ltd
4676/21, First Floor, Ansari Road
Daryaganj, New Delhi 110 002
Phone: +91 11 23263498/43528107
Marketing: kw@kwpub.com
Editorial: production@kwpub.com
Website: www.kwpub.com

Printed and bound in India

Dedicated to

My Parents
for giving me my life,

My Parents-in-laws
for giving me my wife;

My Wife
for giving meaning to my life,

My Children
for always supporting my wife.

Contents

List of Figures, Tables and Maps ix

Acknowledgements xiii

Abbreviations xiv

Introduction: Flight Plan xx

Part I Facets of Combat Aviation

1. Start, Taxy and Take Off 3
2. Scanning Rear Airspace: Historical Perspective of Combat Aviation 17
3. Mission Plan: Imperatives of Combat Aviation Application 33

Part II Five Decades Trajectory of Combat Aviation 1968-2018

4. Cruise Climb – Range Descent: Combat Aircraft Inventory (1968-2018) 51
5. Changing Mission Profile: Technological Innovations in Combat Aviation 71
6. Trigger Live: Air-Launched Weapons: Expanding Capabilities of Combat Aviation 93
7. Mission Buddies: Evolving Alternatives and Combat Enablers 116
8. Top View: Mapping Combat Aircraft Inventory 151

Part III Dynamics of Combat Aviation

9. Cockpit View: Human-Technology Interface and Training 167

10. Gravy Check: Economics of Combat Aviation 193

11. Frontal Scan: Emerging Contours in the Field of Combat Aviation 220

Part IV Combat Aviation Trajectory in India

12. Close Quarters: Combat Aviation Trajectory in India 239

13. Wings and Wheels: India's Internal Factors 257

14. Dry Cranking Engine: Indian Indigenous Defence Industry 278

15. Touch Down 292

Annexures

1. Team Concept 301
2. Battle Space Transparency Spectrum and Techniques 303
3. Threat and Capability - Definitions and Dimensions 308
4. Force Structure Planning Process 311
5. Geopolitics and Military Expenditure 317
6. Development of UK Combat Air Strategy 322
7. Trends in Military Expenditure in Africa 326
8. India's Combat Aircraft Fleet 341

Index 345

List of Figures, Tables and Maps

Figures

4.1:	Total Combat Aircraft in the World from 1968-2018	52
4.2:	Total Types of Combat Aircraft in the World from 1968-2018	53
4.3:	Number of Countries with Combat Aircraft in the World from 1968-2017	55
4.4:	Number of Countries with Combat Aircraft in the World 2018	56
4.5:	Average Number of Combat Aircraft/Country in the World 2018	56
4.6:	Number of Countries with Combat Aircraft in the World in 2018	57
4.7:	Track of the Top Four Nations with the Number of Combat Aircraft in the World from 1968-2017	58
4.8:	Number of Countries with Combat Aircraft in the World in 1968-2017	60
4.9:	Continental Distribution of Combat Aircraft in the World in 1968-2018	61
4.10:	Continental Share of Combat Aircraft in the World in 1968 and 2018	62
4.11:	Percentage Reduction of Combat Aircraft Strength from Peak Strength	63
4.12:	Share of Manufacture of Combat Aircraft of the World	64
4.13:	Chinese Aircraft Industry Performance	65
4.14:	Number of Employees in Chinese Aircraft Industry	66
4.15:	Number of Employees in Hindustan Aeronautical Limited, India	66
4.16:	Relative Strength of Combat Aircraft of the World	68
4.17:	Annual Task for Boeing Company and Lockheed Martin related to Manufacturing/Modification of Combat Aircraft F18/F15 and F16 respectively	68

5.1: Composite Material Share in Structural Weight of Combat Aircraft 73
5.2: MiG-21 and F16 Inventories of the World 79
5.3: Plan and Production of F-22 for the USAF 86
5.4: F-22 Programme Cost Breakdown 86
6.1: Types of Air-to-Surface Missiles in the World 1991-2017 99
6.2: Types of Air-to-Surface Missiles in the World 1991-2017 100
6.3: Effective Range of Air-to-Surface Missiles of the World 102
6.4: Change in Air-to-Surface Missiles Attributes 1991-2017 103
6.5: Kurtosis Analysis of Air-to-Surface Missiles of the World 1991-2017 103
6.6: Air-to-Surface Missiles Matrix of the World 1991-2017 104
6.7: Country-wise Air-to-Surface Missile Matrix of the World 1991-2017 105
6.8: Air-to-Surface Missile Manufacturing Countries of the World 1991-2017 106
6.9: Air to Air Missiles Composition 1991 and 2017 109
6.10: Lethal Range of Air-to-Air Missiles 110
6.11: Lethal Range of Air-to-Air Missiles 110
6.12: Countries Manufacturing Air-to-Air Missiles 111
6.13: World Air-to-Air Missile Matrix 1991 111
6.14: World Air-to-Air Missile Matrix 2017 112
7.1: 2019 US Defence Budget Demand for Aircraft 126
7.2: AEW&C Inventory 2018 132
7.3: Countries with Combat Aircraft and Aerial Refuellers 1998 and 2018 135
7.4: Aerial Refuellers Inventory 1998 and 2018 136
7.5: Countries with Combat Aircraft and Aerial Refuellers 1998 and 2018 137
7.6: USAF Current Force Structure 139
7.7: USAF Accretion Plan 140
7.8: USAF Planned Force Structure 141
7.9: USAF Accretion Plan 142
7.10: Number of Aircraft in the USAF 1950-2008 143
7.11: Schematic Representation of USAF Expansion Plan 144
8.1: Worldwide Arms Deliveries from 1989-1996 in million $ at 1996 Prices 155

8.2:	Worldwide Arms Deliveries from 1989-1996 in million $ at 1996 Prices	156
8.3:	Worldwide Arms Deliveries from 1997-2004 in million $ at 2004 Prices	157
8.4:	Worldwide Arms Deliveries from 1997-2004 in million $ at 2004 Prices	157
8.5:	Worldwide Arms Deliveries from 1989-2015 in million $ at 2015 Prices	158
10.1:	World Defence Expenditure as the percentage of Gross Domestic Production	195
10.2:	World Defence Expenditure as the percentage of Gross Domestic Production	197
10.3:	World Defence Expenditure as the percentage of Gross Domestic Production and number of Combat Aircraft in the World	198
10.4:	World Defence Expenditure as the percentage of Gross Domestic Production and Number of Combat Aircraft in 19 Countries with more than 200 Combat Aircraft in 2018	198
10.5:	World Arms Trade in 1968	200
10.6:	World Arms Trade in 1993	201
10.7:	World Arms Trade in 2017	201
10.8:	World Arms Trade in 1968-2017	201
10.9:	Value of World Arms Trade in 1968-2017	202
10.10:	Share of the Value of Aircraft in World Arms Trade in 1968-2017	203
10.11:	Arms Imports by India in 1968-2017	203
10.12:	Indian Share in World Arms Imports 1968-2017	205
10.13:	Major Arms Importers 2017	205
10.14:	Major Arms Importers 1968-2017	206
10.15:	Major Arms Exporters 2017	206
10.16:	Operational Cost per Flying Hour (in US $) for the United States Air Force from 2008-2012	210
11.1:	Satellites in Orbit	224
11.2:	Forecast Strength of Combat Aircraft in the World	230

12.1: Government Authorisation of Combat Squadrons for Indian Air Force 242
12.2: Government Authorisation of Combat Squadrons for Indian Air Force 242
12.3: Aircraft Accident Rate per 10,000 Flying hours for the Indian Air Force 247
12.4: Share of Top 19 Countries and India in World Combat Aircraft Inventory 249
12.5: Projected Indian Combat Aircraft Strength 2018-2047 250
14.1: HAL-Value of Production/Manpower Cost 285
An 6.1: Military Expenditure 2017 in US Dollars 319
An 7.1: Military Expenditure as the Share of Government Expenditure 327
An 7.2: Average Per Capita Military Expenditure (at current US $ rate) 328
An 7.3: Military Expenditure as Share of GDP 329
An 7.4: Military Expenditure in Africa from 1988-2017 329
An 7.5: Military Expenditure in Africa in 2018 330
An 8.1: IAF Combat Aircraft Squadrons 343

Tables

3.1: Combat Aircraft Potential Assessment Parameters 45
5.1: The Contrast in Material Application Proportions of Some Combat Aircraft 73
5.2: Classification of Combat Aircraft 76
9.1: Comparison of Results of Events in 2008 and 2016 Olympic Games 176
12.1: Combat Aviation Fleet in the Region 252
13.1: Classification of IAF Combat Aircraft 261
13.2: Combat Aircraft Requirement Matrix until 2039 268
14.1: Major Contracts for Aerial Warfare and Training Assets Imported by India since 2000 278

Map

4.1: Map showing 19 countries with more than 200 Combat aircraft in 2018 60

Acknowledgements

Institutions

Indian Air Force
Manohar Parrikar Institute of Defence Studies and Analyses,
New Delhi

Communities

Air Warriors and Air Veterans

Individuals

Adil Rasheed
Alok Deb
Amit Vij
Ashok Mitra
Atul Pant
Bhawna Mungali
Chandra Mohan Thakur
G Balachandran
Hitakshi
Neha Kohli
S Kalyanaraman
S. Samuel C. Rajiv
Shruti Pandalai
Umesh Chandra Jha
Vikas Gupta
Vinay Kaushal
Vivek Chadha
Vivek Dhankar
Vivek Kaushik

The two anonymous referees for their valuable comments and suggestions on the draft manuscript.

I am solely responsible for any error in this publication.

Abbreviations

A2/AD	Anti-Access/Area Denial
A4M	All-Aspect Air-to-Air Missiles
AAH	Armed and Attack Helicopters
AAM	Air-to-Air Missile
ABP	Assumption-Based Planning
ADF	Automatic Direction Finder
AEHF	Advanced Extremely High Frequency
AEW&C	Airborne Early Warning and Control
AI	Air Interception
ALCM	Air-Launched Cruise Missiles
AMRAAM	Advanced Medium Range Air-to-Air Missile
ARRW	Air-launched Rapid Response Weapon
ASM	Anti-Shipping Missile
ASPJ	Airborne Self-Protection Jammers
ASQR	Air Staff Qualitative Requirements
ASTE	Aircraft and Systems Testing Establishment
ATF	Aviation Turbine Fuel
AU	African Union
AUW	All Up Weight
AWACS	Airborne Warning and Aircraft Control Systems
BAS	Battlefield Air Strikes
BDA	Bomb Damage Assessment
BDF	Botswana Defence Force
BH	Boko Haram
BRI	Belt and Road Initiative
BTCS	Battle space Transparency and Control Systems
BVR	Beyond Visual Range

C2	Command and Control
C2ISR	Command and Control, Intelligence, Surveillance and Reconnaissance
CAIDB	Combat Aircraft Inventory Data Base
CAS	Combat Air Strategy/Close Air Support
CBM	Confidence-Building Measures
CBP	Capability-Based Planning
CBRN	Chemical, Biological, Radiological, Nuclear
CCM	Close Combat Missile
CDF	Coastal Defence Flights
CEMILAC	Centre for Military Airworthiness and Certification
CEP	Circular Error of Probability
CFRP	Carbon Fibre Reinforced Plastics
CIWS	Close-In Weapon Systems
CL	Calendar Life
CL20	China Lake 20
CNC	Contract Negotiations Committee
COCOMs	Combatant Commanders
CODE	Collaborative Operations in Denied Environment
COG	Centre of Gravity
COIN	Counter Insurgency
CPSS	Computerised Pilot Selection System
CRPF	Central Reserve Police Force
CSAR	Combat Search and Rescue
CTO	Counter Transparency Operations
DARPA	Defense Advanced Research Projects Agency
DCB	Ditch Cum Bund
DEAD	Destruction of Enemy Air Defence
DEW	Directed Energy Weapons
DME	Distance Measuring Equipment
DMPI	Desired Mean Point of Impact
DPP	Defence Procurement Procedure
DRDO	Defence Research and Development Organisation
EBO	Effects Based Operations
ECM	Electronic Counter Measure
EEZ	Exclusive Economic Zone

EM	Electromagnetic
ETA	Estimated Time of Arrival
EU	European Union
EW	Electronic Warfare
FCS	Flight Control Systems
FLIR	Forward-Looking Infra-Red
FRA	Flight Refuelling Aircraft
GA	Ground Attack
GHE	Ground Handling Equipment
GOI	Government of India
GPS	Global Positioning System
GSE	Ground Support Equipment
GWOT	Global War on Terror
HAHTO	High Altitude and High-Temperature Operations
HAL	Hindustan Aeronautics Limited
HAS	Hardened Aircraft Shelters
HCWS	Hypersonic Conventional Strike Weapon
HMS	Helmet Mounted Sights
HNIW	Hexanitrohexaazaisowurtzitane
HUD	Head-Up Display
IADS	Integrated Air Defence System
IAF	Indian Air Force
IDSA	Institute of Defence Studies and Analyses
IED	Improvised Explosive Devices
IIR	Imaging Infra-Red
ILS	Instrument Landing System
INS	Inertial Navigation Systems
IR	Infra-Red
ISR	Intelligence, Reconnaissance and Surveillance
ISRO	Indian Space Research Organisation
IVTT	Inter-Valley Troop Transfer
JMEM	Joint Munitions Effectiveness Manual
LCA	Light Combat Aircraft
LCC	Life Cycle Cost
LO	Low Observability
LOC	Line of Control

LRIP	Low Rate Initial Production
LVC	Live/Virtual/Constructive
MAD	Mutual Assured Destruction
MAE	Mean Area of Effectiveness
MANPADS	Man-Portable Air Defence System
MCR	Mission Capable Rate
MMRCA	Medium Multi-Role Combat Aircraft
MMW	Millimetre Wave
MOAB	Massive Ordnance Air Blast
MOD	Ministry of Defence
MR	Maintenance Reserves
MRCA	Multi-Role Combat Aircraft
MTBF	Mean Time Between Failures
NAF	Nigerian Air Force
NMO	National Military Objectives
NRSA	National Security Risk Assessment
NSC	National Security Council
OCU	Operational Conversion Units
OEM	Original Equipment Manufacturer
ORBAT	Order of Battle
OTR	Over Target Requirement
PAF	Pakistan Air Force
PAUC	Programme Acquisition Unit Cost
PFM	Pre-Flight Message
PLAAF	People's Liberation Army Air Force
POK	Pakistan-Occupied Kashmir
POW	Prisoners of War
QRSAM	Quick Reaction Surface-to-Air Missiles
R&D	Research and Development
RAS	Robotic and Autonomous Systems
RCMA	Regional Centres for Military Airworthiness
RCS	Radar Cross Section
REE	Range and Endurance Enhancers
RFI	Request for Information
RLG	Ring Laser Gyros
ROA	Radius of Action

RWR	Radar Warning Receiver
SA	Situational Awareness
SAGW	Surface-to-Air Guided Weapons
SAM	Surface-to-Air Missiles
SAR	Synthetic Aperture Radars
SDR	Software-Defined Radio
SEAD	Suppression of Enemy Air Defence
SEPC	Staff Equipment Policy Committee
SFC	Specific Fuel Consumption
SIC	System Induction Costs
SIGINT	Signals Intelligence
SIPRI	Stockholm International Peace Research Institute
SLOC	Sea Lanes of Communication
SOW	Strike Off Wastage
SP	Strategic Partnership
SP/IPA	Strategic Partner/ Indian Production Agency
SSB	Services Selection Boards
SSKP	Single Shot Kill Probability
SSM	Surface to Surface Missiles
STOVL	Short-Take-Off Vertical-Landing
TACAN	Tactical Air Navigation
TACDE	Tactics and Combat Development Establishment
TBA	Tactical Battle Area
TBO	Time Between Overhaul
TBP	Threat-Based Planning
TEAM	Thoughts, Equipment, Application, and Management
TEZ	Target Engagement Zone
TODS	Transparency, Offensive, Defensive and Support System
TOT	Transfer of Technology
TTL	Total Technical Life
TTU	Target Towing Units
UAS	Unmanned Aerial System
UAV	Unmanned Aerial Vehicles
UCAV	Unmanned Combat Aerial Vehicles
UE	Unit Establishment

UGV	Unmanned Ground Vehicles
UMS	Unmanned Maritime Systems
USAF	United States Air Force
VL	Vertical Launch
VOR	Very High-Frequency Omni Directional Range
WASP	Weapon Advisory for Staff Planning
WER	Weapon Effective Range
WPRE	Weapon Precision and Range Enhancers
WSO	Weapon System Operators
XDR	Extended Data Rate

Introduction: Flight Plan

Aviation has been a part of military's kinetic capability for over a century now with combat aircraft playing a pivotal role in many wars. The conceptual and capability changes in a kinetic force remain intertwined with the prevailing and emerging security scenario. Combat aviation, a key kinetic capability, being technology-dependent, needs continuous re-equipping and upgradation. The force structure and organization too need to adapt for an optimal exploitation of available capability. Combat airpower has transformed in the last five decades and expanded its capability in all critical facets. With the changing character of war, there is a need to relook at the capability growth plan for combat airpower for it to be relevant in future. With finite financial outlays, rebalancing various facets of airpower is essential to achieve the desired end goal. This work attempts to answer specific questions. How has combat aviation evolved in the last fifty years? Will combat aviation retain its relevance as a key player in kinetic force application? What role will it play in future?

Combat aircraft, a powerful component of military strength, need a large resource investment in procurement and operations. The world had around 18,000 combat aircraft in 1968 and fifty years later the combat aircraft inventory is again almost at that level today. In five decades, the combat aircraft inventory peaked to near 38,000 in 1988. Changes in the geopolitical landscape, altering character of war, evolving technology and emerging alternatives led to its gradual decline thereafter. Today, there are 106 countries in the world that own and operate around 80 types of approximately 18,000 combat aircraft. But, there are only 19 countries that have more than 200 combat aircraft in their inventories. In this book, the available data of the combat aircraft inventory of the world is analysed for the trends and probable reasons for changes in the holdings before predicting the future trajectory of manned combat aircraft. Additionally, the role of combat aircraft and its interplay with various tenets of Indian air power capability and likely future is discussed.

The book is divided into four parts. In the first part, various facets of combat aviation including definitional aspects, force application history and its methodology are deliberated. In the next part, the trajectory of combat aviation is mapped with specific details of combat aircraft inventory from 1968 to 2018. This section discusses three major factors that impinge on the combat aircraft employment – weapons, alternatives and enablers. Holistic trend analysis and plausible reasons thereof too form part of this section. In the third part, the dynamics of combat aviation covers human resources, financial aspects and emerging trends. A specific case of combat aviation in India is covered in the last part before the final touchdown.

PART I

Facets of Combat Aviation

1. Start, Taxy and Take Off

The armed forces are an effective instrument of a country's political will. Invariably, these forces operate in the realm of uncertainty and are prepared to deal with the confusion associated with war. The fact is, wars produce only victors and vanquished. That is when the kinetic force application is the primary element employed. An analysis of ongoing conflicts across the world indicates that the operational environment, and consequently the force application methods, are transforming. Technology has shaped and improved the operational environment in five critical aspects: battlespace transparency, communication, enhanced effective weapon range, precision targeting, and mobility speed. While these changes have enlarged the kinetic battlespace, the induction of non-kinetic tools has transformed conflicts into a multi-domain multi-dimensional continuous process. Hence, it is difficult to identify the enemy or his intent. Even more difficult is the task to precisely mark the beginning or an end of a conflict. The threats have evolved with advances in technology and communication. Threats that were earlier contained within national boundaries have now become transnational and ideational challenges, which respect neither state sovereignty nor existing governance structures. Hybrid war is a reality and binary outcomes of war are waning.

Aviation has been a part of military kinetic capability for over a century now with combat aircraft playing a pivotal role in many wars since then. Combat airpower has positioned itself to deliver the punch that today's geopolitics may require: swift, deep, effective, precise and contained in terms of collateral. With the changing character of war, there is a need to relook at the capability growth plan for combat airpower for it to be relevant in future. With finite financial outlays, rebalancing various facets of airpower is essential to achieve the desired end goal.

With dynamic changes in the operational environment, the old model of creating self-sufficient independent combat units needs a re-visit. Independent units allowed field commanders a great deal of autonomy to wage their battles. Each unit was assigned a small and specific mission. These small tasks were part of a larger design but the implications of individual battles were rarely known to field operators. The changes in the operational environment have necessitated that a holistic assessment and reassessment be carried out to match or outpace the conflict. Achieving coherence of all small targets for individual units with the evolving big picture, is a difficult task. Thus, now, the battle primarily needs to be orchestrated at a higher level for the enlarged battle space so that the available and useable force can be optimally utilised to achieve the desired goals. This calls for restructuring the way to control the battle space.

The Indian security environment has changed considerably in the last two decades. Peace is elusive and various tenets of hybrid war continue to operate.[1] In this 'no peace, no war' situation, the Indian Air Force (IAF), as a kinetic tool, has undergone many changes to remain relevant in the evolving operational environment. While the character of warfare has transformed, our structures and the capability development model are half a century behind current times. Recognising the transnational nature of threats today, if we do not make a concerted effort to catch up in certain domains, the surprise will be shocking. In any case, except 1971, in all major conflicts thus far, the Indian armed forces have been comprehensively surprised. A well-planned mission in 1971 did bring us an unprecedented victory and 93,000 Prisoners of War (POW).

In a developing country like India, a contest for sharing resources is fierce. Only a small part can be earmarked for defence and security. These resources are finite and need to be utilised to develop capabilities that will protect us from disasters. Going by existing structures, the Indian armed forces are too focused on offensive capabilities as a method of conventional deterrence. Under these challenging circumstances, combat aviation has to evolve. As stated succinctly by a veteran fighter pilot Air Cmde Ramesh V Phadke:

> … there has also been excessive emphasis on the numbers of fighter squadrons and insistence on hi-tech equipment, rather than on new and innovative tactics and strategies, and suitable organisation for their employment.[2]

While the challenges confronting India have multiplied, a cohesive response to them has remained elusive. The changing character of conflict and battle space calls for a changed approach. With each arm constructing frameworks of cooperation for combat, it is time to exchange ideas on countering evolving threats which will define an Indian approach to this issue. Inconsistencies in the combat approach have been exploited considerably and have resulted in frequent failures at the tactical, operational and strategic levels. At this juncture, the Indian Armed Forces must re-evaluate the entire gamut of war fighting. For example, without the requisite battle space transparency, we may not be in a position to employ our offensive capability efficiently. Similarly, new facets of communication, quick mobility, and longer-range weapons need to be synergised in the operational matrix. This can only happen when we change the way we intend to fight. A smaller offensive capability with requisite battle space transparency may be a more suitable solution at a lower resource cost. Additionally, the armed forces need to enforce the concept of assigning responsibility and ensuring accountability within their domains.

Thus, a coherent approach is necessary to mitigate our current and future challenges. To evaluate options, four significant strands that need consideration are: Thoughts, Equipment, Application, and Management (TEAM) (see Annexure 1). The concept of TEAM can assist in developing a well-defined plan and optimise the development of India's military capability to be future-ready. With this direction in mind, the idea is to take the first step of comprehending and evaluating the future trajectory of our armed forces. Thus, in this context, the broad theme is: "Is it time for the armed forces to ameliorate their TEAM?" And this work attempts to answer specific questions. Will combat aviation retain its relevance as a key player in kinetic force application? How has combat aviation evolved in the last fifty years and what role will it play in future? Technological advancement in military aviation in terms of propulsion, control designs, avionics for navigation, and attack systems along with weaponeering have turned aircraft into a complete combat system. The most profound impact of technology is on aircraft deployed for weapon delivery. The standoff ranges for weapon delivery have gone beyond 100 km, yet an accuracy of targeting within three to five meters is retained. Owing to its ability to shape the battle space, combat aircraft is one of the most sought-after military hardware. Therefore, the prime focus of this book is on combat aircraft that have weapon delivery as their primary task.

Framework

The absolute number of combat aircraft in the world has seen a downward trend in the last three decades, from a high of over 38,000 in 1988 under 18,000 as of 2018. Escalating costs and timelines of development of new platforms have shifted focus to the incorporation of new capabilities on existing aircraft, thus leading to a reduction in types of platforms. This study presents data on the worldwide inventory of combat aircraft and thereafter analyses the data, looking for probable reasons and factors before assessing the Indian scenario and emerging trends therein.

Definition

The definition of combat aircraft used in different parts of the world varies. However, the United Nations defines a combat aircraft as having:

> Fixed-wing or variable-geometry wing aircraft designed, equipped or modified to engage targets by employing guided missiles, unguided rockets, bombs, guns, cannons, or other weapons of destruction, including versions of these aircraft which perform specialized electronic warfare, suppression of air defence or reconnaissance missions. The term "combat aircraft" does not

include primary trainer aircraft, unless designed, equipped or modified as described above.[3]

For the collation of data and analyses, a fixed-wing aircraft primarily employed as a weapon platform has been classified as a combat aircraft in consonance with the United Nations' definition. Since inception, the performance of combat aircraft has undergone major changes in terms of speed, manoeuvrability, weapon carriage capacity, onboard sensors, communication systems and data links, Radar Cross Section (RCS), weapon aiming and navigation systems. Today, in different regions of the world, a wide range of aircraft meet this definition criteria, from the low subsonic low load-carrying aircraft to supersonic jets, from aircraft that practically overfly the target while delivering air-to- surface weapons to a range of fifth-generation aircraft capable of launching weapons on a target hundreds of kilometres away. Amongst various states, a wide technological gap exists in this arena. Therefore, using the data to establish the numerical equivalence relationship between various operators, needs to be carried out cautiously.

Observation Period

The functional life of an aviation asset is normally defined in terms of Total Technical Life (TTL) or Calendar Life (CL). The TTL could be a function of the number of hours flown or the number of events of aviation activity. For example, the life of the airframe of an aircraft could be limited by the number of hours it can fly or by the number of landings or any other similar criteria. While CL is life of an aviation asset from its certification date till a pre defined time period. Completion of TTL is primarily a function of rate and quality of utilisation, and ideally should coincide with or be before the completion of CL. The functional life of a combat aircraft varies from 20 to 40 years based on its structure, performance and utilisation quality and rate. To achieve a holistic inventory trend, it, is therefore, imperative that the analysis period encompasses this range completely.

Operational relevance is another factor that impinges on the functional life of a combat aircraft. The operating environment can change with one technological breakthrough. Induction of Air-to-Air Missile (AAM)-equipped combat aircraft in the conflict zone drastically diminished the operational relevance of aircraft equipped with only guns as air-to-air weapons, is one such example. Going with the assertion of military theorist Brigadier Richard Simpkin[4] "for good reason for this rule-of-the thumb figure of 50 years" is apt to assess operational environmental changes. Given all these factors, a period of 50 years from 1968 to 2018 for data collation for analysis is considered apt and in consonance with both the above-mentioned factors. Historically too, this period is significant. The Royal Air Force UK was the first independent air arm established in 1918. In the next 50 years, combat aviation established itself as a significant element in war. The analysis period covers the next 50 years.

Data Span and Sources

Barring aircraft manufacturers and states, there are practically no operators of combat aircraft with an exception of very short time operations by certain non-state actors. The data span in the book covers all operators of combat aircraft of the world. Owing to the sensitive nature of information, data collated from open sources may be at variance with the actual inventory. Being a large population survey, the error in actual data is likely to be normally distributed over various countries and over the planned timeline of 50 years. However, the margin of error is not expected to have a major impact on the trend lines and on the analysis of the data based on the trends. Data has been collected for 50 years from 1968-2018 with specific additional reference points at an interval of five years. The time interval of five years was selected keeping in mind the average calendar life of a combat aircraft and timelines for induction of a new combat aircraft. This time interval gives the requisite data fidelity to assess the trends. For the period 1968 to 2018, data has been collected from the *United Nations Register of Conventional Arms,*[5] *The Military Balance*[6] published by the International Institute for Strategic Studies, *Jane's Year Books,*[7] websites and publications of the Ministries of Defence and armed forces of various countries, and websites and publications of various aircraft manufacturers. The collected data has resulted in a compilation of the Combat Aircraft Inventory Data Base (CAIDB) and this resource is utilised for the production of various graphs.

Genesis of Aviation and Combat Aviation

Man always wanted to fly like birds. A fatal attempt to fly by Bladud, the ninth King of Britain from the Temple of Apollo in Trinnavannum, London using wings covered with feathers around 843 BC, just shows how long the human race has taken to master the art of flying.[8] Many simple and complicated but failed attempts later, the human quest for the skies fructified with hot air balloons beginning in the late 18th century after Father Bartolomeu de Gusmao demonstrated a small model of the hot air balloon that lifted to 3.5 m on August 8, 1709.[9] Jacques Alexandre, Cesar Charles and M. Robert became the first men to make a free flight in a hydrogen-filled balloon covering a distance of 43 km from Les Tuileries to Nesles in France.[10] This concept was low on range, speed, endurance, control, and safety parameters. More than a century later, in December 1903, the Wright Brothers managed a short but path-breaking first controlled flight of a heavier-than-air machine.[11] After this proof of the concept of aircraft, a lot of effort was devoted to stretch the flight duration and enhance control of the machine. As the technology matured and the safety record improved, this ability quickly found its way onto the battlefield. The aircraft permitted an unprecedented top view of the enemy's disposition and increased the line of sight with relatively little threat. From the initial days of military aviation wherein the aircraft were used as observation posts and for imaging enemy troop dispositions, today, they can define the way a nation fights. In current times, aircraft are used as weapon platforms and are equipped with high fidelity long-range sensors for offensive, defensive as well as surveillance tasks.

Scaling up the basic model and fitting on powerful engines to lift more mass expanded the use of aircraft as a fast transporter. The development of transport aircraft changed the parameters of mobility and timelines shrunk for movement of troops and equipment. The intervening terrain and obstacles between the start and end points lost relevance. A quick intercontinental move of troops and military hardware has now become a reality. Within 24 hours, sizeable military contingents can be relocated from one part of the world to another. The ability of some transport aircraft to paradrop troops and hardware, operate from semi-prepared surfaces and with low maintenance requirements, have redefined the logistical process for troop sustenance.

The battlefield underwent another transformation with the development of helicopters that allowed tactical movements besides observation and firepower flexibility. Their vertical take-off and landing capability allowed helicopters to be an integral part of ground troops in the battlefield and also be deployed on ships. Surface forces received a third dimension perspective at the tactical level and ability for vertical envelopment. Heli-lift allowed for quick Inter-Valley Troop Transfer (IVTT) and obviated the need for immediate bridging water obstacles. Helicopters allowed quick positioning of troops and equipment behind enemy lines without the need to clear the intervening obstacles in Ditch Cum Bund (DCB) or minefields. Helicopters have become an intrinsic part of tactical deployment plans of troops in all regions and terrains.

With the induction of Unmanned Aerial Vehicles (UAV) for surveillance with multispectral sensors and targeting with precision weapons, battles are being orchestrated with information dominance and from remote locations. High fidelity sensors and high-speed data links can recreate the entire battle area inside the operation rooms which may be physically located on another continent. A near real-time situation replica of the battle space is now possible. The information gap between field commanders and strategic planners has diminished and micromanagement of deployed combat assets is possible with greater strategic oversight.

Aviation has transformed the two-dimensional battlefield into a three-dimensional battle space. All four facets of military aviation, namely, combat aircraft, transport aircraft, helicopters, and UAVs have a profound impact on battle outcomes. However, the most telling impact is through air delivered kinetic weapons. As opined by Brig Gen Alex Grynkewich:

> Air superiority, often thought of as a mission, is more correctly conceived of as a condition. At its most basic, that condition is achieved when a force possesses the degree of control of the air required for military operations to succeed. Air superiority not only allows coalition and joint force operations to exploit the air domain, but also grants those friendly force operations freedom from attack on the surface. Without air superiority, results can be devastating – witness the rout of the Iraqi Republican Guard as it tried to escape from Kuwait along the so-called "highway of death" in 1991, or the losses suffered by the Taliban in late 2001 on the Shomali Plain in Afghanistan during the opening phase of Operation Enduring Freedom.[12]

The spectrum of conflict that airpower now needs to counter has expanded. At the low-end of this spectrum is a non-state actor without airpower and equipped with the very short-range anti-aircraft weapon system. The selection and identification of target systems against such an adversary are challenging. And targeting small and mobile targets in this scenario is even more difficult despite a very limited threat to the combat aircraft planned for such a mission. At the other end of the spectrum is a conflict against a well-armed state. In this scenario, the combat aircraft will have to penetrate a heavily defended area. The defences often will be multi-layered with multiple sensors providing the inputs. The electronic activity will be high and will cover almost the entire electromagnetic spectrum. The target systems will be defended by surface-based weapons systems, and the air space itself will be contested.

It must be remembered that any platform that can survive in a dense air defence scenario will also be capable of operating in a low-intensity conflict. But the converse is not true. Therefore, a planner would ideally look for a platform that can be operationally deployed covering the entire spectrum of conflict. However, financially, this might not be the most practical option. A large number of high-end platforms with stealth features, ability to operate in a dense electronic warfare scenario and ability to launch long-range weapons will be financially prohibitive. Therefore, most of the armed forces across the world have a mix of combat aircraft scattered across the technology matrix. Michael Buck, a practitioner from the United States armed forces has aptly brought out this aspect in his paper on 'Full Spectrum Close Air Support for the 21st Century'. According to Buck:

> A new, full-spectrum approach to close air support (CAS) must be developed for US forces to optimally operate with ground forces across all levels of conflict. Counterinsurgency and irregular warfare operations in low threat environments will persist for the foreseeable future. Legacy aircraft will be effective in those scenarios, but other future conflicts will take place in highly contested anti-access/area denial (A2/AD) environments. These will contain lethal anti-aircraft threats to which less advanced, non-Stealthy aircraft are intrinsically vulnerable. Fifth-generation aircraft affords survivability in A2/AD environments via stealth.[13]

Combat Aviation in India

On February 26, 2019, the Indian Air Force (IAF) combat aircraft struck a terror training camp at Balakot in Pakistan. The very next day on February 27, 2019, the Pakistan Air Force (PAF) attempted to target military establishments in Jammu and Kashmir at a Brigade Headquarter, a Battalion Headquarter, forward defences and a logistics installation. In the aerial combat that ensued, one F16 of PAF was shot down by an IAF MiG-21 Bison. The F16 crashed and fell across the Line of Control (LOC) in Pakistan-Occupied Kashmir (POK). The IAF lost one MiG-21 in the aerial engagement though the Pilot ejected in POK where he was taken into custody by Pakistan Army and released two days later.[14] After 1971, this was the first-ever offensive use of combat aircraft across the India-Pakistan border and brought to the fore the significance and implication of maintaining and sustaining combat aircraft.

China and Pakistan are India's two nuclear-powered neighbours. With a functional delivery triad, India has a credible second-strike capability in the nuclear domain.[15] However, a credible conventional force too is essential to deter the situation from deteriorating along the national borders. Airpower, in general and combat aircraft, in particular, in combination with other elements of kinetic power plays a significant role in achieving the requisite level of deterrence. Relative combat power between contesting sides defines the outcome of a conflict and also the time and cost. In the case of India-Pakistan, an assessment by Walter C. Ladwig indicates the possibility of a high-cost prolonged conflict:

> Not only is the military capability that India can bring to bear in either type of limited aims offensive far less than the analysts who fret about Indian military modernization appreciate, irrespective of Indian military capabilities, structural and environmental factors such as the terrain, lack of strategic surprise, and the relative military prowess of the two sides will conspire to prevent India from achieving a quick, costless victory.[16]

The number of combat aircraft in the IAF is diminishing. The quest for IAF to achieve the authorised level of 42 combat aircraft squadrons[17] from the existing 31 squadrons,[18] a multi-billion dollar deal to buy 36 Rafale aircraft,[19] operational capability and the induction of indigenous Light Combat Aircraft (LCA), competition between Lockheed Martin F16 and SAAB Gripen for now-cancelled plan for over 100 single-engine fighter aircraft for IAF,[20] and a boost to Prime Minister Narendra Modi's 'Make in India' is being debated by the strategic community, practitioners and academics in the print and electronic media. The latest Request for Information (RFI) issued by the Government of India for 110 combat aircraft covers an important aspect about a strategic partner for making the combat aircraft in India.

> The Ministry of Defence, Government of India, intends to procure Fighter Aircraft for the Indian Air Force (IAF) which is to be Made

> in India. The proposal is to procure approximately 110 fighter aircraft (about 75 per cent single seat and rest twin-seat aircraft). The procurement should have a maximum of 15 per cent aircraft in flyaway state and the remaining 85 per cent aircraft will have to be made in India by a Strategic Partner/Indian Production Agency (SP/ IPA).[21]

The response to this RFI was sought by July 6, 2018. Even till February 2020, no further progress is evident. Besides the six contenders who participated in the shelved plan of procurement of 126 Medium Multi-Role Combat Aircraft (MMRCA), this time Su35 is an additional option.[22] Lockheed Martin unveiled, its F21, a new contender during Aero India 2019. Lockheed Martin had earlier offered its F16 fighter and now claims that the F21 fighter jet is specifically configured for the IAF and will strengthen India's path to an advanced airpower future.[23] The plan for this US defence firm is to build the aircraft in collaboration with Tata Advanced Systems.[24] While the quest for additional combat aircraft for the IAF has been on since 2000-01, the acquisition process has moved at a slow pace. A complicated Defence Procurement Procedure (DPP) has been revised more than six times since then yet, the auditors have had adverse comments about the entire process and have proposed that the Ministry of Defence needs to revisit the entire process of acquisition, to weed out redundant activities and simplify the process.[25] Will another revision of DPP resolve the logjam and IAF finally get additional combat aircraft to stall its drawdown or will the processes and individuals continue to dictate and overpower institutions leading to further decline in the Indian combat airpower capability?

Against this background, it becomes important to assess trends in combat aircraft inventory the world over and evaluate their relevance in the future operational scenario with specific reference to India.

Notes

1. For more on hybrid warfare, see Vikrant Deshpande (ed.), *Hybrid Warfare: The Changing Character of Conflict*, Pentagon Press, New Delhi, 2018.

2. Air Commodore Ramesh V. Phadke (Retd.), Air Power and National Security, *Indian Air Force: Evolution, Growth and Future,* Pentagon Press, New Delhi, 2015, p. 158.
3. "United Nations Categories of equipment and their definitions" at http://www.un.org/Depts/ddar/Register/Categories.html, accessed on May 2, 2018.
4. Brigadier Richard Simpkin was a British Army officer who authored Antitank: an air mechanized response to armoured threats in the 1990s to conceptualise the methods to tackle armoured threats.
5. https://www.unroca.org.
6. International Institute for Strategic Studies (IISS), *Military Balance* for years 1968 to 2018, Routledge, London, Chapman & Hall, 1968 to 2018.
7. IHS, *Jane's World Air Forces*, *Jane's All the World's Aircraft*, *Jane's World Armies* and *Jane's World Navies.*
8. Michael J.H. Taylor, *The Aerospace Chronology*, Tri-Service Press, London, 1989, p. 7.
9. Ibid., p. 9.
10. Ibid., p. 10.
11. Ibid., p. 21.
12. Brig Gen Alex Grynkewich, "An Operational Imperative: The Future of Air Superiority", Mitchell Institute Policy Papers, Volume 7, July 2017.
13. Lt Col Michael Buck, "Full Spectrum Close Air Support for the 21st Century: Leveraging Air Operations with Ground Forces", Mitchell Institute Policy Papers, Volume 8, October 2017.
14. Press Information Bureau, "MoD Press Release Statements by Indian Armed Forces on Prevailing Security Situation", February 28, 2019 at http://pib.nic.in/newsite/pmreleases.aspx?mincode=33, accessed on March 9, 2019.
15. Franz-Stefan Gady, "India Test Fires Second Nuclear Capable Ballistic Missile in a Week", *The Diplomat,* February 9, 2018 at https://thediplomat.com/2018/02/india-test-fires-second-nuclear-capable-ballistic-missile-in-a-week/, accessed on September 4, 2018.
16. Walter C. Ladwig III "Indian Military Modernization and Conventional Deterrence in South Asia", *Journal of Strategic Studies*, Vol. 38, No. 5, 2015.
17. "IAF to reach full squadron strength by 2032: Air Chief", *Business Standard*, October 5, 2017 at https://www.business-standard.com/article/news-ians/iaf-to-reach-full-squadron-strength-by-2032-air-chief-117100501022_1.html, accessed on September 4, 2018.
18. As per Para 55 of *Forty-First Report of the Standing Committee on Defence (2017-2018)* (Sixteenth Lok Sabha), Ministry Of Defence, "Demands

For Grants (2018-19), Army, Navy and Air Force (Demand No. 20)", published by the Lok Sabha Secretariat, New Delhi dated March, 2018 at 164.100.47.193/lsscommittee/Defence/16_Defence_41.pdf, accessed on September 4, 2018.

19. As per Para 3.11 of *Forty-First Report of the Standing Committee on Defence (2017-2018)* (Sixteenth Lok Sabha), Ministry Of Defence, "Demands For Grants (2018-19), Army, Navy and Air Force (Demand No. 20), published by the Lok Sabha Secretariat, New Delhi dated March, 2018 at 164.100.47.193/lsscommittee/Defence/16_Defence_41.pdf, accessed on September 4, 2018.
20. Rajat Pandit, "Govt scraps single-engine fighter plan, asks IAF to go for wider competition", *Times of India,* February 23, 2018 at https://timesofindia.indiatimes.com/india/govt-scraps-single-engine-fighters-plan-asks-iaf-to-go-for-wider-competition/articleshow/63034958.cms, accessed on September 4, 2018.
21. The Ministry of Defence, "Request for Information for Procurement of Fighter Aircraft for the Indian Air Force" at indianairforce.nic.in/sites/default/files/RFI_Fighter_Aircraft.pdf, accessed on September 4, 2018.
22. Huma Siddiqui, "Aero India 2019: Russia offers MiG-35 and SU 35, 'HAL preferred partner for Make in India'", *The Financial Express*, February 21, 2019 at https://www.financialexpress.com/defence/aero-india-2019-russia-offers-mig-35-and-su-35-hal-preferred-partner-for-make-in-india/1494725/, accessed on March 25, 2019.
23. "Lockheed Martin unveils new F-21 fighter jet to be made in India", *Business Today*, February 20, 2019 at https://www.businesstoday.in/current/corporate/lockheed-martin-unveils-new-f21-fighter-jet-to-be-made-make-in-india/story/320634.html, accessed on March 19, 2019.
24. Ibid.
25. *Performance Audit Report of the Comptroller and Auditor General of India on Capital Acquisition in Indian Air Force for the Union Government (Defence Services)* Air Force Report No. 3 of 2019 tabled on the floor of the Parliament on February 13, 2019, p. vi.

2. Scanning Rear Airspace: Historical Perspective of Combat Aviation

---

Although airpower started playing a role in combat operations within a couple of years of the invention of the aircraft, it truly arrived as a combat force during the Second World War. Over the last fifty years, that is, 1968-2018, it has matured and now practically defines and shapes the operational environment. To get a perspective on employment and the role of combat airpower in the past half-century, one conflict from each decade has been selected as case studies for analysis, as listed below:

- The 1970s - Arab- Israel War 1973
- The 1980s - Falklands War 1982
- The 1990s - Gulf War 1991
- The 2000s - Afghanistan War 2001 onwards
- The 2010s - Syrian War 2011 onwards

Not only are these five campaigns located differently on the timeline, but they are also contextually distinct in the application of airpower as a kinetic tool. The Arab-Israel conflict in 1973 was a typical case of settling aspirations within the region for the legitimacy of state boundaries. The Falklands war saw the use of airpower between the two contesting sides in the maritime domain wherein one side had a major locational advantage. The Gulf War I in 1991 redefined the role of airpower as a primary tool of kinetic power to shape the operational environment for exploitation by other elements and a case of multinational force coordinating to overpower a well-defined and militarily powerful state. In Afghanistan, it is a case of a state supported by multinational force to target a non-state actor and in Syria, the definition of opposing sides is even more blurred and several players are operating in the same battle space for their objectives. These are not the only wars that the world has seen in the last half-century. The most significant war in the Indian subcontinent was in 1971 that resulted in the creation of an independent nation as a result of a decisive military victory. That war was being fought on two fronts – on India's East and West. Political goals and therefore, military objectives were very distinct on these two fronts and so were the military strategies from both sides and the role of combat aviation. Amongst many similar conflicts, these five selected wars cover the entire spectrum of application of combat airpower and are indicative of the general trend. A large amount of literature is already available on all these conflicts, therefore only small snippets have been recounted here to highlight the complex nature of combat aviation.

Arab-Israel War 1973

The Arab Israel War of 1973 was fought over a small but densely packed battlefield.[1] Aggressive use of air power to neutralise the opponent both in the air and on the ground was the central theme in spite of the existence of a large number of radars and associated Air Defence Missile Systems. A short and intense 20-day war had combat aircraft from both sides employed primarily to attack enemy airfields, air defence installations and surface forces. In support of the surface forces, combat aircraft were deployed to attack bridges and bridgeheads and defend own troops from enemy air attacks. Over 1500 combat aircraft were in action primarily comprising MiG21, MiG17, Su7, Mirage III, F4 and A4 employed by the Egyptian, the Syrian and the Israeli Air Forces. While actual losses are not available in the open domain for obvious reasons, it is widely believed that between the two sides, 500-600 combat aircraft were lost in aerial combat and to the air defence missiles and guns.[2]

Its importance is reflected in the fact that, for the first time, a multi-layered air defence umbrella with multiple sensors and weapons systems was tested in a realistic scenario against an offensive use of air power. The sensors and weapon systems were potent but a key component in terms of robust and effective communication was missing. Fratricide was a common foe and claimed over 50 aircraft from both sides and on occasions, Israel ground forces were being attacked by their air force. Israel faced a classic two-front war with a combat aircraft numerical inferiority ratio of 1:2. The combined strength of Egyptian and Syrian Air Forces augmented by other players like Iraq in the region started well by capitalising on the concentration of force, a cardinal principle of war. A large-scale offensive strike package of over 300 aircraft across various target systems in the afternoon on a crucial religious holiday in Israel was well-conceived. Long-range air-launched missile Kelt[3] too saw operational service for the first time. Its large size and associated Radar Cross Section and limited speed resulted in some of the missiles being intercepted and those which managed to reach the target had limited impact because of their restrictive weight of attack and accuracy. However, initial offensive momentum was not sustained, probably because the losses were higher than expected and the planned second wave of attacks on Israel never took place. The tactical pause and shift of focus from targeting the Israel Air Force allowed much-needed breathing space to Israel Defence Forces.

A similar response was seen from Israel when the attrition level was much higher than expected during the Israel Air Force's initial missions to thwart the Egyptian land offensive on October 6, 1973. The Air Defence umbrella protecting the Egyptian ground offensive was effective and forced Israel to stop making forays in the tactical battle zone after initial strikes. Strong and successful defensive measures from both sides forced a change of tactics for the employment of offensive airpower. For Egypt, a passive measure like the creation of additional airfields and operating surfaces on each airfield, protected parking space for aircraft, laying out of dummy bridges minimised the effectiveness of Israeli air force's offensive missions. The success of Israeli air attacks for suppression of enemy air defences was also limited. A hole in the Egyptian air defence umbrella was created only when the Israeli ground forces overpowered the Egyptian air defence units after crossing the Suez. This thereafter allowed greater freedom of operation to the Israeli Air Force. This was a classic case of surface forces assisting the air force in operations while the basic theme has always been that it is air power that allows freedom of manoeuvre for the surface forces.

On the Golan Heights, the nature of air operations was slightly different. Syrian offensive missions were aimed at Israeli ground forces to assist their land forces in battle. But the intensity of the air defence mission from Israel was high and effective. This resulted in keeping the Israeli land forces relatively immune from Syrian air attacks. In a classic case of disarray owing to lack of appropriate communication amongst Syrian, Jordanian and Iraqi forces fighting a common enemy in Israel, identification errors from the Syrian side resulted in their aircraft attacking Jordanian forces, Iraqi aircraft targeting Syrian land forces and Syrian air defence shooting down Iraqi aircraft. The Air Defence Barrier in Syria was effective during the initial phase but a successful Israeli attack on its computerised control centre on October 9, 1973, and the Syrian decision to withdraw SA6 batteries to protect Damascus after an Israeli raid, changed the equation.

A major lesson was that when deployed correctly, combat aircraft can be an effective defensive tool against a ground offensive or a supportive tool to fast-track a surface offensive. All three participants in this conflict started the campaigns with a pre-defined strategy but had to change course quickly to accommodate new realisations in the operational environment. The ease with which Israel switched employment of combat aircraft from Sinai to the Golan Heights based on the tempo of battle and necessity, showcased the flexibility and indivisible nature of combat airpower.

Falklands War 1982

Almost a decade after the Arab-Israel conflict of 1973 another conflict raised its head in 1982 in Lebanon's Becca Valley. The same year Argentina and the UK fought for the control of Falklands Islands. While the Becca Valley conflict brought the focus on battlespace transparency and use of non-kinetic electronic warfare to the fore, the story unfolding in the southern hemisphere was starkly different. Argentina had the locational advantage and the UK was fighting with ship-based capability 12,000 km away from the main bases. From the Argentinian occupation of Stanley on April 2, 1982, to its recapture by British forces, the war lasted 74 days. The air battle was fought with 20 Sea Harriers (later joined by eight more aircraft) operated from two aircraft carriers and nearly 150 aircraft including Mirage III, Daggers, Super Etendard and A4 operating from Argentinian airfields.

On May 4, 1982, a Super Etendard of the Argentine Navy hit the *HMS Sheffield* of the Royal Navy with an Exocet air-to-ship missile. This forced both British aircraft carriers to operate east of the Falklands away from Argentinian mainland. The tactic was to minimise the probability of a strike by the Super Etendard, armed with the Exocet missile.[4] On the other hand, the distance between the Argentinian mainland and the Falklands Islands was large and this minimised operational time available to Argentinian combat aircraft. The air battle, thus, was being fought with marginal combat reserve fuel and at the extremes of the radius of action of all combat aircraft. The intensity was low but without any elaborate early warning systems on either side, it was strenuous. Better manoeuvrability and weapons (AIM9L)[5] helped Sea Harriers claim victories in classical combat engagements, but their low numbers and absence of early warning could not stop as many as 25 ships of the UK Carrier Task Force from being hit by air-delivered weapons. Owing to an ultra-low altitude of delivery and consequent non-operation of fuses, most of the weapons that hit the UK ships failed to explode. Although all these ships suffered various degrees of damage, only seven ships of the UK Carrier Task Force sank.

There is a similar story about the use of air-to-air missiles by the Argentinian Air Force. On May 1, 1982, in the first aerial combat during the war, two Argentinian Mirage III fired semi-active Matra R 530 at their targets, UK's Sea Harriers. But the Argentinian pilots, after firing, failed to continue to illuminate Sea Harriers with their radars, resulting in both missiles missing their targets. The Sea Harriers with their Sidewinder missiles shot down both Mirage IIIs. This set the tone of aerial combat between the two forces. Argentina's Air Force became very defensive in aerial combat and confined the operation of Mirage III to mainland defence. Similarly, after an Argentinian Canberra was shot down on the same day, Canberra aircraft were tasked for only night attacks on ships, a ploy with negligible chance of success.

Limited aerial refuelling capability in terms of receivers and refuellers and non-availability of accurate navigation systems, forced a narrow approach corridor to Argentinian aircraft to target UK ships. This assisted in the high interception rate of the Argentinian strikes by ship-based Sea Harriers until an alternative methodology of Pathfinders was adopted. On the other hand, the UK employed Vulcan bombers to target airfields in Falklands with great hope and little scope of success. Vulcans capable of carrying 21 bombs of 1000 lbs and modified to carry Electronic Counter Measure pods and AGM45 missiles, were used to attack Stanley airfield and Argentina Radars in Falklands. Each mission involved multiple aerial refuellings after their launch from Ascension Island. Ageing platforms with limited aids for the success of the mission, resulted in only one bomb (out of 210 planned) hitting the airfield in the ten planned missions, with other missions either aborted or unsuccessful. The losses of UK's aircraft included 10 Harriers and 24 helicopters in enemy fire or accidents or lost along with the ships during the war, and 22 combat aircraft of the Argentinian Air Force were among a total of 54 aircraft/helicopters that were lost.[6]

Despite major technical limitations, both sides tried to use available resources for operations by modifying platforms, their weapons systems, or their roles. The tempo of operations remained low as both sides followed a conservative approach with Argentinian forces concentrated on the mainland and UK aircraft carriers tucked away east of the Falklands. The major lessons from the Falklands War concerned correct force application of available assets and updating professional knowledge. Both sides failed to capitalise on their strengths, the side that erred less, achieved its objectives, albeit at a high cost.

Gulf War 1991[7]

The Gulf War of 1991 was practically a televised war. It was fought between a powerful state with all elements of combat power in adequate strength and a 35-nation coalition force with the most advanced technology on its side. The combat phase, called *Operation Desert Storm*, lasted 42 days, with the ground offensive by the coalition force lasting 100 hours. From the US-led coalition's side, air power was employed as a primary tool, with over 1700 combat aircraft dropping 88,500 tons of bombs. These attacks were against 600 Iraqi aircraft and surface-to-air missiles. Over 140 Iraqi combat aircraft flew out to Iran. Iraq lost 39 aircraft in aerial combat and another 59 were destroyed on the ground in airstrikes. The coalition forces lost 52 aircraft and 23 helicopters. The coalition forces achieved air superiority over a limited area within hours of commencement of operations and gradually expanded to cover the entire battle space.

The foundation of air operations was the ability of coalition forces to achieve a high degree of battle space transparency and denying the same to Iraqi forces.[8] A large number of sensors were deployed before the commencement of operations to accurately map the type, strength and location of enemy combat assets. This was clubbed with extensive electronic warfare operations to minimise the effectiveness of Iraqi sensors. Use of surface and ship-based long-range missiles to target the ground-based sensors and control centres together with an attack by stealth aircraft, practically annihilated the control and reporting system in Iraq. On the other hand, the coalition forces could continually monitor the battle space with airborne and space-based assets.

The war was fought between unequal entities, both in terms of quality and quantity. The discrepancy in the level of battle space transparency along with the availability of long-range weapons tilted the aerial combat heavily in favour of coalition forces. The aerial opposition from Iraq continued to dwindle as the battle progressed because of limited numbers of fighters, relatively inferior air-to-air missiles and diminishing radar cover. Several successful attacks by coalition forces on Iraqi airfields resulted in a loss of operational feasibility and forced Iraq to shift a major portion of its combat fleet to neighbouring Iran. However, Iraqi surface-to-air weapons systems and particularly anti-aircraft guns did take a toll on attacking aircraft and forced a change of coalition force tactics.

The Royal Air Force, having lost a Tornado aircraft every day for the first five days of the war, had to abandon low-level attacks and switch to medium altitude attacks outside the lethal zone of Iraqi anti-aircraft guns. In spite of overwhelming air superiority and a large number of ISR resources, the coalition found it difficult to locate, identify and target mobile Scud launchers.

The air attacks on Iraqi surface forces resulted in a loss of over 2600 tanks/APC and over 1400 artillery pieces. This led to a facile ground victory and served to reiterate the significance of control in the air. With negligible air cover from fighter aircraft and surface-to-air weapons, the much-touted Iraqi Republican Guards were very vulnerable in open desert terrain along with their exposed lines of communications. Precision attacks on several bridges in Iraq practically denied manoeuvre capability to large armour formations of Iraq's Army. A short and swift ground offensive supported by airpower led to a decisive victory for the coalition forces. Coalition forces suffered 340 combat deaths and 774 injuries including 25 per cent deaths and 10 per cent injuries as a result of friendly fire.[9]

Identification of Centre of Gravity (COG) of the opposing force and undertaking Effects-Based Operations (EBO) were the key takeaways at the strategic level. At the operational level, two major lessons that emerged were the use of enhanced tools for battle space transparency that allowed fixing of target locations followed by the use of precision-guided weapons to neutralise the target. The F117, with a 42-aircraft fleet, flew two per cent of the coalition attacks but struck 40 per cent of strategic targets without any loss.[10] In both these facets, technology played a pivotal role. Even with technological and numerical superiority, the coalition forces could neither negate the threat from Scud missiles nor cut down its aircraft losses. Another shortcoming in force application from the coalition forces was in weapon target matching and weapon delivery. Every target identified for precision targeting necessitated multiple-precision weapons. On the other hand, the number of unguided weapons fired too was much higher than warranted by target constituents. Such a force application methodology could become a limiting factor in prolonged conflicts.

Afghanistan War: 2001 Onwards

A force-on-force conflict in Iraq re-emphasized the need for technological superiority for the achievement of objectives with least human losses. However, a decade later, the engagement in Afghanistan was of a different kind. The war was between powerful well-equipped coalition forces against an ill-equipped, ill-trained but highly motivated non-state actor. The realisation of an era of hybrid war had dawned. The enemy was diffused over a large area and rarely concentrated in mass to be an ideal target for application of airpower. Incidentally, this was the strategy that Saddam Hussein in Iraq was advised by his commanders but did not pay heed to.

In Afghanistan, the only threat to an attacker using combat aircraft was from an occasional man-portable surface-to-air guided weapon. The most difficult part of the mission was to locate and identify a target – generally a human being. The concept of employment of airpower had to change to cope with this scenario. Mapping and keeping a large area under surveillance was the first and the most critical step. Once located, the sensor-to-shooter loop had to be quickly closed to ensure the requisite result. The force level required to keep a large area under continuous surveillance was huge, especially because of the long-distance of the target area from available airbases. This role was initially complemented by Unmanned Aerial Vehicles (UAVs) and later completely taken over by them. The unmanned systems had a major advantage compared to manned aircraft in terms of endurance and cost of operations in a benign air defence environment. The UAVs deployed for surveillance allowed detection of potential targets and could track them. With live feed going back to the control room, the identification of the target could be carried out on the ground. Once identified, an appropriate aircraft was designated to carry out the attack in coordination with the UAV.

Keeping manned combat aircraft airborne or on standby for such a strike, though necessary, was difficult to sustain. Here, technology came to the rescue with the development of Unmanned Combat Aerial Vehicles (UCAVs). As the battle progressed without an end in sight, UCAVs replaced a large part of manned combat aircraft. Technology had made that possible and precision attacks could be carried out by UCAVs in this benign air defence environment. Although the number of weapons and their calibre was limited on UCAV as compared to the manned combat aircraft, normally, it was adequate. In any case, when the additional weight of the attack was envisaged, manned combat aircraft could be called in. An attack on April 13, 2017, with the largest non-nuclear weapon, the GBU 43B, to strike a complex of tunnels and bunkers in Achin district in Nangarhar province in Afghanistan, is a case in point.[11]

The UCAV allowed compression of sensor shooter time as it had both sensors and weapons on board and the time required was negligible once a target was designated. Additionally, it obviated the risk to air crew in case of an ejection/bale out in the hostile territory. The ability to loiter on station for long durations for locating and attacking a target was an operational necessity. The UCAVs fitted the bill much better than the combat aircraft in a cost-effective manner. This concept also had peculiar limitations. The sensors on board platforms like UAV/UCAV have a finite scan angle. This provides a straw pipe view to the ground operator. Under certain circumstances, it is difficult to comprehend the entire picture and may lead to wrong decisions.

While the conflict extended geographically and along the timeline, it has become difficult to keep a large area under surveillance with conventional methods. Devising efficient surveillance methods has become a necessity. Alongside, a prompt attacking option is essential. A major lesson in the ongoing Afghanistan conflict is the necessity to devise methods to compress the sensor-shooter loop.[12] Additionally, the failure of *Operation Enduring Freedom* to achieve its objectives of defeating Al-Qaeda and the Taliban by merely air strikes highlighted the need of a strategy with the usage of multiple kinetic and non-kinetic tools in addition to combat airpower.

Syrian War: 2011 Onwards

The ongoing Syrian war in the current decade takes the complexity of hybrid war to another level, with multiple players operating in the same space for different objectives – sometimes coherent and often divergent. The target systems for various contestants are different but they are all diffused and part of heavily populated areas. Collateral damage has been large and the effectiveness in locating and destroying targets, low. In fast-changing operational scenario, combat aircraft continue to play a role but only occasionally, in this long-drawn seemingly interminable war. In July 2012, with Syria shooting down a Turkish aircraft, the aerospace dimension took off. Thereafter, the war in air progressed albeit slowly and gradually. Overall, 120 combat aircraft have been lost in this theatre belonging to Syria, Jordan, Russia, the US, Israel and Turkey. The air war gained momentum with Russia commencing airstrikes in September 2015. The US upped the ante after the alleged use of chemical weapons in April 2017 with a death toll of 58 in Khan Sheikhoun[13] and a year later with a death toll of 70 in Douma.[14] In April 2017, the US carried out missile attacks and in 2018 it was a coordinated attack by the US, the UK and France.[15]

Israel has struck Syria 200 times 2017 onwards to prevent the deployment of Iranian weapons in the region.[16] In a classical mix up of events, a Syrian air defence missile shot down a Russian IL20 aircraft on September 17, 2018, killing 15 personnel.[17] This happened when the Syrian air defence weapons were firing at the attacking Israeli combat aircraft. The Russians blamed Israel for trying to take advantage of the presence of Russian aircraft in the region to carry out their attack on Syrian posts. Although Israel claimed to have informed the Russian side about their plan, the estimated reaction time available to the Russians was only one minute. Israel sent their Chief of Air Staff to Moscow to pacify the situation giving all available details of the strike and events that led to the downing of Russian aircraft by Syria.[18] Syrian airspace has become the first to witness full operational employment of the stealth combat aircraft.[19] Will it also witness aerial combat between stealth combat aircraft? Only time will tell. For the time being, the contest in the Syrian air space is on a low key and the preparations are on for the US to withdraw from the area.[20]

Changing Character of Combat Air Power

In brief, the characteristics of conflict have transformed in the last fifty years. From being primarily a force-on-force war of attrition between well-defined adversaries in well-defined battle space with clearly defined commencements and termination, to the one with blurred boundaries and a diffused enemy. Along with this, the role of combat aircraft has also changed. Instead of leading the offensive and shaping the battle space for exploitation by other elements, combat aircraft in the new form of conflict against a diffused enemy are more succinct. Mission significance and outcomes are dictated more by the deployment of battle space transparency tools to fix the target location than by kinetic weapons that are employed to attack them. Employment of combat aircraft is focused on precise weapon delivery with reduced timeline tolerances, as the targets relocate quickly. In case the air defence environment is docile, this task is given to UCAVs. But in a hostile air defence environment, there is no option other than the employment of combat aircraft.

This assertion by no means indicates that force-on-force conflicts are passé. While the air elements of armed forces are redefining their configuration to tackle various facets of hybrid threats, at the same time they are also gearing up for a force-on-force conflict. So the focus of capability expansion of current air forces the world over is moving in two directions, not necessarily mutually exclusive. On the one hand, the capability of combat aircraft is being enhanced technologically to meet threats from advanced air defence systems and opposing combat aircraft. On the other hand, the role of aerospace power is being refined to tackle hybrid threats from a diffused enemy. In this, the emphasis is on surveillance technology and precise low-calibre attack capability. In this domain, space assets and unmanned vehicles are considered most suitable. While these capabilities can be augmented by manned combat aircraft, the converse is not true. This is evident from the USAF expansion plan over the next decade that envisages 62 combat aircraft squadrons and only 27 UAV squadrons.[21]

Analysis of these five conflicts and application of airpower in these is indicative of force-application methodology and the outcomes. First, force ratios have limited implications for the outcome of air battles. While in the 1973 and 1982 conflicts, the sides with lower numbers prevailed, in 1991, a greater number of combat assets from coalition forces overpowered the Iraqi forces. While in these three wars, combat airpower played a decisive role in the outcome, in Afghanistan and Syria, airpower was reduced to a minor player even though the opposition had limited airpower capability, if any at all.

Technological superiority plays a decisive role in the outcome of combat air operations. Three critical factors in this matrix are battle space transparency, range and accuracy of air-launched weapons and the effort generation rate. The most critical aspect is battle space transparency. This practically is a competition to locate enemy aircraft in the sky before being detected. The main tool for achieving this is ground/ship-based radars. With the miniaturisation of components, radars found their application on aerial platforms. They assisted in creating a situational awareness model beyond the line of sight limitation of surface-based radar platforms.

Once detected, the next step is to engage enemy aircraft. Here, a critical component is the lethal range of weapons on board the competing aircraft. With all other aspects being equal, aircraft with a longer range weapon will invariably win the battle. The ability to launch a missile to target an enemy aircraft before entering the lethal envelope of missiles onboard target aircraft, gives an unprecedented advantage. For this to be practical, the difference in the effective range of missiles on board the competing aircraft has to be substantial, say more than 10 per cent. While range is one criterion, the other is the ability of the missile to home in on the target aircraft. This is dependent on the type of tracking system used. The side that exploits these two aspects of aerial weapons tactically can win the combat even with a marginal disadvantage in terms of technical parameters of platforms or weapons.

The air effort generation rate plays a crucial role in defining the outcome of the war. It is based on the maintenance philosophy of the platform, availability of trained personnel and an efficient logistics chain. The ability of a force to quickly re-arm and re-launch the aircraft can negate numerical inferiority. Additionally, offensive operations in quick succession can unhinge the defender. The ability of the Israeli Air Force to tackle two fronts simultaneously in the 1973 war was based on the concept of a higher effort generation rate than both the adversaries.

The success of combat aviation in shaping the battle space is based on the availability of suitable target systems. In force-on-force military conflict, concentrated force application is desirable to overcome a weak point of the enemy. This, in turn, leads to a conglomeration of various combat assets in a confined space. Such force application presents an ideal target system for airpower. The 1991 Gulf War is a classic case wherein the coalition forces utilised air power to successfully target several surface-based combat units. This helped in a facile ground operation and victory. However, in Afghanistan and Syria, the absence of such concentrated combat elements diluted the impact of combat airpower and stretched the timelines for a conclusive victory.

Combat airpower can define the outcome of a conflict. However, in a contested air space, besides numerical strength, technology plays a crucial role. Combat aircraft need to be supported by suitable battle space transparency tools[22] and need to be equipped with potent weapons. Availability of suitable target systems on the surface also plays a critical role in the success or failure of combat airpower in defining the outcome of the war. A crucial role is also played by the maintenance and logistics subsystems in generating the air effort at a high rate. Reliability of platforms, avionics and weapons along with skill sets of planners and executors are essential parameters to predict the outcome of air combat operations.

Notes

1. For more see David T. Buckwalter, "The 1973 Arab-Israeli War" at http://www.au.af.mil/au/awc/awcgate/navy/pmi/1973.pdf, accessed on March 25, 2019.
2. Air Vice Marshal Tony Mason, "The Air Warfare Requirement", in Phillip Jarret (Ed), *The Modern War Machine, Military Aviation Since 1945,* Putnam Aeronautical Books, London, 2000, pp. 23-24.
3. Kelt (KSR2) was a Soviet origin missile for launch from Tuplov 16 aircraft. It was 8.7 m long and weighed nearly four tonnes and included a 1000-kg warhead. It was equipped with an inertial navigation system and had a range of about 200 km.
4. Lawrence Freedman *The Official History of the Falklands Campaign Volume II,* Routelege, London, 2005 p. 469; Chris Hobson with Andrew Noble, Falklands Air War, Hinckley, Midland, 2002, p. 57.

5. Mike Spick, *Fighters at War: The Story of Air to Air Combat*, Greenhill Books, London, 1997, pp. 131-132.
6. "Part 53. British Aircraft Lost, 22nd April-12th June 1982" Naval History Homepage at http://www.naval-history.net/F63-Falklands-British_aircraft_lost.htm, accessed on February 8, 2018.
7. Air Vice Marshal Tony Mason, no. 2, pp. 25-27.
8. Mike Spick, no. 5, p. 133.
9. Air Vice Marshal Tony Mason, The Air Warfare Requirement, in Phillip Jarret (Ed.), The Modern War Machine, Military Aviation Since 1945, Putnam Aeronautical Books, London, 2000, p. 26.
10. Air Vice Marshal Tony Mason, no. 7.
11. Sune Engel Rasmussen, "US 'mother of all bombs' killed 92 ISIS militants, say, Afghan officials", *The Guardian*, April 15, 2017 at https://www.theguardian.com/world/2017/apr/15/us-mother-of-all-bombs-moab-afghanistan-donald-trump-death-toll, accessed on October 10, 2018.
12. A typical sensor-shooter loop process starts with an assessment of likely conflict area and followed by the deployment of various sensors to monitor the area of interest. Keeping the area under surveillance requires multiple sensors to account for varied ambient light conditions and other environmental factors. The feedback from the sensors is analysed and correlated with other sources of information. This assists in identifying a potential target system. Once corroborated with requisite intelligence, the target is classified and tracked. In a parallel process, on indication of the availability of a potential target, amongst the options available, a suitable option to engage the target is identified and activated. On designation of a system as a target, the instructions are given to the kinetic tool for engagement. Once the platform selected to engage the target reaches the area of interest, it locates and identifies the target and thereafter, the weapons are fired. On completion of weapon firing, the post-strike assessment is carried out to check the result of the strike. If required, the whole process is repeated to achieve the desired outcome. In certain cases, multiple options are activated simultaneously to enhance the probability of success.
13. BBC News, "Syria conflict: 'Chemical attack' in Idlib kills 58", April 4, 2017 at https://www.bbc.com/news/world-middle-east-39488539, accessed on March 25, 2019.
14. BBC News, "Syria War: At least 70 killed in a suspected chemical attack in Douma", April 8, 2018, available onhttps://www.bbc.com/news/world-middle-east-43686157, accessed on March 25, 2019.
15. The Tower, "U.S., U.K., and France Launch Coordinated Attack against Syrian Chemical Weapons Facilities", April 16, 2018 at http://www.thetower.org/6159-u-s-u-k-and-france-launch-coordinated-attack-against-

syrian-chemical-weapons-facilities/, accessed on March 25, 2019.

16. Barbara Starr, Ryan Browne and Nathan Hodge, "Syria accidentally shot down a Russian military plane", CNN, September 18, 2018 at https://edition.cnn.com/2018/09/17/politics/syrian-regime-shoots-down-russian-plane/index.html, accessed on September 25, 2018.
17. Ibid.
18. *Times of Israel,* "IAF chief heads to Moscow to present findings on downing of Russian plane", September 20, 2018 at https://www.timesofisrael.com/iaf-chief-heads-to-moscow-to-present-findings-on-downing-of-russian-plane/, accessed on March 25, 2019.
19. *The Moscow Times*, "Russian Military Unveils Video Footage of New Su-57 Stealth Fighter in Syria", November 19, 2018 at https://www.themoscowtimes.com/2018/11/19/russian-military-unveils-video-footage-new-su-57-stealth-fights-syria-a63532, accessed on March 25, 2019.
20. Karen DeYoung, Louisa Loveluck and John Hudson, "US military announces the start of Syria withdrawal", *The Washington Post*, January 11, 2019 at https://www.washingtonpost.com/world/middle_east/us-military-announces-start-of-syria-troop-withdrawal/2019/01/11/77455bda-1585-11e9-90a8-136fa44b80ba_story.html?utm_term=.33d73d16646e, accessed on March 25, 2019.
21. Stephen Losey, "New Air Force secretary: 'We are too small for what the nation expects of us'," *Air Force Times*, June 6, 2017 at https://www.airforcetimes.com/news/your-air-force/2017/06/06/new-air-force-secretary-we-are-too-small-for-what-the-nation-expects-of-us/, accessed on March 25, 2019.
22. These tools are those systems and subsystems that assist a combatant in localising all combat assets, their movement and likely intention. Radars, electro-optical sensors, communication and electronic signature monitoring systems and associated networks are all battle space transparency tools.

3. Mission Plan: Imperatives of Combat Aviation Application

Airpower is a core component, either as a key enabler of a short ground offensive to seize territory or as a standalone tool for conducting strikes against ground-based targets across the border.[1] Combat aviation, a subset and often the frontend of airpower, is primarily offensive.[2] With this offensive capability, attacks can be carried out on many types of targets and systems. Thus, combat aviation provides a means to achieve ends. The primary or core elements of combat aviation are combat platforms, weapons on combat platforms and combat aviators. This triad – the obverse end of combat aviation – actually needs several other support elements for mission accomplishment. In other words, combat aviation is not an independent vector but is a part of a complex operational system. This chapter attempts to decode the system of combat aviation by listing and defining various elements. Looking at it holistically, from an intended target, a radially outward approach has been adopted to list major factors that impact combat aviation. The process commences with basic operational planning for engaging a target. This approach will assist in understanding the operational factors that define the role and mission requirements of combat aviation.

Operational Imperatives for Combat Aviation

Armed forces operate in the realm of uncertainty and are prepared to deal with the confusion associated with the fog of war. No matter what the higher political direction or intent is, four basic questions that constantly plague the armed forces for operational planning are:

Who all will be engaged militarily?
When will be the military engagement?
Where will be the military engagement?
How will the engagement take place?

On the other hand, in case of a defensive plan, the corollaries to the abovementioned questions are relevant. The situation may demand taking the initiative and commencing operations against an inimical force. In both offensive and defensive options, the decision-makers and commanders need answers to the questions about the enemy's intent, resources, capability, force application plan, criticalities, vulnerabilities and recoverability. Accurate knowledge about location and capabilities of all players in the battle space increases the probability of success owing to better situational awareness and availability of a holistic picture to plan strategic, operational and tactical manoeuvres. The first step in this process is to identify and thereafter localise the position of all combat and combat-support elements of the adversary. The positioning of advance posts, observers on high grounds/platforms to overcome the line of sight limitations were the methods employed ever since conflicts began in human history. Hiding the move behind suitable ground features or in darkness or behind a smokescreen were common tactics to deny access to information to opposing forces. First the invention of telegraphy and then the telephone, found their way into military communications for reporting observations and passing orders. Wireless communications and radars added another dimension to battle space transparency (see Annexure 2). Tracking of the *Bismarck* by the *Prince of Wales* by the use of radars in World War II is a classic example in the maritime domain.

Conflict dynamics undergo a paradigm shift with every technological revolution. The 'Force-on-Force' attrition method prevalent in wars in the 19th century was replaced by blitzkrieg manoeuvres with the availability of faster mobility vehicles and vertical enveloping begun with the advent of airpower. Faster computing power and use of space-based assets allowed engaging longer-range targets with minimal contact battles. Electromagnetic waves and network warfare expanded the speed of operations and enhanced its impact. The lines between uniformed combatants, technical support teams and non-uniformed actors for their roles in a combat situation are getting blurred. Primarily, in the last century, wars have transformed from being an event to a process. This process has no clearly defined commencement or termination point but is continuous with varying intensity. At the lower end of this process are low-intensity conflicts with occasional terrorist attacks/system disruptions/system interferences. The direct involvement of combat forces and the use of kinetic weapons increase the intensity and pace till a full-scale conventional conflict breaks out. Fortunately, barring once by the USA, the intensity has not reached its pinnacle with the use of nuclear weapons. However, the battle space, threat and capabilities have a new meaning in the current context (see Annexure 3).

Operational Planning Process

Although warfare is evolving as a transition out of the industrial age and further into the information age, yet a definable target remains the nodal issue for operational planning.[3] Therefore, identification of a target or target systems is one of the first steps. This selection is inherently linked to the overall aim of the war by asking a basic question, "What, if denied, will force the adversary to capitulate?" History is replete with examples wherein loss of a specific geographical area or collapse of command and control network or negation of a particular kinetic capability led to dramatic consequences. It may not always be possible to target the said centre of gravity for operational reasons. In such cases, subsystems that support the centre of gravity are selected as suitable targets with the ultimate aim of getting to the assessed centre of gravity. Target analysis is the next logical step. This includes assessment of resilience, availability of alternatives, criticality and vulnerability of the selected target system. This allows the attacker to further narrow down the list of physical targets. The next step is to undertake functional, operational and structural analysis of the identified targets. Several tools are utilised to detect, identify and fix the position of target systems. Targets falling within the radius of action of available combat assets from available airbases are further analysed for selection of the desired mean point of impact for weapon aiming. To achieve this, detailed intelligence-gathering missions are undertaken with all possible sensors. This includes Radars, Electro-Optical, Infra-red and Synthetic Aperture Radars (SAR) from airborne platforms or space-based assets. All in all, like all other forms of kinetic force application, intelligence provides the key inputs for application of combat aviation.

In the next step, the vulnerability index of the target is assessed with respect to all possible damage mechanisms. Blast, fragmentation, fire, penetration and shock in isolation or combination are a result of air-launched weapons.[4] These parameters for all weapons available in the inventory are matched with the respective vulnerability indices of the target. Computerised tools like the Joint Munition Effectiveness Manual (JMEM) and Weapon Advisory for Staff Planning (WASP) assist in efficiently carrying out this assessment. The assessment of the operational environment in the target area in terms of terrain, illumination conditions, weather and air defence measures play a pivotal role in the selection of a suitable mode of attack to engage the target. This results in the selection of a suitable weapon-platform-mode of attack combination for targeting. Based on the dimensions and structural strength of the target, the number of weapons required over a target to achieve a requisite degree of damage is calculated. In the next step, the number of platforms required to launch these weapons is computed based on the platform's weapon-carrying capacity. To ensure that the required number of aircraft deliver their weapons, a suitable number of aircraft are planned to account for failures for platform or weapon malfunction and/or enemy action.

Once the basic strike composition is ready with a requisite number of platforms armed with specific weapons, its support package is readied. This includes air defence aircraft that escort the strike package. The air defence aircraft equipped with air-to-air weapons like missiles and guns ensure the protection of strike aircraft from enemy interceptors. To warn the entire package of any enemy aircraft activity, to the extent possible, radar coverage is provided. This radar coverage could be from ground-based radars or airborne platforms like AWACS. To enhance the range and endurance of all airborne platforms, wherever necessary and practical, aerial refuellers provide in-flight refuelling. Additionally, platforms equipped with electronic warfare suits are incorporated in the plan to degrade the performance of electronic sensors of the adversary.[5] Invariably, the surface-based air defence elements protecting the intended target are themselves targeted. This targeting is either permanent by Destruction of Enemy Air Defence (DEAD) missions or transitory through electronic means using Suppression of Enemy Air Defence (SEAD) missions. This enhances the survivability of the strike aircraft and thereby the mission assurance level. Post-strike, to assess the degree of damage, Bomb Damage Assessment (BDA) missions are also planned either by combat aircraft equipped with recce systems or by other means using satellites or UAVs.

Therefore, for a combat aircraft to launch its weapon on a selected target, a large number of support platforms get airborne to gather intelligence, to provide surveillance and air defence cover, for electronic warfare, to suppress enemy air defence, to refuel in air and carry out BDA. Plans also account for ejection over hostile territory and extraction of a downed crew with Combat Search and Rescue (CSAR) missions.

While the motive of any operator is to achieve the objectives, the one on the receiving end too has multiple options to negate the impact of combat aviation assets of the adversary. A strategy to counterbalance the enemy's offensive combat aviation capability can broadly be classified in three subsets – Offensive Operations, Active Defensive Operations, Passive Operations.

Offensive Operations hinge on the use of own offensive combat capability to degrade the offensive potential of the adversary. This can be implemented by a number of methods. Destroying the adversary's combat aircraft on the ground, denying or degrading airfield infrastructure, interdicting weapons and fuel supplies, disrupting command and control centres, degrading battle space transparency sensors, and interrupting communications are some of the common methods. The implementation strategy is based on an objective analysis of these domains in terms of their vulnerability and criticality. These two are then matched with own resources and the available capability to draw up an optimum plan. Overpowering one of the domains in totality will destroy the combat aviation capability of the adversary. The probability of complete success remains very low even if the two sides have major capability differentials. On the other hand, attacking all domains simultaneously needs a large force structure (see Annexure 4). Therefore, normally the final solution is a selection of a combination of domains that are targeted to achieve the objective. Prerequisites for high assurance of the success of offensive operations are battle space transparency along with suitably capable force structures. Successful implementation of this plan can degrade the adversary's offensive combat potential.

Active Defensive Operations are primarily aimed at mitigating the losses in case the adversary uses the offensive combat aviation assets. This strategy is based on the creation of multi-layered defensive shields. The outermost ring is normally by combat aircraft in conjunction with various sensors and command and control tools to intercept the incoming strike before its weapon release line. Invariably, defending aircraft have greater radar coverage from own ground-based radars in addition to airborne assets. However, the initiative remains with the intruder about the plans, force structure, intended target, mode, direction and time of the attack. The defender needs to be ready 24×7 in adequate strength to counter the attack. This uses up a large number of resources by locking up the aircraft, aircrew and operations and maintenance crew. The middle ring of the defensive plan is in terms of Surface-to-Air Guided Weapons (SAGW). It is normally a cost-effective option but has limitations in terms of its range. New systems like S400 with a range of 400 km have expanded the envelope of the middle ring. This frees up combat aircraft from air defence duties in specific sectors. The innermost ring of defensive operation is Close-In Weapon Systems (CIWS) and can be a combination of quick reaction surface-to-air missiles and anti-aircraft guns. Although no defensive system is impregnable, having a potent multi-layered system increases the cost of operation for the aggressor. For an offensive force, the number of weapons that can be delivered on the intended target by the aggressor keep reducing as the intensity and capability of defensive systems protecting it increases.

Airpower has emerged as a central theme in kinetic tool application in the last century. However, the success of air campaigns has hinged heavily on the target systems offered by the adversary. For a successful offensive air attack, the presence of suitable target systems is a prerequisite. Military force application normally focuses on the use of concentrated force at the desired point. This ensures achievement of a favourable force-ratio besides being convenient from the maintenance and administrative points of view. However, a major flaw of this strategy is that it presents itself as an ideal target system for an aerial attack. Dispersion of combat and combat support assets – a passive activity – thus acts as an effective counter to any attack. This, when aided by suitable camouflage and concealment measures, enhances the survivability of assets. The prime objective of such passive operations is to deny the adversary any intelligence on the location of various combat assets.

Assessing Potential of Combat Aircraft

To assess the combat potential of an organisation, a quantitative and qualitative assessment of all its combat components is necessary. In this section, this aspect related to combat aircraft is discussed. A quantitative comparison is easy, based on simple 'Bean Counting', but it will be relevant only if qualitatively the platforms are comparable. The relative pecking order of combat platforms is always a matter of debate amongst practitioners and theoreticians with inputs and claims from manufacturers, operators and technocrats. However, the debate can only be settled in case the platforms are pitted against each other. The results of such a contest will be valid only in case the platforms operate under identical operational environments. That is impossible. So the debate rages on. To put such a debate into perspective, certain relevant parameters are listed here for assessing the combat potential of a combat aircraft. These can be classified into five different classes.

Platform Performance

The combat aircraft retains the central position in any discussion on combat aviation. Conceptualising a combat aircraft and thereafter converting into a physical design is a complex process. While the focus has been to enhance combat potency of each platform, the safety of the platform too has been a key area for the aviation industry. Combat potency is of use only if the platform survives. "Safety, Security and Strike" is the operative principle. Safety and reliability are the basic tenets that need to be beyond doubt before assessing a combat platform. A newly-designed aircraft often would fail on these parameters in its early developmental/operational employment stage. The platform needs to be safe to operate in terms of adequate and reliable systems with sufficient redundancies for basic flying. This covers the 'Safety' aspect in design definition. Thereafter, comes the aspect of 'Security' and it deals with the next test to check that the aircraft should be able to operate in the envisaged operational environment and has systems that help it in detecting and defeating the threats. Lastly, the 'Strike' – the aircraft should be able to deliver the weapons on the designated target – airborne or on the surface, mobile or static, open or camouflaged – as per the operational requirement conceptualisation. While the ability to strike is very distinct, the peculiarity between features for safety and security is getting blurred. Therefore, many automated systems are also being developed for enhancing the safety and security of operations. The latest in the series is an expansion of the Automatic Ground Collision Avoidance System (Auto GCAS) to create a fully-capable combat autopilot. Auto GCAS uses sensors on a fighter aircraft and terrain data for the possibility of a likely ground collision. Based on the aircraft's trajectory, speed, and the lack of inputs from the pilot, the system then calculates the best way to recover to a safe trajectory. It automatically overrides the flight controls and flies the aircraft away from danger. Ground collision is often the result of pilot disorientation, from a scenario such as target-fixation, or gravity-induced loss of consciousness, or a Controlled-Flight-Into-Terrain (CFIT) owing to lack of attention to the flight path. This technology, already integrated into the F-16 and the F-22, is being tested on the

F-35. Further development is on to create a fully- capable combat autopilot that will be able to execute tactical manoeuvres to defeat in-bound kinetic and non-kinetic threats.[6] It then will represent an amalgamation of safety and security features.

Several methods have been explored to arrive at an optimal combat aircraft configuration based on mission requirements, including take-off, climb, cruise, targeting and return phase. At the conceptual design phase itself, based on the mission profile and objectives, the basic definition of gross weight, the wing loading and thrust-to-weight ratio are computed.[7] However, the results from such simplistic approaches have major limitations in designing a combat aircraft and employing it for operational missions. The process of designing does not commence until its feasibility study has been carried out. That meshes design concepts exploring various configurations and amalgamation with available and developing technologies.[8] This is followed by a Project Definition that includes a development contract, design and development, acceptance of type record and transition from development to production.[9] With experience gained after initial operations, a number of design, hardware or software issues emerge that need to be modified to enhance the level of safety and reliability to cross the first stage of assessment. Thereafter, the platform is judged for its ability to take off and land with a planned weapon and fuel load. The take-off roll is an indication of low-speed characteristics of the airframe design and engine performance.[10] Low landing speed and consequent low landing roll are assets for operations from short airfields. The platforms with a vertical take-off and/or landing capability have reduced the dependence of availability of long runways. Other crucial characteristics relate to the time taken for aircraft to take off from the time the pilot reaches the aircraft. This is relevant especially for missions in a reactive scenario like a scramble to intercept an intruder. This time depends on the time taken for initiating engine starting cycle to reach full power. Warm-up and start time of onboard avionics is another factor that adds to this time. Classically, most combat aircraft can take off within three minutes. Once airborne, some critical factors that define the combat potential are thrust-to-weight ratio, level acceleration, maximum speed, rate of climb, combat ceiling,[11] fuel consumption rate, endurance, operational range, the instantaneous rate of turn, sustained rate of turn and low-speed handling characteristics.

Platform Signature

Each combat aircraft has a distinct visual, thermal, radar and electromagnetic signature. The visual signature is defined by aircraft shape, size, colour scheme, and exhaust gas emission trail. This aspect is of particular relevance in combat that is based on visually picking up the aircraft before targeting it. The visual signature plays a vital role not only in aerial combat but also in engagement by surface-based weapons systems that rely on visual or electro-optical sighting systems. Many anti-aircraft guns and man-portable missile systems belong to this category. The thermal signature of a combat aircraft is generated by the engines and the skin of the aircraft. While the heat generated by engines is more prominent in the rear hemisphere of the aircraft, the heat generated by the skin of the aircraft owing to operation at high speed can be detected nearly evenly from all directions. These two distinct heat signatures are in different frequencies and this aspect is utilised in designing homing heads of missile systems. Lower the Infrared signature of a platform, the lower is the probability of a heat-seeking weapon hitting it.[12] The radar signature of a combat platform is its Radar Cross-Section (RCS) as viewed by an electromagnetic wave of radar. The RCS is a predominant factor amongst several radar parameters that define the range at which an aircraft can be detected. The shape and design along with radar absorbing material and radar-absorbing paint are certain methods used to minimize the RCS. The electromagnetic signature of an aircraft is created because of electromagnetic waves generated in the aircraft owing to the operation of a number of onboard systems. The most prominent amongst these are EM emitters like radars, radios, radio altimeters. These, if analysed correctly can give away not only the presence of an aircraft but also its type. Additionally, the audio signature of a combat aircraft can also be mapped but with longer-range weapons for offence and defence;

the salience of this aspect has diminished drastically. However, in areas that are not covered by electronic sensors like radars, an audio signature of combat aircraft is still utilised to detect the presence of a combat aircraft. This methodology is often used in mountainous terrain where combat aircraft flying in the hill shadows or valleys attempt to delay detection by the radars.

Platform Potency

This aspect relates to kinetic weapons that the combat aircraft can carry and deliver. The key parameters in judging and comparing combat platforms in this aspect relate to the number and type of weapons that can be carried, and the efficiency with which these can be fired on the intended targets. This includes both air-to-air weapons and air-to-surface weapons. The aspect of range from the target that a combat aircraft can fire its weapon towards, plays a crucial role in defining its combat potency. While several platforms can fire the same weapon or weapons with identical capability, the role of the platform in providing a suitable interface and ease of targeting is crucial. This could be achieved by an inbuilt system like a radar or laser or an externally carried targeting pod. The ease and accuracy of operation invariably define the outcome of the attack even if the same weapon is used under identical operational conditions.

Platform-Human Interface

It is not the machine but the operator who uses the machine that defines the output. In the case of combat aviation, the comfort level of a pilot in the cockpit has a major impact on the outcome of platform employment. The shape and size of the cockpit, especially its canopy concerning the position of test eye,[13] plays a significant role in defining external visibility for the pilot, an important factor. The position of the control column, the controls on the throttle and stick, the location and information flow on displays in the cockpit, availability of information on helmet-mounted sights, can play a significant role in combat outcome where the time between victory and defeat can be milliseconds.

Platform Environment Interface

The combat aircraft rarely operate as a single entity. A combat aviator interacts with other combat platforms and support systems to enhance situational awareness. The methods used for communication are voice and data. While voice inputs depend excessively on operators and their common understanding, many inputs can be accurately passed on to a combat platform via data links. This could be in terms of location of friends and foes in the region or location and movement of potential targets. Similarly, the output of various onboard sensors can be transmitted to fellow combat aircraft or a ground station using data links. Owing to accuracy, the amount and speed of transmission of information, data links, a platform environment interface, act as a force multiplier. A typical example, in this case, is of a combat aircraft picking up a raider on his radar and transmitting this data to another formation member who silently (without opening up his radar) targets the raider with the raider's radar warning receiver giving no information of the impending attack. The electronic warfare capability of the platform is also part of this, which allows the platform to mask itself from radars; thus, delaying detection and this attribute enhances safety and mission effectiveness. Michael Buck, a practitioner from the United States Air Force, has aptly brought out this aspect in his paper on "Full Spectrum Close Air Support for the 21st Century". According to Buck, the fifth-generation aircraft's role will include the creation of an information cloud about the battle space and:

> New methods of command and control (C2) that capitalize on the situational awareness (SA) created in the combat cloud will permit efficient, decentralized execution at the tactical level. To optimize ground force effectiveness, sensor effect or aircraft will act as "quarterbacks," making on-the-spot decisions and rapidly coordinating the weapons effects of players" across all domains to target enemy forces before they can target our own.[14]

All the above-mentioned parameters that assist in assessing the combat potential of a combat aircraft are detailed in Table 3.1.

Table 3.1: Combat Aircraft Potential Assessment Parameters

Attribute	Characteristics
Platform Performance	Safety, reliability, take-off and landing performance, reaction time, low speed handling, level acceleration, rate of climb, combat ceiling, thrust to weight ratio, maximum speed, fuel consumption rate, endurance, operational range, instantaneous rate of turn, sustained rate of turn and low speed handling characteristics
Platform Signature	Visual, thermal, radar, electromagnetic and audio signature
Platform Potency	Weapon carrying capacity, weapon delivery capability
Platform Human Interface	Cockpit layout, Information display systems
Platform Environment Interface	Voice link, Datalink, Electronic warfare systems

Source: Author's own.

All attributes tabulated in Table 3.1 can be individually assessed very objectively and compared for any two distinct platforms. However, the debate invariably rages on the weight that each attribute is assigned while taking a holistic picture of the combat potential of the aircraft. Another aspect that comes into play is the role assigned to a platform. The majority of combat platforms operational today are multi-role capable. The combat potential of the same platform in different roles differs owing to the distinct configuration. For example, an aircraft for an air defence mission will be configured with air-to-air weapons and the same aircraft for a ground attack mission will have air-to-surface weapons, a targeting pod and an electronic warfare pod. The additional load for a ground attack mission has a telling effect on the performance of the aircraft. So, relative combat potential of different aircraft, is a function of not only platform characteristics but also of the mission assigned to it. This complexity in comparing the combat potential of various combat aircraft and lack of an identical operational environment to test this out makes qualitative assessment very subjective. For this reason, combat aircraft are classified broadly with adequate leeway. Details of one such methodology are covered later in this book.

Summary

A combat aircraft is a significant tool in the battle space and can be employed in a variety of roles. However, to be fully exploited, this tool needs support in terms of battle space transparency. With changing technology helping expand the battle space, it is imperative to focus on capabilities that provide the requisite level of transparency. Without battle space transparency, the effectiveness of offensive and defensive vectors is severely restricted. To sustain operations of both offensive and defensive character, a number of support systems are also required in terms of logistics, maintenance and infrastructure. Force planning and operational planning processes play a vital role in defining the equipment profile and resource allocation to various verticals of military capabilities. Like a balanced diet for human growth, a balanced approach in the development of transparency, offensive, defensive, and support structures is essential for optimizing resource deployment.

Comparing various attributes that play a role in the potential generation of a combat aircraft is an objective process. However, it turns very complex and subjective when a holistic assessment is made about the combat potential of a combat platform. For this reason, combat aircraft are broadly classified with adequate leeway and this takes into account the mission assigned and the operational environment.

Notes

1. Walter C. Ladwig III, Indian Military Modernization and Conventional Deterrence in South Asia, *Journal of Strategic Studies,* Volume 38 Issue 5, May 2015, DOI: 10.1080/01402390.2015.1014473.
2. See Robert Jackson, "Offensive Aircraft in a New Age", in Phillip Jarret (Ed), *The Modern War Machine, Military Aviation Since 1945*, Putnam

Aeronautical Books, London, 2000, pp. 115-139.

3. Lt Gen David A. Deptula, "Interdependent Warfare: Combined Effects Power in the 21st Century", Mitchell Institute Policy Papers, 10, March 2018.
4. For theoretical aspects of explosives see A. Bailey and S.G. Murray, *Explosives, Propellants and Pyrotechnics*, Brasseys, UK, 1989, pp. 1-58.
5. V.V. Rampal, *Photonics in Warfare,* Defence Research and Development Organisation, Ministry of Defence, New Delhi, 2002, pp. 199-215.
6. Garrett Reim, "Edwards Air Force Base begins testing Auto GCAS on Lockheed Martin F-35", *Flight Global,* November 16, 2018 at https://www.flightglobal.com/news/articles/edwards-air-force-base-begins-testing-auto-gcas-on-l-453733/, accessed on November 29, 2018.
7. Peter G. Coen and Willard E.-Foss Jr., "Computer Sizing of fighter aircraft", NASA Technical Memorandum 86351, NASA-TM-86351 19850008450, January 1985, National Aeronautics and Space Administration Langley Research Center, Hampton, Virginia at https://ntrs.nasa.gov/search.jsp?R=19850008450, accessed on November 20, 2018.
8. K. Nagaraj, *Airworthiness Certification of Fighter Aircraft,* Defence Research and Development Organisation, Ministry of Defence, New Delhi, 2015, pp. 3-4.
9. Ibid., pp. 4-7.
10. For certain combat aircraft with low thrust like Jaguar, it is often joked that it takes off from the ground because the earth dips owing to the curvature of the earth especially in high, hot and humid conditions with high-density altitude.
11. Combat ceiling is the altitude at which the aircraft still can sustain a 1000-feet per minute rate of climb.
12. V.V. Rampal, no. 5, pp. 147-162.
13. The cockpit is designed keeping in mind an assessed location of the eye of the pilot. This location is called Test Eye. Irrespective of the height of the pilot, individual pilots adjust the seat height so that their eyes are as close to Test Eye location as that gives the best internal and external view.
14. Lt Col Michael Buck, "Full Spectrum Close Air Support for the 21st Century: Leveraging Air Operations with Ground Forces", Mitchell Institute Policy Papers, 8, October 2017.

PART II

Five Decades Trajectory of Combat Aviation 1968-2018

4. Cruise Climb – Range Descent: Combat Aircraft Inventory (1968-2018)

Combat aircraft provide potent offensive and defensive capabilities within their Radius of Action (ROA). Combat potency is a function of each platform's ability to deliver weapons on other aerial platforms and surface targets on land or sea. In an offensive role, the prime task of a combat aircraft is to deliver kinetic weapons to achieve-K-Kill (Annihilation), M-Kill (Mobility kill) or F-Kill (Functional kill) of the designated target system as per mission requirements. This invariably has to be achieved in a hostile space with the defender employing kinetic and non-kinetic, active and passive means to thwart the attack. On defensive missions, the prime task assigned to combat aircraft is to interrupt an attacker by destroying or disrupting the attack profile to deny launch of a kinetic weapon against friendly forces/assets. The interplay between the offensive and defensive players depends primarily on relative battle space transparency and the relative range of kinetic weapons. Based on the strategy of the states, the role assigned to combat aircraft is either primarily offensive or primarily defensive or a combination of the two. Most of the modern combat aircraft can perform both offensive and defensive roles. Herein lies the origin of the term Multi-Role Combat Aircraft (MRCA).[1]

Currently, there are 18,172 combat aircraft in the world operated by 106 countries. Ironically, the combat aircraft inventory was around the same half a century ago. The number of combat aircraft in the world gradually increased from 1968 to peak in 1988 and thereafter has shown a steady decline as depicted in Figure 4.1. While the quantum of supersonic combat aircraft has followed a

Figure 4.1: Total Combat Aircraft in the World from 1968-2018

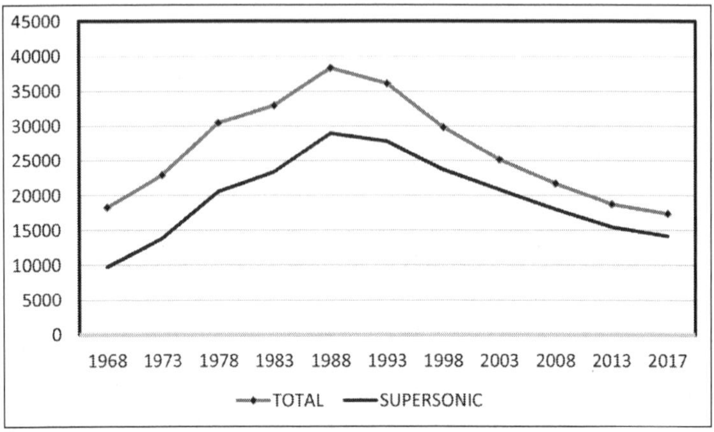

Source: Combat Aircraft Inventory Database.

similar broad pattern but their share has continuously increased from 53 per cent in 1968 to 86 per cent in 2018. The development of powerful engines and understanding of supersonic aerodynamics allowed employment of supersonic military aircraft in the 1950s and the proliferation of this technology allowed replacement of earlier generation of combat aircraft. High speed allows tactical advantage and reduces reaction time to the opposition; therefore a large share of current combat inventory is capable of supersonic operations. Invariably, initially developed and deployed supersonic combat aircraft had relatively poor low-speed handling characteristics. This allowed subsonic aircraft to retain their relevance for specific roles like in Battlefield Air Strikes (BAS). A10 is a classic example in this category and continues to be operationally employed to date. Based on the operational environment and envisaged role, many operators prefer operating subsonic aircraft for their low-speed handling characteristics and fuel efficiency. Good low-speed handling allows the aircraft to be used as tactical trainers besides deployment in low-intensity conflicts. Alpha Jets and Hawks are prime examples in this category deployed in over 20 countries.

Today, there are about 81 types of combat aircraft operating in the world. Quantitatively, the types of combat aircraft have followed

Figure 4.2: Total Types of Combat Aircraft in the World from 1968-2018

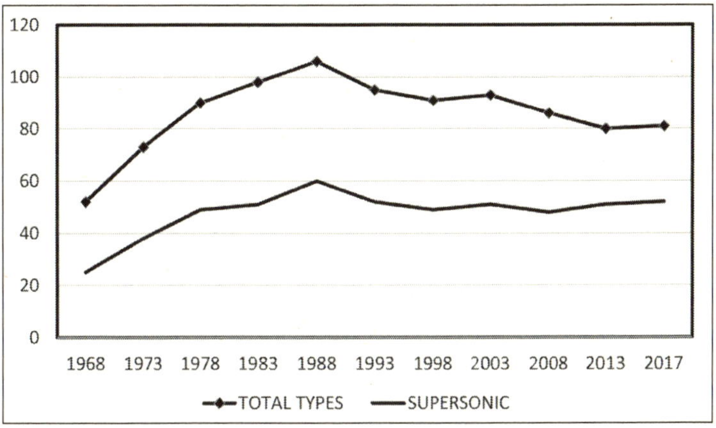

Source: Combat Aircraft Inventory Database.

the pattern of the quantum but not as radically. The types of combat aircraft peaked at 105 in the 1990s and had a gradual decline since as shown in Figure 4.2. Overall, there have been 186 types of combat aircraft employed in the last 50 years with more than 58 per cent of them phasing out. Over 55 types of combat aircraft have been phased out in the last three decades. Practically, every six months, a type of combat aircraft is going into oblivion on termination of operational service. Compared to this, new types of combat aircraft were inducted at an average rate of one per year in the same period. This has resulted in the gradual slide in the types of combat aircraft in operations worldwide.

There are three prime reasons for this trend. First, barring stealth design, there has been no major breakthrough in airframe design after the induction of supersonic aircraft. Stealth technology for aerial platforms is still maturing and is available with only a handful of manufacturers. The number of stealth platforms deployed is relatively low and have not yet altered the operational environment although the process has started. Once the existing operational environment changes with the proliferation of stealth platforms, operational relevance for non-stealth platforms will fall sharply and lead to their phase-out. With limited access to stealth technology, as an alternative, all new technological innovations were incorporated into proven airframe designs and the existing types of aircraft modified. Today, there are several variants of each type based on upgradations and role-specific modifications. Upgradations are normally in terms of avionics for navigation, weapon aiming and weapon delivery subsystems, but sometimes do include additional load-carrying stations or engine configurations or types of external fuel tanks to enhance the safety and performance criteria. The importance of stealth in the air-to-air combat is that it reduces the adversary's detection range, reduces the range at which an active or semi-active air-to-air missile can lock on, and reduces the F-pole, or the distance between the launch aircraft and the target at the time of missile impact.[2]

Second, the concept of MRCA has evolved. With minor changes in weapon configuration or avionics, the same platform could be tasked with the offensive or defensive role. This obviated the need to have two different types for offensive and defensive roles in the same sector. The modular design allowed the same platform to be quickly reconfigured from an Air Defence Mission configuration to a Ground Attack Configuration. A large number of combat aircraft today can carry out air defence missions after having delivered air-to-ground weapons on the designated surface targets. In-flight refuelling has allowed long-duration missions and helped in this quest and *ab initio* configuration to carry a mixed load of air-to-surface weapons and air-to-air missiles.

Lastly, greater sophistication of onboard systems necessitated setting up of vast development and maintenance facilities leading aircraft manufacturers and operators to focus on the commonality of equipment and systems. This is economic and allows a great deal of operational flexibility. The F35 development programme is a classic example with different configurations developed for different users (the United States Air Force, United States Navy and United States Marine Corps) on the same basic platform. A similar concept is adopted for Light Combat Aircraft (LCA) with a version each for Indian Air Force and Indian Navy.

Military aviation commenced its role in the First World War and matured by the Second World War. However, the availability of aviation technology, and specifically military aviation for combat aircraft, was restricted to a few industrialised nations. With the gradual spread of technology, the collapse of the imperialistic British Empire, the creation of new nation-states and inter-state conflicts resulted in a systematic increase in a number of nations with combat aircraft (Figure 4.3). By 1988, more than half the countries in the world possessed and operated combat aircraft. Today, 106 countries own and operate combat aircraft. Asia and Europe are on top with countries that operate combat aircraft and this is closely followed by Africa which has the maximum number of countries that exist without any combat aircraft as seen in Figure 4.4. Barring seven, the combat aircraft inventory of all African nations is less than 50 aircraft each. A similar state exists in South America and Australia Oceania. An overview of combat aircraft per country given in Figure 4.5 is indicative of the low density in Australia Oceania, Africa and South America and a very high density in Asia.

Figure 4.3: Number of Countries with Combat Aircraft in the World from 1968-2017

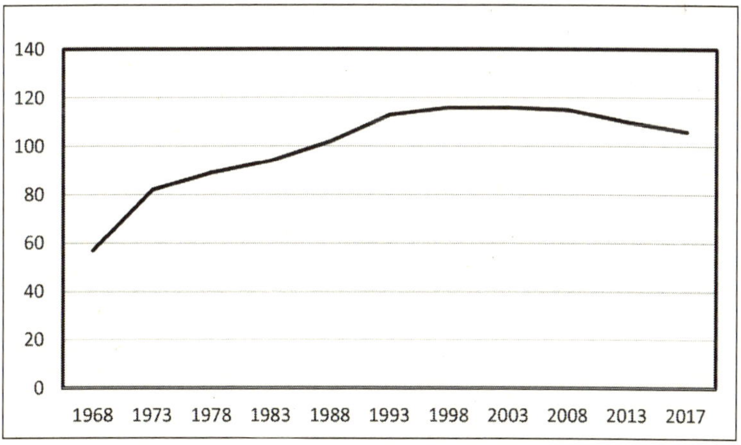

Source: Combat Aircraft Inventory Database.

Figure 4.4: Number of Countries with Combat Aircraft in the World 2018

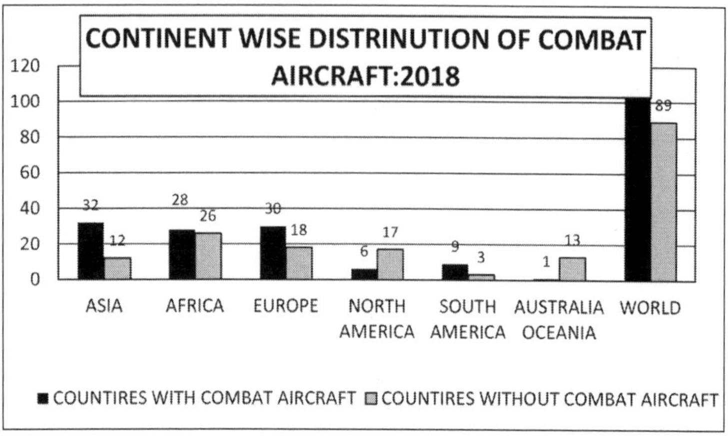

Source: Combat Aircraft Inventory Database.

Figure 4.5: Average Number of Combat Aircraft/Country in the World 2018

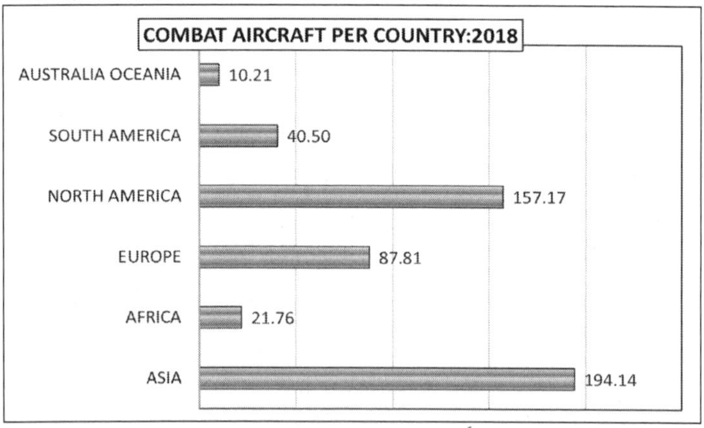

Source: Combat Aircraft Inventory Database.

Inventory-holding of combat aircraft in the world is lopsided (Figure 4.6). The US is the only one with more than 3000 combat aircraft followed by China and Russia in the 1000+ category. India and the Republic of Korea have more than 500 combat aircraft. Nearly one-third of the countries operating combat aircraft have an inventory of less than 20. The top six countries have nearly 50 per cent of combat aircraft in the world and 75 per cent of the inventory is held in just 19 countries. The situation has changed since 1988 when the top three countries – the US, erstwhile USSR and China had more than half of the combat aircraft of the world and at that time their total inventory was more than what the entire world possesses today. In 1988 as many as 12 countries had more than 500 combat aircraft as compared to seven today.

Figure 4.6: Number of Countries with Combat Aircraft in the World in 2018

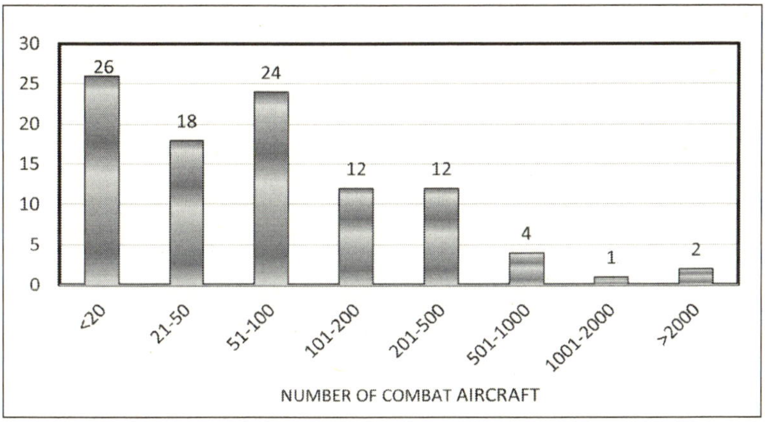

Source: Combat Aircraft Inventory Database.

For over three decades now, the US has retained the top spot in the list of countries with the maximum number of combat aircraft. However, its fleet is ageing and as per the US Aerospace Industry Report:

> The ageing of the U.S. military aircraft fleet remains a significant factor. Anecdotally, it has been said that some of today's pilots are now flying the same equipment as did their fathers – and, in a few cases, their grandfathers. For example, in 2012, the newest B-52 turned 50 years old and those aircraft are projected to fly another 20 years. Overall, the current U.S. Air Force fleet, with planes averaging more than 23 years old, is the oldest in USAF history.[3]

Erstwhile USSR and China had shared the top two positions till the 1980s. The collapse of USSR and distribution of assets including aircraft brought down the inventory Russia holds today. Currently, the US with over 3,463 combat aircraft has a quantitative edge of over 20 per cent over second-placed China and has more than double of the Russian inventory. While these three P5 nations[4] have retained their position, the journey of the other two P5 members is intriguing. Both, UK and France, were at fourth and fifth place respectively in the 1980s with their inventory of combat aircraft. In 2018, France has slipped to 12th position and UK is at 15th. These two countries have systematically decreased the number of combat aircraft by over 70 per cent from their peak holdings in the last three decades. France is scheduled to further trim down its combat aircraft inventory by 20 per cent from its current holding. India placed at the seventh position in 1968 has gradually inched upwards and is steady in fourth place for the last two decades (Figure 4.7).

Figure 4.7: Track of the Top Four Nations with the Number of Combat Aircraft in the World from 1968-2017

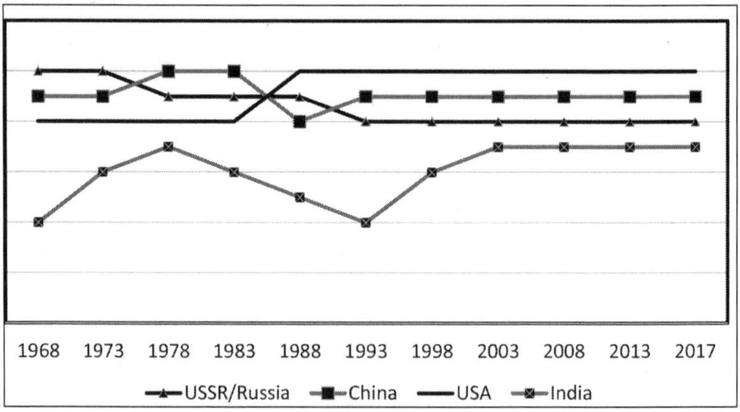

Source: Combat Aircraft Inventory Database.

The qualitative edge that the US enjoyed over other air powers is diminishing. This can be seen from the RAND assessment about the force level required to achieve air superiority in case of a conflict in Eastern Asia. In a period of 1996 to 2017, the US force level required for this mission has seen a 14 to 20 time jump for conflict scenarios in the Taiwan Straits and Spratly Islands respectively.[5] Although quantitatively and qualitatively the US retains the *numero uno* position, the growth in Chinese airpower appears much better owing to a low base effect of PLAAF and PLAN. The closure rate between the US and Chinese airpower is expected to slow down as China closes the gap akin to Newton Law of Cooling.[6] As the capability gap between the two major air powers reduces, the duration of a military conflict, should it take place, will increase and a clear victor may not emerge.

> The United States continues to maintain unparalleled air-to-air capabilities. Even in the most challenging cases examined, the United States does not "lose" the war in the air. However, continuous improvements to Chinese air capabilities make it increasingly difficult for the United States to achieve air superiority within a politically and operationally effective time frame, especially in a scenario close to the Chinese mainland.[7]

There are 19 countries with more than 200 combat aircraft – USA, China, Russia, India, ROK, Taiwan,[8] DPRK, Pakistan, Egypt, Israel, Japan, Saudi Arabia, Turkey, Iran, France, Syria, Greece, Italy and the UK. These are depicted in Map 4.1. While the trend in Europe has been to reduce the combat aircraft inventory, Asia presents a different picture. There are 11 Asian countries in these 19 countries. Although the number of countries operating combat aircraft has almost doubled in the last 50 years, the number of major players has declined. The growth has been in the fringe operators with less than 20 combat aircraft (Figure 4.8). For the first time, the number of countries with less than 20 combat aircraft has overtaken the number of countries with more than 100 combat aircraft.

Map 4.1: Map Showing 19 Countries with more than 200 Combat Aircraft in 2018

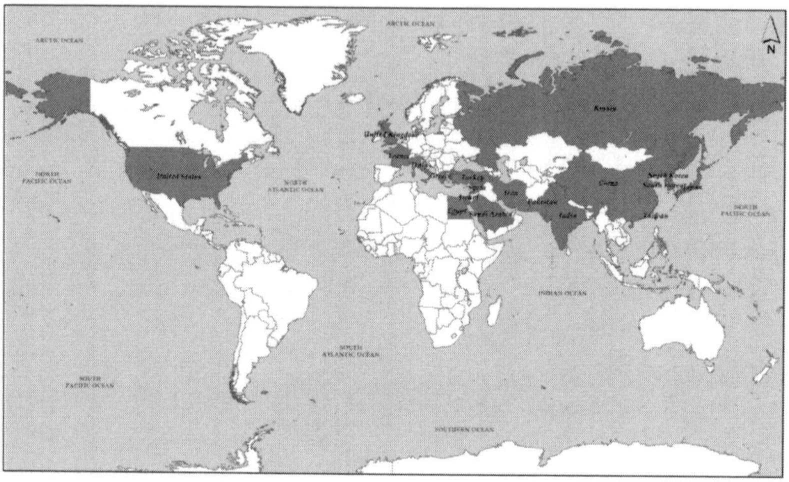

Source: Created by GIS Cell, IDSA, New Delhi based on data from Combat Aircraft Inventory Database.

Figure 4.8: Number of Countries with Combat Aircraft in the World in 1968-2017

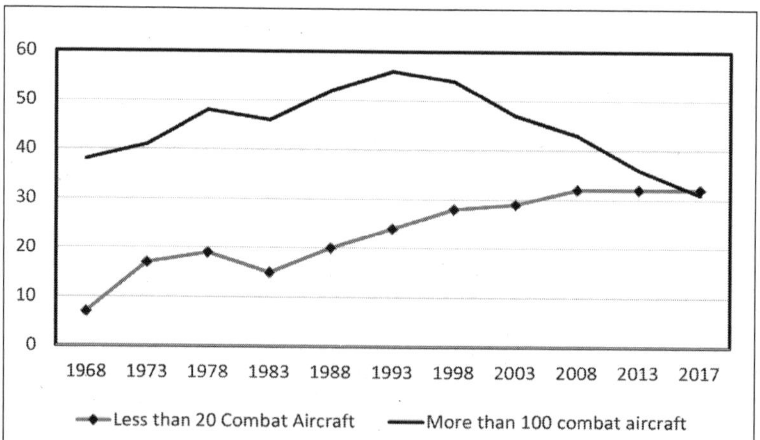

Source: Combat Aircraft Inventory Database.

Availability of combat aircraft was the highest in Europe until 1988 (Figure 4.9). With an end of the Cold War and the breakdown of erstwhile USSR, there was a decline in the number of combat aircraft in Europe. Consequently, Asia emerged as the leader in this respect. This shift was also facilitated by the amalgamation of the combat aircraft inventory of some of the breakaway republics of USSR into the Asian inventory owing to their geographic location. The general absence of inter-state conflicts in Australia Oceania and South America are reflected in the perpetual relatively low density of combat aircraft in these two continents. However, in Africa, the non-availability of technology and economic resources to build infrastructure and operate combat aircraft seems to be the main reason for the low proliferation of combat aircraft. As depicted in Figure 4.10, a tectonic shift has taken place from 1968 to 2018 wherein Europe, with half the share of combat aircraft, has been replaced by Asia today with nearly half (47 per cent) of the world's combat aircraft. In case the American and Russian aircraft deployed in Asia are taken cognizance of, this figure crosses 52 per cent. Today, interestingly, third-placed Russia has more combat aircraft than entire Africa, and second-placed China's inventory is more than the combined strength of combat aircraft in Africa, Australia Oceania, and South America.

Figure 4.9: Continental Distribution of Combat Aircraft in the World in 1968-2018

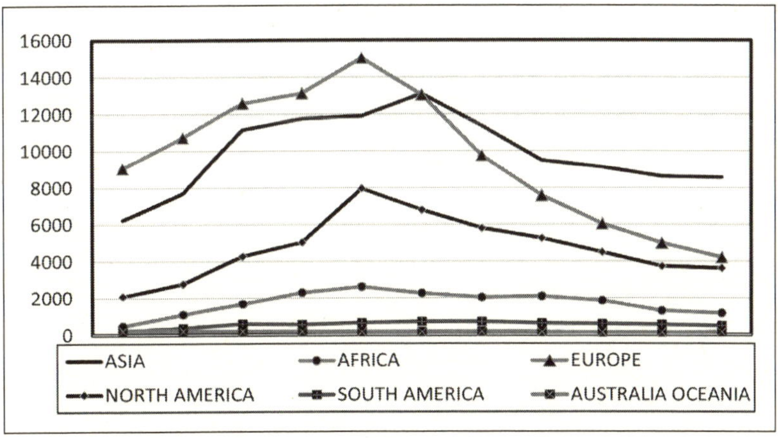

Source: Combat Aircraft Inventory Database.

Figure 4.10: Continental Share of Combat Aircraft in the World in 1968 and 2018

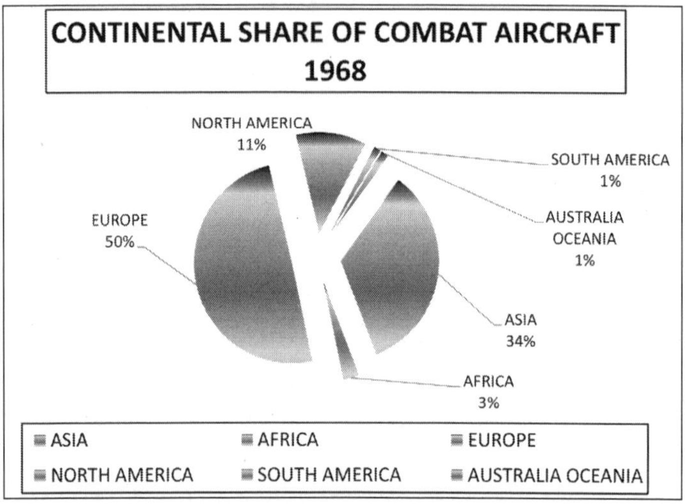

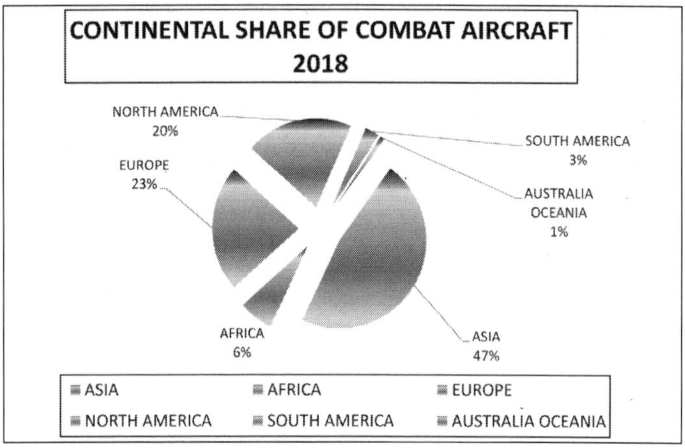

Source: Combat Aircraft Inventory Database.

As is evident from Figure 4.9 that the peak combat aircraft strength was achieved in all continents around 1990 and thereafter it has seen a steady decline. Overall, the world combat aircraft inventory has shrunk by 53 per cent in the last thirty years. Europe which had the highest number of combat aircraft in 1988 has seen a maximum reduction of nearly 72 per cent as depicted in Figure 4.11. Though the Asian inventory has declined from its historic peak by

35 per cent, it is still substantial to retain pole position. A low base effect has led to low percentile reduction in Australia and South America.

Figure 4.11: Percentage Reduction of Combat Aircraft Strength from Peak Strength

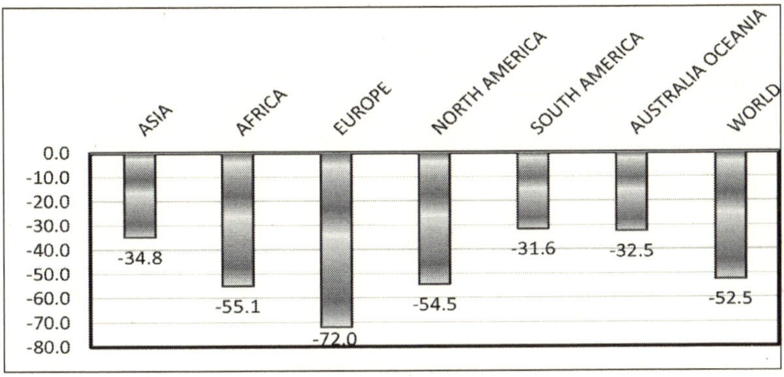

Source: Combat Aircraft Inventory Database.

The Second World War led to a very large manufacturing capacity for military aircraft and by 1945, erstwhile USSR was able to produce 42,000 aircraft in one year compared to British production of 26,000 and 93,000 in the US.[9] A lot of air has passed beneath the wings since then. Complicated designs, high costs and low requirements have resulted in a marked scaled-down military aviation manufacturing base. Now, there are primarily three manufacturing hubs for combat aircraft – the US, Russia and China; and these three countries operate 41 per cent of combat aircraft in the world. While all US and Russian combat aircraft are indigenous, China does operate Russian-made Sukhoi aircraft besides Chinese aircraft. With Light Combat Aircraft (LCA) yet to be inducted in large numbers, India has the dubious distinction of the largest number of foreign combat aircraft in the world. Of all the combat aircraft operating in the world today, 92 per cent have been manufactured by companies established in P5 nations, as indicated in Figure 4.12. The monopoly for aircraft engines is even more severe as indicated by the US Aerospace Industry Report:

The jet engine market is dominated by three manufacturers: General Electric (GE) Aviation; Pratt & Whitney (P&W), a United Technologies company; and Rolls Royce. Given the high barriers to entry, the fundamental market structure for jet engine development and production is not likely to change.[10]

Figure 4.12: Share of Manufacture of Combat Aircraft of the World

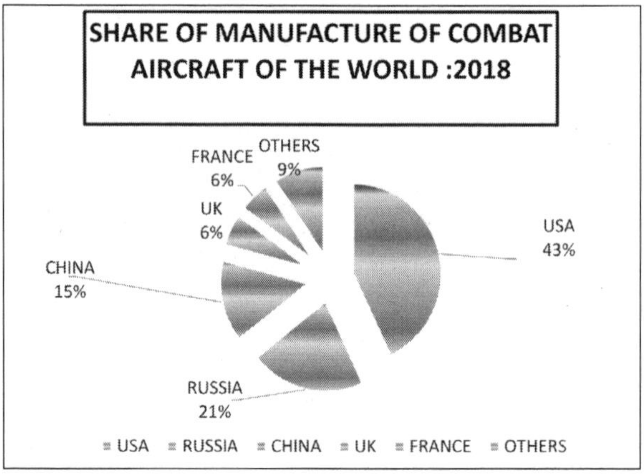

Source: Combat Aircraft Inventory Database.

Overall, the US leads the aviation industry. The US aircraft industry for civil applications grew by 6 per cent in 2017 and delivered 2808 units including 763 transport aircraft, 449 helicopters and 1596 general aviation aircraft. In the military aircraft category, there was compression and only 538 units were delivered including 112 combat aircraft, 42 patrol/C2 aircraft, 321 helicopters, 23 trainers and 40 transport aircraft. This is more than 15 per cent lower than in 2015.[11] Additionally, 469 unmanned aerial vehicles were delivered in 2017, 34 per cent lower than the previous year.[12] The size of Russian aerospace industry is comparatively small but the Russian-designed aircraft, especially the mass- produced military aircraft, have been simple and rugged, austerity-equipped with instrumentation, and seemingly unattentive to pilot safety.[13] The Russian priority on effectiveness has been less apparent in these flying machines. For Russian designers, this priority has meant the studied effort to design aircraft that perform well. These designers have fashioned aircraft that routinely fly in some of the most inhospitable environments in the world.[14] Aleksander S Yakoslve, a leading Soviet aircraft designer summarised their design philosophy in his autobiography *Tselzhizni* (The Aim of a Lifetime) simply as: [15]

- Maximum simplicity for ease of production and reliable operation.
- Evolutionary development to minimise risk and potential impact on production.
- Minimum requirement of field maintenance to operate without regard to climatic conditions and the availability of developed airfields and field support.

On the other hand, although not as big, the Chinese aircraft industry has been steadily expanding in this century as brought out by the data in *Chinese Statistics Yearbook on High Technology Industry 2017* and depicted in Figure 4.13. The export share crossed 10 per cent of revenue in 2005 and has sustained that performance in spite of capacity expansion. A growth of over seven times in revenue since 2000 is accompanied by a one-third reduction in the manpower deployed in the aircraft industry (Figure 4.14). This indicates a major shift toward high-end technology in the Chinese aircraft industry that has enhanced productivity and revenue per employee.

Figure 4.13: Chinese Aircraft Industry Performance

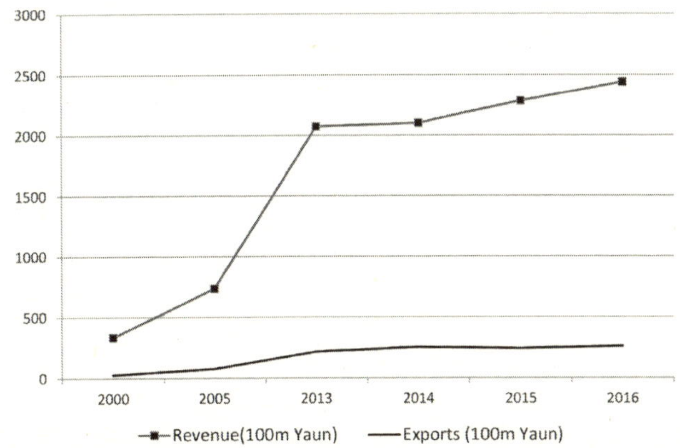

Source: Based on data in *Chinese Statistics Yearbook on High Technology Industry 2017.*

Figure 4.14: Number of Employees in Chinese Aircraft Industry

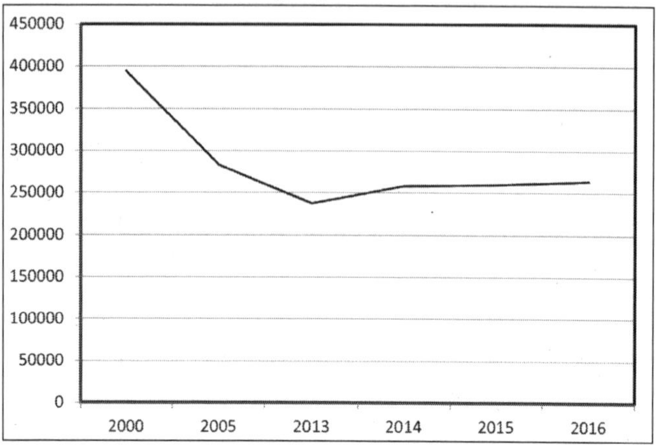

Source: Based on data in *Chinese Statistics Yearbook on High Technology Industry 2017.*

The limited indigenous aircraft industry in India is practically represented by state-owned Hindustan Aeronautics Limited (HAL) headquartered in Bengaluru. Since 2000, the revenue of HAL has gone up with the captive market of the Indian armed forces but the number of employees has not changed much (Figure 4.15). This is indicative of the technologically stagnant industry. More details are covered later in Chapter 14.

Figure 4.15: Number of Employees in Hindustan Aeronautical Limited, India

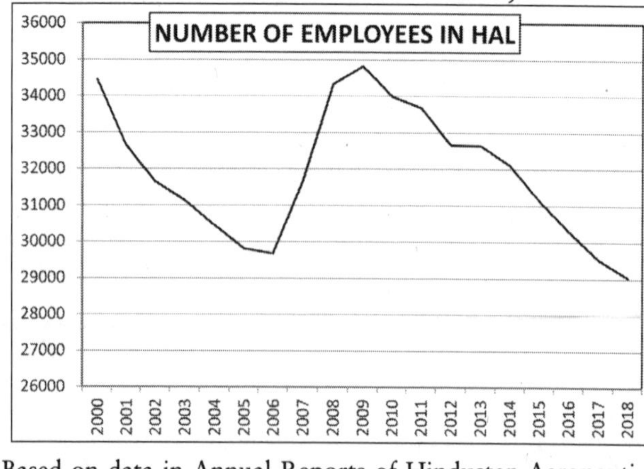

Source: Based on data in Annual Reports of Hindustan Aeronautical Limited 2012-13 and 2017-18.[16]

From 1968 onwards, MiG-21 has been the most popular combat aircraft in terms of numbers closely followed by mass-produced Chinese J6 (MiG-19). Today, only eight types of combat aircraft cover half the world's inventory. The predominance of MiG-21 and J6 has given way to F-16, F-18, and F-15 and these three types form 29 per cent of the world's combat aircraft, with F-16 alone taking 16 per cent share (Figure 4.16). Lockheed Martin has delivered 4588 F-16s to 26 countries.[17] In the last three years, a 44 per cent reduction in work-related to F-18 in Boeing,[18] non-expansion of the F-15 base and non-availability of any orders for the manufacture of F-16 of Lockheed Martin,[19] are indicators that the strength of these three predominant fleets will only go down (Figure 4.17). For F-16, continuous production for four decades at its Fort Worth, Texas plant ceased on November 14, 2017.[20] Order for 19 F-16 aircraft for Bahrain and upgradation work owing to orders from Singapore in 2015 will continue till 2023.[21] Lockheed Martin's F-35 is set to be the leading combat aircraft with 46 aircraft delivered in 2016 and over 50 in 2017. The scheduled production for another two decades with three production lines (Forth Worth, Texas; Cameri, Italy and Nagoya Japan) and an estimated strength of nearly 3000 with United States Air Force, United States Navy and United States Marines Corps as the main users and countries like Australia, Japan, Israel, Turkey, the UK, Denmark, the Netherlands and ROK. Seeking an allocation of resources for procurement of 77 F-35s for the USAF in 2018-19, the US Department of Defense's budget is an indication of this trend. Currently, the F-35 has a vast technological advantage over other combat aircraft. The F-35's footprint will expand as did that of F-16 with a reduction in the technological differential and the necessity to sustain economic viability and employment in Lockheed Martin. All operators of F-16 today will eventually be forced to switch to very expensive F-35 owing to a planned reduction in F-16 maintenance support in the coming decades.

Figure 4.16: Relative Strength of Combat Aircraft of the World

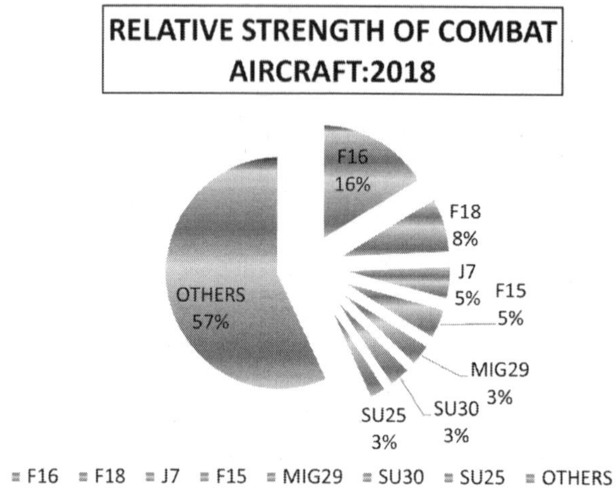

Source: Combat Aircraft Inventory Database

Figure 4.17: Annual Task for Boeing Company and Lockheed Martin related to Manufacturing/Modification of Combat Aircraft F18/F15 and F16 respectively

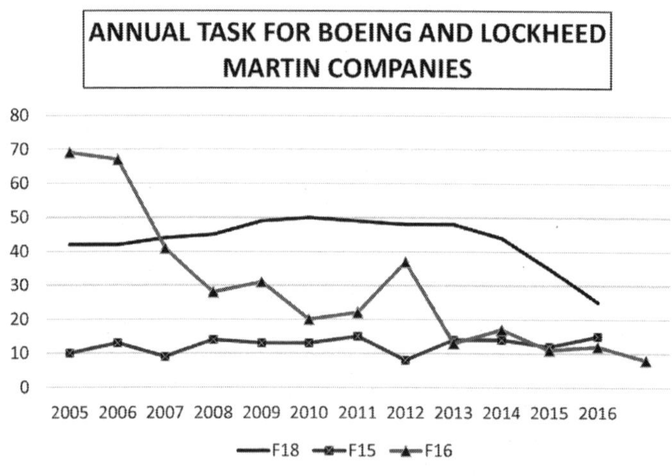

Source: Compiled from the Boeing Company Annual Reports 2006-2016[22] and Lockheed Martin Annual Reports 2006-2016.[23]

In brief, P5 countries have been leaders in designing and manufacturing combat aircraft in the last five decades. Top three spots in the combat aircraft holdings are still with countries from this group. Although diversifying, the world's inventory of combat aircraft is gradually reducing; but this niche market is controlled by the US and Russia, with China moving aggressively upwards.

Notes

1. For more on operational employment of combat aircraft in various wars, see Mike Spick, *Fighters at War: The Story of Air-to-Air Combat*, Greenhill Books, London, 1997, p. 120.
2. Bill Sweetman, *Advanced Fighter Technology: The Future of Cockpit Combat*, Air Life Publishing Ltd, England, 1988, p. 166.
3. *Aerospace Industry Report 2013,* The Aerospace Industries Association of America and the Center of Aviation & Aerospace Leadership at Embry-Riddle Aeronautical University, at http://www.aia-aerospace.org/wp-content/uploads/2016/09/AIR-2012-Book.pdf, Accessed on October 9, 2018.
4. The five permanent members of the United Nations Security Council are referred to as P5 nations.
5. Heginbotham et al, "The U.S. and Chinese Air Superiority Capabilities: An Assessment of Relative Advantage, 1996–2017", RAND Corporation, Santa Monica, CA, 2015 at https://www.rand.org/pubs/research_briefs/RB9858z3.html, Accessed on October 8, 2018.
6. As per Newton's Law of Cooling, the rate of cooling of a hot substance surrounded by a colder mass is inversely proportional to the difference in temperature between the two bodies.
7. Heginbotham et al., no. 5.
8. Taiwan, although not recognised as a country, does maintain its armed forces.
9. Air Vice Marshal Tony Mason, "The Air Warfare Requirement", in Phillip Jarret (ed.), *The Modern War Machine: Military Aviation Since 1945*, Putnam Aeronautical Books, London, 2000, p. 11.
10. Aerospace Industry Report 2013, no. 3.
11. *Annual Report of Aerospace Industry Association 2018 Facts and Figures* at https://doc-14-bk-apps-viewer.googleusercontent.com/viewer/secure/pdf/3nb9bdfcv3e2h2k1cmql0ee9cvc5lole/56eh6aqdmg1efpghfmp9q86h4iv92cnn/1539079875000/lantern/*/ACFrOgCERpfpIFfTwholRJJhgwr3XJS4mANIA_yauyLqWs0IHHc0Dw_kD68FDrtL4Lpfg12M1vEWAut8JU8gFTYO--gcHlspQ3lx6LKFEIj9ns5CFutJ3DrdgXqsbc4vUrT_0BiAzFs5A7O76a3T?print=true, Accessed on October 9, 2018.
12. Ibid.
13. Robin Hingham, John T. Greenwood and Von Hardesty, *Russian Aviation and Air Power in the Twentieth Century*, Frank Cass Publishers, Great

Britain, 1998, p. 1.

14. Ibid.
15. John T, Greenwood, "The Designers: Their Design Bureaus and aircraft", in Robin Hingham, John T. Greenwood and Von Hardesty (Eds.),*Russian Aviation and Air Power in the Twentieth Century*, Frank Cass Publishers, Great Britain, 1998, p. 163.
16. *HAL Annual Report 2012-13 and 2017-18* at https://hal-india.co.in/Common/Uploads/Finance/AnnualReport-2012-13-English.pdf and https://hal-india.co.in/Common/Uploads/Finance/Annual-2017-18.pdf, Accessed on October 29, 2018.
17. Compiled from *Annual Report,* Lockheed Martin Corporation, at https://www.lockheedmartin.com/content/dam/lockheed/data/corporate/documents/2016-annual-report.pdf, accessed on November 1, 2017.
18. *The Boeing Company Annual Report 2016*, pp 32 at http://s2.q4cdn.com/661678649/files/doc_financials/annual/2016/2016-Annual-Report.pdf, accessed on November 1, 2017.
19. *Annual Report,* Lockheed Martin Corporation, no. 17.
20. "Last Fort Worth-built F-16 leaves Lockheed factory" at https://www.flightglobal.com/news/articles/last-fort-worth-built-f-16-leaves-lockheed-factory-443699/, accessed December 1, 2017.
21. 2015 *Annual Report*, Lockheed Martin Corporation, p. 32 at https://www.lockheedmartin.com/content/dam/lockheed/data/corporate/documents/2015-annual-report.pdf, accessed on November 1, 2017.
22. The Boeing Company Annual Reports are available at http://investors.boeing.com/investors/financial-reports/default.aspx, accessed on November 1, 2017.
23. Lockheed Martin, *Annual Reports* at https://www.lockheedmartin.com/content/dam/lockheed/data/corporate/documents/2016-Annual-Report.pdf, accessed on November 3, 2017.

5. Changing Mission Profile: Technological Innovations in Combat Aviation

"What keeps me awake at night is, are we going to miss the next big technological advance? And perhaps an enemy will have that."[1] This statement by General Robert Cone, in fact, is what a military planner goes through every night. New technologies emerge and change combat equations. This calls for a change of plans and maybe goals. The unveiling of a new air-launched hypersonic weapon with a range over 1000 km by Russian President Vladimir Putin in February 2018 is one such event that has forced the military planners and innovators to re-chart their plans.[2] The impact of technology has been most profound on air power. As summarized by the British Defence Minister, Mark Lancaster:

> "Our Armed Forces continue to push the limits of innovative warfare to ensure that we stay ahead of any adversaries or threats faced on the battlefield".[3]

In this chapter, material and structural changes in combat aircraft followed by the impact of technological innovations in military aviation are discussed. The ways core capabilities while designing a combat aircraft have evolved, and the life of a combat aircraft, are covered in the last section along with a case study of F-22 combat aircraft.

Material and Structure[4]

At the beginning of the military aviation, weight, strength and reparability were the three primary key criteria for the selection of material for manufacturing aircraft. Material availability, ease of machining and binding and cost were the other factors that drove the innovation in aircraft designs and material choice. The manufacturing processes too evolved along with material and design for combat aircraft. Before adequate knowledge about aerodynamics was available, the basic aircraft design was biplane and the structure of the wooden frame was strengthened with wire bracing and covered by fabric skin. Cantilevered wings with thicker aerofoils and stronger box spars eliminated wire bracing like in the Fokker Dr1 triplane in 1918. Further, the development of monocoque fuselage with lower weight and drag-enhanced efficiency increased costs. The German Albatross experimented with semi-monocoque construction. In this, load-bearing plywood skin panels were glued to longitudinal longerons and internal bulkheads.

By the middle of the twentieth century, wood was replaced by metal and accordingly semi-monocoque by the stressed skin. In the early days, metals were the main materials in aircraft manufacturing; later, advanced materials such as titanium alloys and composite materials were incorporated into non-bearing structures. With the development in technology, advanced materials are being widely applied in the field of combat aviation, a field that is very sensitive to weight. Composite materials, titanium alloys, and other advanced materials are playing an increasingly important role in both civil and military aircraft. The F-22, a fifth-generation aircraft in service in the USAF, uses composite materials in the fuselage, wings, and tail. Titanium alloy (40 per cent) and composite materials (34 per cent) contribute the most. Manufacturers have gradually broken the original material-use restrictions and transferred the load-bearing structure, moving closer to an all-composite aircraft. Table 5.1 and Figure 5.1 show the material application proportion between various combat aircraft. Barring induction of new materials in terms of various composites and alloys, there have been no major structural changes since then.

Table 5.1: The Contrast in Material Application Proportions of Some Combat Aircraft

Aircraft	Aluminium Alloy	Titanium Alloy	Alloy Steel	Composite Material	Other Materials
F15	0.50	0.34	0.02	0.02	0.12
F22	0.15	0.40	0.06	0.34	0.05
B2	0.24	0.18	0.1	0.38	0.01
F16	0.75	.01	0.11	0.02	0.11
F18	0.51	0.14	0.12	0.11	0.12
B1B	0.42	0.17	0.07	0.33	0

Source: Based on data presented in the 4th Global Conference on Materials Science and Engineering held at University of Macau, Hengqin Island from August 3rd-6th, 2015.[5]

Figure 5.1: Composite Material Share in Structural Weight of Combat Aircraft

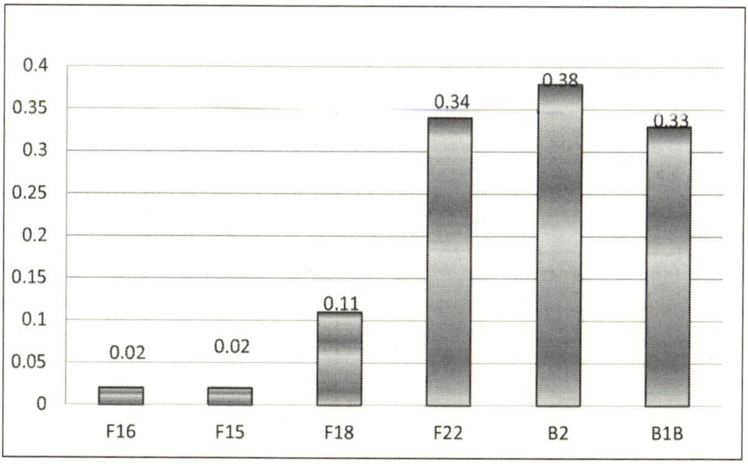

Source: Based on data presented in the 4th Global Conference on Materials Science and Engineering held at University of Macau, Hengqin Island from August 3rd-6th, 2015.[6]

Before the selection of material for various components of the aircraft, during the evaluation of the design, several factors are considered. This involves aerodynamics and computational prediction models, wind tunnel testing, assessing aero loads, hinge moments, stability characteristics and airframe engine compatibility amongst others.[7] With a large number of new technologies, new materials, and new manufacturing processes, aircraft performance has improved rapidly. At the same time, new technologies increase aircraft structures' complexity and the need for precision.[8] While improved capability per platform increases the combat potential of each combat aircraft, it puts downward pressure on the number of combat aircraft that are required for the same mission. Associated with that is the increasing development and manufacturing costs owing to advanced material and engineering techniques required for operational relevance. In sum total, states are gravitating towards high quality and low quantity in the field of combat aviation.

Shifting Core Capability

Acquisition of aviation capability and its amalgamation as an integral military tool were the focus areas in the first quarter of the last century. True to the major precepts of Douhet's[9] theories, with a greater proliferation of aviation assets, a contest in the air was a logical development and called for supremacy in the air. For the first 50 years of military aviation in a combat role, the critical capability was speed. Aft location (guns pointing rearwards) of the cannon and low electronic surveillance capability forced the need for speed to get past and shoot an intruder. While the structural design of combat aircraft changed to achieve higher speeds, it was the aircraft engines that defined this capability. From pistons to jets was a big transition in military aviation.[10]

Engine technology also was gradually refined to achieve better Specific Fuel Consumption (SFC) for better combat range. Brute engine power and sleek design allowed the MiG-21 an unprecedented advantage in combat performance in the 1960s. The MiG-21 design was a disruption and soon catapulted it to *numero uno* position in combat aircraft and its fleet expanded rapidly. Understanding of relaxed stability and ability to control it was the flexion point in structural design for combat aircraft and the proverbial red line of aerodynamic stability breached to achieve greater manoeuvrability by exploiting this new-found knowledge. This forced the transition from speed to manoeuvrability as the key component of combat aircraft.

Lockheed Martin's F-16 stole the march in this arena and ruled the world's combat aircraft space. This was followed by an era of rapid development in sensor technology and its integration in combat aircraft. The F-15, F-18 and Su30 with their onboard sensors allowed each platform to be a complete combat system with a wide-ranging capability and ability to dominate the vast expanses of air space.

Sensor fusion dominated the combat aircraft trend until the emergence of next disruptor. The development of high-fidelity electronic sensors and their long ranges forced this change. Sensors deployed on the ground or their miniaturised versions fitted on airborne platforms including combat aircraft, allowed a high degree of tactical transparency. Now the race was not to outrun or outmanoeuvre an adversary in the air but to out-detect. Beyond Visual Range (BVR) weapons systems placed a premium on aircraft low observability as the most critical attribute. Its development and deployment had started in the last quarter of the last century. Initial design for low observability put a very high cost in terms of aircraft speed and manoeuvrability. Low Observability (LO) including low Radar Cross Section (RCS) is a critical requirement in the operational environment today and is likely to remain so till 2050. By then, the operational environment is expected to undergo another transformation.[11] Michael Buck, a practitioner from the United States army has aptly brought out this aspect in his paper on 'Full Spectrum Close Air Support for the 21st Century'. According to Buck, the fifth-generation aircraft with their sensors collect enormous amounts of data, which they fuse into a picture of the tactical situation. These "sensor-effector" aircraft can share this information with joint forces across all domains—land, sea, space, and cyberspace—as part of a jam-proof construct known as the "combat cloud."[12] This kind of a fused battle space picture helps initiate optimal tactical action.

So the core thrust area for combat aircraft has shifted from speed, manoeuvrability and sensor integration to low observability.[13]Although a classic definition of various generations of combat aircraft does not exist, but based on the core capabilities, it can broadly be classified as listed in Table 5.2.

Table 5.2: Classification of Combat Aircraft

Generation of Combat Aircraft	Key Attributes	Examples
First Generation	Ability to fly at high speed	F100 Super Sabre, MiG 19
Second Generation	Ability to operate at high altitude	MiG25, U2
Third Generation	Ability to achieve high manoeuvrability	MiG21, F16
Fourth Generation	Ability to integrate high range high fidelity sensors and weapons	SU30, Rafale
Fifth Generation	Low Observability (Stealth)	F22, F35
Sixth Generation	Integrated with Artificial Intelligence for greater automation	?

Source: Author

The aircraft developed and operationalised integrate all the technical attributes of the previous generation of combat aircraft with new technology. The development of technology and its integration in combat aircraft are not very well earmarked. It normally takes place in small increments and therefore, is difficult to classically identify the generation of every combat aircraft. A combat aircraft design normally has 50-60,000 drawings; changing all these to design a new platform is time-consuming and inefficient, especially in case some parts represent the best-case solution.[14] To resolve this dichotomy, often, practitioners use terms like 3.5 Generation indicating that the platform has all the capabilities of the third generation and some attributes of the fourth-generation aircraft. At times, a compromise is made in one attribute to enhance efficacy in another. The F-117 which was the first combat aircraft designed with stealth configuration in the 1980s and achieved initial operational capability on September 15, 1983, is a classic example in this category.[15] The core issue in designing this aircraft was to minimise the Radar Cross-Section. However, to achieve that several aerodynamic and engine compromises were made that resulted in the F-117 being a subsonic aircraft. The performance of the aircraft was much below the levels achieved in the previous generations in terms of its speeds, altitude, rate of turn and rate of climb. Once stealth technology was further developed, these shortcomings were overcome with the aerodynamically high-performance aircraft, the F-22. Work is still on in many countries about fifth-generation combat aircraft– two fully operationalized models are the F-22 and the F-35 of the US. The USAF F-22 fighter, also known as the Raptor, is considered as one of "the most capable fighter aircraft ever built, period." The F-22 incorporates a high degree of stealth, as well as supercruise, thrust-vectoring for high manoeuvrability, and integrated avionics that fuse information from on-board and off-board sensors.[16] However, this needs to be seen in the context of the relative combat potential of combat aircraft, as described in Chapter 3.

In the next decade, the Su57 of Russia[17] and the J20 of China[18] are likely to join operational forces in sizeable numbers in their respective countries as fifth-generation combat aircraft. Conceptualisation work has already started for the sixth-generation combat aircraft. The UK's *Project Tempest*[19] and a joint venture between France, Germany and Spain to replace Eurofighter are leading this task at this juncture[20] (See Annexure 5). It will be pertinent to look at the life-cycle of a combat aircraft to understand and estimate the expected timelines for a sixth-generation combat aircraft to take to the skies.

Life of a Combat Aircraft

An analysis of data collated in CAIDB (Combat Aircraft Inventory Data Base) indicates the life-cycle pattern of combat aircraft. It varies between 20-40 years based on its operational capability in the operational environment. It can primarily be divided into six phases commencing with design and development. This is followed by production, operational relevance, pre-eminence and dominance period. Thereafter, the cycle reverses with stoppage of production, and a gradual phase-out commences. The combat aircraft is designed by combining available technology and operational necessity. The

Initial design and development phases vary based on the technological upgradation that has taken place since the development of the last such platform and technological base. This period varies from a couple of years to more than a couple of decades as exemplified by MiG-21 in erstwhile USSR and LCA in India respectively.

Before clearing an aircraft to fly, it is certified for airworthiness. That process is normally carried out by a government-nominated agency. In India, this responsibility rests with the Centre for Military Airworthiness and Certification (CEMILAC), Bengaluru through its Regional Centres for Military Airworthiness (RCMA). It involves all activities leading to certification of aircraft, engines, systems, airborne equipment, software, mid-life upgrade/ life extension of aircraft or stores.[21] On successful testing of prototypes with varying design features and power plants, the production commences followed by its induction in the armed forces. This is the beginning of a period of operational relevance when the new platform combined with its weapon suite forces changes in tactical concepts. As the number of platforms increases, it reaches a position of pre-eminence in altering operational concepts of the force possessing it and the likely opponents. The widespread availability of the platform in large numbers impacts the military-strategic level and this pinnacle in the life-cycle of a combat platform is the period of domination.

All combat aircraft developed do not classically follow the six-phase life-cycle and a large number never peak beyond operational relevance before phasing out. In the period of study, two combat platforms have reached the level of domination – the MiG-21 and the F-16 (Figure 5.2). Over 11,400 MiG-21 produced in USSR and license-built in India and Czechoslovakia, were deployed in nearly 60 countries. Although the number for F-16 pale in comparison with 4,588 platforms in 26 countries, it has had a considerable impact on the prevalent operational environment. Mid-life upgrades have assisted these aircraft to achieve domination status. While the MiG-21 made design and power plant changes, the F-16 relied more on avionics and weapon package upgrade to stay ahead. Today, the MiG-21 is on the verge of phase-out and the F-16 has begun to slide from its position of dominance. The F-16 is likely to be phased out in another 20-25 years on completion of its technical life or once the supply of spares dries up.[22] Although the F-16's manufacturer Lockheed Martin sees a market for 400 new F-16s – mainly in West Asia – after securing Bahrain as a launch customer for the Block 70 variant with delivery starting in 2021. Robert Harward, chief executive for Lockheed Martin Middle-East, describes the fighter as a "workhorse" that "can't be touched by anything that isn't a fifth-generation aircraft."[23] In a category with more than 100 platforms, India is currently the only country with the MiG-21 and there are five nations with the F16 – the US, Israel, the ROK, Taiwan and Turkey.

Figure 5.2: MiG-21 and F16 Inventories of the World

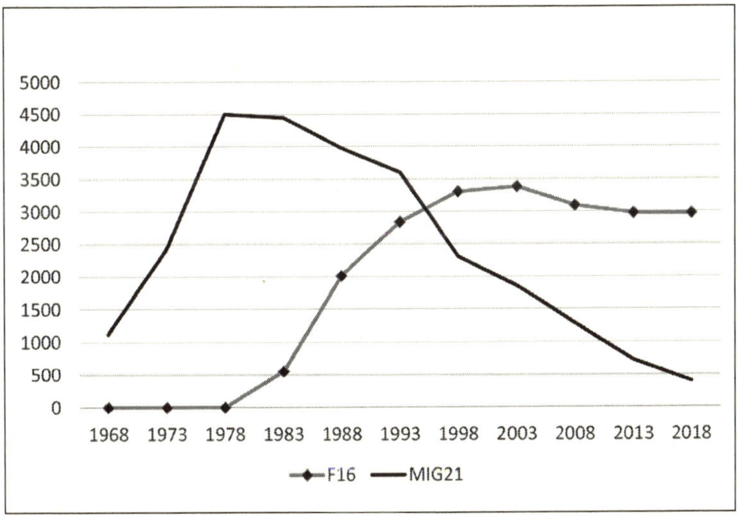

Source: Combat Aircraft Inventory Database.

As manufacturing processes become complex involving advanced material and precision, the repair time and resources also increase. This assertion is supported by the United States Government Accountability Office Report:

> Specifically, we found that the Air Force's organization of its small F22 fleet has not maximized the availability of these 186 aircraft. Availability was constrained by maintenance challenges and unit

organization. For example, maintaining the stealth coating on the outside of the F22 aircraft was time-consuming and significantly reduced the aircraft's availability for missions.[24]

Furthermore, like any other complex system, the combat aircraft on induction and operationalization, have several techno-logistical problems. These may be a result of overlooking some basics or failing to visualize the operational environment or a combination of both. Recalling the F-35 fleet for retrofitting those rivets that were fitted without the anti-corrosion paste during the manufacturing process is one such example. Owing to similar reasons, the support system for a complex machine like the combat aircraft, with parts being manufactured at different world locations, tends to lag behind the plan. This aspect is valid for other types also, with stealth technology. US capabilities to repair F-35 parts at military depots were six years behind schedule, which resulted in average part repair times of 172 days—twice that of the programme's objective.[25] These repair backlogs have contributed to significant F-35 spare part shortages—from January to August 2017, F-35 aircraft were unable to fly 22 per cent of the time because of part shortages.[26] The F-35 support programme typifies this problem and a similar set of problems can be envisaged for indigenous LCA.

Rising Combat Power

The combat power of advanced combat aircraft has increased and thereby negated the impact of reduced numbers. The transformation has been achieved by better airframe designs, engine efficiencies and integrated avionics along with improved weaponeering.[27] A combination of design and material technology has produced low observable combat aircraft, enhancing its survival potential. In the 1960s, improvements in the performance of aircraft were a result of refining the mechanical process in designing and operations; it had its limitations. This changed with computer technology coming of age in the 1970s but its miniaturisation in the 1980s allowed its integration with the combat aircraft. Communication and computing are the two major areas to witness major technological developments in the last three decades. Seamless integration can take place in assessing battle space activities through data links. Enhanced situational awareness is a logical outcome of this.

The miniaturisation of electronic components and higher processing power has allowed replacement of failure-prone mechanical moving parts in various onboard sensors. Multispectral sensors have allowed greater operational freedom and efficient outputs. High-speed computations assisted in the capacity expansion of combat aircraft. Greater Weapon Effective Range (WER) in combination with similar expansion in sensor capabilities has effectively increased the Target Engagement Zone (TEZ) of new platforms. While numbers do play a role, the technological difference has a major bearing on the combat outcome. Countries with access to high-technology platforms are replacing the older generation aircraft with fewer high-combat capability aircraft. Net combat capability for the types of missions envisaged has increased despite the reduced numerical strength of combat aircraft in many regions. The role the technology has played and will continue to play in combat dynamics, is best summarised in *Science, Technology, and the Future of Warfare*:

> In thinking about the future of warfare, one often encounters two ideological camps: those who prioritize the role of technology and those who don't. One must always be cognizant and skeptical of slipping into a technological deterministic mindset. That is the notion that technology alone, or is even the most important factor, can determine the outbreak or outcome of the conflict. The wars of the last decade should also remind us that co-option of broadly available commercial technologies may present the most significant operational threat, e.g., cell-phone activated IEDs in Iraq and Afghanistan. At the same time, to deny or dismiss the role of technology in affecting the outcome (as well as the outbreak) of war and conflict is also perilous. Neither purist ideology is manifested in the operational world. Contemporary analyses often expose the tenuous links or disconnections among mainstream scholarship on international security and war (or strategic) studies, understanding

of the defence technological innovation and acquisition processes, and fundamental understanding of the underlying science.[28]

Weapons'-guidance has improved, leading to a large-scale reduction in Circular Error of Probability (CEP)[29]at relatively low cost. A large number of high-calibre unguided weapons were required to neutralise a typical battlefield target. This was because of high CEP, leading to reduced employment of explosives on the critical part of the target system. Two aspects of targeting have changed in the last three decades: First, high-fidelity sensors can now map the critical area of the battle space to identify vulnerable points to be targeted. The information can be communicated in near real-time to the planners for selection of appropriate weapon-platform combination for employment. With a three-dimensional assessment of the Desired Mean Point of Impact (DMPI)[30] available to the attacker; targeting has become relatively simple and accurate. High-speed computing has allowed accurate terminal- guidance systems on the weapons.[31] This has narrowed down the CEP to under five metres. This translates into the effective utilisation of the explosive content of the weapon on the vulnerable point of the target. Attack by one or two such guided weapons achieves the desired result. Use of guided weapons reduces the number of weapons required for the same impact on a target system, consequently, a reduction in the number of aircraft required for the attack. A lower number of strike aircraft need a reduced number of support aircraft in terms of air defence and electronic warfare escorts. The overall reduced size of the mission package results in a smaller time window required for launch and recovery of aircraft at home bases. This, in turn, reduces the time for creating an air defence umbrella over the launch and recovery bases during the vulnerable period of aircraft take-off and landing. Overall, employment of accurate weapon delivery has had a cascading impact on mission planning and reduced the number of combat aircraft per mission.

The second impact of enhanced battle space transparency is that planners can identify the target systems that need to be neutralised to achieve the desired effect in battle. Unlike yesteryears, when a large number of target systems were planned to be targeted, in the absence of accurate information about the enemy, in the hope that, some of the targets will prove to be crucial for the enemy. And their capitulation will lead to desired battle outcome. So overall, enhanced sensor capability has assisted in reducing the number of targets to be engaged and accurate weapon delivery has necessitated a reduced force. Both these factors have allowed achievement of mission objectives with fewer combat aircraft. The role that a transparent battle space plays in the outcome of a conflict is well articulated by General David Deptula:

> "Information's value extends past the news cycle. Just as wireless connectivity, personal computing devices, and cloud-based applications are revolutionizing life in the civilian sector, these trends are also radically altering how our military forces project power. Faster and more capable networks and computing capabilities are turning information into the dominant factor in modern warfare. Operations over Syria since 2014 validate the assertion that platforms like the F22 are information machines, far above and beyond merely being combat assets."[32]

The definition of a successful combat aircraft has changed. From being able to fly for a specified duration, it now encompasses the ability to undertake missions under the most challenging operational environments, teeming with long-range weapons. The activity of developing a concept and thereafter a combat aircraft on that concept was normally a single-company activity. Added complexities in design and development to meet mission-capable aircraft have forced aircraft developers to coordinate and cooperate to share costs and compress the timelines. Several front-line combat aircraft are a result of co-development, the Eurofighter being the most prominent one with the involvement of four countries[33]. The F-35 manufacturing process involves multiple sources for more than 300,000 individual parts at three locations in Texas (USA), Cameri (Italy) and Nagoya (Japan). Lockheed Martin, Northrop Grumman, BAE Systems and Pratt & Whitney are the main providers amongst more than 1,400 suppliers around the world.[34] Another aspect that has gained momentum is that of transfer of technology to large buyers to establish assembly lines and part manufacturing of combat aircraft components. Turkey and Belgium have F-16 factories. India has under licence produced MiG-21, MiG-27 and Jaguars in the last century and Hawk and SU30MKI in recent times. The development cycle, production and operationalization of the F-22 give a clear picture of the timelines for a complex system like a combat aircraft.

F-22: A Case Study

The US Air Force, the sole operator of the F-22 fifth-generation stealth combat aircraft, commenced its procurement in 1999. A total of 195 (177 production aircraft, 16 test aircraft, and two development aircraft) were procured till 2009. Broad landmarks in this journey are covered in the Congressional Research Service Report 7-5700: [35]

> The F22 program was initiated in the early 1980s to develop a highly capable successor to the F15 that would be capable of defeating all known and projected enemy fighters, including those being developed at the time by the Soviet Union. The F22 program was given a Milestone I approval in October 1986. The first flight of an F22 industry prototype occurred in August 1990, and the first flight of a development version of the aircraft occurred in September 1997. The program was approved for Low Rate Initial Production (LRIP) in August 2001, and the first LRIP F22 was delivered in June 2003. The F22 achieved Initial Operational Capability (IOC) in December 2005.

The initial plan of the US Air Force was to procure around 650 F-22s.[36] However, the plan was frequently revised downward (Figure 5.3). The probable drivers for downward revision were reduced operational necessity given major changes in the geopolitical scenario after the breakup of the USSR and escalating costs. As of December 31, 2010, in the final *Selected Acquisition Report* for F22 procurement, the Department of

Defense (DOD) estimated the total acquisition cost (meaning the sum of research and development cost, procurement cost, and military construction [MilCon] cost) of a 179-aircraft F-22 programme at about $67.3 billion in then-year dollars (meaning dollars across various years that are not adjusted for inflation).[37] This figure includes about $32.4 billion in research and development costs, about $34.2 billion in procurement costs, and $676.6 million in MilCon costs.[38] As of December 31, 2010, the 179-aircraft F-22 programme had a Program Acquisition Unit Cost (PAUC), which is the programme's total acquisition cost divided by the total number of aircraft acquired [including non-production aircraft]) of $369.5 million in then-year dollars, and an Average Unit Procurement Cost (which is the programme's total procurement cost divided by 179 production aircraft) of $185.7 million in then-year dollars.[39] The material used in F-22 also contributed to its high development and production cost. The F-22 structure has 37per cent titanium 6-4, 23per cent thermosetting composite materials, 15per cent aluminium alloy, 10per cent toughened epoxy composite materials, 6per cent alloy steel, 3per cent titanium 6-22-22 and 1per cent thermoplastic materials. This composition and its blending required new manufacturing processes.[40] Composite materials like glass-fibre-reinforced plastics and carbon-fibre reinforced plastics (CFRP) are used in proper form with autoclave cycle to achieve the required consistent properties. This involves controlling both temperature and pressure in a specified way to obtain appropriate strength and stiffness of the component.[41] The F-22 assembly line in Marietta, Georgia (GA), has since been shut down, with its tools and equipment placed in storage.[42] Repair time of an aircraft also impacts the force availability and greater is the time and cost of repair for intricately designed modern combat aircraft as is the case with the Lockheed Martin developed F-22:

> F-22 crash landings are particularly expensive to repair because of the damage they cause to the aircraft's stealth coating and intricate internal structure. For example, an F-22 damaged in 2012 when it

skidded across a runway on its belly took six years to repair and cost $35 million to fix.[43]

Figure 5.3: Plan and Production of F-22 for the USAF

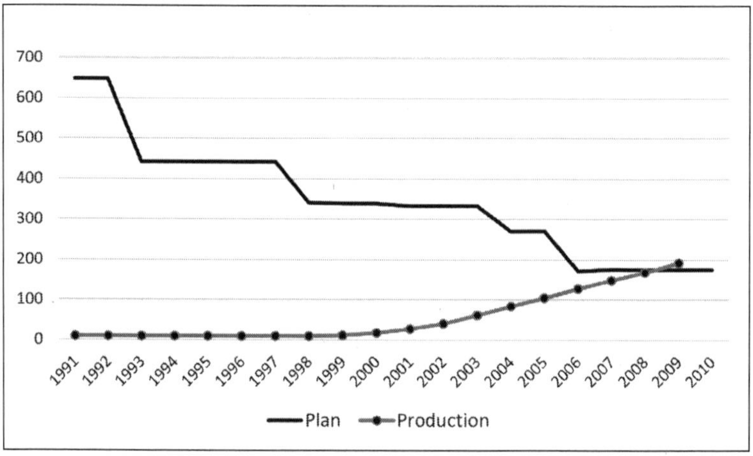

Source: Based on data in Jeremiah Gertler, "Air Force F-22 Fighter Program", *Congressional Research Service Report* 7-5700, L31673 dated July 11, 2013.

Figure 5.4 : F-22 Programme Cost Breakdown

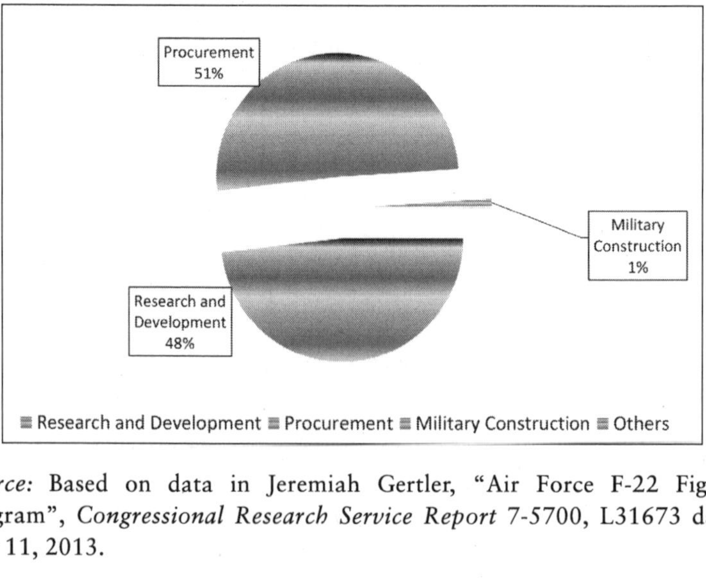

Source: Based on data in Jeremiah Gertler, "Air Force F-22 Fighter Program", *Congressional Research Service Report* 7-5700, L31673 dated July 11, 2013.

The Light Combat Aircraft (LCA) in India was approved at the same time as was the initial conceptualisation of the F-22. However, both have followed very different trajectories. The F22 is probably the most potent platform in the world for over a decade and the LCA has finally achieved its Full Operational Clearance (FOC) in 2019. The difference can be attributed to a combination of technology, approach, bureaucracy, resources and human endeavour – not necessarily in that order. As Douglas Birkey puts it succinctly, "In evaluating future challenges, technology will probably not represent the top impediment. Instead, it will likely be humans and various bureaucracies."[44] A look at Figure 5.4 indicates that half the expenditure is for research and development even in a large programme for the production of nearly 200 aircraft. Unless a focussed approach combines with a large number of resources for research and development, the project timelines will keep extending as has been the case for the LCA.

Sum Up

Based on intent and capability, plans are made to utilise the kinetic elements. A broad strategy for guiding force development is essential. The United Kingdom released its *Combat Air Strategy 2018* (CAS 2018) which indicates the impact of developments in the arena of combat aviation in the coming decades. For a country like India, with a huge demand for combat aircraft, three clear messages underpinning the Team Tempest concept outlined in CAS 2018 are relevant. First, the development of complex military hardware like a combat aircraft is expensive and time-consuming. An international collaborative mechanism is a necessity. Within the country, such high-risk projects need to be undertaken under the rubric of public-private partnership. The entire process needs to be audited objectively and the failure to meet specific goals ought to lead to project termination. Second, continuous upgradation of current systems and making them future-ready is an economic strategy, as these subsystems can directly fit into a developing platform. Small and medium-sized local industry can effectively carry out this kind of work. This approach helps local industry to flourish besides reducing the cost and time of development. Third, all platforms, being designed, need to have an open architecture. This facilitates plugging in of subsystems developed elsewhere and for other purposes. It permits faster and cost-effective integration. This methodology also helps in the expansion of the dual-use technologies basket. Furthermore, commercial use of subsystems thus developed leads to financial offsets. How far and how fast these progress will have a major impact on combat aviation in the second half of this century.

The role of combat aircraft has changed to keep pace with the changing nature of warfare and force application. Technology too has played a role in enhancing combat power per platform, thereby reducing the quantum of force required for specified objectives. Greater engine efficiencies allowed longer flight duration for combat aircraft and longer ranges for propelled weapons. Increase in availability of Airborne Warning and Control Systems (AWACS) and Flight Refuelling Aircraft (FRA) in combination with an increased range of aircraft and weapons allowed an increase in the TEZ of each combat aircraft. This practically translated into a reduction in the number of aircraft required in the combat zone of specified dimensions. Enhanced targeting accuracy resulted in reduction in the Over Target Requirement (OTR)[45] to cause requisite disruption in a target system and which in turn resulted in the requirement of a lower number of combat aircraft.

Better sensor and communication technology allowed high-fidelity battle space transparency and therefore the ability to accurately select the targets in a system of targets. This reduced the number of targets to be engaged to achieve the desired outcome in a sector and thus reducing the number of combat aircraft required. All these technological factors result in a reduction in the number of combat aircraft for achieving the same goal against a technologically disadvantageous adversary. With a large number of new technologies, new materials, and new manufacturing processes, aircraft performance has improved rapidly. At the same time, new technologies increase the complexity of aircraft structures and the need for precision.[46] Notwithstanding the changing dynamics, this niche market is tightly controlled by the same set of countries in the last 50 years and the status quo is reinforced year after year.

Notes

1. General Robert Cone, Commander US Army TRADOC, from Mike Morones, "Interview with Gen Robert Cone," *Defense News,* December 16, 2013.
2. Russian News Agency, Putin: Work on advanced Tsirkon hypersonic missile proceeding on schedule, TASS, February 20, 2018 at http://tass.com/defense/1045576 (Accessed on March 29, 2019).
3. The UK Ministry of Defence and The Rt Hon Mark Lancaster TD MP, "British Army set to redefine warfare with joint Autonomous Warrior", June 20, 2018.
4. For more see Dr David Barker, "Aerodynamics and Structures", in Phillip Jarret (ed), *The Modern War Machine, Military Aviation Since 1945*, Putnam Aeronautical Books, London, 2000, pp.71-94.
5. A. W. Shen, J. L. Guo and Z. J. Wang, "Analysis of the influence of advanced materials for aerospace products R&D and manufacturing cost", 4th Global Conference on Materials Science and Engineering (CMSE 2015) IOP Publishing IOP Conf. Series: *Materials Science and Engineering* 103, 2015, 012004 DOI:10.1088/1757-899X/103/1/012004 at iopscience.iop.org/article/10.1088/1757-899X/103/1/012004/pdf (Accessed on October 10, 2018).
6. Ibid.
7. K. Nagaraj, *Airworthiness Certification of Fighter Aircraft*, Defence Research and Development Organisation, Ministry of Defence, New Delhi, 2015, p. 15.
8. A. W. Shen, J. L. Guo and Z. J. Wang, no. 5
9. General Giulio Douhet was an Italian general and air power theorist. He was a key proponent of strategic bombing in aerial warfare. He wrote *Rules for the Use of Airplanes in War* (*Regole per l'usodegliaeroplani in guerra*) — one of the first doctrine manuals of its kind in 1912 and *The Command of the Air* (*Ildominiodell'aria*) in 1921.
10. Jerry Scutts, "The Jet Revolution", in Phillip Jarret (ed), no. 4, pp. 53-69.
11. J.P.R. Browne and M.T. Thurbon, *Electronic Warfare*, Brassy's UK Limited, 1998, pp. 225-233.
12. Lt Col Michael Buck, "Full Spectrum Close Air Support for the 21st Century: Leveraging Air Operations with Ground Forces", Mitchell

Institute Policy Papers, 8, October 2017.

13. For early developments see Mike Spick, *Fighters at War: The Story of Air to Air Combat*, Greenhill Books, London, 1997, pp. 102-113.
14. K. Nagaraj, no. 7, p 14.
15. Michael J. H. Taylor, *The Aerospace Chronology*, Tri-Service Press, London, 1989, p. 280.
16. Jeremiah Gertler, "Air Force F-22 Fighter Program",*Congressional Research Service Report* 7-5700, L31673, July 11, 2013.
17. TASS News, :"Russia ready to discuss deliveries of Su-57 fifth-generation fighter jets to India", February 25, 2019 at http://tass.com/defense/1046248 (Accessed on March 29, 2019).
18. Tyler Rogoway, "China's J-20 Stealth Fighter Stuns By Brandishing Full Load Of Missiles At Zhuhai Air Show", *The Drive*, November 11, 2018 at https://www.thedrive.com/the-war-zone/24841/chinas-j-20-stealth-fighter-stuns-by-brandishing-full-load-of-missiles-at-zhuhai-air-show (Accessed on March 29, 2019).
19. George Allison, "UK unveils new next-generation fighter jet called Tempest", *UK Defence Journal*, July 16, 2018 at ttps://ukdefencejournal.org.uk/uk-unveils-new-next-generation-fighter-jet-called-tempest/ (Accessed on March 29, 2018).
20. Clement Charpentereau, "Spain to join French-German next fighter jet program", *Aerotime News Hub*, February 12, 2019, at https://www.aerotime.aero/clement.charpentreau/22358-spain-to-join-french-german-next-fighter-jet-program (Accessed on March 29, 2019).
21. K. Nagaraj, no.7, p xvii.
22. *Annual Report*, Lockheed Martin Cooperation 2016, at https://www.lockheedmartin.com/content/dam/lockheed/data/corporate/documents/2016-annual-report.pdf (Accessed on November 1, 2017).
23. Murdo Morrison, "Lockheed sees a 400-strong market for new F-16s", *Flight International*, November 15, 2018, at https://www.flightglobal.com/news/articles/lockheed-sees-400-strong-market-for-new-f-16s-453667/ (Accesed on November 18, 2018).
24. *United States Government Accountability Office Report GAO-19-120T on Air Force Readiness; Actions Needed to Rebuild Readiness and Prepare for the Future,* October 10, 2018, at https://www.armed-services.senate.gov/imo/media/doc/Pendleton_10-10-18.pdf (Accessed on October 12, 2018).
25. Ibid.
26. Ibid.
27. For a detailed account of development in military avionics see Norman Friedman, "Military Avionics Since the Second World War", in Phillip Jarret (ed), no. 4, pp. 95-114.

28. Margaret Kosal, "Science, Technology, and the Future of Warfare", Modern War Institute, West Point, October 2, 2016 at https://mwi.usma.edu/science-technology-future-warfare/
29. To compute the accuracy of a weapon in conjunction with its delivery system, several trial firings are carried out. Further, once the weapon system is inducted in a combat force, continuous training using the weapon generates data about the likely error that may occur while using a weapon. Based on this data, a mathematical figure named Circular Error Probability is derived and is indicative of the radius of a circle, with the aiming point at its centre, within which 50 per cent of the weapons fired will fall under the defined delivery parameters. This assists the operational planners to assess the number of weapons that are required to be planned to achieve a pre-defined level of assurance of the requisite degree of damage to the target system.
30. Desired Mean Point of Impact (DMPI) is the point selected within a target system and weapons are aimed at that. This is selected based on functional and vulnerability analysis of the target system and matching it with the damage mechanism of the weapon planned to be used. Based on the relative size and strength of the target system and the weapon, multiple DMPIs could be required within a target system. These DMPIs are targeted individually to achieve the desired overall outcome.
31. V.V. Rampal, *Photonics in Warfare*, DRDO Monographs/Special Publications Series, Defence Research and Development Organisation, Ministry of Defence, New Delhi, 2002, pp.147-162.
32. Lt Gen David A. Deptula, "Beyond Goldwater-Nichols: Roles And Missions Of The Armed Services In The 21st Century", Mitchell Institute Policy Papers, 1, March 2016.
33. The four partners of Eurofighter Typhoon development and manufacturing are Germany, UK, Italy and Spain.
34. "Building the F35" at https://www.f35.com/about/life-cycle/production (Accessed on November 06, 2017).
35. Jeremiah Gertler, no. 16.
36. Ibid.
37. Ibid.
38. Ibid.
39. Ibid.
40. A. W. Shen, J. L. Guo and Z. J. Wang, no. 5,
41. K Nagaraj, no. 7, pp. 74-75.
42. Jeremiah Gertler, no. 16.
43. Garrett Reim, "Second F-22 crash landing in 2018", *Flight Global*, October 11, 2018, at https://www.flightglobal.com/news/articles/second-f-22-crash-landing-in-2018-452620/ (Accessed on October 12, 2018).

44. Douglas Birkey, Lt Gen David Deptula, and Maj Gen Lawrence Stutzriem, "Manned-Unmanned Aircraft Teaming: Taking Combat Airpower to the Next Level", The Mitchell Institute Policy Papers, 15, July 2018.
45. Over Target Requirement (OTR) is the number of weapons required for a target to achieve requisite level of damage and is calculated based on the target system, its functional and vulnerability analysis along with weapon characteristics and the parameters of its damage mechanism like Blast Over Pressure, Dynamic Pressure, Pressure Pulse, Penetrative Index, Fragmentation Pattern, Shock and Fire Indices in the given attack profile.
46. A. W. Shen, J. L. Guo and Z. J. Wang, no. 5.

6. Trigger Live: Air-Launched Weapons: Expanding Capabilities of Combat Aviation

Aviation transformed the battlefield – a two-dimensional entity – into battle space by adding the third dimension.[1] Aircraft were the vehicles that commenced combat operation in the newly-added dimension. As the flying capability of aircraft improved, so did their combat potential. Developments in the field of metallurgy, aerodynamics, propellants and sensor technology translated into increased potency of combat weapons and combat aircraft.[2] Enhanced combat capability could achieve the desired results with greater precision with air-launched weapons as its fulcrum. "Weapons differentiate between Air Forces and Flying Clubs" is an often-heard adage. Weapons capability is an integral part of an Air Power matrix and the critical component of combat aircraft. Weapons are the deliverables that are responsible for tactical, operational and strategic implications by damaging/destroying the intended targets.

Development of weapons is complicated and their integration in the aerial platform is a very complex and time-consuming process. The F-35 made its first flight in 2006 and was inducted in the US armed forces nine years later in 2015. However, the first combat training drop of the GBU-49 from the F35A in November 2018 was three years later.[3] This indicates the time for operationalization of various facets of combat aviation. Looking at the future, the US Department of Defense has granted Lockheed Martin an $83.1 million contract on November 15, 2018, to make the aircraft dual-capable – with the ability to launch conventional or nuclear weapons

– by February 2024[4] ; this means, besides substantial resources, a processing time of 18 years from the first flight of the platform to full operational functionality for this fifth-generation combat aircraft. Even the indigenous Light Combat Aircraft (LCA) with modest capabilities as compared to the F-35, did struggle to achieve Full Operational Clearance (FOC) primarily for this reason.[5]

The development of weapons is taking place in different directions and dimensions. On the one hand, development of efficient kinetic weapons minimizes collateral damage and on the other, the focus is on developing a different set of capabilities like Directed Energy Weapons that use electromagnetic power for causing damage.[6] It is, therefore, important to analyze changes in this field of weapons in the past decades before analyzing the combat aircraft inventory data. Broadly, the weapons for combat aircraft can be classified into two categories – Air-to-Surface Weapons and Air-to-Air Weapons. Development in these two areas in the last three decades has played a major role in redefining the role of combat aircraft. This chapter discusses combat platform capability enhancement through weapons.

Air-to-Surface Weapons

Air-to-surface weapons are characterized by three primary criteria – Damage Mechanism, Range and Precision. The interaction between primary damage mechanisms of the weapon (like blast, fragmentation or penetration) with the vulnerability of the target system defines the weapon's effect on a target. The amount of explosive in the warhead, the nature and type of casing along with the explosion- initiation mechanism and the timing determine the nature and extent of the damage.[7] The damage caused by each weapon assists in calculating the number of weapons required to achieve the requisite degree of damage on the target system. Although a macabre narrative, the most devastating air-delivered weapons were nuclear bombs dropped on Japan by the United States Air Force (USAF) in August 1945. A large area was affected. The USAF made no pretence of avoiding civilian deaths when it attacked Japanese towns. Such weapons owing to large Mean Area of Effectiveness (MAE) can absorb large weapon delivery errors. A similar attack with conventional weapon GBU 43B –Massive Ordnance Air Blast (MOAB – popularly known as Mother of All Bombs) was carried out by the USAF in Afghanistan on April 13, 2017.[8] It is the largest conventional air-delivered weapon ever used with 8.5 tonnes of explosive and estimated equivalent yield of 11 tonnes of TNT.[9] While large-yield weapons do not require very high weapon delivery accuracy but collateral damage to various environmental systems and the civilian population in their blast wave reduces their employability. The alternative is to have small weapons that will lead to only the requisite level of damage at the desired point of impact. Two aspects that make this possible are accurate information about the location of the target and matching weapon delivery accuracy.

The first use of aircraft as a weapon platform exploited the aircraft's ability to take the weapon high in the air and then be fired or dropped over the intended target. These were dumb weapons. The distance these covered was based on the altitude, attitude and speed of the mother aircraft and the ballistic trajectory followed till impact with a surface (land or water). Higher release height and speed resulted in the longer range. This brought in a problem of sighting and aiming at the target from long distance. Additionally, the long flight time exposed the weapon to winds that altered its flight path. Aiming at a static target at high speed was also a problem which was further accentuated in case of a moving target. The inclusion of gyroscopes in aiming sights brought some relief and improved the accuracy but the effort required to neutralize a target was still cumbersome. The second problem being faced by military aviators was their inability to carry large ordnances owing to structural limits and engine limitations of the aircraft. Modern aircraft engines like the XF9-1, which can produce a 33,000-lb thrust (147kN) with afterburner, give multiple options to the aircraft in terms of weapon load.[10]

A large explosion could offset the weapon aiming inaccuracies. But it was a technical limitation. Weapon development took place in two different directions. One – to develop non-flight path weapons that are propelled. In this category, a rocket motor assisted the weapon and its flight path was a result of initial launch, rocket motor and winds. This increased the kinetic energy of the weapon and thus reduced the amount of explosive required. More importantly, it reduced the time of flight of the weapon considerably, thus assisting in reducing the terminal error and easier aiming. On the other hand – ballistic weapons were aided by aerodynamic surfaces to elongate the time of flight and range with better predictability of the flight path. Both these developments increased the accuracy of weapons. This was further aided by computer-based weapon aiming systems after the development of miniaturized computers, suitable for fitment in combat aircraft. Other add-ons included sensors that exploited the LASER and electro-optical or Infra-Red spectrum to home-in on the target.[11] Terminal weapon guidance brought in precision strike capability. The circular error probability of the weapons reduced to sub-10 meters. During *Operation Desert Storm*, the F-117 consistently achieved an accuracy of fewer than 10 feet.[12] Greater weapon delivery accuracy, in turn, reduced the explosive content required in the weapon to achieve the necessary degree of degradation in the target system.

Having achieved precision in delivery, the focus shifted back to enhance the range of air delivered air-to-surface weapons to beat the burgeoning threat from the surface-to-air guided weapons. To mitigate the increasing threat from accurate air-delivered weapons, a range of surface-based weapons systems were developed to counter aerial attacks. Mastering the RADAR technology and using it to guide weapons to intercept high-speed aircraft, changed the equation in the battle for air supremacy. The ability of high-power radars to locate and establish the position of flying aircraft was combined with higher-frequency radar systems for weapon guidance by accurately fixing the location of the missile and the intended target. High-speed computation allowed missiles to manoeuvre and converge onto the intended high-speed aircraft. The development of proximity fuses[13] further improved the success rate of the interception of incoming aircraft with ground-based surface-to-air weapons. Carrying out attacks against targets defended by multi-layered air defence weapons systems has attendant risks. A non-stealth aircraft in a ground attack configuration has a large Radar Cross Section (RCS), given the imperative of carrying multiple external weapons. This leads to early detection by adversary surveillance and tracking systems. Besides early detection by the terminal weapon radars, the aircraft's configuration imposes a severe limitation both on its speed and manoeuvrability. Unless protected by multiple high-powered Electronic Warfare (EW) warning and counter-measure systems, there is a high probability that terminal weapons would be able to engage strike aircraft.[14] This leads to either aborted attacks or loss of aircraft. All this can be avoided by attacking from outside the lethal engagement zone of the terminal weapon systems. For that, an air-launched weapon with a range greater than the lethal zone of terminal weapons is required. The BrahMos Air-Launched Cruise Missile – the world's fastest supersonic cruise missile – exemplifies this process. Although BrahMos itself can be intercepted, owing to its relatively smaller RCS and high speed in the range of 2.8 to 3 Mach, interception is much more difficult than intercepting a fully loaded aircraft. This leads to a high assurance level of success of an attack. On November 22, 2017, the Indian Air Force (IAF) successfully fired the BrahMos from a Su30 fighter aircraft. With a warhead weighing 300 kg, this 2.5-tonne missile has an engagement envelope of 400 km– [15]a classic case of enhancing standoff range, as it combines the advantages of a missile system with the flexibility of airpower. A standoff range of 300 to 400 km keeps the launch aircraft outside the lethal zone of all known terminal defence weapons. If need be, the launch aircraft can go deep inside the adversary's territory with requisite combat support and attack target systems hitherto not reachable. In practical terms, with this long-range weapon, the effective range for engaging targets (radius of action) increases by 25 to 30 per cent and the size of the engagement zone[16] doubles.

The number of weapons that an aircraft can carry is based on the hard points (or suspension points) on the aircraft and the weight and size of the weapons. In the early 1960s, each combat aircraft on an average had five hard points – two under each wing and one under the central fuselage. In most cases, two hard points were utilized to carry external fuel tanks, leaving only three hard points to carry weapons. With the availability of high-power engines and better structural technology, this has changed. Availability of nine hard points in current-generation combat aircraft is not unusual. However, for the internal carriage of weapons in a concealed manner to reduce the RCS, there are still severe limitations. Additionally, operations from High-Altitude and High-Temperature (HAHTO) conditions reduce the maximum All-Up Weight (AUW) for take-off and this forces reduction in weapon load. However, this can be offset by high weapon delivery accuracy – in case the Circular Error of Probability (CEP) is comparable to the dimensions of the vulnerable portion of the target around the aiming point or the Desired Mean Point of Impact (DMPI).[17]Therefore, the terminal accuracy attains great significance. An accurate attack can result in damaging the critical subsystem to make the target system non-functional and achieve the desired effect. With 200 kilogramme of the warhead, sub-10-metre accuracy is ideal for most target systems.[18]

With conflict zones expanding to cover urban areas, to minimize the probability of collateral damage, it is necessary to accurately identify and lock on to the target system. This forced the development of multiple methods of honing the terminal guidance for the air-launched missiles.[19] Quantitative comparison of the world's air-to-surface missile inventory indicates a rise in types in this class by 257 per cent in the last 25 years.[20] Even the maximum range of air-to-surface missiles has gone up by 67 per cent. [21] Barring nuclear missiles, the type of missies in all other categories has grown substantially in the last three decades (Figure 6.1). The starkest increase, almost five-fold, is in the types of land-attack missiles. A prime reason is the proliferation of basic missile technology and a significant improvement in sensor technology to defeat various environmental conditions like clouds, fog, smoke and dust that prevail. The basic heat signature to lock on to a target using the Infra-Red (IR) band has severe limitations in such an environment. The development of LASER designator pods to illuminate a target with a receiver in the missile homing head to home -in to the source of reflected LASER energy has been the most popular method for short-range ASM, especially for anti-tank operations.[22] Environmental attenuation restricts the use of limited power LASER from airborne platforms to small ranges normally within 10 km. Electro-optical sensors allow large ranges but need clear weather conditions to be fully effective. Development and integration of Imaging Infra-Red (IIR) sensors, Millimeter Wave (MMW) radars, Global Positioning System (GPS) and Inertial Navigation Systems (INS) have allowed the ASM to increase their effective accuracy.[23] The development of various sensors for ASM has allowed the creation of multiple variants of the same basic missile to be employed in different environmental conditions and for different target systems. Selection of a suitable weapon sensor for a particular target system is based on attributes of the target system that can be captured with a high degree of probability. For example, the use of the LASER receiver in a semi-active ASM is most suitable for targets that have high reflectivity.[24] Targets that have a distinct and discernible heat signature as compared to the surrounding environment are suited to be engaged by missiles with Infra-Red homing heads.

Figure 6.1: Types of Air-to-Surface Missiles in the World 1991-2017

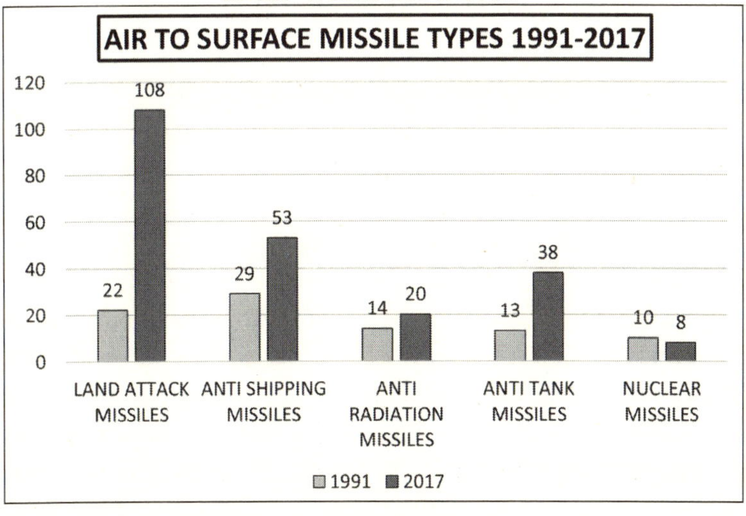

Source: Combat Aircraft Inventory Database.

Figure 6.2: Types of Air-to-Surface Missiles in the World 1991-2017

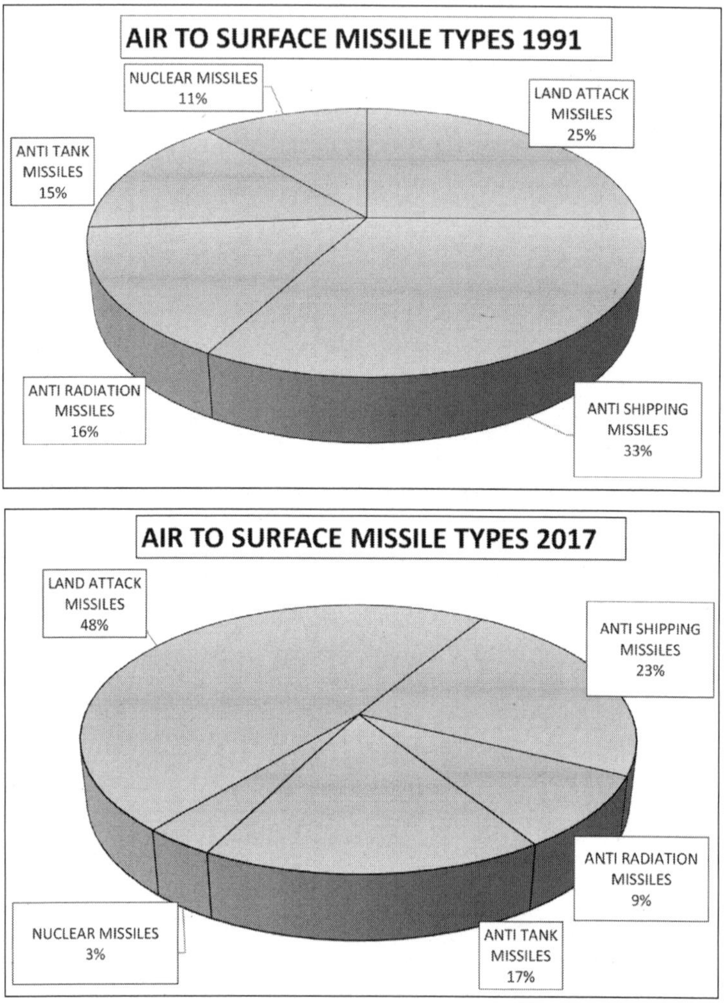

Source: Combat Aircraft Inventory Database.

As indicated in Figure 6.2, the share of the anti-shipping missiles has declined while that of land attack missiles has grown.[25] These changing dynamics are indicative of the changing character of warfare. The fact, that, there have been almost no major wars in the seas since the Falklands War of 1982, can be a primary reason. This is further supported by the relative ease with which localization of a naval platform can be carried out by an electronic sensor, owing to its operation in the almost even background. These two reasons have limited the development of variants in this segment. Effective range enhancement has been the major aspect that has changed to counter the ever-increasing range of ship-based defensive systems. Relatively low growth in the Anti-Radiation ASM segment is because of the passive nature of the homing head that can cover a wide range of frequencies.

Combined with sensor and homing technology, enhanced fuel efficiency in ASM power plants has allowed these weapons to travel longer distances. This has opened up its engagement zone. This has also been complemented by the development of high-capacity propellants that allow greater thrust-to-weight ratio to the weapon and longer burn time to impart greater kinetic energy to the weapon. This assists the ASM to travel a longer distance. Hexanitrohexaazaisowurtzitane, (HNIW and commonly known as China Lake 20 or CL-20) is a classic case and is used in propellants owing to its better oxidization ratio, with 20 per cent more energy than traditional propellants. As depicted in Figure 6.3, the range expansion has taken place in all types of ASM with the maximum increase in ASM with more than 100 km range where the types of missiles have grown four to six-fold. On an average, the range of ASM has increased by 46 per cent and the median range by 53 per cent since 1991 (Figure 6.4). This practically indicates the opening up of the engagement zone of a combat platform by 11.8 per cent, taking weapon range at a nominal 5 per cent of the platform Radius of Action (ROA).

The destructive power of an ASM is based on the energy that it can impart to the intended target. It normally is a combination of kinetic energy owing to the high-speed movement of the ASM and the explosive power of the warhead. While there has been a change in the kinetic energy with the development of hypersonic weapons, the ASM's average speed has not changed significantly. On the other hand, greater fortification of land-based targets has increased their robustness against an ASM attack. To overcome this challenge, the warhead size of the ASMs have gradually been increasing. As depicted in Figure 6.5, the average size of the warhead of the ASM has increased by 26 per cent but what is more significant is that the weight of the median warhead has grown by nearly 60 per cent. This indicates a shift in the employment philosophy of the ASM as a kinetic tool. Heavy warheads lead to a larger destruction area. With the explosive doubling from 100 to 200 kg of TNT, the range for the incident pressure of 13.28 KPa increases from 50 m to 63 m. This translates to an 58.76 per cent increase in the destruction area concerning targets susceptible to the nominal overpressure of 13.28 KPa. Additionally, longer incident impulse by 57.73 per cent (measured in KPa-ms) and longer positive pulse duration by 16.91 per cent (measured in ms) will result in a greater extent of the damage.[26] The Kurtosis analysis of warhead weights and the effective ranges of the ASM since 1991 as given in Figure 6.6, further support the notion of the changing employment philosophy of the ASM. Warheads with greater destructive power reduce the number of weapons that are required to achieve the requisite level of damage in a target system. This, in turn, reduces the number of platforms required to hit a target system and enhances the efficiency of combat air operations.

Figure 6.3: Effective Range of Air-to-Surface Missiles of the World

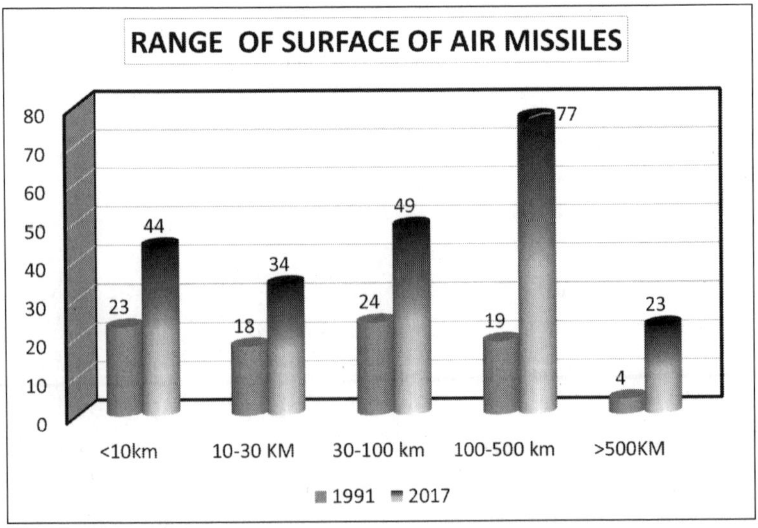

Source: Combat Aircraft Inventory Database.

Figure 6.4: Change in Air-to-Surface Missiles Attributes 1991-2017

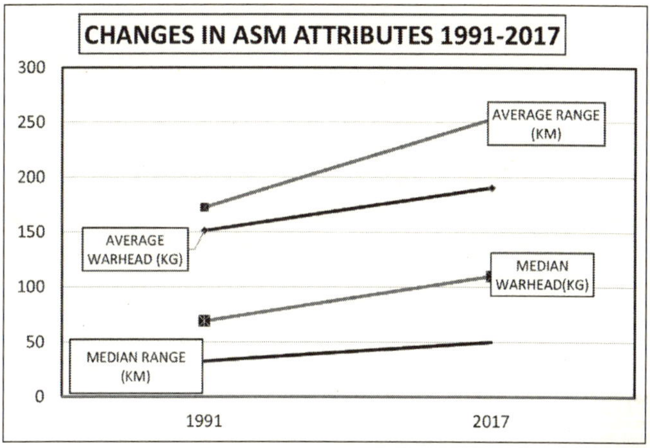

Source: Combat Aircraft Inventory Database.

Figure 6.5: Kurtosis Analysis of Air-to-Surface Missiles of the World 1991-2017

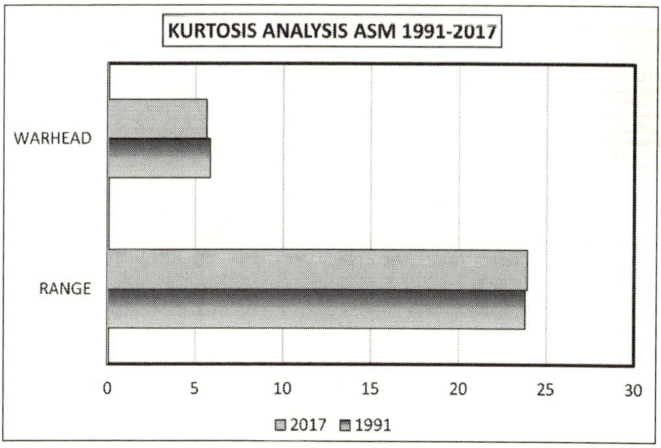

Source: Combat Aircraft Inventory Database.

The air-to-surface missiles can broadly be classified into three categories based on the sensors employed to home-in to the intended target. While most of the long-range ASMs are equipped with inertial navigation systems, satellite navigation or GPS sensors for the initial phase and mid-course updation of their travel to the intended target, it is the terminal phase homing system that determines the classification. An active ASM has an on-board Electromagnetic Emitter, that is used to illuminate the target area. Based on the reflection of the electromagnetic waves emitted, identification and the homing function are executed according to pre-fed algorithms. A majority of long-range anti-shipping missiles fall in this category. In the case of a semi-active ASM, the homing head has a receiver to accept the electromagnetic radiations reflected by the target. Target illumination is carried out by the airborne or surface-based pods.

Figure 6.6: Air-to-Surface Missiles Matrix of the World 1991-2017

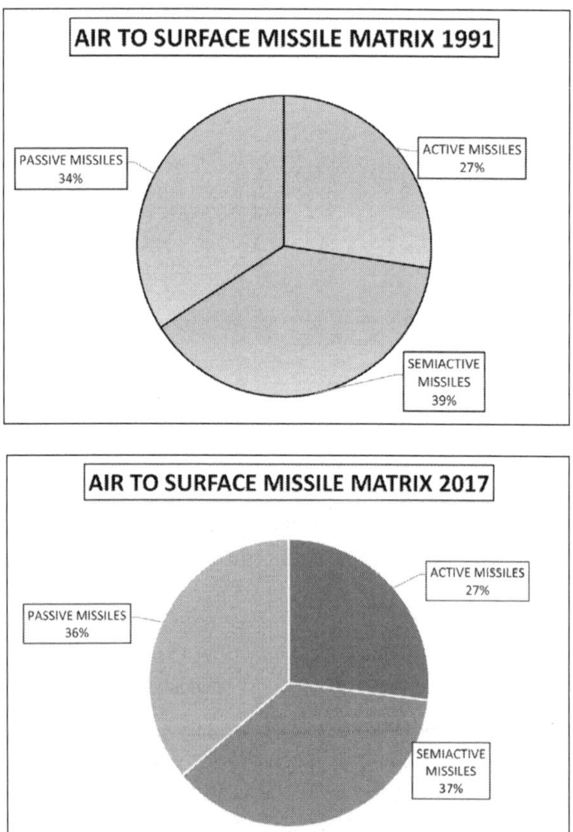

Source: Combat Aircraft Inventory Database.

LASER illumination is the most prevalent technique and is often the choice for anti-tank missiles.[27] In the case of a passive ASM, homing logics are based on the radiation pattern of the target system. Most anti-radiation missiles fall in this category. Besides, several ASMs use Infra-Red and Imaging Infra-Red bands to lock onto their targets. The relative strengths and weaknesses of these three types have remained nearly static since 1991 as can be figured out from their composition charts depicted in Figure 6.6.

The US, Russian, Chinese and French dominance in ASM technology has remained unchanged since 1991, garnering almost 2/3rd of the ASM space (Figure 6.7). The most significant changes are the emergence of China ahead of France and Russia, overtaking the US.

Figure 6.7: Country-wise Air-to-Surface Missile Matrix of the World 1991-2017

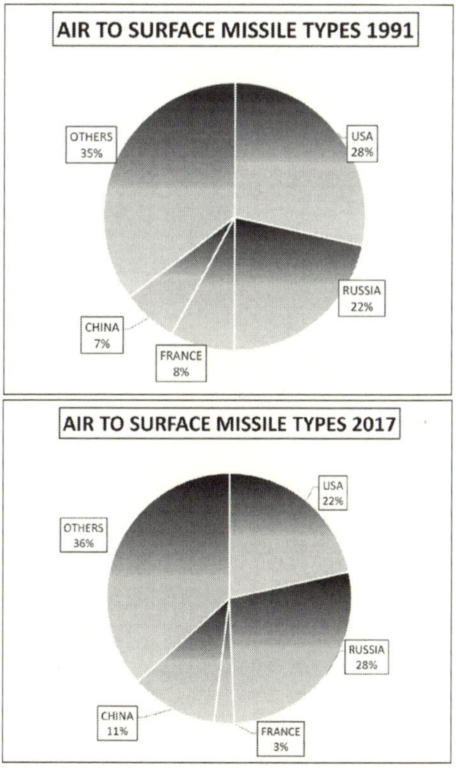

Source: Combat Aircraft Inventory Database.

A gradual increase in the number of countries manufacturing the ASM from 13 to 18 since 1991, indicates the need felt by major air powers to design and develop their air-launched precision long-range weapons (Figure 6.8). However, projects with international collaboration have nearly doubled in the same period. This indicates that countries are focussing on super specialisation in certain techniques and are willing to collaborate with like-minded nations to share the cost and risks of co-development of new weapon systems. Besides cutting the developmental costs, such a methodology helps compress the timelines and optimises resources. Overall, all these figures indicate that crucial homing technology for weapons is still very tightly controlled.

Figure 6.8: Air-to-Surface Missile Manufacturing Countries of the World 1991-2017

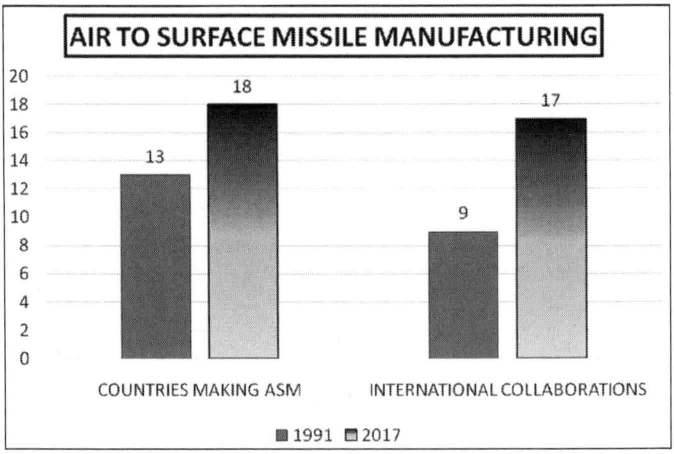

Source: Combat Aircraft Inventory Database.

Air-to-Air Weapons[28]

While the air-to-surface weapons extended their ranges and precision, a similar metamorphosis was witnessed in the development of air-to-air weapons. Till the early 1960s, the air-to-air guns with an effective range of 600-800 m were the prime weapons to shoot down an intruder in aerial combat. Location of a gun on a combat aircraft necessitated a minimum distance between the gun and line of sight for accurate firing. The gun fitment had to ensure that there was no probability of damage to the mother aircraft structure or equipment as a result of gun recoil and blast along with the stability of electrical systems and airflow for the engine.[29] The target had to be brought within the frontal cone of less than one degree before opening fire. Close combat skills of the air crew and the performance of the platform played a major role in defining the outcome of the aerial combat. However, the induction of air-to-air guided missiles changed that but only marginally, as the engagement range increased to about 1500 m and firing cone opened up to 15 degrees. The missiles were required to be fitted externally on the aircraft and normally under-wing. Some aircraft like the F-16 have provisions for carrying lightweight missiles on the wingtips and over the wing in case of Jaguars. The key parameters that are tested before fitting a missile on the aircraft are the strength of the suspension, physical clearance of the missile, alignment of the weapon, sway braces, separation characteristics, and mechanical and electrical release requirements.[30] The Infra-Red (IR) radiation from the engine of the target aircraft was used by the missile seeker head to lock-in on the target. As sensor technology and computation power increased, All-Aspect Air-to-Air Missiles (A4M) allowed the target to be fired from any aspect as the sensors could lock on to even the skin friction heat signature of the target aircraft. This technology also expanded the engagement envelope as it used the speed of the target aircraft to its advantage, and the head-on engagements allowed a kill from 5000 m. In the next stage of transformation, technology to miniaturise radars and communication with computation speed were exploited, leading to Semi-Active and Active AAM. In a semi-active missile, the radar from the mother aircraft illuminated the target and the receiver in the missile used the reflected energy from the target aircraft to guide itself.[31] The effective ranges increased beyond 10 km. Alternatively, the location of the intended target as assessed by the radar on the mother aircraft is communicated to the missile electronically, for it to manoeuvre to intercept the target. In active missiles, after initial designation, the missile goes autonomous and uses in-built radars to locate and home-in on the target aircraft.[32] The weapon ranges increased beyond 30 km and now have reached beyond 200 km. Such an increase in the weapon ranges increases the lethality of the combat aircraft and the area that each aircraft could sanitise. In other words, the number of combat aircraft required to ensure the defence of a specified area, reduced. However, this capability, to be fully exploited, had to be deployed in conjunction with high-fidelity surveillance systems and near real-time electronic transfer of data through secure data links.

The enhancement of computational technology and miniaturization has allowed expansion of an array of active air-to-air missiles as can be seen in Figure 6.9. In 1991, the majority of air-to-air missiles were of the passive category, homing-in on the Infra-Red signature of the intended target aircraft. While this technology remains relevant even today, its share in the air-to-air missile matrix has diminished. Its relevance is based on such a missile giving little electronic warning to the intended target of an impending attack, whereas a semi-active and active missile electronically illuminates the target aircraft and invariably, a Radar Warning Receiver onboard the target aircraft gets activated, warning the combat air crew of an impending missile attack. This becomes a critical input to initiate an evasive manoeuvre and increases the probability to defeat the missile attack. Without such a warning, a passive missile scores in these scenarios. However, as passive sensors lock on to their targets utilizing the target's radiation signature, atmospheric attenuation limits their effective lethal range. The sensor's capabilities in various Infra-Red bands were enhanced and additional correlation features were added, to keep these short-range air-to-air missiles relevant. Additionally, these missiles are of the 'fire and forget' variety, leaving the attacker air crew free to plan and execute their next manoeuvre.[33]

Figure 6.9: Air to Air Missiles Composition 1991 and 2017

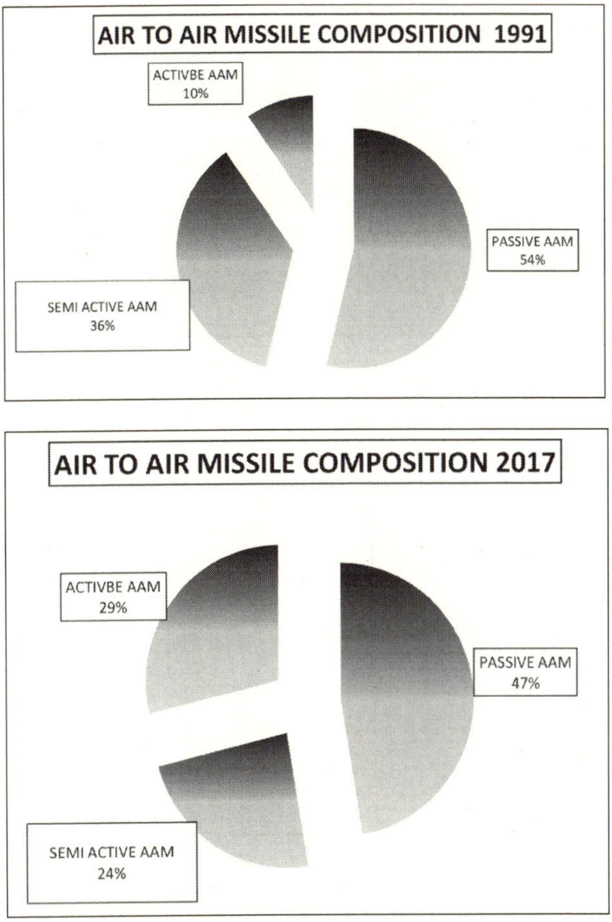

Source: Combat Aircraft Inventory Database.

Since 1991, the types of air-to-air missiles in the short-range – and mostly passive – have declined (Figure 6.10). On the other hand, there have been some new missiles in long (more than 20 km) and very long-range (> 80 km). The average range of air-to-air missile in 2017 was almost three times the average range of those in 1991 and the range median had increased five-fold (Figure 6.11). The Kurtosis analysis indicates a more even distribution of the lethal range of air-to-air missiles prevalent today.

Figure 6.10: Lethal Range of Air-to-Air Missiles

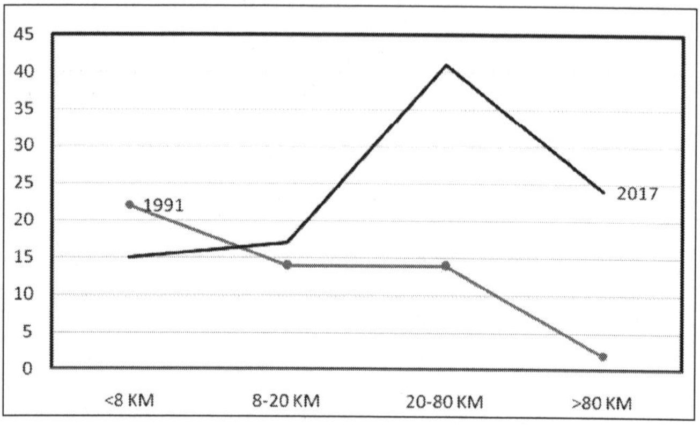

Source: Combat Aircraft Inventory Database.

Figure 6.11: Lethal Range of Air-to-Air Missiles

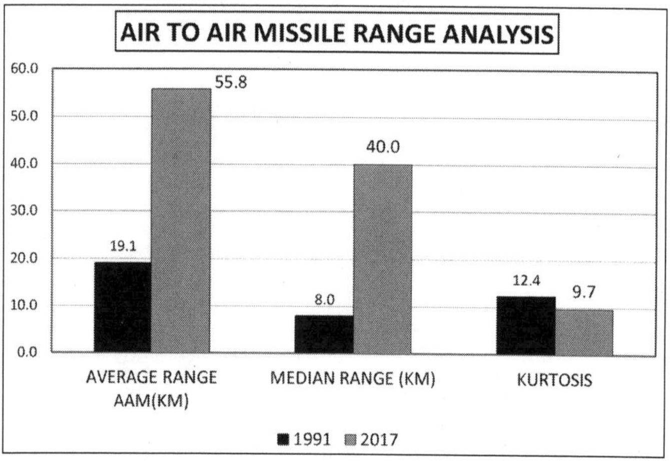

Source: Combat Aircraft Inventory Database.

The number of countries manufacturing air-to-air missiles has increased since 1991 (Figure 6.12) but this number is lower than the countries that manufacture air-to- surface missiles. This is because special technology is required to hit a dynamic high speed and manoeuvring target like a combat aircraft. In international collaborations also, the stories of air-to-surface missiles and air-to-air missiles are different. Unlike air-to-surface missiles, the number of international collaborations to manufacture air-to-air missiles has remained static. This is indicative of the inability of various nations to share their niche technologies to commence joint development and production. Like their air-to-surface counterparts, the air-to-air missile matrix is dominated by the US, Russia, China and France, with 3/4th the share (Figure 6.13). There has not been much change since 1991 barring interchange of the position of Russia and the US for the top slot.

Figure 6.12: Countries Manufacturing Air-to-Air Missiles

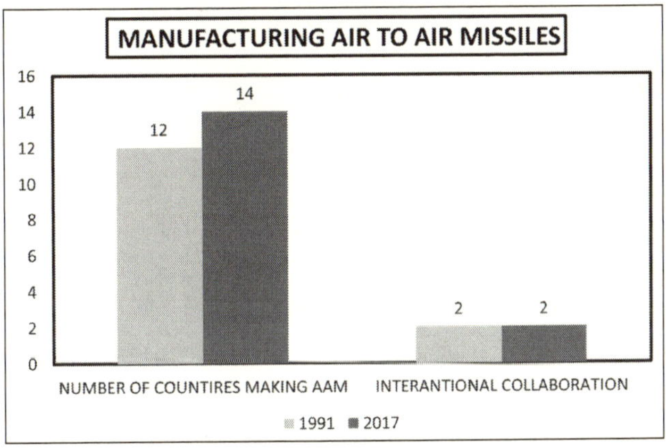

Source: Combat Aircraft Inventory Database.

Figure 6.13: World Air-to-Air Missile Matrix 1991

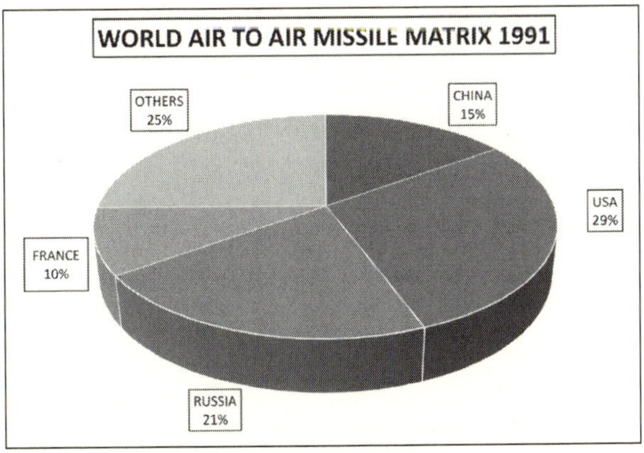

Source: Combat Aircraft Inventory Database.

Figure 6.14: World Air-to-Air Missile Matrix 2017

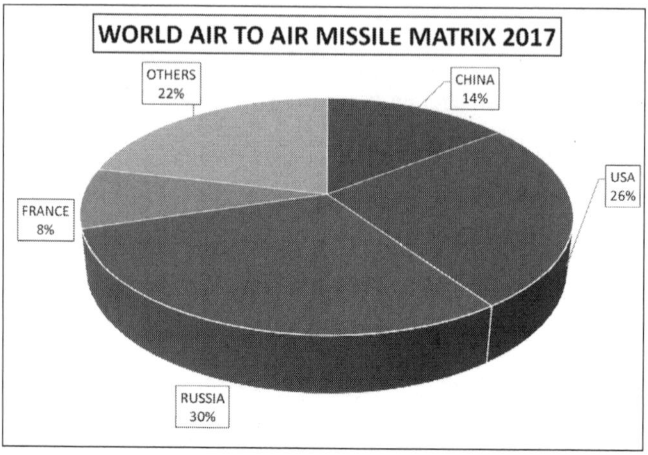

Source: Combat Aircraft Inventory Database.

To control the rising costs and optimize inventory, logistics and maintenance, air-to-air missiles are being configured for multiple tasks. For example, the AIM-9X Sidewinder missile is an Infra-Red-tracking, short-range missile for air-to-air, air-to-surface or surface-to-air applications, with no modifications.[34] The current version, the AIM-9X Block II missile, is in its 16th year of production.[35] Its updated electronics enable the lock-on-after-launch capability using a weapon data link to support beyond-visual-range engagements. It is configured for installation on a wide range of modern aircraft, including the F-15, F-16, F/A18, E/A18G, F-22 and F-35 fighters. It is actively deployed by 23 countries.[36]

Implications of Weapon Capability Enhancements

Weapons have played a crucial role in defining the combat potency of combat platforms. Specifically, in the last three decades, with improved power of computation and communication along with sensor technology, effective ranges and accuracies of air-launched weapons have shown a marked improvement.[37]Although the field of weapon technology is still dominated by a few select countries, gradually more countries have joined the club of air-launched weapon manufacturers. Technology has assisted combat aircraft to carry out multiple-precision attacks with small weapons from long standoff ranges. This reduces the Over Target Requirement (OTR) and Force Levels, leading to the use of a reduced number of combat aircraft to achieve the desired outcome. The proliferation of technology to manufacture these advanced weapons has improved the combat potential per platform across the spectrum. These long-range and accurate weapons in the air-to-surface and air-to-air categories reduce the number of combat aircraft required for covering a specified number of target systems in a pre-defined area for offensive or defensive missions. The ranges of weapons are getting longer and their accuracies are improving. Overall, the size of the battle space is expanding. Battle space transparency has become the key to fully exploit the capabilities of combat aircraft and their weapons. While this attribute has reduced the requirement of combat aircraft, it lays more emphasis on the availability of battle space transparency tools like radars, AWACS, data links and surface-mapping electronic systems, backed up by robust EW systems.[38]

Notes

1. Conflict, manoeuvre and force application in the land and maritime domains were along x-axis and y-axis, in two dimensions. With the induction of airpower, kinetic force application from z-axis became a reality. So the two-dimensional battlefield turned into three-dimensional battle space.
2. A. Bailey and S.G. Murray, *Explosives, Propellants and Pyrotechnics*, Brasseys, UK, 1989, pp. 99-114.
3. Garrett Reim, "F-35A drops GBU-49 precision bomb for the first time in combat training", *Flight Global,* November 19, 2018 at https://www.flightglobal.com/news/articles/f-35a-drops-gbu-49-precision-bomb-for-first-time-in-453766/ (Accessed on November 20, 2018).
4. Ibid.
5. Ministry of Defence, Government of India, "Final Operational Clearance of LCA Tejas MK I for Indian Air Force", Press Release, February 20, 2019, at http://pib.nic.in/newsite/pmreleases.aspx?mincode=33 (Accessed on February 21, 2019).
6. Amitav Malik, "High Power Lasers- directed Energy Weapons, Impact on Defence and Security", Defence Research and Development Organisation, Ministry of Defence, New Delhi, 2012, pp. 99-121.
7. A. Bailey and S.G. Murray, no. 2, pp. 21-47.

8. Helen Cooper and Mujib Mashal, "U.S. Drops 'Mother of All Bombs' on ISIS Caves in Afghanistan", *New York Times,* April 13, 2017 at https://www.nytimes.com/2017/04/13/world/asia/moab-mother-of-all-bombs-afghanistan.html (Accessed on March 28, 2019).
9. BBC News, "Mother of all bombs: How powerful is US mega-weapon?" April 13, 2017 at https://www.bbc.com/news/world-asia-39596333 (Accessed on March 28, 2019).
10. Greg Waldron, "Tokyo contemplates its future fighter plans", *Flight Global,* November 19, 2018 at https://www.flightglobal.com/news/articles/analysis-tokyo-contemplates-its-future-fighter-pla-453253/ (Accessed on November 20, 2018).
11. V.V. Rampal, *Photonics in Warfare,* DRDO Monographs and Special Publications Series, Defence Research and Development Organisation, Ministry of Defence, New Delhi, 2002, pp.147-162.
12. Air Vice-Marshal Tony Mason, "The Air Warfare Requirement", in Phillip Jarret (ed), *The Modern War Machine, Military Aviation Since 1945*, Putnam Aeronautical Books, London, 2000, p. 26.
13. Proximity fuse gGets activated when the target is within pre-defined miss distance from the missile. This obviates the need for a direct collision between the missile and the target, a very difficult task with a low probability of success because of very high crossing speed between a manoeuvring missile and a manoeuvring aircraft.
14. V.V. Rampal, no. 11, pp.199-219.
15. Press Release, Press Information Bureau, Ministry of Defence, Government of India, November 22, 2017at http://pib.nic.in/newsite/pmreleases.aspx?mincode=33 (Accessed on November 23, 2017).
16. The area in which an aircraft is capable of engaging a target with onboard weapons with adequate fuel to return to its parent base. It is calculated as the circular area with the parent base as the centre and radius equal to the sum of the maximum operational range of onboard weapon and maximum distance the aircraft can go in combat configuration with adequate fuel to return to the parent base. The friendly area is negated in this calculation.
17. Circular Error of Probability (CEP) is the distance in metres from the aiming point on the target within which the impact of 50 per cent of the weapons fired takes place.
18. The number of aircraft required to attack a target reduces significantly by improving weapon delivery accuracy. Halving the CEP generally reduces the number of attack aircraft required by 75 per cent for a typical combat zone target.
19. V.V. Rampal, no. 11, pp.147-162.
20. Combat Aircraft Inventory Database based on *IHS Jane's Air-Launched Weapon*, Editions from 1991-2018.

21. Ibid.
22. Amitav Malik, no. 6, pp.147-162.
23. V.V. Rampal, no. 11, pp.147-162.
24. The reflection co-efficient R for normal angles of incidence from air to opaque perfect flat clean metal surface can be computed using the following formula: $R=[(1-n)^2+k^2]/[(1+n)^2+k^2]$ and the absorptivity A of opaque metal surface is: $A= 1 - R =4n/[(n+1)^2+k^2]$ Where n is the refraction co-efficient of material, k is the extinction co-efficient of material. Both values are based on the constituent material. These optical properties are functions of radiation wavelength and vary with temperature. Other factors that define the amount of reflection are the wavelength of LASER and angle of incidence. Environmental conditions dictate the reflection energy at a specific range.
25. Combat Aircraft Inventory Database, no. 20.
26. "Blast Effect Calculator" at https://www.un.org/disarmament/un-saferguard/kingery-bulmash/ (Accessed on November 18, 2018)can be used to calculate these basic details about the explosive power.
27. Amitav Malik, no. 6, pp.147-162.
28. See Mike Spick, *Fighters at War: The Story of Air-to-Air Combat*, Greenhill Books, London, 1997, pp.114-134.
29. K. Nagaraj, *Airworthiness Certification of Fighter Aircraft*, Defence Research and Development Organisation, Ministry of Defence, New Delhi, 2015, p 160.
30. K Nagaraj, Ibid., pp. 163-167.
31. Mike Spick, no. 28, p.111.
32. Ibid., pp.114-134.
33. Jerry Scutts, "From Nuclear Bombs to Cruise Missiles", in Phillip Jarret (ed), *The Modern War Machine: Military Aviation Since 1945*, Putnam Aeronautical Books, London, 2000, pp. 29-51.
34. IM-9X Sidewinder Missile details available on https://www.raytheon.com/capabilities/products/aim-9x?WT.mc_id=aviationweeksponsoredcontentrms_sas_iis_airdom&utm_source=aviationweek&utm_medium=sponsoredcontent&utm_content=rms_sas_iis_airdom_f35_hyperlink_aim9x_sc&utm_campaign=rms_sas_iis_airdom (Accessed on September 10, 2018).
35. Ibid.
36. Ibid.
37. Mike Spick, no, 28, p.141.
38. For more see Mike Spick, "Tactical Support", in Phillip Jarret (ed), no. 33, pp.165-186.

7. Mission Buddies: Evolving Alternatives and Combat Enablers

War is unforgiving. Threat matrices continuously undergo change. Geopolitics, economics and technology play critical roles in defining these matrices. Therefore, armed forces across the world continuously attempt to re-equip, re-organise, re-structure and re-define their force structures in order to enhance their operational capabilities. The focus of these processes invariably is to build proficiency in the relevant domains for present and future conflict scenarios. With finite financial resources, there is a perpetual debate between domains, quality and quantity.

Induction of aircraft in war zones saw the advent of combat aviation. Rapidly, combat aircraft achieved an iconic status amongst all types of combat equipment. With enhancement of combat power of each platform, combat aircraft have started playing a decisive role in military strategy and tactics. Though that position has not changed much in the last five decades, a number of competing alternatives have evolved. While technology was assisting in augmenting combat capability of combat aircraft, it was also engaged in developing other alternatives. Unmanned Aerial Vehicles (UAV) and Unmanned Combat Air Vehicles (UCAV), Surface-to-Surface Missiles (SSM) and Surface-to-Air Missile Systems (SAM) with accurate explosive delivery mechanisms starting competing with manned combat aircraft and have become an integral part of most combat forces. These alternatives sometimes compete with combat aircraft for undertaking a mission and at other times complement it in mission execution. Although Armed and Attack Helicopters (AAH) have a significant role in combat operations in the Tactical Battle Area (TBA), they invariably complement the combat aircraft in offensive missions and therefore are not discussed here as an alternative. This chapter gives a brief overview of SSM, UAV and SAM domains. Thereafter, force enablers for combat aviation like AWACS and FRA are discussed and in the end is a case study of the United States Air Force Expansion Plan, indicating the changing relative significance of combat aircraft in its primary roles of attack and to defend.

Surface-to-Surface Missiles (SSM)[1]

The first-ever rocket was launched in China in 1232.[2] Technology and force application of this attribute has come a long way since then. A surface-to-surface missile (SSM), a modern version of a rocket, is a guided weapon powered by a power plant to carry a warhead to the intended target. Based on their power plants, these can be broadly classified as Ballistic Missiles (BM) or Cruise Missiles (CM). Ballistic missiles do not depend on atmospheric air for propelling themselves to the exosphere before free-falling. A cruise missile has an air breather propulsion plant and normally remains below an altitude of 45,000 feet. In most cases, the missile heads towards a pre-programmed target location and no further interventions are necessary. These weapons provide an alternative to the manned combat aircraft. A case in point is the development of such long-range missiles in Pakistan which are intended to provide target coverage deep inside India's large territory, over distances that are beyond the reach of its fighter aircraft .[3]

Delivery of explosives to destroy an intended target can also be carried out by a combat aircraft. Therefore, for the offensive role, both SSM and combat aircraft are designed to deliver the weapon load on the intended target – so in some sense, they are competitors. There has been a never-ending debate on the relative efficacy of SSMs vis-a-vis manned combat aircraft. The dynamics were tilted highly in favour of combat aircraft as initial operational SSMs were not very accurate. That forced the operator to use a large number of missiles to achieve requisite assurance levels of target neutralization. This led to the requirement of large stocking of SSMs and associated cumulative cost. However, for large Mean Area of Effectiveness (MAE) weapons like nuclear weapons, prime dependence is on missiles as a Circular Error Probability (CEP) of over 100 metres is well within acceptable limits. This is because of very large area that can be affected by the exploding nuclear warhead. As is the impact of technology on combat aircraft, so is it on the missiles. With greater terminal guidance accuracy, the CEP has come down. Improvements in navigation systems and terminal guidance systems have reduced the CEP of missiles to less than 100 metres with some high-end missiles capable of CEP of 3-5 metres. Greater accuracy reduces the number of weapons that need to be fired to neutralize a specified target.

Improvements in power plant technology have enhanced the capabilities of both combat aircraft and SSMs. But its impact is more pronounced on combat aircraft. While it is common for a combat aircraft to carry a weapon load of 4000-6000 kg, the average warhead of an SSM is less than 500 kg. This means that multiple SSMs, normally more than ten, can replicate weight of attack by a combat aircraft. Along with SSMs attribute of non-reusability, this aspect makes attacks by SSM very expensive. This, to some extent, is compensated by negligible infrastructure, operational and maintenance cost of SSM as compared to a manned combat aircraft. The SSM also scores over combat aircraft in terms of its sustenance costs. Combat aircraft procurement, maintenance, training especially for the air crew, is a cost-intensive activity but necessary to achieve the requisite levels of professional capability. Additionally, operators have to spend considerable resources on the regular training of combat pilots to retain requisite skill sets. During training, a number of aircraft are lost in accidents and that adds to the overall cost of maintaining combat aircraft fleet. Additionally, combat aircraft, for full effectiveness, depend on force multipliers like AWACS and in-flight refuellers on the one hand and ground-based radars and associated infrastructure on the other. Acquisition, operation, maintenance and training of all such systems add on to the cost of combat capability through combat aircraft. There are no such expenditures for SSMs.

Non-reusability, inability to recall after launch and vulnerability of static launch sites are other major limitations of SSMs as compared to manned combat aircraft. But long-range SSMs and mobile launchers provide an unmatched alternative to the planners. Such SSMs can be launched from far distances from the intended targets thus retaining the element of surprise, whereas combat aircraft may have to re-deploy to a base closer to the target so that the target system is within its radius of action. This reveals the intentions and practically eliminates the element of surprise. Although with aerial refuelling, this limitation can be overcome to some extent. Some critical aspects of SSMs are covered here.

Targeting

The targeting process commences with fixing the location of the intended target system. A missile attack is envisaged only on fixed/ large targets and adequate data can be collected about such a target system with the use of satellites over a period of time and archived to be used on an as required basis. However, the approach for targeting a mobile system needs to be different. Detecting, identifying and tracking mobile target systems in hostile territory is possible only within the sensor range of existing aerospace assets.

Deployment of aerial assets for surveillance in the hostile airspace is a high-risk mission and distance wise, may not be possible in areas that need to be targeted. The area that can be brought under surveillance of aerial assets is minuscule as compared to the targeting zone of SSMs. A time lag between satellite revisits and time for data download and interpretation makes satellites unsuitable for tracking and lending assistance to the targeting of a mobile system. Overland, the possibility of a mobile target to conceal itself exists, which negates mission success for an SSM attack. Therefore, a very low assurance level is expected in case a long-range SSM is employed against a mobile target in hostile territory with a conventional warhead.

Maritime Targeting

Sea Lanes of Communication (SLOC) are the lifeline of the world economy. Naval surface and sub-surface assets ensure their security. Maritime domain awareness tools in conjunction with combat ship deployment, augmented by combat and combat support aircraft, can dominate a vast area and help in safeguarding the rules-based order. However, the equation will change in the case of deployment of aircraft carriers. Aircraft carriers are invariably deployed as a part of the Carrier Battle Group (CBG) with a number of combat and support ships for operational and logistical imperatives. As compared to land, in case of a ship, a mobile target, in international waters, detecting and tracking are comparatively easier as airborne sensors can be deployed with minimal risks and the target cannot conceal itself easily. In such a scenario, air-launched long-range cruise missiles (ALCMs) like BrahMos can provide effective deterrence, but the continuous deployment of air power over the long range is resource-intensive. Alternatively, a conventional warhead SSM with MIRV can be a cost-effective tool. Additionally, ballistic missiles with their elliptical high-angle trajectory and hypersonic speed limit the efficacy of most of the ship-based air defence systems. A coordinated attack by cruise missiles and ballistic missiles will test the limits of even the most advanced air defence systems and such an attack will have a high probability of success.

Based on the expected speed of the target system and time gap between its launch and the Estimated Time of Arrival (ETA) of the missile in the area, the sensors on board SSM will have to scan an area of approximately 3,000 square kilometres for its intended target system. A time lag between the last detection of a target and missile launch will increase this area further. Manoeuvring at hypersonic speed to converge onto a mobile target adds to the mission complexities. Overall, the current sensor-shooter combination for SSM against a mobile target system is sub-optimal as compared to a manned combat aircraft wherein the pilot can identify and track the intended mobile target and carry out an attack. Once these two major technological challenges — identifying and locating the target and terminal homing, are overcome, SSMs can boost deterrence in the maritime domain as a cost-effective alternative to combat aircraft deployment.

Unmanned Aerial Vehicles (UAV)[4]

Manned aircraft were first inducted in warfare as high-ground observatories to monitor enemy troop movement. Aerial reconnaissance, with an observation by the pilot and later with a still camera, was the first operational role of aircraft. The next step involved the air crew carrying small bombs and dropping them manually from the cockpit. Thus was born the role of ground attack. In the next phase, aircraft were equipped with guns to engage enemy aircraft in the air and so commenced the aerial combat role. Besides these, the development of bigger airframes and powerful engines enabled the development of transport aircraft, which were subsequently modified with the fitting of radars, jammers and fuel tanks for surveillance, electronic warfare and in-flight refuelling, respectively. These roles are being performed by manned aircraft albeit with much better technology and accuracy than was possible during the 20th century.

Technological advancement in computing and communication facilitated the development of Unmanned Aerial Vehicles (UAV). Controlled from a ground station, the UAV either fly a pre-planned path or can be dynamically controlled.[5] While the roles of UAVs are gradually increasing in the civil sector, ranging from the delivery of packages to the shooting of high-quality aerial films, a debate is on about the end of an era for manned aircraft for operational missions. As was the case with manned aircraft about a century ago, the operational roles of UAVs are following a similar trajectory. Besides being used as a weapon, the first operational role for UAVs was of aerial reconnaissance, wherein the UAV was fitted with optical cameras. The development of sensor technology and its miniaturization along with better computation and communication allowed transmission of real-time data in various electromagnetic bands, a boon for a military commander. UAVs scored substantially over manned aircraft in this role, owing to their longer endurance. Coupled with satellite imagery capabilities, UAVs have practically driven out manned aircraft from the reconnaissance role except in a very few critical cases where their low speed remains an operational impediment. However, UAVs have been able to overcome their speed limits to a certain extent by their low Radar Cross Section (RCS), making it difficult to detect and engage them.[6]

Going by the precedent of manned aircraft, the next role UAVs were assigned was of ground attack. This required more powerful engines and larger airframes for enabling the UAV to carry weapons. Here too, technology played a pivotal role in enhancing weapons delivery accuracy, thus reducing the weapon size required for the same extent of impact on the target. This role by UAVs is being carried out successfully in Afghanistan with Hellfire missiles from the USAF MQ9. The UAV's long endurance allows a high success rate for search and strike missions as compared to a manned fighter aircraft with comparatively limited endurance. The success rate of UAV ground attack missions is to a large extent dependent on their operation in a benign air defence environment.

The full development and employment of UAVs in an air defence role is still some distance away owing to the prevailing technological challenges. In the same vein, switching to unmanned transport aircraft for transporting personnel may also take a few decades.

There are three critical components involved in the employment of UAVs instead of manned aircraft in combat, viz., basic flying (take off, landing and planned navigation), tactical flying (situation appreciation and changing the plan midway) and weapon delivery (correct and timely targeting). While progress has been made in all three verticals, it is yet to reach a level that would enable the complete replacement of manned aircraft. Factors that need to be considered in this debate are:-

Sensors and Dynamic Situation Processing

In a benign air defence environment and uncontested airspace, UAVs are efficient in mission accomplishment. When decision-making autonomy is required or there are rules of engagement or a developing air situation that cannot be explicitly expressed mathematically, human interface is essential. The current generation of sensors does not have the capacity to replicate the appreciation by a human eye and poses a limitation in operations because the UAV operator is not fully aware of the situation in real time. The major drawback of the current generation systems is their inability to capture high-fidelity data, process, encrypt and transmit it and based on directions from the ground station, receive, decrypt and process it to execute a command.[7] Based on the type of processor and communication systems, this process may take anywhere from 600 milliseconds to three seconds – a very long duration in combat operations. Communication capabilities form the backbone of operations and more so for unmanned systems. The USAF with the launch of the fourth Advanced Extremely High Frequency (AEHF) satellite on October 17, 2018, completed the constellation requirements for global Extended Data Rate (XDR) connectivity online. This enhanced the communications throughput ten times over the existing Milstar. The goal of such a satellite constellation is to provide survivable, global, secure, protected and jam-resistant communications for high-priority military ground, sea and air assets. Increased speed allows the transmission of real-time video, battlefield maps and targeting data to help combatant commanders and national leaders make optimal tactical and strategic decisions.[8] The development of Artificial Intelligence will reduce dependency on communication from the base station and enhance the level of autonomy to the UAV.

Speed and Manoeuvrability

UAVs are generally characterized by their low speed and consequent low manoeuvrability as compared to manned fighter aircraft, and this makes them vulnerable. At the same time however, a low RCS and greater endurance are design features that assist UAVs in mission accomplishment. Some UAV manufacturers like Kratos USA involved in making target drones, are also dealing with tactical UAVs that are manoeuvrable to more than 9g.[9]

Weapon Carrying Capacity

Owing to their power, UAVs are capable of carrying low calibre/ low weight weapons in limited numbers as compared to manned aircraft. But this limitation can be overcome by converting fighter aircraft into UAVs or through the use of special weapons with high accuracy to reduce Over Target Requirement (OTR)[10] in terms of number and size of weapons.

Quantity and Costs

UAVs do not need some of the safety and operating systems that manned aircraft need and thus enjoy better cost-efficiency. As compared to manned aircraft, the major factor in the cost matrix is the safety features for the pilot. The pilot's safety is a critical function in combat aircraft design. This aspect can be clearly understood from the design configuration for a Flight Control System (FCS). To enhance combat capability, the aircraft are designed with relaxed stability. The X-29 was designed with a thin, supercritical wing for improved supersonic performance, a form of variable wing camber and canard fore planes, trimmed so that the fore plane and wing would almost equally load at high speed for the lowest possible supersonic drag. The platform was very unstable at very low speed. To counter the chances of failure of the FCS, the digital flight control system had three independent channels, with each monitoring the other two for possible failures and as a standby to these three, a fourth analogous FCS was deployed, should the digital system fail. So practically, four layers of redundancy to ensure that the pilot had a reasonable chance of ejecting should things go wrong. [11] This is where a UAV scores over the manned aircraft. This normally translates into greater numbers of UAVs for the same cost as compared to a combat aircraft. The Valkyrie, a tactical UAV under development, could be built for less than $2 million. The low-cost nature of these tactical systems means that it would be cheaper to finance an air war against an adversary. The air defence system is expensive, and advanced air defence missiles may cost up to $5 million. Such missile engagement for a relatively cheap UAV of $500,000 is a good barter. The cost equation for employing tactical UAVs in high-threat zones becomes very effective.[12] However, autonomous aviation technology is yet to mature and UAV accident rates are four to five times higher than that of manned aircraft. This negates the cost-effectiveness partially as of now, but is likely to improve with better technology.

Endurance and Risks

UAVs practically eliminate human endurance as a factor for mission duration. Autonomous in-flight refuelling could keep the UAV in the air for days. In July 2018, Zephyr set the world record for flight endurance after staying aloft using solar cells for 25 days, 23 hours, 57 minutes.[13] The aircraft flew as high as 74,000ft during daytime.[14] Risk to life and of capture of operators is fully eliminated. However, the control of UAV is heavily dependent on electromagnetic waves, which are susceptible to interference/jamming/technical malfunctions. Any delay in the transmission of critical commands could be lethal. Another aspect of the absence of an aircrew in UAVs is the limited ability of on-board systems to diagnose any system malfunction, especially owing to an external factor. An air crew can diagnose instrument failure and react to save the aircraft, but a UAV with instrument failure will most probably be lost.

The long-term trend in the field of UAVs field is indicated in the US Congressional Research Service Report which noted that DOD spending on Unmanned Aerial System (UAS) had increased from $284 million in FY2000 to $3.3 billion in FY2010.[15] With effect from 2010, the induction of UAVs has outnumbered that of manned aircraft in the US armed forces. And since 2011, the US Air Force has trained more UAV pilots than fighter/bomber pilots. As per the US *Congressional Research Service Report*:

> "Conventional wisdom states that UAS offer two main advantages over manned aircraft: they are considered more cost-effective, and they minimize the risk to a pilot's life. For these reasons and others, DOD's unmanned aircraft inventory increased more than 40-fold from 2002 to 2010. "[16]

But most of the financial allocations the world over, including in the US, are still being made for manned aircraft development and procurement (Figure 7.1). This will change once better processing capacities, artificial intelligence and communication equipment are developed and incorporated into the UAVs.

Figure 7.1: 2019 US Defence Budget Demand for Aircraft[17]

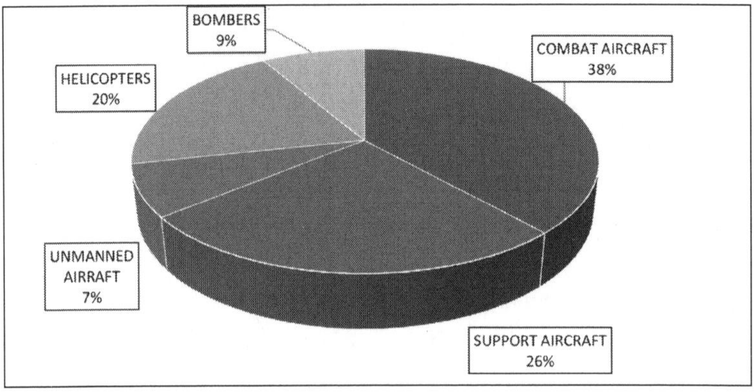

Source: Based on data in the FY 2019 Program Acquisition Costs by Weapon System of United Stated Department of Defense Fiscal Year 2019 Budget Request by the Office of the Undersecretary of Defense (Comptroller)/ Chief Financial Officer, February 2018.

The conversion of fighter aircraft to UAVs for undertaking training missions has been tried and tested in the case of the F-4 and F-16 in the US Air Force and the F-6 in the People's Liberation Army Air Force (PLAAF). The same could be developed further for undertaking high-risk operational missions. Technology involving a swarm of UAVs operating in a group and being mutually supportive is at an advanced stage of development and will assist UAVs in garnering a greater share of operational missions. A critical component of such a programme is development of autonomous flight controls, to allow a single operator, on the ground or in another aircraft – such as the pilot of a combat aircraft – to manage the missions of several UAVs at once. The mission could be controlled from the ground, through direct line-of-sight, through a relay, a satellite relay, or through another aircraft.[18] This technology will expand the operational applicability of the UAVs.

In the foreseeable future, an optimal solution is a mix of manned aircraft and UAVs until technology can support a better appreciation of situational awareness and command and control aspects. Currently, the most suitable missions for UAVs are the five Ds – Detect, Designate, Dirty, Destructive and Dangerous. Detect missions require long endurance and are pre-planned and repetitive in nature like surveillance over a large area for a prolonged duration to detect a possible development. Designate missions are used in conjunction with Detect missions or as a standalone to designate a target system/subsystem using laser designators (fitted on board the UAV to illuminate a target system and attack aircraft use the laser reflected from the target to guide its weapons) for an attack by an armed aircraft/UAV. Dirty missions are undertaken in an NBC environment in order to negate the risk to human life. Destructive missions involve a UAV equipped with explosives and its use as a weapon, and Dangerous missions involve those against a heavily defended target to either attack the defences or force the adversary to expend missiles on UAVs. Enhancement in the number of tactical UAVs is a response to growing threats to aircraft from adversaries with advanced air-defence networks. A group of aircraft against an enemy air defence system may cause short-term decision paralysis or part saturation. This increases the probability of survival of the manned aircraft in the engagement zone of the lethal air defence system. Gradually, an additional role as a communication hub is evolving for UAVs; [19] a mission that can only be accomplished by an unmanned system.

Israel and the US are pioneers and leaders in UAV technology and operations. Now all major combat forces are equipped with UAVs. China is taking a lead in manufacturing and exporting UAVs to countries such as Jordan, Saudi Arabia, Egypt, and the United Arab Emirates.[20] The US estimates China could produce almost 42,000 UAVs, with a sale value more than $10 billion, in the decade up to 2023.[21]

With the current state of technology, UAVs are the best bet for operations in an uncontested airspace for surveillance and search-and-strike missions with low- calibre high-accuracy guided weapons. However, operations in a moderate-to- dense air defence environment will need manned aircraft to react appropriately. UAVs can be of great value though to reduce the risk to manned aircraft by saturating the airspace and attacking air defence systems, thus compelling an adversary to expend his missiles. UAVs are essential ingredients of a combat force and their role will continue to increase along with their capability.

A quantum jump in the operational role for UAVs can be expected only with a breakthrough in AI. Until that happens, the role of UAVs will increase gradually to reach about 50 per cent of combat operations over the course of the next three decades.[22] Till a requisite number of mission-capable UAVs are inducted, some of the operational missions will have to be carried out by manned aircraft, albeit in a sub-optimal way. The Unmanned Systems Integrated Roadmap of the United States armed forces till 2034 gives a glimpse of the operational role unmanned systems will play in the future battle space:

> In today's military, unmanned systems are highly desired by combatant commanders (COCOMs) for their versatility and persistence. By performing tasks such as surveillance; signals intelligence (SIGINT); precision target designation; mine detection; and chemical, biological, radiological, nuclear (CBRN) reconnaissance, unmanned systems have made key contributions to the Global War on Terror (GWOT). As of October 2008, coalition unmanned aircraft systems (UAS) (exclusive of hand-launched systems) have flown almost 500,000 flight hours in support of Operations Enduring Freedom and Iraqi Freedom, unmanned ground vehicles (UGVs) have conducted over 30,000 missions, detecting and/or neutralizing over 15,000 improvised explosive devices (IEDs), and unmanned maritime systems (UMSs) have provided security to ports.[23]

Surface-to-Air Missiles (SAM)

It may appear as an oxymoron that the weapon system designed to thwart the employment of combat air power is actually competing to occupy the same space. The development of surface-to-air weapons started immediately after air power was used as an offensive tool for the first time. However, it was only after the development of radars to scan the sky, and homing heads to lock the incoming aircraft, that SAMs actually turned a leaf. A number of methods are employed to detect, identify and track an incoming hostile aircraft, but invariably, radars form the most significant component in the air defence chain.

Radars from low to ultra-high Frequency are for detection, and higher frequency radars with better resolution are utilized for tracking an aircraft prior to engaging it with surface-based missiles. Integration of a number of techniques to intercept an incoming aircraft with high-speed computing has made the SAM systems not only intercept incoming combat aircraft but also engage incoming cruise and ballistic missiles. With high resolution and sensitivity, certain systems have a high probability of intercepting air-launched weapons with low radar cross-section.[24]

The effective range of a SAM system is based on its ability to detect and react, besides the amount of kinetic energy that can be imparted to the missile. SAMs keep losing speed after the boost phase and consequently lose their ability to manoeuvre to catch the incoming aircraft or missile. Therefore, the type and size of the propellant plays a vital role in defining the effective range of a missile. SAMs with a range of 3 to 400 kilometres exist. While small-range SAMs have the utility to defend a point target, it is the long-range surface-to-air weapons that are redefining combat aviation. Deployment of a long-range surface-to-air weapon creates an air defence umbrella to limit the exploitation of the third dimension by the hostile forces. This allows other elements of combat power to operate. While not foolproof, this kind of arrangement reduces the need for combat aircraft to perform the defensive role. On the other hand, in case of a requirement to attack a target system defended by a long-range SAM, the attackers need to deploy a combination of an electronic shield, long- range air-to-surface weapons with tactical ploys of decoys and saturation.[25] To augment the combat power, in spite of dwindling numbers of combat aircraft, India is focussing on this aspect as brought out clearly by multiple tests undertaken by the Defence Research and Development Organisation (DRDO) in February 2019:

> The Defence Research and Development Organisation (DRDO) successfully test fired indigenously developed Quick Reach Surface-to-Air missiles (QRSAM) from ITR Chandipur, off the Odisha Coast. The two missiles were tested for different altitude and conditions. The test flights successfully demonstrated the robust Control, Aerodynamics, Propulsion, Structural performance and high manoeuvring capabilities, thus proving the design configuration. Radars, Electro-Optical Systems, Telemetry and other stations have tracked the missiles and monitored [them] through the entire flights. All the mission objectives have been met.[26]

The proliferation of surface-to-air weapons also impacted the design philosophy of the combat platforms. While qualifying the requirements of a combat aircraft, higher speed and higher combat ceiling are sought to eliminate the threat from short-range SAMs and minimize exposure to large-range SAMs. This "High- Fast Sanctuary" was the key criteria for designs for SR 71 and MiG25.[27] Shooting down of the US' U2 high-altitude reconnaissance aircraft by SA2 over erstwhile USSR on May 1, 1960, did alter the myth about the invincibility of higher and faster and brought focus back onto the significance of better surface-to-air weapon systems.

Combat Enablers (or Force Multipliers)

The combat power of a nation is greater than the total potential of all the combat elements it possesses. This is because some combat elements magnify the potential of others. Such boosters are normally referred to as force multipliers. An exponential enhancement of combat power takes place by a process that combines the effects of multiple force multipliers. In the current operational scenario, force multipliers can be classified in three broad categories – Battle space Transparency and Control Systems (BTCS), Range and Endurance Enhancers (REE), and Weapon-Precision and Range Enhancers

(WPRE) for targeting.[28] BTCS include all sensors and networks that assist an accurate assessment of the location, potential and intent of all combat assets in a pre-defined battle space as well as help control own assets for force application. These include ground/sea-based and airborne/ space-based electronic, optical and infra-red sensors in combination with the requisite communication networks to create the battle space awareness for friendly elements and deny the same to the hostile elements. Amongst these, airborne sensors are the most flexible and can be deployed in the area of interest at very short notice. Airborne sensors overcome the line of sight limitation of surface-based sensors and help in effective surveillance and control particularly in mountainous terrain. Airborne Warning and Control Systems (AWACS), Airborne Early Warning and Control (AEW&C) aircraft and Electronic Warfare aircraft are classic force multipliers in this category.[29]

For application of combat aviation, Airborne Early Warning and Control (AEW&C) and Airborne Early Warning and Aircraft Control Systems (AWACS), serve as advanced battle space transparency tools.[30] With radar mounted on a heavy aircraft, AWACS/ AEW&C help overcome the limitations of line of sight from a ground-based radar system. Being airborne, AEW&C/AWACS are a difficult platform to jam or target although it has a major limitation in terms of on-station time for surveillance and control tasks based on the fuel it can carry. Normally, the on-station time for various platforms in this category is between six to eight hours before it is refuelled either in the air or after landing. Based on the type of radar fitted, this airborne system either has a 360 degree coverage or a sectoral coverage on either side of the aircraft track of around 240 degrees. Three popular AEW&C/AWACS configurations are based on Boeing, Ilyushin and Embraer aircraft across the world. The niche technology associated with this tool is still restricted to a few countries. While defensive operations for defending one's own territory can be carried out with the use of ground/ surface-based radars, this is not true for the maritime domain and for operations over hostile territories. As such, any expeditionary force, that expects an aerial threat, needs to be supported by airborne radar systems as

AEW&C/AWACS. This explains as to why the US owns nearly 46 per cent of the world's inventory in this category. (Figure 7.2).

Figure 7.2: AEW&C Inventory 2018

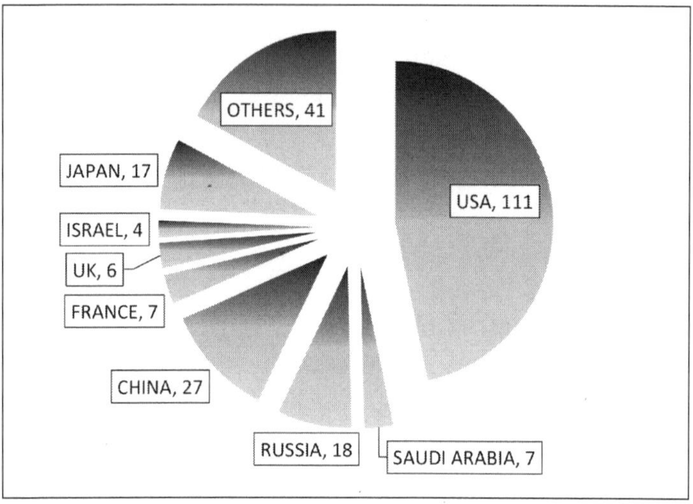

Source: Military Balance 2018, IISS.

REE are aircraft capable of dispensing fuel to other aircraft in the air in order to enhance the range and endurance of aerial platforms. The concept of aerial refuelling is nearly a hundred years old, with the first recorded refuelling occurring on June 27, 1923.[31] Aviation, in general, and military aviation in particular, has come a long way since then. Effective mission duration of a combat aircraft is a subset of its endurance. One of the major shortcomings of combat aircraft is its low endurance. The high-performance engines fitted on combat aircraft have a very high rate of fuel consumption. On an average, a modern combat aircraft carries between 3000-5000 kg of fuel. Based on the type of aircraft, configuration, altitude and speed, during air combat, the fuel consumption can be as high as 300-500 kg per minute. This high rate of fuel consumption poses severe limitations on the range to which a mission can be undertaken and its duration.

Transit time between the parent base and operating area and the fuel required for a possible diversion during recovery has to be managed within overall platform endurance. During hostile conditions, the base of operation is required to be in-depth to minimize the risk of an enemy attack while the aircraft is on the ground for refuelling or servicing. This reduces the time a combat aircraft can remain on station for operational tasks. In a typical combat mission profile, the "on-station" duration varies between 70 to 80 per cent of platform endurance. However, in case of missions over the sea and far from any friendly/safe air base, this could reduce to 30 or 40 per cent. After each mission, the aircraft requires to be refuelled and serviced on the ground. This process is time-consuming and can take up to three hours. The combination of these two factors (on-ground time and transit time to mission area) limits the effective mission duration for each platform. In a 24-hour cycle, a combat aircraft will be mission-effective for about six hours. The remainder is spent on the ground refuelling and servicing, as well as transiting to and from the operational area for each sortie. In case the aircraft is refuelled in the air, at or near its operational area, there is a major change in its mission-effective time. For a combat aircraft, aerial refuelling for ten minutes enhances its endurance by about two hours. In practical terms, the mission-effective time increases to twelve hours in a 24-hour cycle. Simply stated, aerial refuelling reduces the number of platforms for round-the-clock missions in a specified area from four to two. This can be operationally employed by bringing a larger area under mission cover. Another aspect that this technology took care of was longer mission durations especially related to air defence and Intelligence, Reconnaissance and Surveillance (ISR). These missions are endurance-dependent and not range-dependent. In that, the output of the mission is based more on its "on-station" time. Resorting to multiple aerial refuelling improves this matrix further. However, this has to be within the overall limit imposed by crew fatigue as well as maintenance imperatives in terms of replenishing other consumables (oil/gases) and replacing/servicing components (due after a specified duration of operation). An additional advantage of such a profile is reduced "on- ground" time. This reduces the vulnerability of the aircraft. This dimension is significant for aircraft that do not have hardened aircraft shelters for protection and are most vulnerable when on the ground. Aerial refuelling helps fighter/bomber aircraft to stay in combat for a longer duration or reach targets farther than their in-built fuel capacity permits. It also enables them to carry more weapon load and less fuel to stay within the safe operational limits especially at high and hot airfields. After take-off, these aircraft take in the balance fuel from the aerial refueller as per the mission requirement.

For aerial refueling, primarily two methods are employed of 'Probe & Drogue' and 'Boom and Receptacle'.[32] In the Probe and Drogue system, the tanker aircraft reels out a refuelling hose with a drogue chute at its end. The receiver aircraft has to manoeuvre the aircraft in such a fashion that the refuelling probe engages the socket inside the drogue. Once the contact is established and the probe engages the socket, refuelling can commence. The latitude available to the receiver is very small in terms of longitudinal range and vertical range during refuelling. In case the receiver exceeds the limits in any dimension, the probe and socket engagement terminates and refuelling ceases. However, in case of the Boom and Receptacle method, the receiver positions the aircraft aft (behind and below) of the tanker, and the Boom Operator in the tanker manoeuvres a boom to slot it in the refuelling receptacle of the receiver. Once engaged, the refuelling can commence and the rate of refuelling is generally two to three times higher than the Probe and Drogue method.

Aerial refuelling technology was available only on very limited platforms in the last century. This was also true for aerial tankers and their availability was restricted. However, as battle space expanded, the need was felt by more states to expand the range of their combat platforms. Figure 7.3 indicates that the number of countries with combat aircraft and aerial refuelling capability increased in the past two decades from 22 to 30. Aerial refuelling provided a cost-effective method to do so.

Figure 7.3: Countries with Combat Aircraft and Aerial Refuellers 1998 and 2018

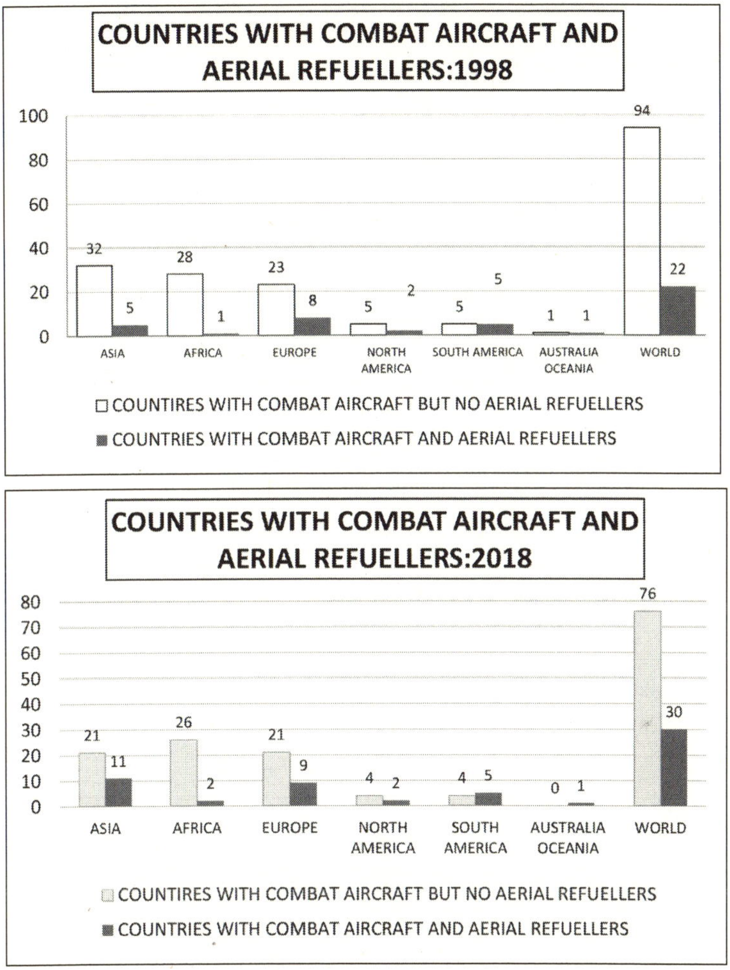

Source: Based on data extracted from *Military Balance* 1998 and 2018.

In the last two decades, although the number of aerial refuellers has gone down from 745 to 712 the inventory base has expanded from 22 to 30 countries.[33] With ongoing missions across the globe, the US has the largest fleet of aerial refuellers. In absolute terms the US tanker fleet has shrunk by 13 per cent and its world share has declined (Figure 7.4). This primarily is related to more countries adapting this technology to enhance their combat power and the gradual reduction in the number of receivers in the US.

Figure 7.4: Aerial Refuellers Inventory 1998 and 2018

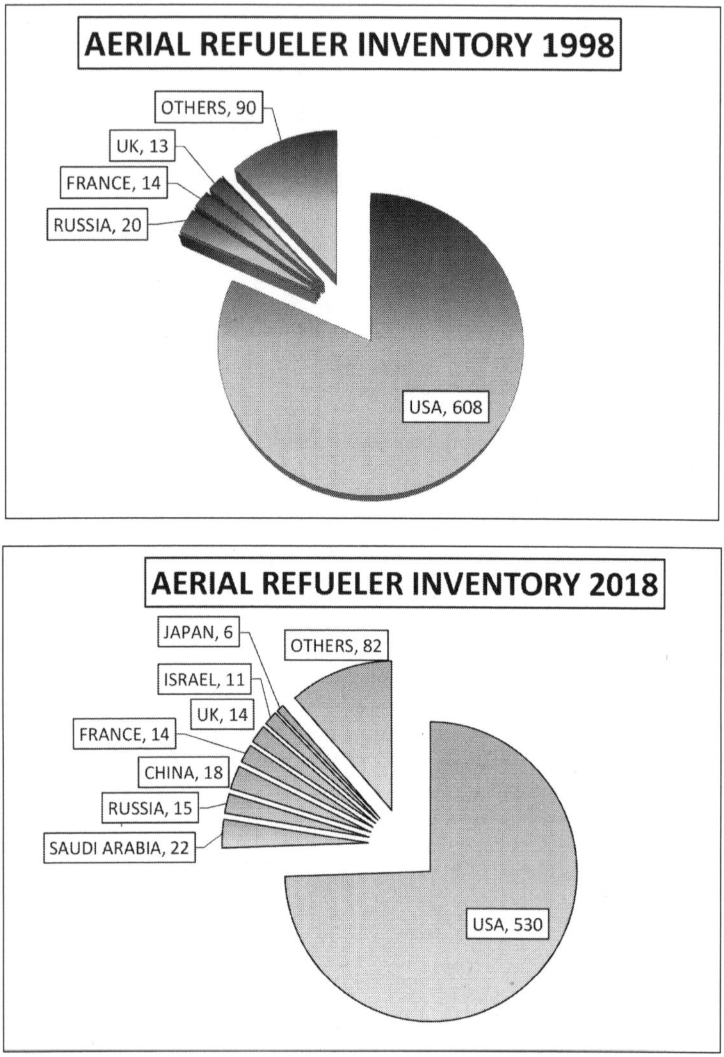

Source: Based on data extracted from *Military Balance* 1998 and 2018.

The most significant impact of aerial refuelling on combat aviation can be gauged from the fact that in the last twenty years, the world's combat aircraft inventory in countries with aerial refuelling has increased from 46 to 71 per cent (Figure 7.5). Today, nearly two-third of the fighter/bomber aircraft deployed worldwide are capable of receiving aerial refuelling. As of now, all combat aircraft in countries with aerial refuelling may not be capable of receiving fuel in air. But that too will change gradually. As a classic case, the profile of the Indian combat aircraft fleet is synchronising with this reality too. In a few years, with the phasing out of the MiG-21 and MiG-27 fleets, the entire Indian combat aircraft fleet will be capable of receiving aerial refuelling.

Figure 7.5: Countries with Combat Aircraft and Aerial Refuellers 1998 and 2018

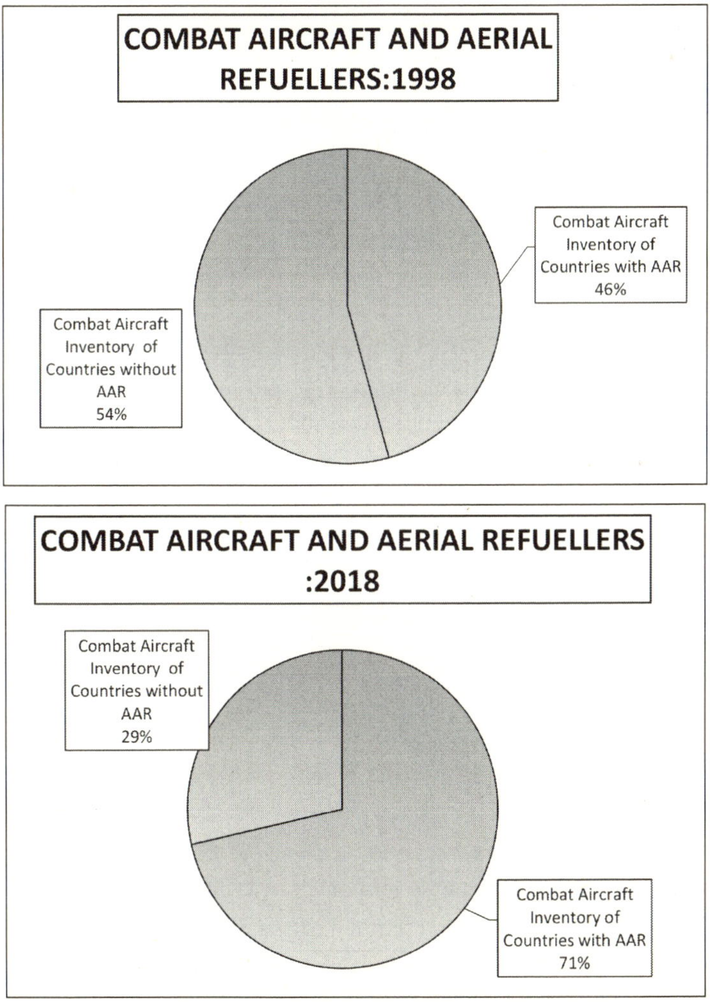

Source: Based on data extracted from *Military Balance* 1998 and 2018.

That sums up the impact of aerial refuelling on the combat aircraft inventory. As more countries adopt this facet of combat aviation, the number of combat aircraft required will gradually come down for the same mission definition. However, normally expanding capability triggers ambition too. That factor also impinges on the profile and numbers of combat aircraft. Tankers have become a central figure and competition between various alternatives is well understood by a case study about USAF Expansion Plans.

USAF Expansion Plan[34] – A Case Study

The United States Air Force (USAF) is presently in restructuring mode and is looking to expand capacity through quantity. "The Air Force is too small for what the nation expects of us," the USAF Secretary Heather Wilson reiterated at the annual Air, Space and Cyber Conference in National Harbor, Maryland, on September 17, 2018.[35] She articulated her intentions last year for a bigger air force when assuming charge.[36] But before making any long-term decisions on the force structure, she wanted to have a better idea of what threats the United States would face in the coming years, stating, "I'm a believer that threat drives strategy, strategy drives force posture."[37]

The USAF's expansion plan is to primarily counter growing military challenges from Russia and China.[38] The broad plan unveiled after a long study for the expansion of the USAF seeks to add 74 more squadrons to the current strength of 312.[39] The exact details of the study are still awaited and about six more studies on force restructuring are likely to be submitted to refine the current assessment. Broadly, the expansion plan is based on the 2018 United States National Defense Strategy that calls on the USAF to defend the homeland, provide a safe and effective nuclear deterrent, meet a peer threat and deter a near-peer threat while maintaining campaign momentum against global extremism.[40]

On the human resource front, the active personnel strength of the USAF reduced from 357,000 in 2006, hitting a low of 311,000 in 2014, before rebounding to roughly 322,800 now, with the intention of hitting 350,000 by about 2024.[41] Nearly US$ one billion per annum is being spent by USAF to retain personnel, including incentive pay and bonuses. As of mid-2017, the force was 3,000 personnel below strength in terms of aircraft-maintenance staff and around 1,200 short of tactical-combat-aircraft pilots.[42] Making good the existing shortfall and then planning for future expansion will be a herculean human resource mobilization task. It is estimated that the full implementation of the plan would need an additional 40,000 personnel.[43]

Looking at the current inventory mix of the USAF, the emphasis on fighters and airlift capabilities are apparent (Figure 7.6). Fighter aircraft try to achieve airspace control so that other kinetic elements can operate freely. Additionally, these aircraft provide long range, and accurate delivery of kinetic weapons to achieve tactical and operational objectives. The transport fleet is required to achieve a high mobility quotient for the combat forces. With a global outlook for military operations and current deployment in almost all parts of the world, the necessity for very high airlift capability is essential.

Figure 7.6: USAF Current Force Structure

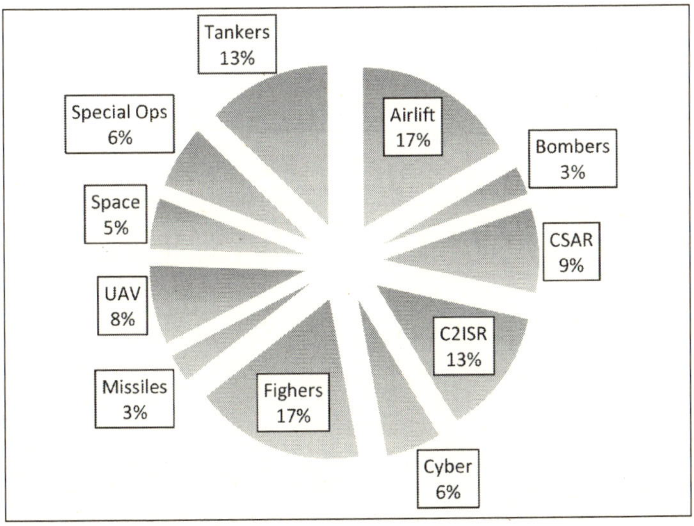

Source: Based on USAF data.[44]

Aerial refuellers (tankers) and Command and Control, Intelligence, Surveillance and Reconnaissance (C2ISR) assets are also in substantial strength. The tanker force helps in the deployment and employment of combat power, minimizing *en route* halts. This compresses the deployment timeline and additionally, helps in retaining an element of surprise by allowing combat aircraft to project force far away from their operating bases.

Insofar as C2ISR assets are concerned, their significance is related to the ability to enhance battle space transparency for the accurate planning and controlling of missions for safe execution. Invariably, these, along with space resources, are the first assets to be employed to gain a picture of the battle space.

The USAF expansion plan envisages an addition of 74 squadrons. An analysis of these additional squadrons brings to the fore the changing character of likely combat engagements. The two most prominent verticals being planned for expansion are C2ISR platforms and aerial refuellers (tankers) (Figure 7.7). Moreover, an additional seven squadrons for fighter combat aircraft and five squadrons for bombers are being planned. But no accretions are envisaged for the cyber and missile force: their capability enhancement would be through equipment upgradations only. And although UAVs have expanded their operational role, no major expansion is planned in this field.

Figure 7.7: USAF Accretion Plan

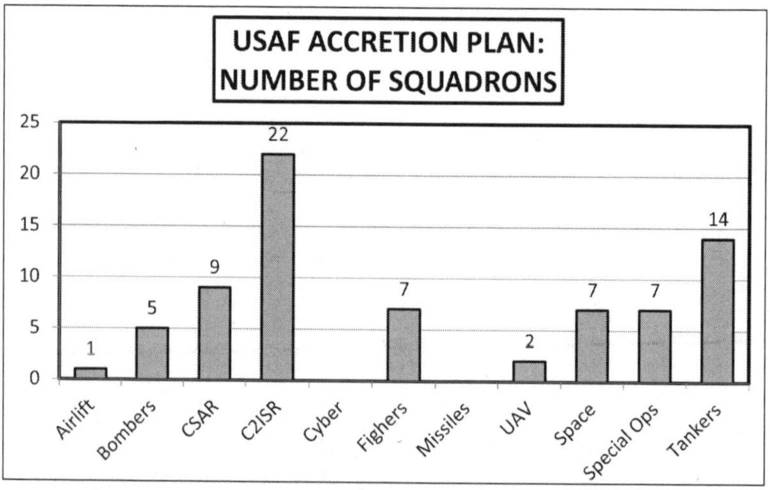

Source: Based on USAF data.[45]

The prime reason for such a lopsided approach in favour of manned combat aircraft is the limitations of UAVs in a hostile air defence environment. Russia and China have developed and deployed advanced air defence systems. A number of countries are in the process of acquiring high-technology air defence systems from Russia and China. The proliferation of such advanced air defence systems will limit the efficacy of UAV operations. That may be a possible reason for the limited expansion envisaged for the UAV fleet in the restructuring plan. With an increase in manned combat aircraft, an increase in resources for Combat Search and Rescue (CSAR) is an obvious fallout. Consequently, the plan envisages an additional nine squadrons for CSAR.

Once the proposed accretions fructify, the USAF force structure will, for the first time, have an equal number of squadrons for C2ISR and fighter aircraft (Figure 7.8). In the heavy aircraft category also, parity will be achieved between tankers and airlift aircraft for the first time. Special operations squadrons and space units will increase their share from current levels.

Figure 7.8: USAF Planned Force Structure

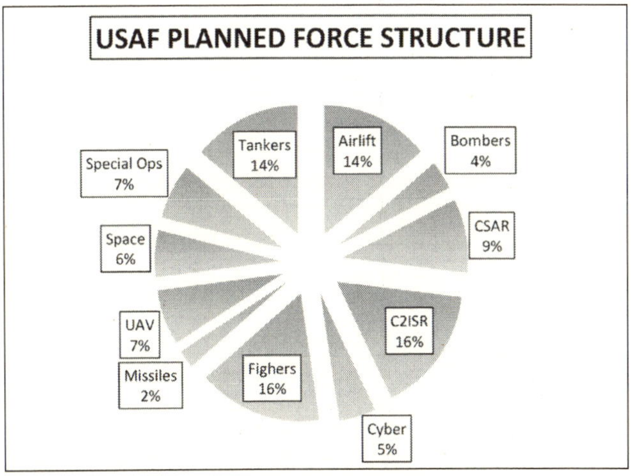

Source: Based on USAF data.[46]

A close examination of force accretion planned over and above the existing inventory given in Figure 7.9, indicates that the current USAF dispensation feels an acute shortage of bombers, C2ISR and space assets for likely missions in the coming decade. The expansion plan increases their quantity by over 50 per cent. A major increase in C2ISR and space assets is indicative of an increased requirement to monitor a larger area for a longer duration and with multiple sensors. This kind of surveillance and reconnaissance has become a necessity owing to the changing character of war. Unlike during the Cold War when the focus was on major military manoeuvres with large formations as the key threats, now small teams can operate to achieve critical objectives with strategic implications. This calls for greater monitoring of the area of interest. Hence an increase in C2ISR and Space assets is an obvious assessment.

An added implication of this changing character of war is on special operations. Gradually, their relevance in kinetic operations has increased and these operations are becoming the first option for planners. In certain situations, special operations help achieve the objectives without large-scale force-on-force engagement. With hybridization of war, the salience of special operations will only increase. It is probably this assessment that has led the USAF to project a 35 per cent increase in the number of special operations squadrons. As the majority of aerial platforms of the USAF are capable of aerial refuelling, an increase in receivers would entail a corresponding increase in tankers. To retain the existing tanker-receiver ratio, the tanker force is to enjoy a 35 per cent accretion in numbers.

Figure 7.9: USAF Accretion Plan

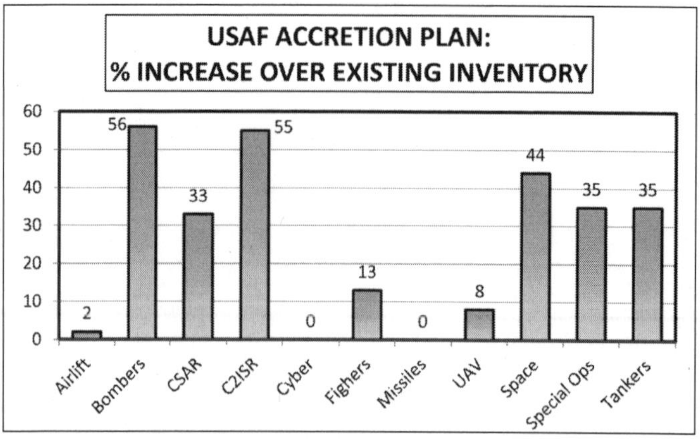

Source: Based on USAF data.[47]

For one of the largest air forces in the world, to ambitiously expand by nearly 25 per cent seems contrary to the long-term trend. Notwithstanding a number of new facets like cyber, Space and missiles added to the arsenal of the USAF, its number of aircraft has been declining steadily for decades since the peak strength of 26,104 aircraft in 1956 (Figure 7.10). The USAF aircraft inventory has shrunk by over 80 per cent during the last sixty years.

Figure 7.10: Number of Aircraft in the USAF 1950-2008

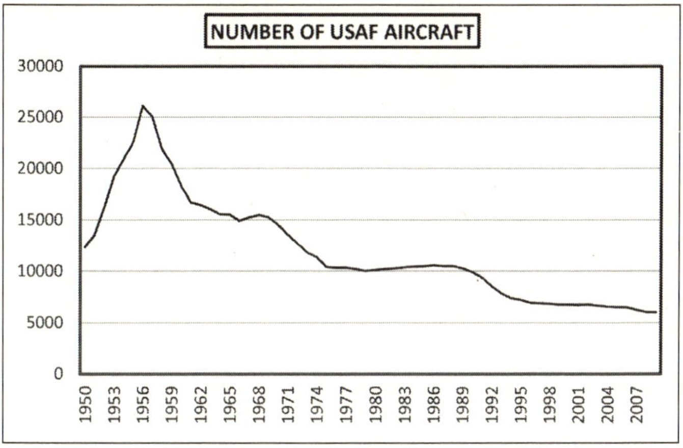

Source: Based on data in the Mitchell Institute Study, 2010.[48]

To fulfil the requirements of the expansion plan, an addition of over 400 aircraft will have to take place during the next decade. This will be over and above the replacement of ageing aircraft like the F-16 with the F-35. It is likely that other arms of the US military organization will have a similar wishlist to expand capabilities, citing the 2018 United States National Defense Strategy. The additional demand for aviation assets from the US Army, US Navy, US Marine Corps and US Coast Guard is likely to be expected soon. A similar 25 per cent increase by all of these entities over the next decade will have major implications on force levels and finances. Fulfilling these requirements could be a major challenge for the Pentagon. If the plan were to be sanctioned, it will indeed be a bonanza for the aviation industry.

Once all the restructuring studies are submitted and a comprehensive USAF restructuring plan is made, the project costing will be done. Based on types of aircraft and equipment planned for induction and the associated increase in manpower, the overall financial outlay for the USAF may have to increase by at least 25 per cent from current levels assuming that no quality compromises are made. That will mean an increase in the USAF's share in the defence budget.

Figure 7.11: Schematic representation of USAF Expansion Plan

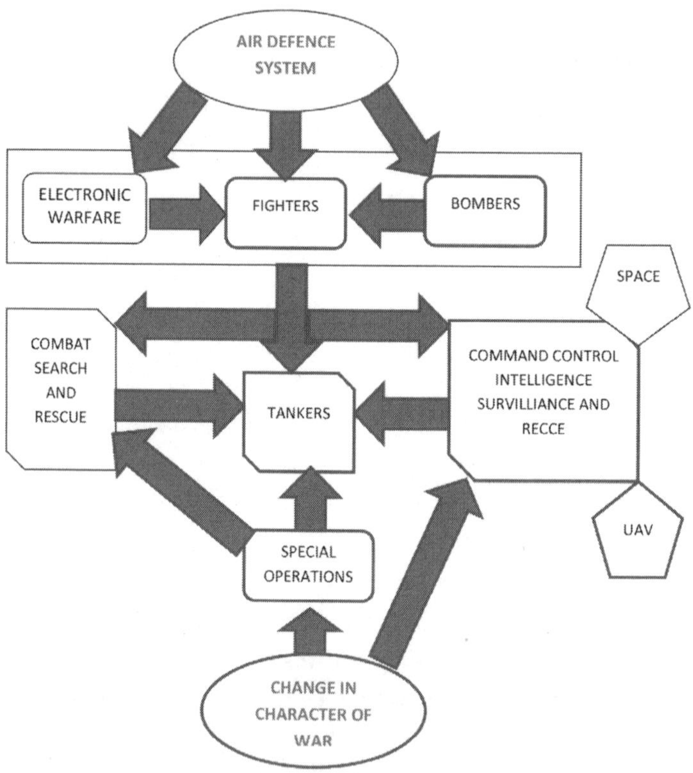

Source: Author's own.

Schematically, the USAF expansion plan is depicted in Figure 7.11. Primarily, it indicates two drivers. The deployment of potent air defence systems like the S400, and an associated increase in combat power of two main rivals, Russia and China, has forced an increase in the requirement of the bomber and fighter force. To protect that additional force, more electronic warfare (EW) assets are essential. Increase in bombers and EW aircraft again put upward pressure on the number of fighter aircraft required for creating a suitable operational environment. More combat aircraft necessitate greater number of controlling assets like AWACS, increase in in-flight refuellers and a larger fleet of Combat Search and Rescue aircraft.

The Second driver is the changing character of warfare. The hybridization of war requires the monitoring of larger areas and the concomitant need to enhance surveillance fidelity. This calls for increase in the number of Command, Control, Intelligence, Surveillance and Reconnaissance (C2ISR) platforms along with additional space-based assets and unmanned aircraft. On the other hand, the significance of special operations increases and so does the force structure designed to carry out such operations. Additional special operations squadrons necessitate more C2ISR assets. Along with this, a larger number of refuellers and CSAR platforms are required.

Another factor that will play a major role in redefining the USAF's restructuring plan is the creation of the Space Force. The new organization will probably hive off space assets of the USAF for consolidation under one agency. Furthermore, this entity will probably have a priority for budgetary allocations and further compress the resources that could be made available to the USAF. Before treading on a restructuring path, taking the US Congress along and pacifying other contenders for the annual defence allocation will be the key battles that the USAF will have to fight and win.

The outcome of these battles will define the course of the force's restructuring. Going by the history of such ambitious expansion plans across the globe, it is safe to assume that the restructuring plan will have to be scaled down qualitatively or quantitatively. Nonetheless, USAF Secretary Wilson told the Senate Armed Services Committee in prepared remarks that the service is making headway on some fronts. For example, the USAF believes it can get 204 of its 312 operational squadrons to 80 per cent combat readiness by 2020. The remainder would achieve 80 per cent readiness by 2023.[49]

Overall, all elements in the field of aviation are directly linked to each other in terms of operational efficacy. Lt Gen David A. Deptula's remarks about the need to achieve jointness between services are equally applicable as regards the imperative to achieve synergy between various elements within a service:

> When a single service attempts to achieve warfighting independence instead of embracing interdependence, "jointness" unravels, warfighting effectiveness is reduced, and costly redundancies and gaps likely abound.[50]

This model in essence is likely to be followed by all proponents of air power in the coming decades. The extent of its implementation will be based on intent, financial resources and technical prowess.

Gestalt

Capabilities in the real and virtual domains can challenge a state. While cyber and communication tools in the virtual domain can subjugate individuals, institutions and significant parts of a state, military capabilities act in the real domain to inflict physical damage. The 21st century is witnessing a greater amalgamation of virtual and real tools in the form of hybrid threats to states. Yet kinetic weapons, like long-range SSMs, UCAVs and SAMs, play a significant role in the prevailing 'no war no peace' conditions. This debate just proves that these systems, along with combat aircraft, actually complement each other in providing deterrence to retain peace, stability and freedom of movement, so essential for the world's growth and development.

In the last five decades, combat aircraft have significantly enhanced their combat power, not only in terms of platform performance but also by their weapon mix. The area that can be dominated by a combat aircraft has increased and led to the reduction in the number of platforms required for a specified sector. Additionally, these three alternatives, in terms of SSMs, UAVs and SAMs, along with combat enablers have complimented the combat aircraft in force application. With the development of these three credible alternatives, prime dependence on combat aircraft for rapid force projection has reduced. A combination of these factors has changed the way combat forces are equipped and this is evident in the changes that have occurred in combat aircraft inventory the world over.

Notes

1 Based on Kishore Kumar Khera, "Agni 5 Tested: What Next?" January 25, 2018 at https://idsa.in/idsacomments/agni-5-tested-what-next_kkkhera_250118 and "Weapons are the Combat Differentiators: The BrahMos Air Launched Cruise Missile", November 27, 2017 at https://idsa.in/idsacomments/weapons-are-the-combat-differentiators_kkkhera_271117, accessed on March 28, 2019.

2 Michael J. H. Taylor, *The Aerospace Chronology*, Tri Service Press, London, 1989, p. 7.

3 Rodney W. Jones, "Conventional Military Imbalance and Strategic Stability in South Asia", SASSU Research Paper No. 1, March 2005 at http://www.policyarchitects.org/pdf/Conventional_imbalance_RJones.pdf, accessed on February 25, 2019.

4 Based on Kishore Kumar Khera, "Has the Time Come to Replace Manned Combat Aircraft With Armed Unmanned Aerial Vehicles?" IDSA Comment, August 16, 2017 at https://idsa.in/idsacomments/replace-manned-combat-aircraft-with-armed-unmanned-aerial-vehicles_kkkhera_160817, accessed on March 28, 2019.

5 J. Jayaraman, *Unmanned Aircraft Systems: A Global View,* DRDO Monographs/Special Publications Series, Defence Research and Development Organisation, Ministry of Defence, New Delhi, 2014, p.15.

6 J.P.R. Browne and M.T. Thurbon, *Electronic Warfare*, Brassy's UK Limited, 1998, pp. 109-113.

7 J. Jayaraman, no. 5, pp. 113-117.

8 Daniel Cebul, "The Air Force launched its next protected communications satellite", C4ISR Net, October 17, 2018 at https://www.c4isrnet.com/special-reports/satcom/2018/10/17/the-air-force-launched-its-next-protected-communications-satellite/?utm_source=Sailthru&utm_medium=email&utm_campaign=Space%2010.31.18&utm_term=Editorial%20-%20Military%20Space%20Report, accessed on November 1, 2018.

9 Garrett Reim, "Kratos more than doubles tactical UAV development projects", *Flight International,* November 16, 2018 at https://www.flightglobal.com/news/articles/kratos-more-than-doubles-tactical-uav-development-pr-453659/, accessed on November 18, 2018.

10 Over Target Requirement (OTR) is the number of weapons required over a target to achieve requisite level of damage and is calculated based on target system, its functional and vulnerability analysis along with weapon characteristics and parameters of its damage mechanism like Blast Over Pressure, Dynamic Pressure, Pressure Pulse, Penetrative Index, Fragmentation Pattern, Shock and Fire Indices in the given attack profile.

11 Bill Sweetman, *Advanced Fighter Technology: The Future of Cockpit Combat*, Air Life Publishing Ltd, England, 1988, p. 85.

12 Kishore Kumar Khera, no. 4.

13 Garrett Reim, "US Army eyes high-altitude UAVs like Airbus Zephyr", *Flight Global*, October 10, 2018 at https://www.flightglobal.com/news/articles/us-army-eyes-high-altitude-uavs-like-airbus-zephyr-452551/, accessed on October 12, 2018.

14 Ibid.

15 Jeremiah Gertler, "US Unmanned Aerial Systems", *Congressional Research Service Report* for Congress, January 3, 2012, pp. 7-57 at www.crs.gov R42136 at https://fas.org/sgp/crs/natsec/R42136.pdf, accessed on August 2, 2018.

16 Ibid.

17 "Defense Budget Overview", United States Department of Defense, Fiscal Year 2019 Budget Request at comptroller.defense.gov/Portals/45/Documents/defbudget/fy2019/FY2019_Budget_Request_Overview_Book.pdf, accessed on March 28, 2019.

18 TEC Communication aspects of Unmanned Aircraft System (UAS) by Radio Division available at tec.gov.in/pdf/studypaper/uav, accessed on December 15, 2019.

19 Vicente Mayor, Rafael Estepa, Antonio Estepa, German Madinabeitia, Deploying a Reliable UAV-Aided Communication Service in Disaster Areas, Wireless Communications and Mobile Computing Dated April 8, 2019, Volume 2019 available on https://doi.org/10.1155/2019/7521513, accessed on December 15, 2019.

20 Jeremy Page and Paul Sonne, "Unable to Buy US Military Drones, Allies Place Orders with China," *The Wall Street Journal*, July 17, 2017, http://www.wsj.com/artiles/unable-to-buy-u-s-military-drones-allies-place-orders-with-china-1500301716, accessed on August 10, 2018.

21 Ibid.

22 Kishore Kumar Khera, no. 4.

23 Department of Defense, USA, FY2009–2034 "Unmanned Systems Integrated Roadmap",April 6, 2009, p. xiii.

24 J.P.R. Browne and M.T. Thurbon, no. 6, pp. 176-178.

25 Ibid., pp. 272-276.

26 "Twin Success for Quick Reaction Surface-to-Air Missile", Press Release,

Press Information Bureau, Ministry of Defence, February 26, 2019 at http://pib.nic.in/newsite/PrintRelease.aspx?relid=188958, accessed on March 9, 2019.

27 Bill Sweetman, no. 11, p. 75.

28 Kishore Kumar Khera, "Aerial Refuelling of Airborne Early Warning and Control Aircraft", IDSA Comment at https://idsa.in/idsacomments/aerial-refuelling-of-airborne-early-warning-and-control-aircraft_kkkhera_061217, accessed on March 29, 2019.

29 J.P.R. Browne and M.T. Thurbon, Electronic no. 6 , pp. 149-152.

30 Ibid.

31 Kishore Kumar Khera, no. 28.

32 Aerial refuelling is considered as one of the most challenging exercises, more so in the probe and drogue method like in the IL78. The tanker trails a drogue with refuelling pipe and the receiver aircraft manoeuvres to plug-in its probe to make a contact for refuelling. This method is defined as a controlled collision between the probe and the drogue. In the other method of the boom and receptacle employed in KC135, it is simpler in terms of execution. The boom operator in the refueller controls the flying boom into the fuel receptacle for refuelling while the receiver aircraft maintains in close formation with the tanker. It is relatively simple for the receiver pilot. The rate of fuel transfer too is approximately four times faster than in the probe and drogue method.

33 International Institute for Strategic Studies (IISS), *Military Balance 1998 and 2018*, Routledge, Chapman & Hall, London.

34 Based on author's IDSA Comment "Decoding the Expansion Plans of the United States Air Force", September 28, 2018 at https://idsa.in/idsacomments/expansion-plans-of-the-united-states-air-force-kkkhera-280918, accessed on September 30, 2018.

35 Stephen Losey, "New Air Force Secretary: 'We are too small for what the nation expects of us'," *Air Force Times*, June 6, 2017 at https://www.airforcetimes.com/news/your-air-force/2017/06/06/new-air-force-secretary-we-are-too-small-for-what-the-nation-expects-of-us/, accessed on September 27, 2018.

36 Lee Hudson and Jen DiMascio, "Can The U.S. Air Force Add 74 Squadrons? *Aviation Week & Space Technology*, September 24, 2018 at http://aviationweek.com/defense/can-us-air-force-add-74-squadrons, accessed on September 27, 2018.

37 Stephen Losey, no. 35.

38 Ken Dalecki, "Air Force Secretary Wilson highlights plans to expand the air force at NPC luncheon", The National Press Club, September 26, 2018 at https://www.press.org/news-multimedia/news/air-force-secretary-wilson-hi..., accessed on September 27, 2018.

39 Chuck Broadway, "SecAF Wilson provides Air Force update," USAF, September 17, 2018 at https://www.af.mil/News/Article-Display/Article/1635645/secaf-wilson-provides-air-force-update/, accessed on September 27, 2018.

40 Lee Hudson and Jen DiMascio, no. 36.

41 Stephen Losey, no. 35; International Institute for Strategic Studies (IISS), *Military Balance 2018*, Routledge, Chapman & Hall, London, p. 46.

42 Ibid., p. 32.

43 Lee Hudson and Jen DiMascio, no. 36.

44 Secretary of the Air Force Public Affairs, USAF, "The Air Force We Need: 386 operational squadrons", September 17, 2018 at https://www.af.mil/News/Article-Display/Article/1635070/the-air-force-we-need-386-operational-squadrons/, accessed on September 27, 2018.

45 Ibid.

46 Ibid.

47 Ibid.

48 Col. James C. Ruehrmund Jr., USAF (Ret.) and Christopher J. Bowie, "Arsenal of Airpower: USAF Aircraft Inventory 1950-2009:", Mitchell Institute Study, November 2010at https://higherlogicdownload.s3.amazonaws.com/AFA/6379b747-7730-4f82-9b45-a1c80d6c8fdb/UploadedImages/Mitchell%20Publications/Arsenal%20of%20Airpower.pdf, accessed on September 27, 2018.

49. Garrett Reim, "USAF faces challenges to grow fleet, boost readiness", *Flight Global,* October 11, 2018 at https://www.flightglobal.com/news/articles/usaf-faces-challenges-to-grow-fleet-boost-readiness-452584/, accessed on October 12, 2018.

50. Lt Gen David A. Deptula, "Beyond Goldwater-Nichols: Roles And Missions of the Armed Services in the 21st Century", Mitchell Institute Policy Papers, 1, March 2016.

8. Top View: Mapping Combat Aircraft Inventory

Military strategists were aware of the significance of airpower; its profound impact was visualized by non-military personnel during the televised Gulf War 1991. The impact of airpower on the outcome of the war and the way it was orchestrated was profound. However, instead of the increase in quantum, that period witnessed the beginning of the fall in numbers of combat aircraft worldwide.

In the last fifty years, the number of countries operating combat aircraft has almost doubled. However, the overall combat aircraft inventory has declined. The reduction in the number of combat aircraft in various regions of the world has come in the last thirty years after an upward surge in the 1970s and 1980s. Primarily, now there are more operators and each operator is managing a smaller inventory. Average inventory holding per country was over 320 aircraft in 1968 and peaked at 375 in 1988 before commencing its downward journey. For the first time in the last fifty years, the average combat aircraft inventory per country has dipped below the 150 mark. The geographical spread of combat aircraft deployment has increased but its density has reduced substantially.

This seems contrarian as more users would have led to the growth of the inventory. This chapter looks at two probable reasons leading to this reversal in the trend. It initially looks at geopolitical reasons for the slide in combat aircraft inventory. Thereafter, it covers the impact of the changing character of warfare and operational imperatives.

Geopolitics

Post the Second World War, the world gradually gravitated towards two powers – the US and the USSR. Formation of military alliances became an operational necessity. For major powers, the purpose was to bolster military strength and influence and for smaller nations, it was a security insurance policy. Two major alliances of the era–NATO and the Warsaw Pact – defined security paradigms and Europe was the central theme. Although nuclear capabilities existed on both sides, yet conventional capabilities kept growing to thwart any attempt to achieve operational success below the nuclear threshold. A Mutual Assured Destruction (MAD) capability on both sides with a vast nuclear arsenal, ruled out the possibility of any dominance in the nuclear domain. The space in conventional capability was contested. It was difficult to accurately assess the capability, deployment and intent of the other side. The relative capability assessment between these two military alliances oscillated as brought out by the US Congressional Budget Office Report in 1977.

> The official U.S. view of the NATO/Warsaw Pact military balance shifted from pessimism in the 1950s to optimism in the 1960s. In the 1970s it seems to have slipped back toward pessimism—far back enough to worry some defence planners about NATO's chances of defeating or deterring a Pact attack.[1]

To negate the element of surprise and bid time for mobilization of the surface forces, a large number of airbases in Europe maintained combat aircraft on standby to react to any incoming threat. Additionally, a large number of weaponized combat aircraft were kept on airborne standby to react without any delay. Continuous aircraft operations demanded a large inventory and the numbers of combat aircraft kept increasing. Between members of NATO and the Warsaw Pact, a quantitative expansion of the combat aircraft inventory till 1990 was an obvious outcome of this competition.

Besides the Cold War centred on Europe, another geopolitical reality was playing out in the developing world in Asia. A large number of countries had just emerged from colonial rule and were coming to grips with the geopolitical realities. National security was the main agenda and the growth of armed forces for self-protection was considered an essential activity. Inter-state conflicts across Asia from the Korean Peninsula to the Indian subcontinent to West Asia ensured that a large number of resources were diverted towards developing military capabilities. Combat aircraft were available at friendship prices from the two superpowers as it allowed them to expand their zone of influence, and shore up their alliance systems. This resulted in doubling the combat aircraft inventory in Asia and increasing operators from 19 in 1968 to 31 in 1993. Both the geographical spread and density of combat aircraft in Asia increased and surpassed Europe. A similar story unfolded in Africa where the number of countries with combat aircraft witnessed a ten-fold increase and the number of combat aircraft went up by five times from 1968 to 1993. The density of combat aircraft in Africa remained low owing to a lack of supporting infrastructure and focus on internal consolidation in various states, rather than contesting neighbouring states.

No major changes were witnessed in the number of countries possessing combat aircraft in North America, South America and Australia Oceania. Barring the Falklands War in 1982, the absence of classical inter-state conflicts may be the major cause. However, combat aircraft density increased in North America, primarily through the US, to play its role in the Cold War. These geopolitical factors resulted in the doubling of the number of combat aircraft in the world in twenty years from 1968-1988 and a similar increase in the number of countries that possessed these from 57 to 113.

The breaking up of the USSR heralded the end of the Cold War period between the two major power blocs and established the US as the sole superpower in the last decade of the 20th century. The disintegration of the USSR changed the threat matrix for NATO members and consequently there was a reduction in their requisite military capabilities. Russia and other members of the erstwhile USSR focused on economic consolidation for their survival and military capability development or even sustenance was a low-priority area. Practically, both sides of the Cold War scaled down their conventional arsenal and combat aircraft inventory diminished markedly in Europe. Another significant geopolitical event that reshaped Europe was the formation of the European Union (EU). Integration of major powers of Europe in the economic arena and their enhanced interdependence diminished the chances of inter-state conflicts and enlarged the scope of collective defence against common threats. Sustenance of individual military capabilities was still essential albeit at lower scales. Many NATO members reduced their defence expenditure below one per cent of their GDP. While there was an overall reduction in the military capabilities across the spectrum, the most visible effect was on the fleet of resource-intensive combat aircraft. Today Europe has about half the number of combat aircraft operating in Asia while in 1968 it had 45 per cent more than the Asian inventory.

After the Second World War, erstwhile USSR was the source of a large share of the worldwide combat aircraft inventory. That was the 'Golden Age' of their aviation industry as analyzed by John T. Greenwood in the book on Russian Aviation:

> The 'Golden Age' of Soviet Aviation was in the 1950s and 1960s when national strategic priorities provided continuing requirements for new military and civilian aircraft and almost unlimited funds to support research, development, and production. Inefficient, loud, gas-guzzling engines were tolerated because they were powerful and gave soviet fighters a better thrust-to-weight ratio compared with Western jet fighters. [2]

The breakup of the USSR also had an impact on the maintenance support capacity for various combat aircraft manufactured there and operated by various countries. The aircraft industry in USSR had a diverse geographical base for manufacturing. After USSR's breakup, parts of the aircraft industry were now in different countries and under the control of different governments. Coordinating and sourcing of spares and maintenance facilities became increasingly difficult. All newly- formed states were looking to build up their resources by exploiting their strengths. Sale of aircraft, spares, manufacturing facilities and maintenance support was one arena. Economics had overtaken the geopolitical battle. Its most profound impact was in the developing countries that operated small numbers of combat aircraft that had their origins in erstwhile USSR. Setting up of maintenance facilities was uneconomical for small fleets especially when adequate support was available from the USSR. The breakup of the USSR changed all that. The absence of low-cost and prompt supply of spares and maintenance facilities accelerated the phasing out of many combat aircraft originally from the USSR, and often without replacements. A sudden dip in business for companies directly or indirectly involved in military aviation in Russia, forced smaller players to close down or relocate with international partners. This reduced the size of the military aviation industry in Russia and other breakaway republics. The domino had started rolling and the first casualty was the availability of combat aircraft. Figure 8.1 is indicative of this reality. In the 1989-1996 period barring a marginal increase in exports from the US, there was a marked decrease in military hardware exports from all other major players. The impact on Russia was most notable, with nearly 80 per cent reduction.

Figure 8.1: Worldwide Arms Deliveries from 1989-1996 in million $ at 1996 Prices

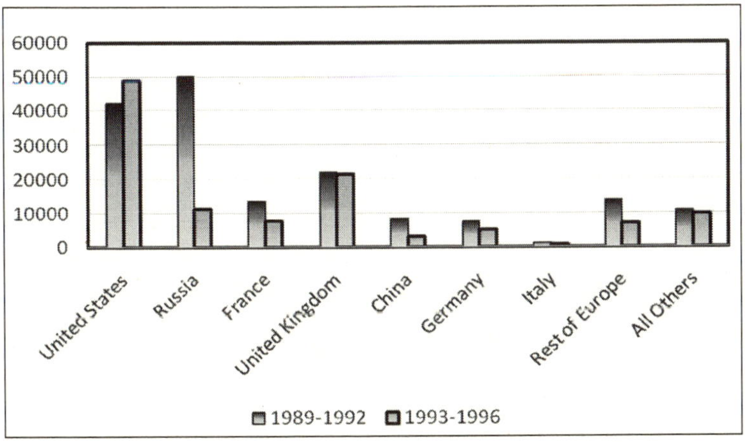

Source: The US Congressional Research Service Report for the Congress on Conventional Arms Transfers to Developing Nations, 1989-1996[3]

The Russian share in global arms exports declined from 30 per cent in the 1989-1992 period to 10 per cent between 1993 and1996, as indicated in Figure 8.2. The space ceded by Russia was quickly taken over by the US primarily for lack of other alternatives and reduced overall demand.

Figure 8.2: Worldwide Arms Deliveries from 1989-1996 in million $ at 1996 Prices

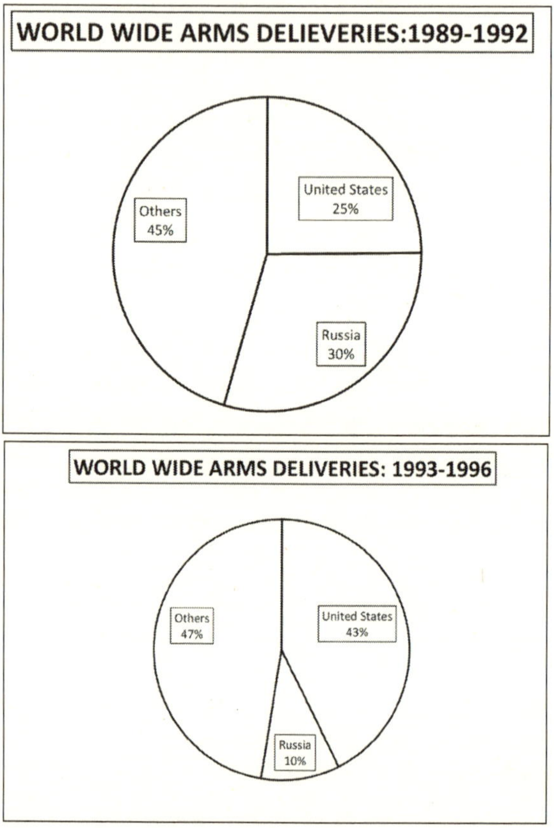

Source: The US *Congressional Research Service Report* for the Congress on Conventional Arms Transfers to Developing Nations, 1989-1996[4]

This trend in global arms trade reversed in the subsequent period wherein Russia was the only country with increased exports in 1997-2004 (Figure 8.3). This was primarily due to a low base effect for Russia coming from a really low level. Otherwise, the global trend of reduced military hardware trade was indicative of new geopolitical realities.

As Russia consolidated and remodelled its defence industry, especially combat aircraft, with the formation of a central organisation to coordinate all aspects related to exports as Rosoboronexport, its share increased from 8 per cent in 1997-2001 to 13 per cent in 2002-04 (Figure 8.4).[6] Today, after consolidating operations, Russia supplies military hardware to 116 countries and has nearly 25 per cent of the world military hardware trade share.

Figure 8.3: Worldwide Arms Deliveries from 1997-2004 in million $ at 2004 Prices

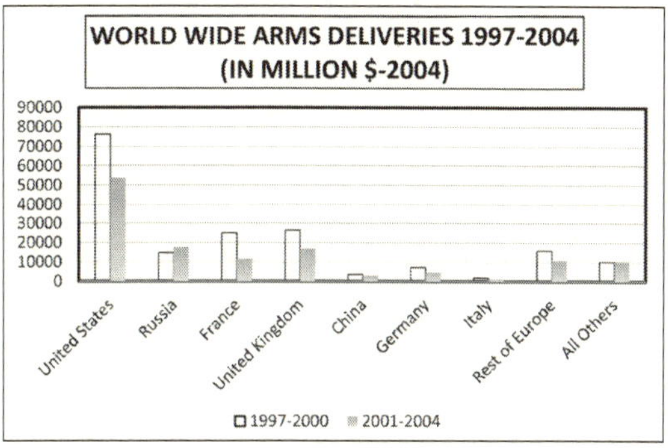

Source: The US *Congressional Research Service Report* for the Congress on Conventional Arms Transfers to Developing Nations, 1997-2004[5]

Figure 8.4: Worldwide Arms Deliveries from 1997-2004 in million $ at 2004 Prices

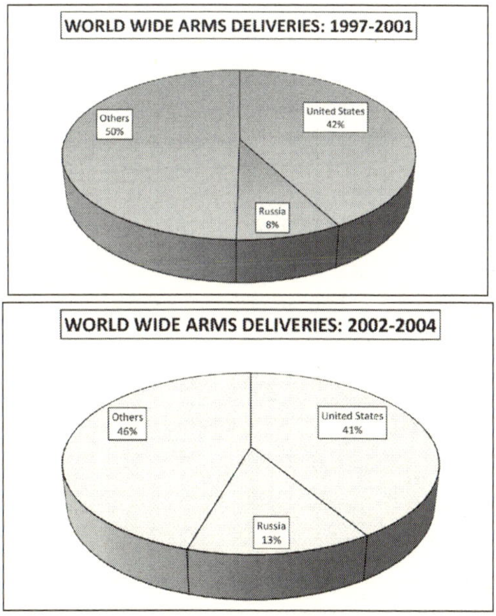

Source: The US *Congressional Research Service Report* for the Congress on Conventional Arms Transfers to Developing Nations, 1997-2004[7]

Figure 8.5: Worldwide Arms Deliveries from 1989-2015 in million $ at 2015 prices

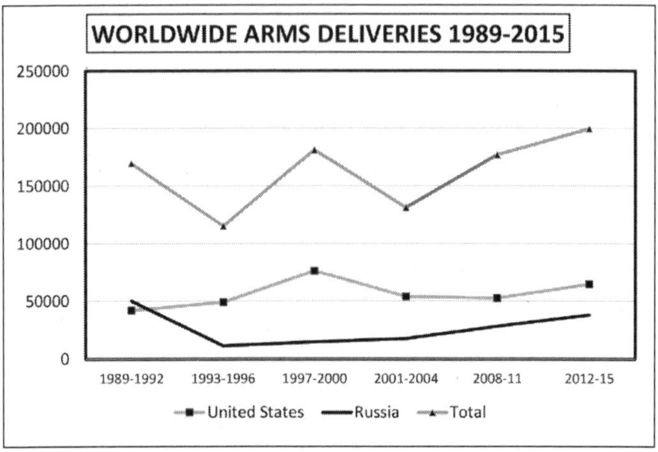

Source: Based on data extracted from the US *Congressional Research Service Report* for the Congress on Conventional Arms Transfers to Developing Nations for period of 1989-2015[8]

After the end of the Cold War, the world was unipolar. Reshaping of the world order after the breakup of USSR has practically kept the world's arms trade nearly static (Figure 8.5). A near-stagnation in value of weapons delivery in the 1989-2015 period is indicative of a gradual decline in relevance of military hardware. A large number of states preferred a policy of collective security and forged alliances leading to an expansion of NATO. Economics governed this and resulted in the downsizing of the combat capabilities of individual states and their combat aircraft inventories. During the period after the Cold War, the dynamics of geopolitics in the developing world were in stark contrast with the European experience. West Asia exemplified that. Intra-state and inter-state conflicts fuelled by the vested interests of the developed world resulted in unstable governance and fragile geopolitical scenarios. This disintegrated inherent military powers of the state into smaller factions. These entities could not operate and maintain resource-sapping combat aircraft. Afghanistan, Yemen, and Iraq post the Gulf War are some of the typical examples.

The net result of geopolitical changes in the last fifty years was that the world's combat aircraft inventory increased at a rapid pace in the first thirty years primarily as a result of the Cold War and inter-state conflicts in Asia. But in the last twenty years, there has been a decline owing to the changed world order and geopolitical realities (See Annexure 5).

The Character of Warfare and Operational Imperatives

War strategists, from NATO and Warsaw Pacts countries, based on their lessons from the Second World War, measured military capability in terms of quantity and its deployment speed. During the Cold War, a major threat that NATO envisaged was a large-scale armour movement of Warsaw Pact countries in Europe. To counter such a threat and break its momentum, several tactical nuclear weapons were deployed in Europe. It was a fear of the Hobbesian trap. Deployment of a large number of combat aircraft was an operational necessity by both sides to gain an initial advantage in the war of attrition that was envisaged. Combat aircraft were to be the first respondents for both offensive and defensive missions. Tools for battle space transparency were still not mature. First mover advantage was assessed as significant. The critical role for combat aircraft in the battle space was summarised in the US Congressional Budget Office Report in January 1977 as:-

> Should war occur between NATO and the Warsaw Pact, U.S. tactical airpower could make a critical difference in NATO's prospects of defeating a Warsaw Pact invasion, especially if the attack came before ground forces were in place. The flexibility of tactical airpower is such that it can be brought to bear quickly in a battle and can move more rapidly than ground forces to areas where enemy forces are concentrated. The primary role of tactical airpower in the land battle is to support friendly ground forces by contributing firepower against enemy ground forces and by warding off enemy air attacks on friendly forces.[9]

Enhancing the number of combat aircraft to outmatch the adversary was a compulsion. The outcome was that Europe in the 1980s had more combat aircraft than the entire world has today. Not only have the geopolitical compulsions changed in the last twenty years, so have the kind of conflicts and therefore, the operational requirements of the armed forces.

An analysis of ongoing conflicts in the world indicates that the character of warfare has transformed. Focus has shifted from 'force on force' inter-state conflicts to a hybrid war with the use of non-state actors and non-kinetic means. In such a scenario, the battle space expands and the enemy is diffused. Multiple hybrid warfare tools are often in play simultaneously. While airpower remains relevant, its application methodology has to be recalibrated. Large-scale airpower dominance with the use of multiple combat aircraft has very little relevance against an adversary operating in very small teams in urban, mountainous or jungle areas. During the Second Lebanon War of 2006, a professional force like the Israeli Air Force with total air superiority and backed by robust intelligence, targeted over 7000 sites in Lebanon and yet failed to comprehensively defeat a small Hezbollah force sans air support.[10] The ongoing conflict in Yemen is also indicative of a similar outcome, wherein all elements of the Yemeni Armed Forces, including airstrikes, were used to counter the Houthi movement since 2004. The situation has hardly altered even after the coalition led by Saudi Arabia, the largest military force in the region, has been undertaking airstrikes against the Houthi-held areas since March 26, 2015. This reiterates that in a conflict against a dispersed and diffused opponent, the concepts of use of airpower developed to tackle a conventional threat are of little use. In hybrid warfare, airpower utilization needs to be transformed from an overtly offensive arm to a supporting, precise, intelligent and restrained component, to avoid collaterals and yet assist in achieving the laid out objective.[11]

Technology is already playing an important role and will probably increase its influence on greater diffusion of the battle space and enhance the hybrid nature of conflict.[12] State and non-state actors are resorting to methods of hybrid warfare involving the use of military means below the threshold of a conventional war, to undermine a state. This approach combines various civilian and military means and instruments in a way that does not reveal their actual aggressive and offensive intentions until all the pieces of the puzzle have been brought together.[13] In turn, conflicts in future will have an application of all facets of power and the battle space and battle timelines poorly defined. The conflicts will have political, ideological, social, economic and military sides and the battle for supremacy will not only be with military hardware but also with information and economy. Military employment will include conflict, irregular war, proxy war and guerrilla war simultaneously and in the same space as direct 'force on force' engagement.

Warfare is transformed from military-to-military direct struggle to a system-to- system engagement. Threats to the state and society are not always easy to predict. The opportunities offered by globalization, new technologies and the digital age are redefining the conduct of the conflict. States will have to adapt to accommodate the cyber and information domain, digitalization, autonomous systems, and hybrid tactics.[14] This holds an important lesson about the type of forthcoming threats for states and societies and to be prepared accordingly. Changing the nature of warfare has diminished the need for a large number of combat aircraft to tackle a grey zone threat but has major implications for conventional confrontation. Combat aircraft are no longer considered the visceral means of death and destruction. The ability of states to achieve their goals by resorting to means other than kinetic force has reduced the salience of military power.[15] Changing the character of warfare has contributed to compression of the combat aircraft inventory to half in the last three decades. In Annexure 6, a case study of the UK's Combat Air Strategy is discussed to assess how the next couple of decades will pan out for combat aviation.

Summing up, it is geopolitics that has triggered a slide in combat aircraft inventory and transformation of conflict dynamics that has changed the application and role of combat aircraft. A combination of these two factors has resulted in the steady reduction in the world's inventory of combat aircraft.

Notes

1. "Assessing The NATO/Warsaw Pact Military Balance", Budget Issue Paper of The Congress of the United States Congressional Budget Office, December 1977 at https://www.cbo.gov/sites/default/files/95th-congress-1977-1978/

reports/77doc579.pdf (Accessed on December 19, 2018).

2. John T. Greenwood, "The Aviation Industry, 1917-97", in Robin Hingham, John T. Greenwood and Von Hardesty (Eds.), *Russian Aviation and Air Power in the Twentieth Century*, Frank Cass Publishers, Great Britain, 1998, p.152.
3. Richard F. Grimmett, The US *Congressional Research Service Report* for the Congress on Conventional Arms Transfers to Developing Nations, 1989-1996, August 13, 1997.
4. Ibid.
5. Richard F. Grimmett, The US *Congressional Research Service Report* for the Congress on Conventional Arms Transfers to Developing Nations, 1997-2004, August 29, 2005.
6. Originally, the Soviet (Russian) system of military-technical cooperation with other nations started with the Chief Engineering Board, which was set up in 1953 as a unit of the Ministry for Domestic and Foreign Trade, according to a resolution of the Council of Ministers of the USSR. As areas of military-technical cooperation ("MTC") were evolving, other bodies of specialized foreign trade also emerged. In the 1990s, the system of Russia's MTC underwent crucial changes. By the end of the decade, the country had two state-controlled intermediaries in the military trade sector, namely Rosvooruzhenie, a state-owned company and a federal state unitary enterprise (FSUE), and Promexport, also a federal state unitary enterprise (FSUE). Besides, there were a few other entities involved in MTC, in particular, military-industrial enterprises. To enhance the efficiency of their operations in the external market, the establishment of the "presidential vertical" for the management of MTC by the federal government was required, which helped reinforce coordination and control over arms exports and eliminated competition among Russian entities involved in MTC. On November 4, 2000, the President of the Russian Federation issued Decree No. 1834, to merge the two state-controlled intermediaries and establish a single state-controlled special exporter named Rosoboronexport, a federal-state unitary enterprise (FSUE). By July 1, 2011, pursuant to Decree No. 1577 of the President of the Russian Federation, privatization of the asset portfolio of Rosoboronexport (FSUE) had been completed, and the Company was converted into an open joint-stock-company (OJSC), keeping the functions of the only state-controlled intermediary in carrying out foreign trade operations with respect to the entire range of military goods. According to Federal Law No. 99-FZ, dated September 1, 2014, Rostec State Corporation passed a resolution on November 10, 2015, to amend the Company's Articles of Association so far as its corporate name was concerned. The Company was renamed into Joint-Stock Company Rosoboronexport or JSC Rosoboronexport for short.
7. Richard F. Grimmett, no. 5.

8. The US *Congressional Research Service Reports* for the Congress on Conventional Arms Transfers to Developing Nations, for period from 1989-2015 published from 1997 to 2016 including Catherine A. Theohary, Conventional Arms Transfers to Developing Nations, 2008-2015 dated December 19, 2016.
9. "Planning US General Purpose Forces: The Tactical Air Forces", The Congress of the United States Congressional Budget Office Budget Issue Paper, January 1977, at https://www.cbo.gov/sites/default/files/95th-congress-1977-1978/reports/77doc693_0.pdf (Accessed on December 19, 2018).
10. Kishore Kumar Khera, "Lebanon–Yemen Marathon: Hezbollah Head and Houthi Legs", in Vikrant Deshpande (Ed.), *Hybrid Warfare: The Changing Character of Conflict*, Pentagon Press, New Delhi, 2018,p.112.
11. Kishore Kumar Khera, no. 10.
12. As brought out in the White Paper on German Security Policy and the Future of Bundeswehr, 2016: "Challenges will continue to change in the future, and attackers will search for vulnerabilities in our open society. In their efforts, they will make use of the opportunities offered by technological progress to remain undetected. Against the backdrop of a dynamic security environment and attribution problems, strengthening our resilience will become increasingly important. Besides making an effective contribution to deterrence, the objective of resilience is to improve the ability of both state and society to withstand and adapt to disruptions, such as those caused by environmental disasters, severe system failures, and targeted attacks. The objective is to enable the state, the economy and society to absorb adverse events while continuing to function. Overall resilience can be strengthened by continuously building up resilience in the areas mentioned above the Alliance is also preparing for asymmetric and hybrid threats, including cyber attacks. The distinguishing feature of hybrid warfare, namely a blurring of the lines between war and peace, presents particular challenges when it comes to invoking Article 5 of the North Atlantic Treaty Complex security challenges such as in particular transnational terrorism, cybersecurity, and hybrid threats can only be countered through a comprehensive approach."
13. *White Paper on German Security Policy and the Future of Bundeswehr, 2016*, No, 47.
14. Ibid.
15. Kishore Kumar Khera,no. 10, pp.112-116.

PART III

Dynamics of Combat Aviation

9. Cockpit View: Human-Technology Interface and Training

With courage and integrity as their distinguishing traits, warriors are respected. Skilful warriors, like military aviators, have created a special place for themselves in society. In this class, a very small section of fighter pilots has attained iconic status. Oft- quoted adages, for example, –'all men are born equal, then a few become fighter pilots', support this perception. Myths and perceptions about fighter pilots, their interaction with combat aircraft and through that with the battle environment have been creatively brought out by Steven A. Fino in his book *Tiger Check*.[1] Steven, an F-15 pilot in the United States Air Force, brings to fore multiple aspects of the impact of the infusion of technology in combat aviation in the period between 1950 and 1980. But combat aviation is not about combat pilots alone. There are many more important verticals, the first being a group of technologists who convert concepts to designs and deliver the combat machine. They are also responsible for its maintenance and keep it combat-worthy. The calibre and dedication of the technical personnel and their understanding of aerial combat attributes is an essential element of combat aviation. The combat controller is the third facet of human resource for combat aviation. The combat controller plays a significant role is deciphering the combat environment and assisting the combat aviator in undertaking the designated mission. Thus, the output of combat aviation is a team effort, comprising the combat aviator, technician and combat controller. Other members of the team that play a significant role in the launch of combat missions at the tactical level are logisticians and infrastructure providers, on the one hand, and operational planners on the other.

This chapter discusses the changing roles and responsibilities of the combat aviators over the last five decades. The first section covers details of how the instrumentation of the cockpit impact the skillsets required to be a successful combat aviator. The next section takes the reader through the journey of combat aviation; also addressed is the change in cockpit configuration—from being a two-crew to one crew, and reverting to two-crew designs. The next section covers the manning requirement for combat aircraft classically defined as the Pilot Cockpit Ratio. The final section deals with women in combat aviation.

Shifting Core Skillsets

While in flight, the aviator requires various aids to assess the flight path of the flying machine—be it a hot air balloon or a combat aircraft. The first flying instruments to aid the pilot were designed to measure altitude, speed and direction. That these gadgets exist in modified form even today in all flying machines is a testament to their necessity, even as the methods employed to assess altitude, airspeed and direction have undergone considerable transformation. But most aircraft still retain these instruments based on the basic environmental conditions as a backup. This is because these basic instruments, although coarse in their output, are not dependent on any power supply. The air density and thus the static pressure assess the altitude; the difference in dynamic and static air pressure indicates the airspeed, and the magnetic compass lays out the direction of movement. The incorporation of gyroscopes in their mechanical forms and later as Ring Laser Gyros (RLG) has found many applications in flight instrumentations. Artificial Horizon and Turn and Slip Indicators have assisted in flying operations during adverse weather conditions with no external view for reference.

The manual assessment of the accurate ground position continuously is a difficult task. The task becomes complex in a high-speed aircraft that is manoeuvring. Initially, an assessment based on speed and direction, and correlation with ground features and maps helped pilots fix their positions. This was not very difficult in clear weather and unlimited visibility. But this system had various limitations in adverse weather and at night or over large water bodies with no features for reference. Guiding beacons and radio and navigation aids to assist the pilots like Automatic Direction Finder (ADF) were developed in the 1920s as a necessity. Several radio waves-based navigation aids were developed in the class of pilot-interpreted aids in the cockpit. Distance Measuring Equipment (DME), Tactical Air Navigation (TACAN), Very High-Frequency Omni Directional Range (VOR) and Instrument Landing System (ILS) – all developed or greatly improved in the 1950s – fall in this category. Simultaneously, in the class of ground-interpreted aids, several of these came into being for the ground controller. Radars for detection of aircraft are the most significant tools applicable in this category developed in the 1930s, and radio transmission-based direction finders are also widely used.

The navigational workload has practically been hived-off the pilots with the development of Inertial Navigation platforms. Although the same principle was used in German V2 rockets in the Second World War, its optimisation made it a practical component for fitment in the combat platforms in the 1960s. In the 1990s, there was a big leap in navigation systems for combat aircraft with the induction of the Global Positioning System (GPS). This system worked on accurate time measurement of the order of three nanoseconds from various satellites orbiting the earth at different inclinations, to accurately compute the position of the receiver. Greater accuracy and reliability of satellite-based navigation systems like the Global Positioning System (GPS), GLONASS, BeiDou and Gagan, have eased the workload further. The basic navigation from a point to another – a bugbear till the middle of the last century for combat aviators – is a non-issue today.

With basic flying and navigation issues being addressed simultaneously, the effort was directed to improve the combat effectiveness of the combat platform. The first major development in this arena was a gun sight in the intervening period between the two World Wars.[2] The sight had to assist the pilot in aiming at the target accurately taking the flight parameters and the relative position of the intended target. With a simple crosshair or fixed sight, the results were far from satisfactory. The three critical factors in assessing the correct aiming point in aerial combat were the flight parameters, target range and relative motion. In terms of assessing the speed, altitude and direction of the flight path, the pilots were generally accurate. But assessing the range and relative motion of the intended target needed help. The gyroscope-based gun sights and later computer-based gun sights in the 1970s operating in conjunction with laser and on-board radars were developed to overcome these shortcomings. As a result, aerial firing became more accurate. Accurate and fast computing by on-board computers can calculate the velocity jump and gravity drop of the bullets leaving the mother aircraft for target and make its depiction in real-time possible. This has minimised the aiming errors.

While the instrumentation was being upgraded for the missions of firing guns on other aircraft, the development of air-to-air missiles changed the dynamics of aerial combat. Instrumentation now had to come up with a different solution. A visual and audio indication for missile lock-on to the target was a natural development. Incorporation of weapons attack parameters on Head-Up Display (HUD) along with basic flight parameters made combat easy as the pilot could remain aware of all critical parameters without having to glance inside the cockpit. Replicating the HUD and radar parameters on the visor of the helmet led to the development of Helmet-Mounted Sights (HMS). This facilitated the ability of the pilot to lock-on by turning his head towards the intended target thus obviating the need to turn the aircraft.[3] The cockpit is getting homogenized and physical dials are giving way to digital screens. However, the total screen space available in a combat aircraft cockpit is smaller than the usable screen area of a personal computer – so the sensor information must be miniaturized and morphed.[4] Even the latest cockpits do only a mediocre job of relaying information to the pilot.

A similar revolution has taken place in combat aircraft instrumentation for ground attack missions. The assessment of the accurate relative position of the aircraft in real-time concerning the intended target in terms of height, track and distance together with flight parameters, allows onboard computers to generate accurate weapon release points. This used to be a manual assessment that led to a large number of air-launched weapons to miss their targets. Radio altimeters, Laser and Radar operate in conjunction with Inertial and satellite-based navigation systems to minimise weapon aiming errors. The wind correction required for air-to-ground weapons is also computed and factored-in automatically.

In a nutshell, the instrumentation and aids in the combat aircraft have seen remarkable changes in the last fifty years. This has also reflected in the human resource for combat aviation. Often, the combat aviators were compared to knights in the air but now they look more like scientists.[5] Flying by the feel of the seat in yesteryears and visual assessments has been replaced by decoding information from a plethora of sources to optimally select a weapon and its firing mode from multiple options. The skills required for basic flying remain the same but the degree of difficulty in mission execution has changed. The timeline has not changed for both incarnations of the knights and the scientists. One second is still far too long for combat aviators and often the pause between defeat and victory.

Single-Twin-Single Transition

Looking back at the initial cockpit designs of the combat aircraft, two things stand out. First, the workload was distributed between two occupants of the cockpit and primarily related to flying and weapon firing respectively. But as the front firing weapons became possible, the focus was to have a single-person cockpit. This was operationally beneficial due to the reduction in the overall weight of the aircraft and number of aircrew required. This allowed launch of a greater number of aircraft with existing aircrew. Gradually, most of the combat aircraft were designed with a single pilot concept and twin-seaters were limited to a restricted role for training. The second seat was added often by reducing the operational capability of the single-seater version to account for added weight and space required for the second pilot. Fuel, weapons and avionics were often the casualties. The two-seater version of the MiG-21 has very limited fuel as compared to the single-seat version and the Jaguar twin-seater had one gun removed from the single-seater version.

With increased assets onboard the combat aircraft, it became difficult for a single pilot to effectively manage all the systems optimally and exploit the entire battle space transparency picture available. Data linking allowed the aircraft's multi-functional displays to not only depict the output of onboard sensors but also from the friendly sensors in the vicinity. Situational awareness was available from other members of the same formation and airborne or ground-based radars in the area. Although all details available were not always relevant in aerial combat or for mission accomplishment, these helped in optimising force application. Data linking allowed a coordinated attack by various elements of the formation against several hostile targets. This helped in enhancing mission efficiency as the best-positioned combat aircraft took the responsibility for attacking while the other formation members repositioned for alternative targets. This increased the pilot workload as it entailed continuous monitoring of all relevant players in the arena and assigning various responsibilities to formation members in a dynamic way.

Another aspect that changed the human resource matrix in a combat aircraft is the role that was assigned. At the beginning of military aviation, the roles were clearly defined for bomber or ground attack and air defence or fighter aircraft. The technology did not permit amalgamation of these roles, as the basic characteristics required for the aircraft to perform these roles were distinct. Better engines and airframe designs, computer-based computations for weapon solutions and miniaturization of various sensors and their integration in small-sized combat aircraft changed the basic concepts. The aircraft are now designed to perform multiple roles including basic ground attack and air defence. Most of the combat aircraft in the current inventory fall in the category of multi-role. The number of specifically designed aircraft like the F-22 for air superiority or purely ground attack aircraft like the Jaguar is diminishing. With the concept of multi-role, many missions assigned to the crew have an element of both, the ground attack and of air defence. This makes system management rather complex for a single person to handle effectively. These factors have led to the re-creation of the two-member cockpit configuration. The Su30 is a classic example in this category.

Pilot-Cockpit Ratio

How many pilots are needed for each cockpit, is a crucial human resource question. While there are many complex modules designed to arrive at the force level required for a specified strategy, the calculation for manning of cockpits is rather simple. Based on the mission type, mission time duration can be computed that includes mission preparation, mission execution and mission de-brief. Accounting for rest and recuperation too is essential. Based on the environmental condition, this rest period could vary between 8 to 12 hours in a 24-hour cycle. Under hot and humid conditions, recuperation to achieve optimal response status may be longer. In a 24-hour cycle, the maximum number of missions that each air crew can undertake is calculated by subtracting the resting period from 24 and dividing the remainder by the mission time duration. Now this time needs to be compared with the aircraft turnaround time in terms of its servicing, replenishment of consumables like fuel, oil and rearming. This turnaround period in combination with the mission duration defines the number of missions that a particular aircraft can undertake in a 24-hour cycle. Typically, a combat aircraft can be utilised for 8-12 hours in a 24-hour cycle with the rest of the time devoted to servicing and replenishing. The way a force intends utilizing its combat fleet defines the pilot-to-cockpit ratio. It normally varies between 1 and 2.5. A pilot- cockpit ratio of 2.5 means that for every cockpit, the force trains 2.5 pilots. Practically, for every combat aircraft unit with 18 single-seat aircraft, the force will have strength of 45 pilots. In case the aircraft are twin seaters like the Su30, the numbers will be 45 pilots and 45 Weapon System Operators (WSO). All aircrew are normally not on the strength of the combat aircraft unit. They are deployed for various staff and training appointments but are trained and ready to be deployed for operational tasks on an as required basis.

Training of combat air crew is time-consuming and expensive. As per an assessment, a fighter pilot requires approximately five years of training to be qualified to lead flights, at a cost of about $3 to $11 million depending on the specific type of aircraft.[6] And retaining the skill sets also requires an adequate amount of continuity training for combat pilots. For example, in Canada, to maintain and develop new skills to sustain the fighter force's capability, CF18 pilots are expected to fly 140 hours per year.[7] Once such an investment is made in terms of time and resources, the organisations loath to part with the trained combat pilots. However, unless appropriately incentivised, most organisations find it difficult to retain trained pilots. The US Air Force was short of 192 fighter pilots (5 per cent of authorizations) in 2006 and this gap increased to 1,005 (27 per cent of authorizations) in 2017.[8] The same story exists in Canada too as brought out by the Auditor-General of Canada to their Parliament:[9]

> ..... National Defence identified that it had only 64% of the trained CF-18 pilots it needed to meet the government's new requirement, so it would need to considerably increase the number of trained pilots. National Defence is unlikely to be able to do so because pilots have been leaving the fighter force faster than new ones could be trained. According to National Defence, between April 2016 and March 2018, the Royal Canadian Air Force lost 40 trained fighter pilots and produced only 30 new ones.

The problem in the field of trained maintenance personnel is not much different. In case of lack of an adequate number of trained maintenance personnel, it is difficult to generate the rate of effort required even for peacetime training. The situation would get worse during the operations. The Report of the Auditor-General of Canada to the Canadian Parliament in 2018 on Canada's Fighter Force sums up the human resource aspect of the fighter fleet in Canada, highlighting the domino effect of inadequate qualified personnel on operational readiness.

> ....the fighter force did not have enough experienced technicians and pilots. As of April 2018, according to National Defence, 22 per cent of technician positions in CF-18 squadrons were vacant (8%) or were filled by technicians not yet fully qualified to do maintenance (14 per cent). ...between December 2016 and April 2018, CF-18 technicians were able to prepare on average about 83 per cent of the aircraft needed. ... from 2014 until 2018, the average maintenance hours needed for every hour that a CF-18 flew increased from 21 to 24. .....Unless there are more experienced technicians to perform maintenance, the number of flying hours available for each CF-18 pilot will decrease. We found that in the 2017–18 fiscal year, 28 per cent of pilots flew fewer than the minimum 140 hours.[10]

Women in Combat Aviation

Is combat gender-independent? Are women as capable as men in combat operations? Answers to such questions are relevant while formulating human resource policies for combat forces. This gains even more traction in the field of combat aviation wherein the cost of training is substantially higher than other combat fields. Historically, combat, in general, has always been dominated by men. Physical attributes played a major role in defining the gender ratio within the combat forces the world over since times immemorial. And yet, throughout history, society has debated the suitability of women in combat. That notwithstanding, there were women combatants and leaders like Boudicca of Iceni, Tomyris of Scythia, Sultan Razia, Chand Bibi, Kitturu Chennamma, and Laxmi Bai, the Rani of Jhansi.[11]These examples proved the irrelevance of gender in commanding forces and even leading them in battlefields. However, such examples are rare in human history. With the advent and organization of modern military forces, the role assigned to women varied from negligible to support roles based on the societal structures and necessity. Today, countries like Eritrea and Israel have the largest share of women in the armed forces at 33 per cent.[12] Major factors in this debate about the role of women in combat, in general, and combat aviation in particular, are capability, compatibility and economics.

Capability

Key capabilities required of a combatant are in physical, mental and psychological domains. In the physical domain, the combatant must be able to have the requisite strength, stamina and speed. The objective standards for such attributes are well laid down by the armed forces across the world along with the basic minimum physical standards. These form the basis of selection of an individual for training in the combat arm. The physical standards that must be achieved during initial training for a candidate to graduate to be a combatant are also well documented. Genetic and physical attributes of the two genders are different. Just a cursory glance at any sporting event that tests the strength, stamina and speed of the participants indicates this gap. Data for the 2006 Beijing Olympics and 2016 Rio Olympics tabulated in Table 9.1 indicates the difference between the best of men and women in their respective events testing their speed, stamina and strength.

Table 9.1: Comparison of Results of Events in 2008 and 2016 Olympic Games

Event	Year	Men	Women	Performance Difference of Women as compared to Men
100 m	2016	9.81 s	10.71 s	9.17% slower
	2008	9.69 s	10.78 s	11.24% slower
Marathon	2016	2h08m44s	2h24m04s	11.91% slower
	2008	2h06m32s	2h26m44s	15.96% slower
Shot Put	2016	22.52 m	20.63 m	8.4% shorter
	2008	21.51 m	20.56 m	4.5% shorter

Source: Olympic Games data available at https://www.olympic.org/olympic-games.

A point that needs to be clearly understood here is that physically, the women do not have the same strength, stamina and speed as their male counterparts. But a woman with a timing of 10.71 seconds for a 100-metre dash will be able to defeat over 99% of the world's male population. Practically, so long as a candidate meets the basic physical requirements to be a combatant, gender should not play a role. Now the key question is, should the physical standards be different based on the candidate's gender? Should women be given a handicap in this regard to compete with the male counterparts in meeting the requisite standards? Supported by data about speed, stamina and strength, looking at the basic disadvantage that the women have in the physical domain, organizations tend to give a handicap of about 10 per cent in physical standards. Even if such a handicap is not given, many women will still make the cut and be able to join as combatants.

Besides physical attributes, combat aviation is about the ability to assimilate inputs from multiple sources and conjure up an appropriate response in a timely fashion. The time limit for initiating an action in combat aviation may be less than a second. In this specific domain, gender is practically irrelevant. This attribute is of greater significance than the basic physical attributes for being a competent combat aviator. To test the response and basic limbs and eye coordination, several static and dynamic tests exist and are put to use to select appropriate candidates for aviation. The Computerized Pilot Selection System (CPSS) being used in India is one such format. This is carried out at the Services Selection Boards (SSB) for short listing candidates suitable for aviation. This test can be undertaken just once in a lifetime and the candidates who do not make the required grade in this test cannot join military aviation.

Overall, there are means and methods to test the capability of individuals in an objective manner. So long as the laid down standards are met, the gender of the candidate becomes irrelevant.

Compatibility

In some societies, the pride is associated with the protection of women of the clan. Should women fall prey to an enemy, it is considered as a major failure. With such deep-rooted societal values, women were kept in the safe innermost ring. However, as the necessity of combatants increased, the men were relieved of combat support jobs and these went to women. Most of the armed forces have had women in the medical support team for a fairly long time. As demands increased, gradually women came into combat support operations in communication and logistics and accounts departments of the armed forces. This was not to bring in gender parity but was an operational necessity to free up more men for combat duties. Such backroom jobs had a low scope of women falling to an advancing enemy. Gradual changes in society and the necessity of fielding most capable combatants, the situation changed and several armed forces started inducting women in combat roles. In the UK as late as 2018, women have been cleared to join all combat arms.

How will society and the state react should a woman combatant become a Prisoner of War (POW)? The answer to this question has withheld the induction of women in combat. A threat of physical abuse of the women POWs keeps the state and society apprehensive. But looking at the record of a front-ranking country like the United States of America in Abu Ghraib prison camps – cases of torture, prisoner abuse and sub-human treatment to Iraqi POWs, or the mutilation of bodies of Indian soldiers by the Pakistan Army, the irrationality and gender irrelevance comes to fore. Treatment of a POW will be decided by the captor and not on the basis of the gender of the captive. Societies will gradually accept this fact of life.

The last aspect of women's compatibility in combat forces comes from the internal dynamics of the force. How do women fit into a predominately male bastion without being exploited? The US Senator Martha McSally, the first female US Air Force fighter pilot to fly in combat, was sexually assaulted by a superior officer, and later, when she tried to talk about it to military officials, she "felt like the system was raping her all over again." [13] Such exploitation is not uncommon in militaries. The militaries derive their values and ethos from the society and reflect the behavioural pattern of the society at large. Theoretically, all militaries invariably have adequate checks and balances to ensure freedom from exploitation and several legislations to back up the process. Several culprits have been punished by the military judicial systems. However, militaries being very hierarchal with a restrictive framework, do not have optimized structures and systems to eliminate such instances. This is a major limitation at present. [14]

Economics

Training combatants is time and resource-intensive, more so for combat aviation. Therefore, organizations like to view the cost-effectiveness of the entire process more critically. Besides additional tests to check the suitability of the candidates for combat aviation in terms of the medical condition, physical ability, response mechanism and psychological profile, their availability is also considered. This is where women have a distinct disadvantage. During cyclic physiological changes in their bodies, for about three days out of 28, they may not be in the best of physical and mental condition. Although not applicable to all, during such a period, some women may not be fit to fly owing to a lower level of attentiveness or because of physical discomfort. This is based on the individual's constitution. Secondly, during pregnancy too, a combat aviator is unable to undertake missions. That will be physically challenging for both the expectant mother and her unborn child. The combined effect of these two factors will be unavailability approximately for 10 per cent of women aviators as compared to their male counterparts. This is a key point while auditing the cost-effectiveness of the entire process. In practical terms, the mission that requires 100 male combat aviators will necessitate approximately 110 women. Training and sustaining additional 10 per cent combat aviators needs to be factored into the planning and budget. The economics are tilted against the induction of women in combat aviation. However, this is a small price to pay for bringing competent combatants in combat aviation based only on capability and not on gender.

Induction of women in combat forces has an administrative side-effect too. Several women in the combat forces tend to find a life partner within the combat forces. Economically, this arrangement benefits the organization in terms of reduced requirement of resources like accommodation, medical and travel facilities for one family instead of two. But for human resource managers, it becomes difficult to manage co-location for such couples.

Like most combat arms, to begin with, combat aviation was an exclusively male domain. The number of women in aviation was very limited and in military aviation even more scarce in the first half of the 20th century. Many women combat aviators have etched their names in the annals of combat aviation history. The erstwhile USSR was first off the blocks and raised three women's air force regiments. Apart from the pilots, even engineers, technicians and other ground crew were women. Women pilots also served in overwhelmingly male regiments. The ace fighters of the Second World War—Lydia Litvyak (15 kills) and Yekaterina "Katya" Budanova (9 kills),[15] along with Irina Feodorovna Sebrova with over 1000 bombing missions[16]— are legends.

In the United States, in 1993, a 45-year ban on women flying fighter jets and bombers ended.[17] Even though restrictions on women flying aircraft in combat were lifted 25 years ago, the percentage of military pilots who are women remains around 6.5 per cent — and is comparable in the commercial industry, where many pilots land after training and careers in the armed services.[18] Gradually, women are now allowed to be part of combat aviation in many countries. Although induction of women in the Indian Armed Forces (other than the medical branch) started in 1992, it has been a long, arduous journey.[19] India joined the group of other about 25 countries in 2017 that allow women to join combat aviation.[20] However, there are still areas that need to be ironed out as brought out by the Ministry of Defence Press Release in March 2019:[21]

> Insofar the Indian Air Force is concerned, all Branches, including Fighter Pilots, are now open for women officers. In Indian Navy, all non-sea going Branches/Cadre/Specialization has been opened for induction of women officers through the Short-Service Commission. In addition to education, Law & Naval Constructor branch/cadre, women SSC officers have been made eligible for grant of Permanent Commission in the Naval Armament branch, at par with the male officers. The proposal for induction of three new training ships for the Indian Navy is underway. This will provide the requisite infrastructure for training of both men and women officers. Indian Navy will start inducting women in all branches, once the training ships are in place. Women officers will be granted Permanent Commission in the Indian Army in all the ten branches

where women are inducted for Short-Service Commission. So, besides the existing two streams of Judge Advocate General (JAG) and Army Education Corps, now PC will be granted in Signals, Engineers, Army Aviation, Army Air Defence, Electronics and Mechanical Engineers, Army Service Corps, Army Ordnance Corps and Intelligence also to women officers.

The combat aviation domain is still dominated by men. Combat aviation allows no particular gender advantage and has a limited role for physical strength. Anyone with responsive hand-eye coordination and the ability to assimilate situations based on multiple inputs in a multitude of formats can be drafted into combat aviation. Thereafter, it is sheer hard work to understand the nuisances and various facets of combat aviation. Some of these are analyzed in a case study of aerial combat on the Indo- Pakistan border in February 2019.

What matters in Aerial Combat? Balakot Strike and the Aftermath – A Case Study

On February 14, 2019, 44 Central Reserve Police Force (CRPF) personnel died and 70 others were injured in the suicide car bombing carried out by the Pakistani terrorist group Jaish-e-Mohammed at Pulwama, Jammu and Kashmir.[22] In tune with the policy of countering terror, at 03:30 AM local time on February 26, 2019, Indian Air Force combat aircraft attacked the Jaish-e-Mohammed terrorist camp at Balakot in Pakistan's Khyber Pakhtunkhwa province. The Indian Foreign Secretary Vijay Gokhale referred to credible intelligence about Jaish-e-Mohammed cadre undergoing training at the Balakot camp for carrying out further terrorist attacks in India.[23] The extent of the damage caused by this aerial attack and number of terrorist killed is not known accurately. The estimates vary between a figure from 30 to 300.

As a response, the next day on February 27, 2019, Pakistan Air Force (PAF) combat aircraft crossed the Line of Control to strike Indian military targets.[24] Though PAF aircraft failed in their primary task, the aerial combat between IAF and PAF aircraft resulted in both sides losing one aircraft each.[25] The pilot of the IAF aircraft Wing Commander Abhinandan Varthaman, flying a MiG-21 Bison, crashed in Pakistan- occupied Kashmir (POK) and was taken as a prisoner. The PAF pilot flying an F-16 that was shot down succumbed to injuries on February 28, 2019, after ejection followed by mob lynching in the POK.[26] The MiG-21 Bison fired a R-73 Air-to-Air missile and parts of the debris of the AIM-120C Advanced Medium Range Air-to-Air missile (AMRAAM) recovered in Jammu and Kashmir give an indication of the weaponry on board the F-16.[27] Although Pakistan has not yet confirmed the loss of a PAF aircraft but an accurate assessment can be made based on the press conference on February 27, 2019 by Major- General Asif Gafoor, Director-General, Inter-Services Public Relations Pakistan, and later reiterated by Pakistan's Prime Minister Imran Khan, that one pilot has been captured and the other is undergoing treatment in the military hospital in Pakistan.[28]Although, Major-General Gafoor denied participation of the F-16 in the mission that day, parts of the AIM-120C recovered in the combat zone irrevocably prove the presence of the F-16 as that is the only aircraft in PAF's inventory capable of being armed with this missile. Additionally, at that juncture, the Pakistani establishment did not know the identity of the second pilot who was critically injured. On realization that he was a PAF pilot, the narrative from Pakistan conveniently ignored covering his status in follow- up briefings.

By looking at the scoreline 1-1 in this short aerial combat in the Indian subcontinent after nearly five decades, it appears that F-16 and MiG-21 Bison can be equated. The PAF package had around 24 aircraft including the Mirage V and JF-17 besides the F-16 and the IAF defended with a package of eight aircraft including the MiG-21 Bison, the Mirage 2000 and the Su30.[29] The ingression of PAF aircraft into Indian airspace was very limited thus reducing combat space and time. While the outcome of the combat is known, it is still not certain as to which aircraft and which weapon finally achieved the kills and would be known in due course of time. However, five critical factors that need to be deliberated upon, are covered here that dictate the outcome of aerial combat.

First, the relative capability of combat platforms engaged in combat. In this, the key operational parameters that play a pivotal role in aerial combat are maximum speed, acceleration, instantaneous and sustained rate of turn, rate of climb, combat ceiling, and low-speed handling. In most of these parameters, the F-16 outscores the MiG-21 Bison. The F-16 is a product of the US' Light Weight Fighter Program, designed to outmatch the MiG-21. However, a significant caveat, while comparing combat performance is that both types of aircraft are configured for the same role, as both the F-16 and the MiG-21 Bison are capable of multiple roles. The Mig-21 Bison was clearly in an air defence configuration as it was scrambled from the Operational Readiness Platform (ORP) for intercepting the incoming hostile aircraft. The aircraft in this configuration would have air-to-air missiles and guns loaded. However, without official confirmation from the Pakistan Air Force or a look at the wreckage of the aircraft, it will be difficult to assess the role assigned to the downed F-16. As per the stated intent of Pakistan's armed forces, the mission's objective was to demonstrate the intent and capability of PAF to attack targets inside India as per DG ISPR's press briefing on February 27, 2019.[30] Towards this, the F-16 could have been in a Ground Attack (GA) role, equipped with a targeting pod and air-to-surface weapons. The probability of this is low owing to the presence of a dedicated ground-attack platform like Mirage V in the package. The F-16 could have been in an Electronic Warfare (EW) role with the Electronic Counter Measure (ECM) pod slapped on. Alternatively, the F-16 was in an air defence configuration for protection of the aircraft against the interceptors. In such a case, it would be equipped with AAM and guns. In an air defence configuration, the F-16 would retain the platform-capability advantage over the MiG-21 Bison but in case of a GA or EW mission for the F-16, the same will not be valid based on the exact external load at the time of combat engagement.

The second aspect pertains to the relative performance of onboard sensors for combat aircraft. Onboard avionics relevant to aerial combat are the Air Interception (AI) Radar, the Radar Warning Receiver (RWR) and the Electronic Warfare (EW) suite.

The AI radar allows the combat pilot to scan the area ahead for any hostile aircraft and thus helps in assessing the location and intention of the adversary. While the update rate of the radar picture in almost all AI radars is similar, the differentiating factors are the scan zone in terms of lateral and vertical field of view of the radar and the maximum range. In all these attributes, the F-16's radar AN/APG series and the MiG-21 Bison's Kopoyo are comparable but with different functional features. The RWR monitors the radar's waves impinging a combat aircraft and thereafter converts them into usable information for the combat pilot in the cockpit. With a pre-programmed Pre-Flight Message (PFM), the impinging radar waves are displayed as symbols in the cockpit that the pilot needs to decode. Based on the radar signature, the pilot assesses the type of radar painting his/her combat aircraft. These include surveillance radars, ground-based weapon radars, tracking radars and AI radars. Even the status and modes of the AI radar can be assessed based on the accuracy of the PFM to indicate if the hostile aircraft are searching, tracking or are locked-on to the combat aircraft. The RWR can also indicate an imminent missile launch and a lock-on by the AAM. Additionally, to defend itself a combat aircraft can use electronic warfare suites fitted on the aircraft like the Airborne Self-Protection Jammers (ASPJ), and chaffs and flares. The ASPJ helps in delaying or deceiving lock-on by the hostile aircraft using the AI radar. This makes a crucial difference in aerial combat where a time of even a couple of seconds makes a difference between victory and defeat. Similarly, intelligent use of the chaff can deceive an active missile and flares can decoy a passive missile. This entire package fitted onto the MiG-21 Bison along with the innovation and tactical acumen of IAF pilots did surprise the USAF F-15 and F-16 in *Exercise Cope India* in 2004 and 2005.[31]

The third factor was the weapons on board the combat aircraft–the MiG-21 Bison equipped with two R77 and two R73 AAM and the F-16 with the AIM120C AMRAAM. The difference in performance between these weapons is huge. The R73 is a passive short-range Close-Combat Missile (CCM) and has an Infra-red homing head. It locks-on to the heat signature of the target aircraft and homes on to it. Such missiles are prone to deception by use of appropriate flares that replicate the heat signature of the aircraft. Once fired, the combat pilot has no control over the missile. R77 is a mid range active AAM but was not used possibly because of low reaction time available and faster lock on by the R73. On the other hand, the AIM-120C is one of the best in class Beyond Visual Range (BVR) AAM. Its claimed range under ideal conditions is over 100 kilometres, more than four times that of the R73. Besides, it is an active AAM, meaning that the missile has radar and uses it to guide itself to the intended target. So practically, the aircraft equipped with a BVR AAM like the AIM-120C can take multiple shots at an aircraft armed with CCM before becoming vulnerable. However, at closer ranges, the advantage of the BVR gets neutralized and the aircraft with the better interface has an edge. In this context, a Helmet-Mounted Sight (HMS) that allows an easier and quicker lock-on to the target can define the victory parameters.

The fourth factor is the operational environment. Combat aircraft do not operate in isolation and the operational environment impacts their combat capability. This aspect concerns situational awareness. Ground-based radars or airborne radars like the Airborne Warning and Aircraft Control System (AWACS) play a significant role in this. The radar on board the combat aircraft has limited capability in terms of the area under coverage which is also partially lost when the same radar is used to track a target and is locked-on for a weapon launch. In aerial combat, owing to speed and freedom of movement in three dimensions, a combat pilot cannot scan the area around his aircraft and keep track of hostile aircraft in the vicinity. The matter aggravates when several aircraft in the region are armed with a BVR AAM. The volume of airspace that needs to be watched is beyond the capability of any combat pilot. Here, the radar controllers (normally called fighter controllers or combat controllers) in ground-based radars or AWACS play a crucial role. They monitor the combat airspace and keep updating the combat pilot about whereabouts of hostile and friendly aircraft. Instead of an individual effort of a combat pilot in aerial combat, it is a team effort between the fighter controller and combat pilot that plays a significant role. The time available to communicate between a combat pilot and a controlling fighter controller is very short. Unless they understand each other well and can convey their intentions in a cryptic yet unambiguous manner, the outcome will not be optimal. To obviate human dependence in such a critical aspect of combat aviation, a data link helps in assisting the combat pilot wherein the data related to airspace around his combat aircraft is transmitted electronically and a fused air picture depicting friendly and hostile aircraft in the area is reproduced in the cockpit. Additionally, tactical coordination between various members of the formation plays a crucial role in defining the combat's outcome. In this matrix, communication jamming too plays a pivotal role, especially for the voice mode between the pilot and the fighter controller. Jamming voice communication is not very difficult and a large number of militaries own equipment for such a mission. This can to a large extent be obviated by the use of encrypted communication equipment like Software Defined Radios (SDR). In the absence of such communication equipment, calls between pilot and fighter controller can be jammed by sheer noise or by deception. Both can lead to a loss of tactical information that may be crucial for mission accomplishment. Once details of combat engagement are declassified in due course, it will be possible to ascertain if the non-availability of SDR is a primary cause for loss of the MiG-21 Bison.

The fifth factor is human resource. It is not the equipment that fights but the humans operating it. A clear understanding of all aspects of aerial combat and professional training helps in defining the outcome of aerial combat. Training of combat pilots and fighter controllers individually and their integration as a combat team play a vital role in the outcome of aerial combat. With similar seniority and experience of pilots on both sides, the level of expertise is expected to be similar. Here, multiple international exercises carried out by the IAF with and against the F-16 from various countries would have given IAF pilots and controllers a very clear understanding of the capabilities of that platform. Once details are declassified, it will be known in case the Bison fell in a classic Shooter- Drag trap or the warning by the controller of impending threat was lost owing to high noise level in the cockpit at very high speed or the controller failed to notice the tactical ploy of the attackers. On the PAF side, was the drag attempt executed a bit slower than the required rate or the combat controller failed to appreciate closure rate of Bison or the pilot- controller team failed in assessing range of weapons on board the Bison. The result was the loss of two aircraft.

On all technical and equipment capability parameters, the F-16 scores well as compared to the MiG-21 Bison. Yet, the outcome is one-all. Motivation and courage too play a vital role in deciding aerial combat. At this juncture, it is difficult to assess whether the motivation and courage of the MiG-21 Bison's pilot outweighed that of his F-16 counterpart. While both pilots were operating as per mandates of their respective services, being with a just cause could have tilted the scale in favour of the MiG-21 Bison.[32]

Another moot point that comes out as an after-effect of such an operation is about gender neutrality in combat aviation. India categorically refused to link the release of the captured pilot Wing Commander Abhinandan Varthaman to de-escalation of the situation and instead continued to state that de-escalation will take place only after tangible and verifiable action is initiated against terror networks in Pakistan by the Government of Pakistan. Would it have been the same response had the downed pilot been a woman? At this juncture, a hypothetical question, as women combat aviators in India are yet to reach operationally deployable status. However, it is just a matter of time when such a situation could arise. How, as a state and as a society, would India respond? Both the Indian state and Indian society need to change their current frame of reference in this context and prepare themselves for such a situation. Faced with such a situation, it ought not to become an emotive issue and result in a deflection of policy.

Now, a grave question: Two pilots – one each from IAF and PAF– ejected after hostile firing and both landed up in Pakistan-occupied Kashmir. Besides physical discomfort from ejection, on landing with the help of their parachutes, both pilots faced a hostile mob. The armed forces are legally bound to protect the enemy soldier in their custody as per the Geneva Convention and also consider it as an asset to glean information. On both these counts, a combatant's priority after landing in hostile territory is to escape.; if not feasible, they would prefer custody by rival armed forces than face hostile and often irrational local populace. During hostilities, the general populace tends to be hostile towards an enemy soldier. However, they may or may not have the skills to identify the nationality of the captured pilot. The period from facing a mob to the arrival of a representative of the unit of the armed forces deployed in the area, is crucial. Wing Commander Abhinandan Varthaman of the IAF on February 27, 2019, managed to survive this phase in a hostile land but the PAF F-16 pilot who crashed in friendly territory, was lynched and later succumbed to his injuries. He probably could not verify his identity to the irrational mob. A sad way for a combatant to lose his life.

With this small sample, the probability of a pilot after ejection surviving a hostile mob is 50 per cent. In a patriarchal society like in the Indian sub-continent, the situation would have been more precarious had the ejected pilot been a woman. Would she have survived an irrational mob? How would society and state react in case her video with a blood-covered face and tattered clothes (as happened in case of Wing Commander Abhinanadan Varthaman) were doing the rounds on social media? Would the rage in society, in that case, force the state to act differently? Will a threat of such a situation force deployment of women combat aviators away from combat zones? That will defeat the basic tenets of gender neutrality. When a society moves towards gender neutrality, such challenges will come. Based on how robust the will of the society is to steer this course under challenging circumstances, gender neutrality will grow or decay and its manifestation will be seen in combat forces as well.

Conclusion

The character of warfare is changing; so is the space occupied by combat aviation. The combat aviator– the cutting edge– has transformed from being a knight to a scientist in the last five decades. With hybridization of the conflict, their role is likely to further transform. The combat aviators must train to fight effectively in a much more decentralized and degraded set of conditions.[33] Irrespective of how advanced the aircraft are, the (wo)man-machine interface will still dictate terms of combat outcome in the coming decades.

Notes

1. Steven A. Fino, *Tiger Check: Automating the US Air Force: Fighter Pilot in Air-to-Air Combat 1950-1980*, Johns Hopkins University Press, Maryland, 2017.
2. Mike Spick, *Fighters at War: The Story of Air to Air Combat,* Greenhill Books, London, 1997, pp. 10-35.
3. Ibid.,pp.132-133.
4. Bill Sweetman, *Advanced Fighter Technology: The Future of Cockpit Combat*, Air Life Publishing Ltd, England, 1988, p 127.
5. Steven A Fino, no. 1.
6. Garrett Reim, "USAF faces challenges to grow fleet, boost readiness", *Flight Global*, October 11, 2018 at https://www.flightglobal.com/news/articles/usaf-faces-challenges-to-grow-fleet-boost-readiness-452584/ (Accessed on October 12, 2018).
7. "Fall Reports of the Auditor General of Canada to the Parliament of Canada, Report 3—Canada's Fighter Force—National Defence", 2018 at http://www.oag-bvg.gc.ca/internet/English/parl_oag_201811_03_e_43201.html (Accessed on November 27, 2018).
8. "United States Government Accountability Office Report GAO-19-120T on Air Force Readiness Actions Needed to Rebuild Readiness and Prepare for the Future", October 10, 2018 https://www.armed-services.senate.gov/imo/media/doc/Pendleton_10-10-18.pdf (Accessed on October 12, 2018).
9. Fall Reports of the Auditor General of Canada to the Parliament of Canada, no. 7.
10. Ibid.
11. Manimugdha S. Sharma, "Not fit to fight? These women warriors prove otherwise", *The Times of India* (New Delhi edition) December 23, 2018.
12. Ibid.
13. "Was raped in Air Force by a superior officer: First US female fighter pilot to fly in combat", *The New Indian Express*, March 7, 2019 at http://www.newindianexpress.com/world/2019/mar/07/was-raped-in-air-force-by-superior-officer-first-us-female-fighter-pilot-to-fly-in-combat-1947987.html (Accessed on March 30, 2019).
14. Jude Eden served in the US Marines from 2004-2008 and was stationed at Camp Lejeune with 8th Comm Bn. She was deployed for eight months over 2005-6 to support Camp Fallujah's communications network and was also assigned entry checkpoint duty working with the Marine Infantry and

frisking women for explosives on Fallujah's outskirts. Of sexual tension in the military, she writes: "Whether it's a consensual relationship, unwanted advances, or sexual assault, they all destroy unit cohesion. No one is talking about the physical and emotional stuff that goes along with men and women together. A good relationship can foment jealousy and the perception of favouritism. A relationship goes sour, and suddenly one loses faith in the very person who may need to drag one off the field of battle. A sexual assault happens, and a woman not only loses faith in her fellows but may fear them. A vindictive man paints a woman as easy, and she loses the respect of her peers. A vindictive woman wants to destroy a man's career with a false accusation, and its poison to the unit. All this happens before the fighting even begins." Rob Schwarzwalder, *Women, Special Operations Forces, and Selective Service Inclusion*, Issue Brief, July 2016 at https://downloads.frc.org/EF/EF16G12.pdf, (Accessed on April 15, 2019).

15. Manimugdha S. Sharma, no. 11.
16. "The Fearless Young Soviet Women Who Played A Huge Part In World War II", War History Online at https://www.warhistoryonline.com/world-war-ii/soviet-fearless-female-fighters-wwii.html (Accessed on September 17, 2018).
17. Rowan Scarborough, "She has the right stuff: Female combat pilots have been flashing their skills for 20 years", *The Washington Times*, March 25, 2013 at https://www.washingtontimes.com/news/2013/mar/25/more-than-a-sound-barrier-female-pilots have displ/ (Accessed on September 17, 2018).Top of Form Bottom of Form
18. Belly Kennedy, "What it Was Like to Be One of the First Female Fighter Pilots", *The New York Times*, March 2, 2018 at https://www.nytimes.com/2018/05/02/magazine/women-pilots-military.html (Accessed on September 17, 2018).
19. Since the Government of India is a signatory to important international conventions, in particular, the Convention on the Elimination of All Forms of Discrimination against Women (CEDAW), as well as the Convention on the Rights of the Child, it must ensure gender-sensitization in the forces. Efforts must be made to ensure that all members of the armed forces receive the same benefits and are treated equally, as mandated by the Constitution. Women's participation in the armed forces is as crucial today as is her active participation in all the other spheres of society. There may be certain operational issues in employing women in combat roles. Hopefully, in the years to come, the defence system will be more technologically advanced and battles will increasingly depend on technology, rather than mere muscle power. It is also hoped that the physical and psychological differences between men and women will be taken into consideration in future training and functional environments to include women in combat roles. The Government should rely on generals and not on activists in deciding whether women could be assigned combat roles in the armed forces.

20. "Meet the country's first women fighter pilots", *The Times of India*, June 18, 2016 at https://m.timesofindia.com/Meet-country-first-women-fighter-pilots/listshow/52805557.cms (Accessed on September 18, 2018).
21. "Permanent Commission to Women", March 5, 2019, Press Release, Press Information Bureau, Ministry of Defence at http://pib.nic.in/newsite/pmreleases.aspx?mincode=33 (Accessed on March 9, 2019).
22. "Union Home Minister reviews security scenario in J&K at a high-level meeting in Srinagar on February 15, 2019", PIB Press Release at http://pib.nic.in/PressReleseDetail.aspx?PRID=1564834 (Accessed on March 11, 2019).
23. "Statement by Foreign Secretary on 26 February 2019 on the Strike on JeM training camp at Balakot", at https://www.mea.gov.in/media-briefings.htm?dtl/31090/Statement_by_Foreign_Secretary_on_26_February_2019_on_the_Strike_on_JeM_training_camp_at_Balakot (Accessed on March 11, 2019).
24. "Statement by Official Spokesperson of Ministry of External Affairs", February 27, 2019 at https://www.mea.gov.in/media-briefings.htm?dtl/31098/Statement_by_Official_Spokesperson_on_27_February_2019 (Accessed on March 11, 2019).
25. "Statements by Indian Armed Forces on Prevailing Security Situation", February 27, 2019 at http://pib.nic.in/newsite/pmreleases.aspx?mincode=33 (Accessed on March 11, 2019).
26. "Nirmala Sitharaman Says She Knows the Identity of Pak Pilot Whose Aircraft was Shot Down by Abhinandan", *India Today*, March 13, 2019 at https://www.indiatoday.in/india/story/pakistan-pilot-abhinandan-nirmala-sitharaman-1476251-2019-03-12, (Accessed on June 14, 2019).
27. PIB Press Release, Press Statement dated March 5, 2019, at http://pib.nic.in/newsite/pmreleases.aspx?mincode=33 (Accessed on March 11, 2019).
28. "DG ISPR Press Conference", February 27, 2019 at https://www.youtube.com/watch?v=EkGeXOiGhBU (Accessed on March 31, 2019).
29. "Statements by Indian Armed Forces on Prevailing Security Situation", February 28, 2019, Press Release, Press Information Bureau, Ministry of Defence at http://pib.nic.in/newsite/pmreleases.aspx?mincode=33 (Accessed on March 9, 2019).
30. DG ISPR Press Conference, no. 28.
31. Rakesh Krishnan Simha, "Cope India: How the IAF rewrote the rules of air combat", *Russia Beyond*, February 16, 2014 at https://www.rbth.com/blogs/2014/02/16/cope_india_how_the_iaf_rewrote_the_rules_of_air_combat_33111 (Accessed on March 30, 2019).
32. Is Jammu and Kashmir turning into a new generation Kurukshetra? As per Indian epic *Mahabharat,* Kurukshetra was the scene of the final battle between two sides of the same Kuru family viz., Kauravas (sons of

Dhritarashtra) and Pandavas (sons of Pandu). Two of the best archers of the time Karna and Arjuna, though sons of the same mother, were fighting from the opposing sides. Karna, the elder and more competent archer, but with an immoral side, died in the battle after losing to Arjun. That led to the eventual defeat for the Kauravas.

33. Lt. Gen. David A. Deptula, "Interdependent Warfare: Combined Effects Power in the 21st Century", Mitchell Institute Policy Papers, 10, March 2018.

10. Gravy Check: Economics of Combat Aviation

States' spend on defence is based on their strategic goals and the capabilities required to achieve them in the prevailing and emerging security scenario. After the First World War and then again after the Second World War, the world order changed and the world map was redrawn. The last shots fired in the Second World War were heralding an era of a new arms race. Use of nuclear weapons on Hiroshima and Nagasaki ushered in an age of nuclear weapons. The devastating war had not taught any significant lesson about peace and co-existence to mankind. Competition rather than cooperation was the central theme for survival. Two major military blocs, built based on different ideologies, emerged, led by the US and the erstwhile USSR. A race to stay ahead in terms of the military arsenal led to a large share of resources being diverted into the defence sector. This period also saw significant technological innovations in military and defence technology, especially aviation.

Combat aircraft are technology-dependent and need a long gestation time for maturity. As the field of combat aviation is just about a century old, the rate of success of ventures in this arena is low and needs a large financial outlay for associated research and development. This is where the key stakeholders face a dilemma. How much investment is adequate? Should a project be aided by additional allotment of resources or foreclosed to cut losses? Additionally, the classical guns versus butter debate or the basic demand and supply cycle are critical issues. Then, there are competing sectors within the armed forces trying to garner financial resources from a finite pie. At the end of it all, a lot of things boil down to plain economics. An assessment of the scale of resources can be gauged from the fact that an entity like the Indian Air Force of about 1,10,000 personnel signed contracts of capital acquisition with a total value of over Rs 95,000 crores between 2012-13 and 2017-18.[1]

This chapter focuses on the financial aspect of combat aviation. Before going specifically into details about combat aircraft, it will be pertinent to look at the big picture of defence-related expenditure and the data about arms trade in the last five decades. Thereafter, the next section covers the costing methodology for combat aircraft with specific reference to the Life Cycle Cost (LCC) methodology. Although this process has been tested by many states, it was adopted by India for the first time in the now-scrapped Medium Multi-Role Combat Aircraft (MMRCA) acquisition proposal. As per the Indian Auditors, the model used for calculating the life-cycle cost of acquisitions had several deficiencies and needs to be fine-tuned and improved further.[2] It indeed is difficult to reach a reasonable and accurate assessment of the cost of owning and operating a combat aircraft.

The Big Picture

After the Second World War, the geography was reshaping. One end of the spectrum had an intense cold war between two military blocs and on the other, newly-formed states were emerging from the shadows of colonialism. The levels of aspirations varied; so did the resources that were available. The major lesson from the Second World War was that military power is essential to survive. A race for potent weapons began, to ensure relevance. This needed resources and almost across the spectrum, in the guns versus butter debate, a significant share was being diverted to the military hardware – more out of compulsion than desire – to keep pace with the armoury of likely adversaries. Defence expenditure figures from 1968 indicate that the world collectively spent 5.6 per cent of the total Gross Domestic Product (GDP) on defence (see Figure 10.1). Europe, the centre of both World Wars was re-militarising. Conflicts in Asia, and specifically in Korea and Vietnam in the East and South Asia, had forced states to spend substantial resources on the military. However, the share of military expenditure as part of GDP has declined continuously since then, barring a minor peak in the 1980s. It was only in 1991, that the world's defence expenditure came below three per cent of the GDP. Today, the defence sector with 2.2 per cent of the world GDP, retains a significant share in the world economy and trade. During this period, the economic activity in the world also spurted and moved from US $ 2,440,686 million in 1968 to US $ 80,737,567 million in 2017 at the current valuation for US dollars.[3] This is a rise of over 33 times in the fifty years.

Figure 10.1: World Defence Expenditure as the percentage of Gross Domestic Production

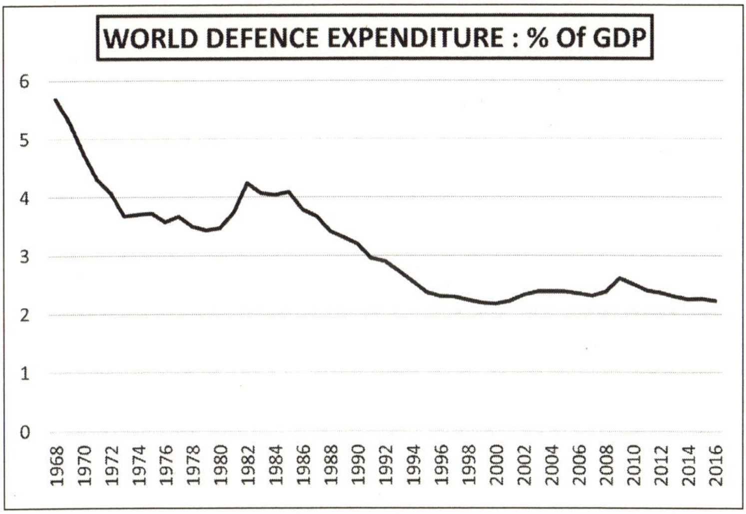

Source: Based on the World Bank Data from 1968 - 2018.[4]

In absolute terms, there has been an increase in defence expenditure in the last five decades. However, the growth in defence expenditure is lower than the GDP growth, and this has led to a continuous reduction in its share. There may be three major reasons for the decline in defence-related expenditure as the percentage of GDP:

- The first is the definition of defence expenditure. International financial institutions lay out strict guidelines for defence expenditure before sanctioning financial assistance to various states. This has led the states to redefine their defence expenditure by removing certain components like pensions, medicare and infrastructure expenditure associated with the armed forces or creating paramilitary forces outside the purview of the Ministry or Department of Defence.

- Secondly, while the trend is indicative of reduced competition amongst states, what is missing from the data set is the resources utilised by the non-state actors. Funding for non-state actors and other means of hybrid war are not accounted for directly as defence-related expenditure. In case such details are added, the annual world defence-related expenditure will be higher than the current assessment of 2.2 per cent of the GDP.
- Lastly, technology has played a major role in cutting the costs of the kinetic tools and bringing in a plethora of non-kinetic tools at very low costs to achieve the strategic objectives without a force-on-force attrition conflict. Technology and trade denial sanctions are being used frequently to achieve geopolitical objectives. This has helped in scaling down the share of defence expenditure the world over.

As the money bag for defence is finite and shrinking in real terms, its impact is visible on the high-value combat assets namely, aircraft carriers and combat aircraft. Not outrightly denying the new acquisitions to the armed forces to meet the threats and challenges, the governments all over the world are resorting to the second-best option – delay. This, in the hope that the economy will grow at a fast pace, making more resources available for defence and in the interim period non-military means are utilised to minimise risks. An associated hope is that the security environment will improve and the necessity to acquire expensive military capability will diminish if not altogether disappear. But this has not happened universally. As depicted in Figure 10.2, 19 countries that possess and operate more than 200 combat aircraft today, are still spending over 3.14 per cent of their collective GDP on defence. It must be remembered that besides combat aviation, there are multiple claimants to the share in the defence budgetary pie. These include demands for aircraft carriers, submarines and tanks at the high-end of the spectrum to the large number required for relatively low-cost capital equipment like weapons for the infantry. So, overall, the race at the top continues, albeit at a slower pace.

Acquisition and operational sustenance of combat aircraft are resource-intensive. As the overall defence expenditure diminishes, the combat aircraft inventory is expected to shrink. But one aspect that is evident from Figure 10.3 is that combat aircraft inventory lags behind in defence expenditure by about two decades. This relationship seems better defined in the countries with a current inventory of more than 200 combat aircraft as seen in Figure 10.4. This is because combat aircraft are manufactured only on the placement of a firm order and can rarely be bought off the shelf. Once the process of acquisition is set in motion, initial manufacturing and delivery of the first aircraft takes about 18-36 months and thereafter the delivery stabilises to one to three aircraft per month per assembly line. The manufacturing rate is based on the complexity of the process and availability of raw material and technical expertise.

Figure 10.2: World Defence Expenditure as the percentage of Gross Domestic Production

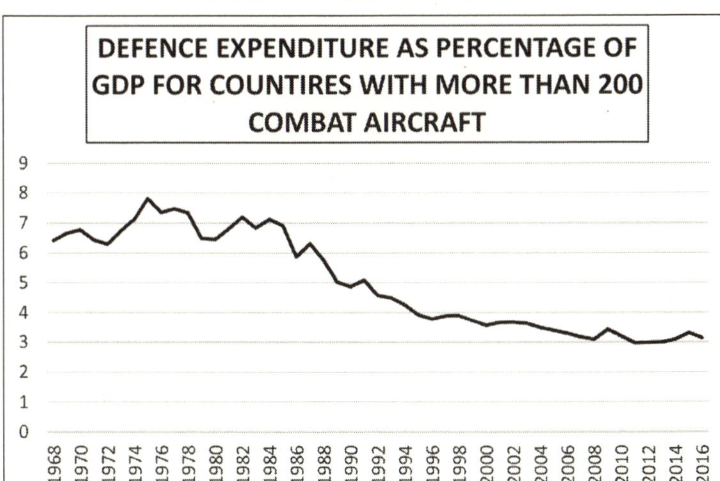

Source: Based on World Bank Data.[5]

Figure 10.3: World Defence Expenditure as the percentage of Gross Domestic Production and number of Combat Aircraft in the World.

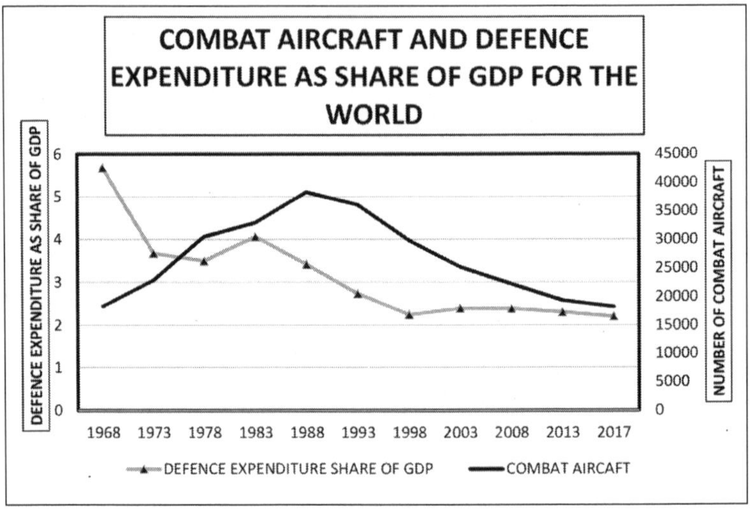

Source: Based on CAIDB and World Bank Data.[6]

Figure 10.4: World Defence Expenditure as the percentage of Gross Domestic Production and Number of Combat Aircraft in 19 Countries with more than 200 Combat Aircraft in 2018

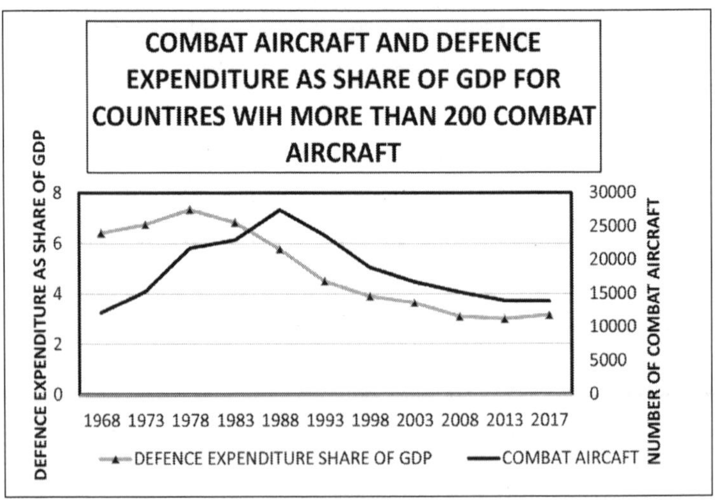

Source: Based on CAIDB and World Bank Data.[7]

A reduction in the defence expenditure translates into a lower combat aircraft inventory. In 1992, after the collapse of the Soviet Union, the Russian government reduced its defence orders by 70 per cent.[8] Even if the trend is reversed and the defence expenditure is enhanced, its impact on the combat aircraft inventory will be felt only after a gap of two decades. That is primarily because of a very long gestation time for design and development for the manufacturers and for the buyers, the timeline required to make payments after generally a very long processing time to finalise the product to be bought. From the time a process was initiated by the IAF to procure an additional 126 combat aircraft in 2000, the contract was finally signed for only 36 aircraft in 2016 and the delivery is expected to be over by 2022– the entire process culminating after nearly a quarter of a century since it was first initiated.[9]

The increase in defence expenditure from the current level of 2.2 per cent of the GDP to tackle current or emerging threats, is unlikely to stabilize the combat aircraft inventory at current levels. Going by the worldwide trend in the defence expenditure, in general, and for the top 19 countries with more than 200 combat aircraft in particular, the world combat aircraft inventory is expected to go down below 10,000 in the next two decades. However, the 2014 pledge by NATO members to increase their defence spending up to 2 per cent of their GDPs within ten years, has seen some traction. On June 28, 2018, the French parliament adopted a bill on military planning for 2019-2025, envisaging the increase of defence spending of up to 2 per cent of the country's GDP, which means that French military expenses should reach 295 billion Euros by 2025. But the focus could be on information rather than means of combat. This was apparent with France planning to spend 3.6 billion Euros (over $4 billion) for renewal of military satellites so that France could "just know who approaches" as per the French Defence Minister Florence Parly during her interview on the French radio station Europe 1 on September 9, 2018.[10]

Global weapons and combat equipment manufacturing have a very limited base but its users are spread evenly across the globe. Even though the major manufacturers have robust domestic consumption in this category, the trade in arms and weapons gives a good indication of the outlook for combat equipment. Aircraft accounted for nearly half the global arms trade in 1968 (Figure 10.5). That is because of a very limited number of aircraft manufacturers and a robust global demand. Trade in armoured vehicles was a distant second with only 16 per cent by value. By 1993, the share of aircraft in world trade dipped to 41 per cent (Figure 10.6) but regained to 47 per cent by 2017 (Figure 10.7). In case a holistic assessment is made for the last five decades, it is clear that aircraft with 46 per cent of the world's arms trade constitute the most significant numbers (Figure 10.8). The Soviet aviation industry took a hit on the break up of erstwhile USSR, although Russia inherited 85 per cent of the industry, with 300 research institutions, design bureaus, production associations and series production plants and three million workers. By 1994-95, total production had dropped to 60-70 per cent compared with the levels in the mid-1980s.[11]

Figure 10.5: World Arms Trade in 1968.

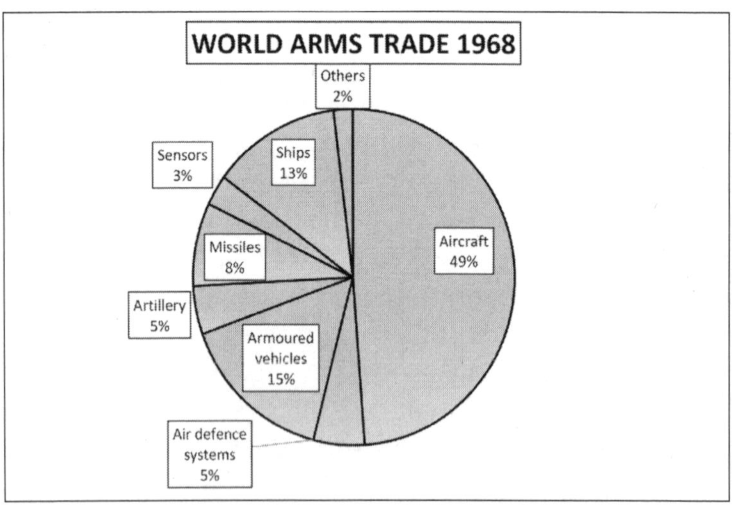

Source: Based on the SIPRI Database.[12]

Figure 10.6: World Arms Trade in 1993

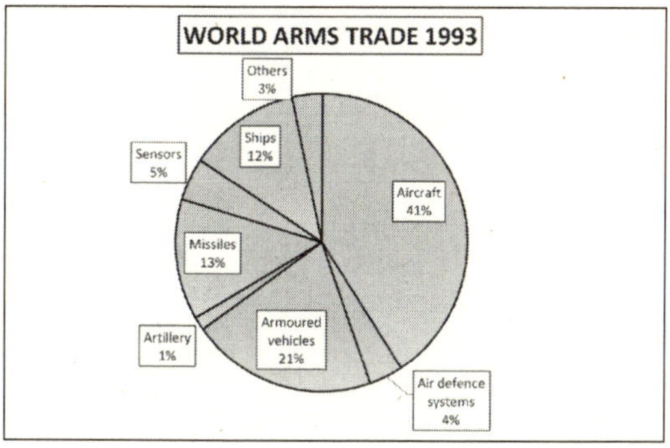

Source: Based on the SIPRI Database.[13]

Figure 10.7: World Arms Trade in 2017

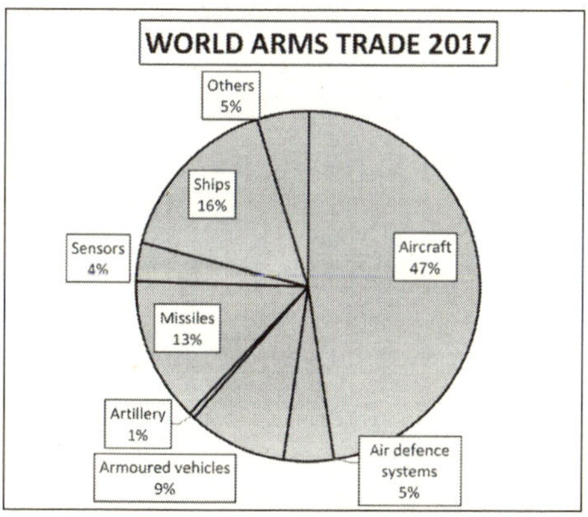

Source: Based on the SIPRI Database.[14]

Figure 10.8: World Arms Trade in 1968-2017

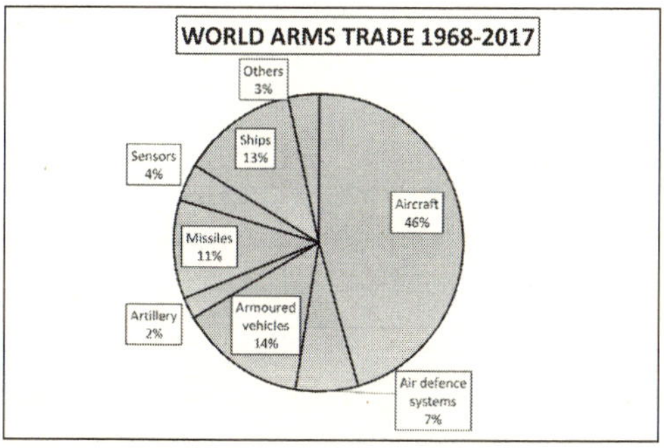

Source: Based on the SIPRI Database.[15]

Figure 10.9: Value of World Arms Trade in 1968-2017

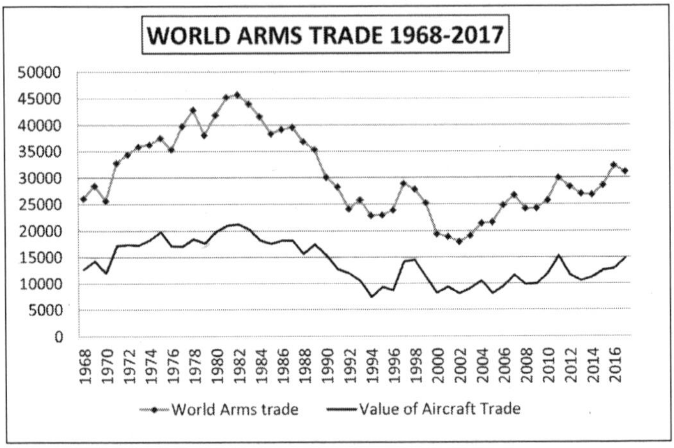

Source: Based on the SIPRI Database.[16]

The overall value of world arms trade gradually and systematically picked up by about the mid-1980s (Figure 10.9). Thereafter, there had been a decline for about two decades before its marginal resurgence. The graph depicting the value of world arms trade in Figure 10.9 moves in spurts. The main reason for such rough edges is that the demand for arms and its supply is a time-consuming process almost everywhere in the world. The contracts for the supply of arms especially with 46 per cent devoted to high ticket items like aircraft are of very high value. These high-value contracts create minor peaks and their absence in the following year(s) creates a trough. But overall, looking at the trend, it is clear that arms trade kept an upward trend during the Cold War era and declined thereafter for almost two decades.

The share of aircraft in the world arms trade has hovered around the midway mark consistently for the past five decades (Figure 10.10). This is indicative of a very small manufacturing base for a large market. Corroborating this trend with the overall combat aircraft inventory the world over, it is clear that the volume of aircraft trade has declined but its value has not followed a similar trend. The cost of combat aircraft has gradually increased along with its combat potential in the last fifty years. This has led to aircraft retaining its share in world arms trade during this period.

Figure 10.10: Share of the Value of Aircraft in World Arms Trade in 1968-2017

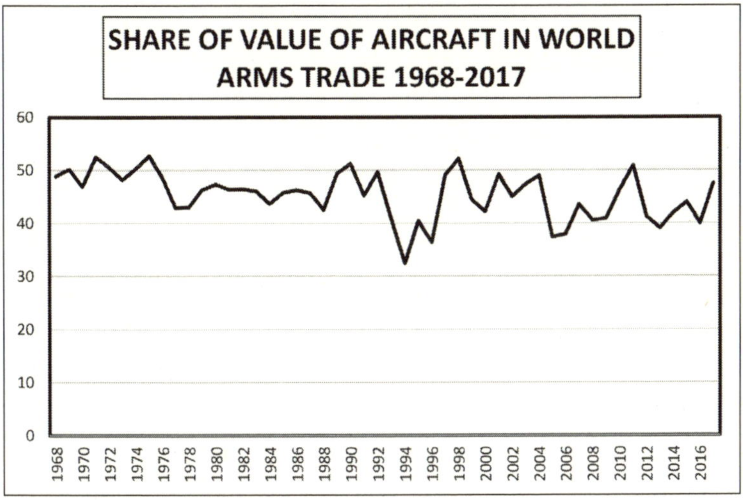

Source: Based on the SIPRI Database.[17]

Figure 10.11: Arms Imports by India in 1968-2017

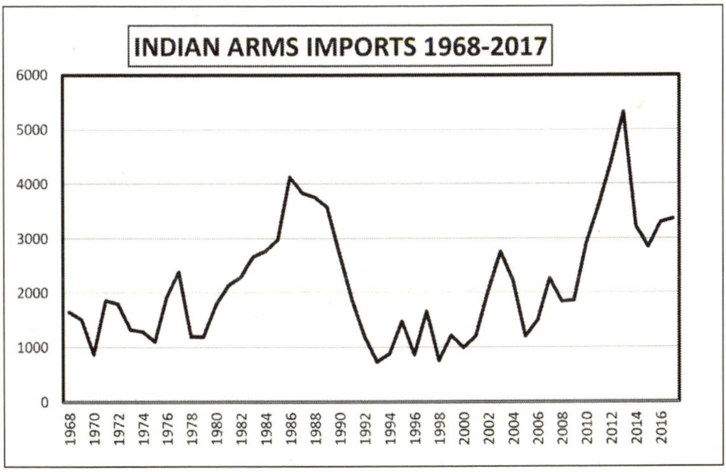

Source: Based on the SIPRI Database.[18]

The arms imports by India in the last five decades as indicated in Figure 10.11 are interesting. Currently, India is a leading importer of arms and spends about Rs 78,000 crores on an average annually on the capital acquisition of a defence system. The share of the Indian Air Force (IAF) is about 40 per cent of the total defence capital acquisition budget. Further, the IAF spends 65 per cent of its total budget on capital acquisitions.[19] While India was growing gradually with a sub-four per cent of the GDP till 1980, the defence budget as also the arms import bill was moderate. But in the 1980s, the arms import bill was increased to re-equip the Indian Armed Forces. It primarily comprised new inductions in terms of combat aircraft (Jaguar, Mirage 2000, MiG-23, MiG-27, MiG-29) and an increase in armoured and artillery units in the Indian Army. But this tempo of upgradation of combat equipment inventory and its simultaneous expansion could not be sustained economically. Combined with a global economic crisis, the Indian economy entered a very difficult phase and was on the verge of defaulting in payment. To tide over an immediate Balance of Payment crisis, 47 tonnes of gold was sent to the Bank of England as collateral for $ 405 million.[20] This economic turmoil took its toll on the defence budget and in particular on induction of new combat equipment. The sharp fall in the defence expenditure at the beginning of the 1990s is a reflection of this state.

Another factor that nearly halted arms imports was the opaque process of arms imports and associated corruption charges. The case of acquisition of Bofors Guns from Sweden became synonymous with corruption and had major fallout in domestic politics. A low phase continued for almost a decade. With the economy gradually picking up and new threats emerging to national security, defence capital acquisition was reprioritized. After a terrorist attack on Parliament followed by a military standoff as *Operation Parakaram*[21] for almost a year, a spurt in arms imports is witnessed at the beginning of 21st century. In terms of combat aircraft, this period saw the induction of the Su30 in the Indian Air Force in large numbers. A major spike in Indian arms imports in the current decade relates to new acquisitions in all three wings of the Indian Armed Forces in large numbers. The most significant acquisition included an aircraft carrier and submarines for the Navy, the replacement of ageing equipment for the army and induction of various force multipliers for the Air Force. The most notable deal for combat aircraft in this period was for 36 Rafale from France, signed in 2016.

Figure 10.12: Indian Share in World Arms Imports 1968-2017

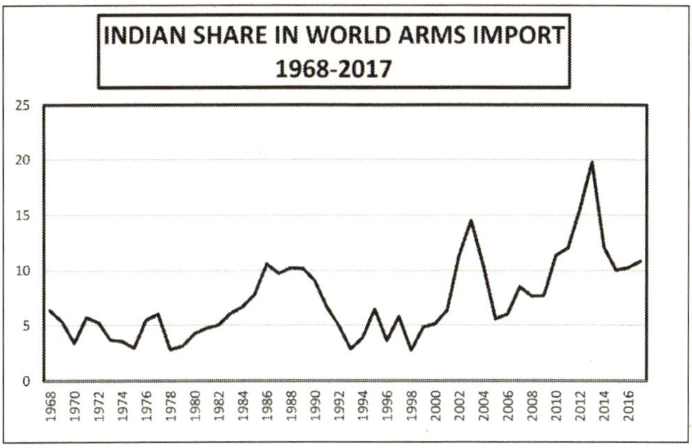

Source: Based on the SIPRI Database.[22]

Figure 10.13: Major Arms Importers 2017

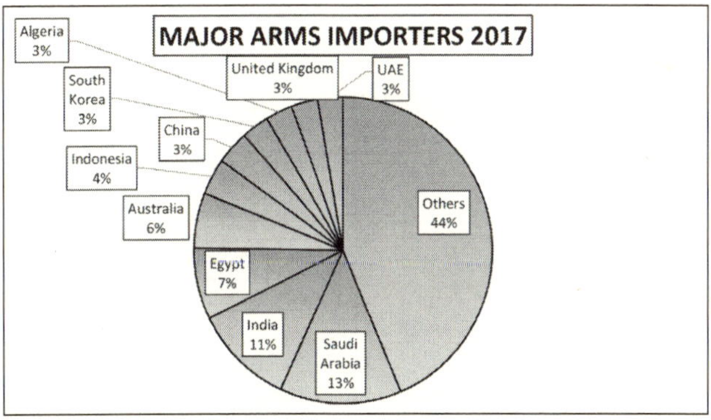

Source: Based on the SIPRI Database.[23]

Figure 10.14: Major Arms Importers 1968-2017

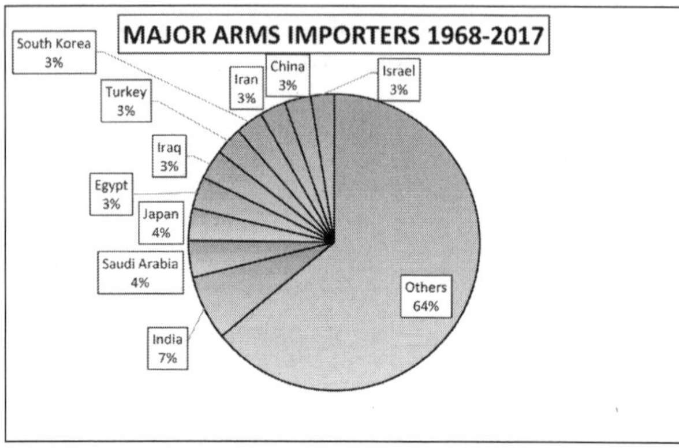

Source: Based on the SIPRI Database.[24]

Presently, Saudi Arabia leads among arms importers, with India as close runners up and Egypt with 7 per cent of the world's arms import at the third place (Figure 10.13). But looking at the last five decades, India wins this race handsomely with 7 per cent of the world's arms imports in the last fifty years (Figure 10.14). Indian arms imports since 1968 are almost double of second-placed Saudi Arabia. With the second-most populous country in the world, it is difficult to say as to who has failed India more in this regard – the policymakers, the policy implementers, or their nexus.

Figure 10.15: Major Arms Exporters 2017

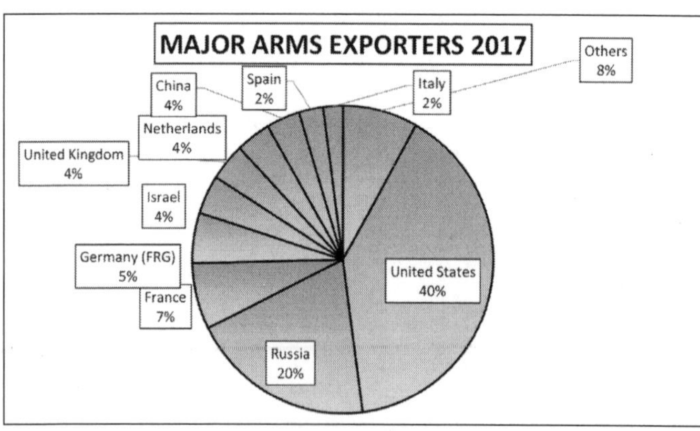

Source: Based on the SIPRI Database.[25]

Figure 10.15 gives a clear picture of current stakeholders in the world's arms trade as exporters. Just three countries– the US, Russia and France – export more than two-thirds of the world's arms. Israel, a small country, has a disproportionately large share of 4 per cent of arms exports. Investments in defence technology, research and development have paid rich dividends in several cases.

Costing Model

An accurate cost estimation of military equipment plays a crucial role in the acquisition strategy. Defining the cost of a combat aircraft is a very complex process. At the beginning of aviation equipment development, the requirement has many unknown factors and the equipment design is uncertain, which means that there is uncertainty about the equipment's cost.[26] However, once the concept is proven, the technology monetisation takes over, to recover the input costs and make a profit.

Traditionally, the L1 model (Bid won by the lowest financial quote) was followed for capital acquisition in India to select the final product amongst those which met the laid down Qualitative Requirements (QR). The acquisition cost of the material and equipment procured was the sole criteria in determining the L1. The equipment costing model followed by the erstwhile USSR and then Russia, led to a low unit price and it was difficult for the non-Russian firms to match that price. So the logic of computing Life Cycle Cost (LCC) to define the L1 came into being in India in the mother of all defence deals for the proposed acquisition of 126 MMRCA. Notwithstanding the reasons for this tectonic policy shift in the bidding process, its merits are obvious. For the computation of LCC1 or the lowest bidder for the life cycle cost of the equipment, it is important to calculate not only the initial acquisition cost but also the sustenance cost for the capability throughout the scheduled life of the equipment. This technique was designed in the early 1960s for procurement purposes in the US Department of Defense.[27] This concept is now becoming a central concern and increasingly being considered in many military procurement processes. [28]

The LCC includes acquisition cost, operations cost, maintenance cost and disposal cost. On average, about two-thirds of the total life cycle cost of a major defence system lies in post-production—in its operation and sustainment over its useful life.[29] The acquisition cost includes the purchase price of the basic equipment along with its required support systems and accessories. The operation costs include the costs associated with the operation of the equipment including consumables and services. Maintenance cost includes the cost associated with both scheduled and unscheduled maintenance. Scheduled maintenance is preventive and is recommended in terms of frequency and type by the manufacturer. Unscheduled maintenance is a result of equipment failure or is used to recover damaged equipment. The maintenance cost includes expenditure related to repairs and stocking of spares. Disposal cost is incurred when equipment is withdrawn from service. [30] The LCC model can assist in estimating the overall costs of equipment and help in decoding the optimal resource utilisation model.[31]This attribute offers a more balanced competition for greater financial efficiency. Even as the optimal methodology for procurement is being debated, the Comptroller and Auditor General of India (CAG) observed that it needs to be considered whether the present 'Lowest Price Technically Acceptable (LPTA)' method of bid evaluation – wherein the contract is awarded to the lowest priced offer which is technically acceptable – is suitable for all procurements. For procuring highly technical products, the use of the Best Value method or a "Quality-cum-Cost" assessment, may yield better value for money.[32]

Ageing assets experience a decline in value and productivity over several years of use. Normally, Russian combat aircraft have a scheduled calendar life of 25 years as compared to 40 years of combat aircraft manufactured by some other countries. In fact, in some cases, the calendar life is not specified, leading to possible utilization of the combat aircraft without any restriction till completion of its Total Technical Life (TTL). It is assessed that for military aircraft the maintenance and repair expenditure is primarily for field maintenance (47 per cent), airframe (20 per cent), engines (17 per cent) and components (16 per cent).[33] Some examples of various aircraft are indicative of this process and relative costs. The Canadian Arcturus fleet had approximately $2.2 million as the initial operational and maintenance cost of the aircraft. With ageing, this cost increased at a rate of 3.6 per cent per annum.[34] If that rule were to hold, with a charge of roughly $79.0 billion to buy the F-22, the sustainment costs could be roughly $160.0 billion. Moreover, under its `structures retrofit program', over the next few years, the United States Air Force will need more than $100.0 million to retrofit the F-22 fleet just to ensure these aircraft can fly for the full 8,000 hours for which they were designed.[35] A very high operational cost per flying hour of F-22 in USAF in the period 2008-12 in Figure 10.16 is indicative of this resource-sapping platform. The F-35 has projected sustainment costs of over $1 trillion over a 60-year life cycle.[36] Figure 10.16 also indicates that the operation cost of a certain class of unmanned aircraft systems is much higher than that of manned aircraft, clarifying a myth about operational costs.

Figure 10.16: Operational Cost per Flying Hour (in US $) for the United States Air Force from 2008-2012

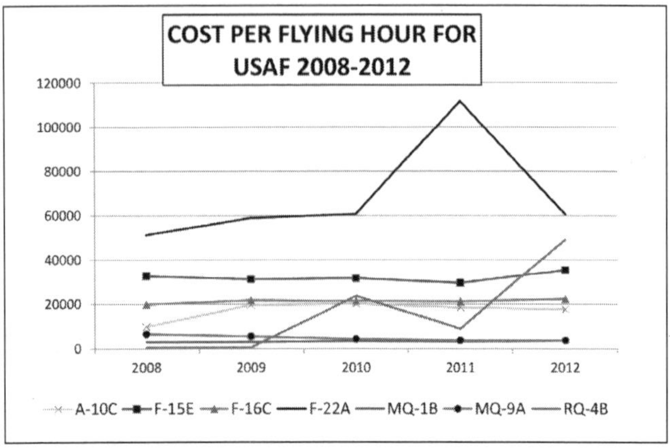

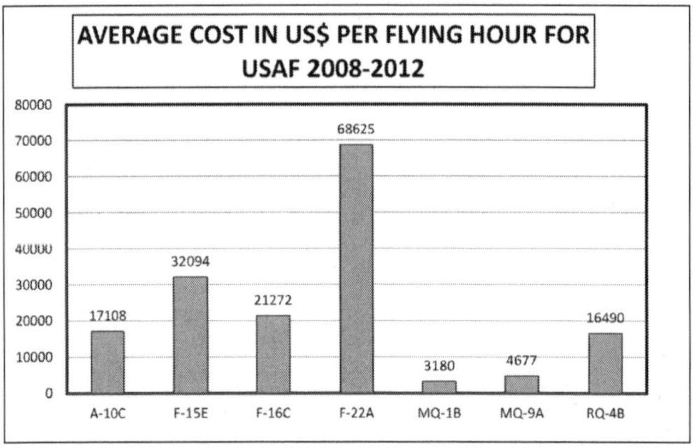

Source: Based on data from *Time* Magazine.[37]

Determination of Total Life Cycle Cost- MMRCA Project

As has been enumerated above, for the first time, the concept of Life Cycle Cost was introduced in Indian defence procurements for the 126 MMRCA project. The RFP required the price bid to be submitted for the Life Cycle Cost of the aircraft and stated that the total life cycle cost would be the criteria for identifying the lowest bidder (L1). The price bid was required to give the detailed cost break-up of all the seven components, M1 to M7.[38]

- M 1 – Direct cost of acquisition, i.e., cost of flyaway aircraft, cost of kits for license production, cost of infrastructure for manufacturing, cost of infrastructure for Intermediate and Depot-level maintenance, cost of maintenance equipment for aircraft, operational and maintenance cost of weapon, cost of training aids and cost of documentation and initial training of pilots and technicians.

- M 2 – Cost of Total Technical Life (TTL) based Reserves– the cost of all spares required to be held during the life of aircraft for the prescribed scheduled maintenance, including overhaul.
- M 3 – Cost of Time Between Overhaul (TBO) and Mean Time Between Failures (MTBF)-based Reserves.
- M 4 – Cost of Scheduled Intermediate-Level maintenance.
- M 5 – Cost of Depot-Level Overhaul and maintenance.
- M 6 – Operating Cost – Cost of flying the aircraft.
- M7– Cost of Transfer of Technology – Transfer of Technology fees, technical assistance, training.

In an ideal scenario, the method worked out in the RFP would lead to the selection of the product based on the best Life Cycle Cost. However, in case the same objectivity is not observed in the follow-up process, this can lead to unacceptable deviations as happened in the MMRCA case. Commercial Bids of M/s Dassault Aviation (DA) and M/s EADS were opened in November 2011 and the contract negotiations in January 2012, recommended M/s DA as the lowest bidder based on Life Cycle Costing,[39] although M/s DA did not submit its price bid in the format prescribed by the RFP which contained a detailed cost breakup of the seven cost elements prescribed in the RFP, which were crucial for price evaluation.[40] The firm had instead disclosed its price in two parts – Price of Direct flyaway aircraft and price of ToT.[41] M/s EADS, on the other hand, had submitted its price bid in conformity to the prescribed RFP format, giving the detailed cost breakup of the seven elements.[42] This created difficulty in comparing the prices of the two firms. In the absence of a complete cost breakup of the seven components for the price bid of M/s DA, the price evaluation L1 sub-committee derived the price of these components with whatever information was available in the bid.[43] The independent validation of these costs regarding the Total Technical Life (TTL), Time Between Overhaul (TBO) and Mean Time Between Failure (MTBF) data given by the vendor in their technical proposal, was not possible.[44] The price bid for M1 M/s DA did not quote for the capital expenditure for setting up the licensed production of the aircraft. It had stated that the price would be provided later. The L1 sub-committee, while comparing the prices took this price as nil while calculating M1 for the Rafale aircraft. But capital expenditure for production was included in the price bid of M/s EADS.[45] So practically, the execution was flawed in terms of a good systematic construct.

Is the LCC model an ideal methodology to select a combat aircraft? As with any methodology, it has both advantages and disadvantages. The LCC model offers an optimum cost-benefit matrix to choose a system among various valid competitors that, over a specified period, will allow specific capability at the least cost. In that sense, it offers an optimal solution in comparing combat aircraft suitable for procurement. A major drawback of this system is that it does not account for the cost of induction of a new system in the operational, maintenance, logistical and human resource environment. To understand this nuanced aspect of costing, a planned procurement of a combat aircraft needs to factor-in the operationalization cost of the system.

The induction of a new combat aircraft results in capability enhancement owing to additional numbers and associated operational performance. For example, the induction of the Rafale, after the signature of the contract in 2016, commenced in October 2019 in the Indian Air Force. The aircraft are expected in India by Mid 2020. This will have a major impact on a large spectrum of air operations owing to its capability in both air defence and ground attack roles. Induction of a new platform necessitates several other changes in an organization to ensure its optimal absorption. Each complex system like a combat aircraft sourced from a foreign Original Equipment Manufacturer (OEM) leads to induction of associated Ground Handling Equipment (GHE), Ground Support Equipment (GSE), associated weapons, maintenance facilities, logistical chain and training facilities for various sections of human resources. A considerable amount of time, effort and resources are required for the integration of the newly-inducted system into an operational environment in terms of communication, data linkages, and data transfer. These physical changes have a price. For ease of reference, let the costs associated with the induction of a new system be called System Induction Costs (SIC). The SIC will include all components of LCC associated with the new system.

A typical example of SIC is associated with the induction of the large-sized Su-30 in the IAF. Before its induction, all combat aircraft of the IAF, except for bomber Canberra, were with the wing-span of fewer than 14 metres and a proportionate length of the order of 17 metres and a height of 5 metres. The blast pens and Hardened Aircraft Shelters (HAS) to host these aircraft, were designed accordingly. The induction of the Su-30 changed that. Barring a handful, all existing blast pens and HAS were unsuitable to accommodate a Su-30. This made the aircraft very vulnerable while on the ground. An unprotected Su-30 on the ground could easily be damaged and their large surface area that was exposed necessitated a low volume of attack by an invader. As a result, many HAS suitable to accommodate the Su-30 were created, or the existing ones modified. All this is a SIC that is rarely accounted for in the overall economic matrix of a system. This expenditure can be justified as the operational capability of the Su-30 which was much higher than the prevailing IAF combat fleet's inventory. However, this may not always be the case.

An important component of the SIC will be the support a new system needs from force-multipliers. The adoption of the new system in the data linkage planned for transmission and reception of operational information for battle space transparency and force employment will be a necessity. Modification would be required in the communication, mission computer, display systems and maybe the antenna configuration. Alternatively or additionally, one of the external store-carrying stations may be permanently employed to carry an external pod for the requisite data link subsystem. This will effectively reduce the weapon-carrying capacity of the new platform.

This is a small price to pay in case the overall operational capability is likely to transform by multiple notches through the induction of the new system. However, this needs to be factored-in as SIC while comparing various options for induction.

In other fields of force-multipliers, the equation is lopsided in favour of existing systems. This is the arena of Flight Refuelling Systems. Primarily, there are two types of operations in the world for combat aircraft – Probe and Drogue systems and Boom and Socket System, as explained in Chapter 7. The Indian Air Force currently employs the Probe and Drogue system and accordingly, all combat aircraft and the newly-inducted AEW&C aircraft are compatible with an existing inventory of the Flight Refuelling Aircraft (FRA) fleet of the IL-78.

Now, should an aircraft be inducted that uses Boom and Socket methodology, there are three distinct scenarios: First, the in-flight refuelling capability is not utilised on the newly-inducted system. This will impose a severe operational restriction on employment of the new systems and a large portion of its capabilities would remain under-utilized. This will primarily defeat the very purpose for which a new system is considered for induction, that is, to boost existing operational capability. In the second scenario, a new set of FRA aircraft is inducted to support the newly-inducted combat aircraft. The overall package cost will make such a proposition economically unviable for a defined degree of enhancement in the operational capability. In the third scenario, modifying the existing fleet of FRA for dual usage by Probe and Drogue on the outstations and Boom and Socket on the central station, although technically feasible, will add to the overall SIC in terms of economics. While at this juncture, IAF is looking to augment its small single type of FRA, the case has been pending for almost a decade without fructification.[46] Should a system with only a Probe and Drogue fuel dispenser system be finally selected, the SIC for boom and socket type of combat aircraft will turn out to be very high. In case a dual-method fuel dissension system is selected, i.e., with Probe and drogue as well as boom and socket, then a significant part of this newly-added capability will remain unutilized as the IAF does not have any receiver with boom and socket at present. Action in this regard in anticipation of possible induction of a combat aircraft with boom and socket, will always be viewed with suspicion to favour a specific vendor of combat aircraft. It is a case of the Hobson's choice.

Another crucial aspect is the integration of new combat aircraft with an existing or planned inventory of weapons. With very negligible indigenous capability to manufacture precision weapons, India imports most of its specialist weapons. Integration of a weapon system imported from country A with an aircraft imported from country B requires a huge amount of effort and cost in generating protocols and communication systems that will make the process of weapon launch safe and efficient. The costs associated with such an operational integration are not a part of the LCC calculus. Another operational aspect that adds to the SIC relates to the flexibility of operation, a key element of airpower. Combat aircraft are deployed in various places as per operational plans for operational tasks assigned to them. These may or may not be their peacetime bases. This entails that the GHE/GSE and weapons specifically for the combat aircraft are moved to the operating base or are additionally procured and pre-positioned there. Both approaches have inherent costs and form part of the SIC.

One aspect is fixing the price for current procurement and the other is related to financial outlays for cost-escalation. This is significant as the entire procurement process till delivery of the last item contracted for takes many years, and in the case of combat aircraft, this could stretch to over a decade. Therefore, there is a need for adopting a transparent price escalation/variation method.[47] Defence procurements, especially in India, have been marred by controversies and undue delays. The entire process proceeds at a very slow pace even for procurement of non-complex products like the Doppler Weather Radar. While the Ministry of Defence (MoD) took eight years to conclude the contract, the same radar was procured by the Indian Meteorological Department in just nine months.[48] The MoD took eight months for contract negotiation which was completed in one month by the Indian Meteorological Department.[49] So much about efficiency in the procurement process in the Indian Ministry of Defence!

In overall terms, it is sub-optimal to induct a system with high System Induction Costs without an increase in operational capability over the prevalent inventory. All aspects of LCC and SIC need to be considered while computing the overall cost of the project to induct a new system for the armed forces. The CAG has recommended that the MoD may consider adopting the Best Value method of bid evaluation (both Technical and price) based on a quantitative assessment matrix to ensure value for money in acquisitions.[50] And this needs to factor-in the SIC too. In the end, only one objective question needs to be answered – Is the new system giving optimal 'bang for the buck'? To clearly understand this aspect in the larger context of military expenditure, there a case study of military expenditure in Africa with specific examples of two African nations – Nigeria and Botswana. These two countries, to mitigate their security threats, have distinct approaches towards combat aviation and this may be indicative of their aspirations in the region. The lessons from this can also – with relevant modification – be extrapolated to the larger picture of state aspiration linked to military capability. This case study of Africa with Botswanian and Nigerian subsets is placed at Annexure 7.

Gestalt

Governments all over the world can allocate only finite resources for their armed forces. It is incumbent on the armed forces to assess the operational environment realistically and then draw out an appropriate equipment procurement strategy. To acquire the right product at the right price, it is essential that the qualitative requirements truly reflect the user's functional need; maximum possible competition is generated, and technical and price evaluation is done objectively.[51]Assets to tackle the existing security challenges must be provided for and only thereafter should the capabilities for tackling future threats be built up. Many debates are on about the usefulness or otherwise of spending a large amount especially by a developing country on building a military capability that may never have to be used. But building military capability is a time-consuming process. It is better to gradually build the national capability to face likely threats, so that the nation is ready when the need arises.

Notes

1. *Performance Audit Report of the Comptroller and Auditor General of India on Capital Acquisition in Indian Air Force for the Union Government (Defence Services),* Air Force Report No. 3 of 2019 tabled on the floor of the Parliament on February 13, 2019, p. iii.
2. Ibid., p. v.
3. As per World Bank Data available at https://data.worldbank.org/indicator/NY.GDP.MKTP.CD?end=2017&locations=US-1W&name_desc=false&start=1961 (Accessed on March 22, 2019).
4. World Bank Data available at http://databank.worldbank.org/data/reports.aspx?source=2&series=MS.MIL.XPND.GD.ZS&country=# (Accessed on February 13, 2018).
5. Ibid.
6. Ibid.
7. Ibid.
8. John T. Greenwood, "The Aviation Industry, 1917-97", in Robin Hingham, John T. Greenwood and Von Hardesty (Eds.), *Russian Aviation and Air Power in the Twentieth Century*, Frank Cass Publishers, Great Britain, 1998, p.153.
9. NDTV News, "First Rafale Fighter Arrives In India By September": Nirmala Sitharaman, January 4, 2019, at www.ndtv.com/india-news/nirmala-sitharaman-says-first-rafale-fighter-jet-will-arrives-in-india-by-september-1972625 (Accessed on March 30, 2019).
10. Sputnik News, September 9, 2018, "France to Spend Over $4 billon on Military Satellites Renewal -- Defense Minister"at https://www.globalsecurity.org/wmd/library/news/france/france-180909-sputnik01.htm?_m=3n%252e002a%252e2380%252eju0ao0d60s%252e26w1 (Accessed on September 10, 2018).
11. John T Greenwood, no. 8.
12. "SIPRI Database" at http://armstrade.sipri.org/armstrade/page/values.php ((Accessed on August 1, 2018).
13. Ibid.
14. Ibid.
15. Ibid.
16. Ibid.

17. Ibid.
18. Ibid.
19. "Performance Audit Report of the Comptroller and Auditor General of India on Capital Acquisition in Indian Air Force for the Union Government (Defence Services)", no. 1, p. 1.
20. Gayatri Nayak, "When 47 tonnes of gold was in the middle of the road", *The Economics Times*, July 5, 2017, at https://economictimes.indiatimes.com/news/economy/finance/when-47-tonnes-of-gold-was-in-the-middle-of-road/articleshow/59447917.cms (Accessed on March 22, 2019).
21. Brig. Gurmeet Kanwal, "Lost opportunities in Operation Parakram", *Indian Defence Review*, December 13, 2011 at http://www.indiandefencereview.com/spotlights/lost-opportunities-in-operation-parakram/ (Accessed on March 22, 2019).
22. "SIPRI Database", no. 12.
23. Ibid.
24. Ibid.
25. Ibid.
26. Huang Zhaodong, Luo Rongxuan, Jin Jing, "Development and Production Costs Estimating for Aviation Equipment Based on Uncertainty Design", *Procedia Engineering*, 99, 2015, pp. 143-149 at https://www.sciencedirect.com/science/article/pii/S1877705814036327 (Accessed on October 9, 2018).
27. Abder Rahmane Sokri, "Life Cycle Costing of Military Equipment", Paper No. 45, Proceedings of the International Conference on Control, Dynamic Systems, and Robotics, Ottawa, Ontario, Canada, May 15-16 2014 at https://pdfs.semanticscholar.org/e28e/a1db8770fcc2c96a0f80905781f1ca5ed555.pdf (Accessed on October 10, 2018).
28. Ibid.
29. Jeremiah Gertler, "Air Force F-22 Fighter Program", *Congressional Research Service Report 7-5700, L31673* dated July 11, 2013.
30. Abder Rahmane Sokri, no. 27.
31. Ibid.
32. "Performance Audit Report of the Comptroller and Auditor General of India on Capital Acquisition in Indian Air Force for the Union Government (Defence Services)", no, 1, p.vi.
33. "Aerospace Industry Report 2013", Aerospace Industries Association of America and the Center of Aviation & Aerospace Leadership, Embry-Riddle Aeronautical University at http://www.aia-aerospace.org/wp-content/uploads/2016/09/AIR-2012-Book.pdf (Accessed on October 9, 2018).
34. Abder Rahmane Sokri no. 27.

35. Jeremiah Gertler, no. 29.
36. "United States Government Accountability Office Report GAO-19-120T on Air Force Readiness Actions Needed to Rebuild Readiness and Prepare for the Future", October 10, 2018, at https://www.armed-services.senate.gov/imo/media/doc/Pendleton_10-10-18.pdf (Accessed on October 12, 2018).
37. Data extracted from a link on Mark Thompson, "Costly Flight Hours", *Time Magazine.com*, April 02, 2013 at http://nation.time.com/2013/04/02/costly-flight-hours/ (Accessed on August 9, 2018).
38. "Performance Audit Report of the Comptroller and Auditor General of India on Capital Acquisition in Indian Air Force for the Union Government (Defence Services)", no. 1, pp.121-122.
39. Ibid.
40. Ibid.
41. Ibid.
42. Ibid.
43. Ibid.
44. Ibid.
45. Ibid.
46. Shaurya Karanbir Gurung, "IAF starts the process for procuring six tanker aircraft", *The Economic Times*, January 25, 2018 at https://economictimes.indiatimes.com/news/defence/iaf-starts-process-for-procuring-six-tanker-aircraft/articleshow/62654532.cms (Accessed on March 30, 2019).
47. "Performance Audit Report of the Comptroller and Auditor General of India on Capital Acquisition in Indian Air Force for the Union Government (Defence Services)", no. 1, p. 23.
48. Ibid., p. 26.
49. Ibid.
50. Ibid., p. 25.
51. Ibid., p. v.

11. Frontal Scan: Emerging Contours in the Field of Combat Aviation

Technology plays a major role in the development of military capability. The pace of technology development in combat aviation and its associated cost will be a key factor in defining the battle space of tomorrow. Several hybrid tools will be in action and technology will play a significant role in that too. Most probably, the individuals will be targeted with kinetic weapons and institutions will be targeted by non-kinetic means. Large-scale use of kinetic weapons will be rare. It is unlikely that a weapon like GBU 43/B Massive Ordnance Air Blast[1] will have any operational relevance. Development and employment of Directed Energy Weapons (DEW) in battle space will gain traction and be used even in space for defensive and offensive purposes.[2] Economics and military capabilities are intertwined with technology. This may change future conflicts to a technological contest, though the history of warfare advances in technology that provided significant new capabilities, have played a key role in determining the combat outcome. Yet, technology advances alone cannot lead to military success. Success depended on how new technologies made key capabilities possible. The ability to modify or even develop new doctrines to exploit new capabilities led to success.[3] In this ever-changing technological landscape, the role of manned combat aircraft will be redefined and so will be its inventory. Emphasising the role of new technology on warfare, the UK's Chief of the General Staff, General Mark Carleton-Smith, aptly summarised:-

> "We need a more proactive, threat-based approach to our capability planning, including placing some big bets on those technologies

that we judge may offer an exponential advantage because given the pace of the race, to fall behind today is to cede an almost unquantifiable advantage from which it might be impossible to recover".[4]

The combat aircraft inventory pattern the world over has changed. The major reasons were the end of the Cold War and the disintegration of erstwhile USSR along with an economic slowdown leading to major cuts in military spending on high-value assets like combat aircraft. This was further pushed by the technological revolution in computing and weaponry, leading to an expansion of combat engagement zones of combat aircraft with greater ranges and better accuracy. The combat potential per platform increased, thus necessitating fewer numbers to perform the same task. One of the major outcomes of the first Gulf War (1990-91) was that militaries started giving greater weightage to quality at the cost of quantity. The older generation combat aircraft were replaced by newer generation aircraft and with fewer numbers. However, in case the aspirations are to enhance the area under influence, then greater numbers will be required to cover the larger area. The interplay between the level of aspiration and the technological capability of combat aircraft will determine the combat aircraft inventory in future. Will there be surprises in aerial combat with the induction of new technology? Comparing the processes involved in designing and developing a new combat platform for the Western world and the then Soviet (and now Russian) aircraft industry, Bill Sweetman had summarised [5]:-

> The time taken to bring a new aircraft into large scale service is considerable, in both cases and this should reduce the risk of surprise. The laws of aerodynamics and the principles of aircraft design are a constant, and given the approximate size and shape of a prototype aircraft– data that a satellite can acquire accurately– an analyst can guess, with reasonable confidence, what that aircraft will be capable of doing and what its mission is most likely to be.

However, much has changed concerning dependencies on aerodynamics and shape and size of the combat aircraft for combat capability. The focus has shifted to sensors and integrated weapons. While basic flying parameters in terms of altitude, speed and range do matter, these have been relegated to secondary status. With battle space expansion in hybrid conflicts, battle space transparency has gained pre-eminence. Battle space transparency primarily comprises integration, synchronization and analysis of information from multiple sources and domains within specific time and space parameters. This allows an asymmetric decision advantage at tactical, operational, and strategic levels. Ideally, battle space transparency can assist in shaping the real-time battle space in advance.[6] To achieve this against an adversary in a contested environment, the core concept is to link information across all domains to enhance their combined effectiveness, while compensating for their vulnerabilities.[7] The armed forces across the globe need to rapidly adapt themselves to leverage new technology, foster innovative concepts of operations, and shape their structural and cultural barriers to enable the diffusion of new ideas.[8] This has resulted in a need for smaller but highly agile force structures and combat tools with greater potency per unit. New-generation combat aircraft with low observability, networked and longer lethal range are set to dominate the operational environment in the coming decades. The number of support systems will grow in number to assist greater flexibility to combat aircraft. Role-specific designed combat aircraft will continue to phase out, to be replaced by multi-role aircraft and supplemented by UAVs and other kinetic tools, as brought out in Chapter 6. But the development of complex combat aircraft to fit in the future operational environment will have its teething problems, as is evident in the case of the F-35:-

> The worldwide fleet of Lockheed Martin F-35 Lightning II aircraft was grounded for inspections after a problem with the aircraft's engine fuel tube was discovered, which is believed to be related to the first crash of the stealth fighter.[9]

Stealth technology will gain prominence in combat aviation in the next two decades. However, technology will find a suitable solution to negate the advantage of low observability that the Stealth platforms currently enjoy. Quantum radars are one such solution.[10] Initial reports on their development have been encouraging. But it may take a decade to master this new art for operational deployment. Once that happens, the advantages of Stealth designs will be neutralised. Developments in passive sensors that rely on disturbances created by the passage of an aerial vehicle, could go beyond the current laboratory testing stage. These passive sensors too will counterbalance the stealth capability of aircraft.

Power plants are another area that may change combat aviation in the coming decades. The fuel efficiencies are increasing and may improve further. This will allow for longer duration missions. The super cruise—the ability to cruise at supersonic speed without the use of afterburner—presently in a limited number of platforms like the F-22 – will be an attribute in a greater number of platforms. The kind of fuel these power plants use itself may change. A mix of bio-fuel along with the conventional fossil fuel, ATF (Aviation Turbine Fuel) is being tested on aircraft.[11] On the other hand, the electric-powered aircraft are still small in size and with limited capability. The power storage solutions are transforming the systems on the ground with longer duration batteries.[12] Once the power-to-weight ratio improves further, these batteries may find their way in the aviation industry as a source of power.

Space

In the foreseeable future, the combat aircraft will continue to operate utilizing the medium of air but their dependence on space-based assets for mission effectiveness will gradually grow. Time synchronization is one aspect that has been implemented well across the spectrum using space-based assets. Currently, space-based navigation systems like the Global Positioning System (GPS), Glonass, BeiDou, and Gagan are an integral part of many aerial platform navigation systems. While GPS and Glonass are well established and the Indian Gagan has a limited regional application, the Chinese BeiDou is expanding its capacity. Named after the Chinese term for the Big Dipper constellation, the BeiDou system started operations in China in 2000 and grew its footprint to cover the Asia-Pacific region in 2012. On November 19, 2018, China sent two new satellites of the BeiDou Navigation Satellite System (BDS) into space on a Long March-3B carrier rocket from the Xichang Satellite Launch Center in Sichuan Province. [13] These satellites will operate in coordination with 17 other BDS-3 satellites already in space, thus completing the BDS constellation. Overall, these are the 42nd and 43rd satellites of the BDS satellite family. China plans to provide navigation services with the BDS-3 to countries participating in the Belt and Road Initiative. The positioning accuracy of the BDS-3 system is expected to be 2.5 to 5 metres. China plans to launch another six BDS-3 satellites to the medium earth orbits, three satellites to the inclined geosynchronous earth orbit and two satellites to the geostationary earth orbit. Thereafter, the system is expected to have a global footprint by 2020.[14] The dominance of a select few countries in the space domain is obvious, as depicted in Figure 11.1.

Figure 11.1 Satellites in Orbit

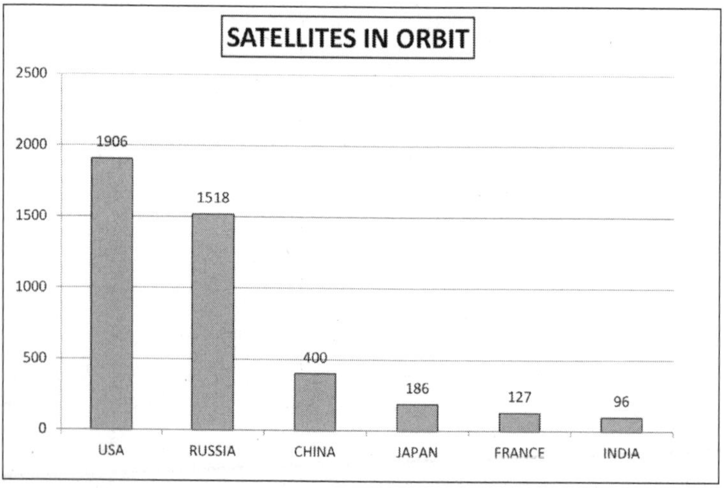

Source: Times of India.[15]

While the dependence on accurate space-based satellite systems for combat aviation and weapon delivery has increased, so has the susceptibility to external interference. In reality, dependency on space-based navigation systems has become a key concern and vulnerability. This was evident during NATO's exercise 'Trident Juncture' from October 16 to November 7, 2018, in Norway that included soldiers from 31 countries. A Norwegian statement about GPS jamming during the exercise from the Russian forces on the Arctic Kola Peninsula reiterated the disruption that such jamming can cause.[16] Understanding this critical vulnerability, the combat aircraft are planned to be modified to carry anti-jam GPS.[17] Gradually, space applications will expand to other functional domains of combat aviation. Currently, data links for uploading intelligence inputs and downloading inputs from combat platform sensors are predominantly based on the line-of-sight principles with direct communication or through an airborne relay platform. However, this is gradually changing. With a greater need to orchestrate combat from a nodal point to optimise effort, there is an increase in the distance at which the combat aircraft operate from the combat planners. Space-based communication systems have made this possible and gradually larger number of platforms will have this option. A new concept of 'Fast Space' will grow in applicability. The Fast Space construct is an ecosystem of concepts, capabilities, and industrial partnerships that make speed the defining attribute of advantage in space, with regard to both supply and demand.[18] Detection of a missile launch is another aspect of space-based systems that will see a greater role in the coming years. To expand the capabilities of defensive systems against a potential missile attack, several satellites are being deployed in space to detect and track hostile targets.[19]The growing significance of space in combat operations is best articulated by the US Deputy Defense Secretary, Patrick M. Shanahan:-

> ".....Space, known as the final frontier, is something the Defense Department would like to explore. And, Congress and the president's administration want the DOD to accelerate its abilities to deliver capabilities in the space domain. Other DOD priorities, in addition to space, include cyber and hypersonics. These are "super priorities....."[20]

With the growing dependence on space for various kinetic and non-kinetic capabilities, it is but natural for various stakeholders to device ways to deny the use of space to competitors. Development of the concept of space dominance and space control is just a matter of time and it will be an extension of the control of air concepts but the methods may predominantly be non-kinetic and effect-based for short durations in specific geographical areas. The capability in the kinetic domain is still available with a limited number of states and India is the latest entrant. On March 27, 2019, India jumped the queue in space capabilities by testing the Anti-Satellite (ASAT) Missile as part of 'Mission Shakti'. This has made India the fourth country to acquire such a specialised and modern capability and that too indigenously.[21]

Denial of communications and inputs for operations during the mission will be a reality. The war fighters will have to operate in standalone mode. Therefore, the commander's intent needs to be understood by all the war fighting elements. Even when disconnected, they still need to contribute to the overall mission objectives. Such an ability to operate in degraded structures is essential and must be part of the training processes.[22] This will change the way combat aviators operate today. Mitchell Institute Policy Papers clearly bring this out as,[23]

> ... achieving air superiority in 2030 would require an integrated and networked family of both penetrating and standoff capabilities, operating not just in the air but across space and cyberspace as well.

Artificial Intelligence

With the development of practical applications of artificial intelligence, the character of force application in war or warlike situations will change. Deployment of lethal autonomous weapons will take away the major load from combatants. In the coming decades, a similar approach is expected in the field of combat aviation as well. The Collaborative Operations in Denied Environment

(CODE) Program of the Defense Advanced Research Projects Agency (DARPA) is an example of likely future scenarios. In its test at the Yuma Proving Ground in Arizona, the CODE-equipped Unmanned Aerial Systems (UASs) adapted and responded to unexpected threats in an anti-access area denial (A2AD) environment.[24] During the three-week ground and flight test series in a live/virtual/constructive (LVC) environment, up to six live and 24 virtual UASs served as surrogate strike assets, receiving mission objectives from a human mission commander. The systems then autonomously collaborated to navigate, search, localize, and engage both pre-planned and pop-up targets protected by a simulated Integrated Air Defense System (IADS) in communications– and GPS-denied scenarios. The UASs efficiently shared information, cooperatively planned and allocated mission objectives, made coordinated tactical decisions, and collaboratively reacted to a dynamic, high-threat environment with minimal communication. The air vehicles initially operated with supervisory mission commander interaction. When communications were degraded or denied, CODE vehicles retained the mission plan intended to accomplish mission objectives without live human direction. This ability will enable dynamic, long-distance engagements of the highly mobile ground and maritime targets in the contested or denied battle space.[25] A similar programme, Army Warfighting Experiment, is being pursued by the UK to test as Project Autonomous Warrior.[26] This is the result of collaboration between the British Army, Royal Navy, Royal Air Force, US Army, UK Ministry of Defence, and around fifty industry participants. The initial four-week long experiment started on November 12, 2018, was focused on autonomous last-mile resupply. Autonomous Warrior tested a range of prototype unmanned aerial and ground cargo vehicles to reduce the danger to troops during combat. British soldiers tested and evaluated the effectiveness of Robotic and Autonomous Systems (RAS) in the battlefield. Autonomous Warrior is planned to develop capabilities in surveillance to improve the effectiveness of long-range and precision targeting. The land-based exercise follows on from the 'Unmanned Warrior' of the Royal Navy that demonstrated autonomous systems diving, swimming and flying together to engage in surveillance, intelligence-gathering and mine countermeasures.[27]

Application of such a technology in combat aviation will allow higher efficiency and mission efficacy. This will reduce the number of manned aircraft in the entire operational gamut and increase similarly capable platforms operated by Artificial Intelligence (AI). The change will take at least a couple of decades as the technology is still maturing. As a first step, the technology will find space in the cockpit and will assist the pilot in taking decisions and action. Once such prototypes are tested, in the next stage, AI operations will be under the supervision of the pilot, with the pilot having the ability to override the decisions. On achieving an enhanced level of reliability, gradually, the role of man in the cockpit will reduce. All such systems will invariably be tested on the unmanned system and be gradually implemented on manned combat aircraft. Probably by the middle of this century, unmanned aerial vehicles with embedded AI, will have a major stake in combat aviation.

Hypersonics

A hypersonic vehicle can fly at a speed greater than 5 Mach (five times the speed of sound). Russia, China and the US are considered the most advanced nations to possess hypersonic technologies. In August 2018, China reportedly conducted the first flight of an unmanned hypersonic test vehicle, Starry Sky 2, reaching speeds of Mach 5.5 for more than six minutes, and topping off at Mach 6.[28] During the flight, the vehicle climbed to an altitude of about 98,000 feet and completed several manoeuvres. The US Air Force is also aiming for a 2020 initial operational capability for its Hypersonic Conventional Strike Weapon (HCSW), an air-breathing, ram-jet-powered cruise missile being developed by Lockheed Missiles and Space for $928 million.[29] The USAF also awarded a separate $780 million contract to Lockheed Missiles and Fire Control in 2017 to develop the Air-launched Rapid Response Weapon (ARRW), a boost-glide hypersonic system, which uses a rocket to accelerate its payload to high speeds, before the payload separates from the rocket and glides unpowered to its destination at up to Mach 20.[30] Russia, too, is in the fray, in fact as a leader to deploy hypersonic weapons. The intent was disclosed by the Russian President Vladimir Putin about a new weapon, in 2018.[31] By December 2018, a test of Russian Avangard with a claimed speed of 27 Mach (approximately 30,000 kilometres per hour) provided the proof.[32] The Avangard as of now is the fastest weapon. This high speed combined with its random manoeuvring makes the prediction of its flight path difficult. This practically negates any possibility of its interception. A statement by the Russian Deputy Prime Minister Yuri Borisov, "*There's almost no missile that can shoot it down*" sums up the capability of this new weapon.[33]

Hypersonic weapons will redefine the way to defend air space. This will initiate rethinking on the conceptualisation, designing and application of combat aviation assets. Entire air defence missile systems will transform tackling a hypersonic weapon. With further development of this technology, the hypersonic weapons will find a way in the combat aircraft arsenal. That will take the offensive potential of combat aviation at a new level by further compressing the time to defend. While the race to deploy hypersonic weapons in on, the DARPA is planning for counter-hypersonic weapons as part of its Glide Breaker Program. The Glide Breaker Program aims to achieve an advanced interceptor capable of defeating manoeuvring hypersonic vehicles in the upper atmosphere.[34]

Future Combat Aircraft Inventory

How will all the emerging technology impact combat aviation and its future? What is the timeline that we are looking at for these technologies to mature and their translation in battle space force application? Will there be a single entity leading or a collation? Malcolm Davis, Senior Analyst, Defence Strategy and Capability at the Australian Strategic Policy Institute conjures,

> "The terminology of 5th gen, 5.5 gen, 6th gen seems increasingly passé and runs the risk of another 20-30 year multibillion-dollar programme that delivers capability too slowly. We need to think in terms of rapid development, spiral acquisition and experimentation towards a systems-of-systems approach – rather than an exquisite, very expensive single platform that does it all."[35]

Although development of combat aircraft continues, some tentative conclusions present themselves. The guiding force for a future generation of combat aircraft will be its ability to operate efficiently and stealthily with use of low-calibre precision weapons in a networked environment with adequate onboard sensors to execute the tasks autonomously with the ability to operate with minimal infrastructural support.[36] Going by the trend that the world's combat aircraft inventory has followed in the last fifty years in general, and in the last three decades, in particular, a downward trajectory is expected over the next three decades (Figure 11.2). Extrapolating the trend of the last three decades with a constant change of rate, the expected combat aircraft inventory will go below 10,000 by 2037 and shrink further to about 7000 by 2047.

Figure 11.2: Forecast Strength of Combat Aircraft in the World

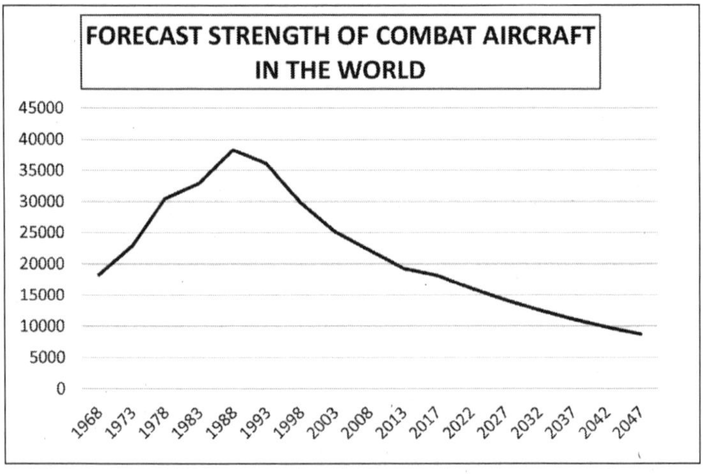

Source: Extrapolated from data extracted from CAIDB.

This forecast is based on the current assessment of future geopolitics, the operational environment, technological advances, emerging alternatives, expanding capabilities of platforms and weapons, and a hope: that mankind will look for alternative methods of resolving disputes. War or a threat of war will/should not be the prime option. This is simplistic and based on the continuation of a similar pattern of geopolitical, technological and operational changes. Any deviation in this will alter the outcome. One aspect that can dramatically alter this is the development of AI. This field is in its infancy right now. Once this matures, the need for manned combat aircraft will rarely be felt. Miniaturized unmanned vehicles in SWARM will be able to destroy key elements of a combat or support system.

There are a few caveats that need consideration. First, technology develops and percolates further to allow the creation of a nearly seamless society. This will enhance transparency, a precursor to unmask individuals, institutions and organizations with hidden motives and agenda. In an equal, just and rule-based society, the chances of conflicts leading to war are minimized. Two significant factors in this debate are the ethics and the politics of technology. These two, especially the politics of it, will also be present/grow simultaneously. An example is nuclear proliferation. The way new world leaders will view this aspect and try to use these cards for national interests will hold the key. There are regional politics and extra-regional politics to investing in assets like technology. There's a justification for building/investing in particular technology regionally, forced by environmental compulsions in the region; for example, procurement of a weapon system by the neighbouring country forces development of its counter. But in case of the extra-regional dimension, objectives are to generate/build technology to seek to regulate it henceforth and thus deny it to some and deny opportunities to develop the same to others, especially those who acquire it from the generators. Will humanity prevail over nationality? The ethics debate is integral to AI especially, and in cases where slowly technology is being given a certain decision-making authority. Whether war is ethical or not, it is sought to be justified. It has been bad enough in cases where humans were making decisions but how does it change/mutate with an increasing use of technology? Will the transformation take place with greater risk? Associated with the above is the question of legality that brings in the second caveat. States as part of the international community will be able to prevail over any agency or institution or a fellow state from going rogue. A lot of mechanisms put in place in the post-Second World War age are unravelling or, if not that dramatic, are ineffective to a considerable degree. This is the politics of it – the part that follows the long-drawn-out politics of creating international rules-based order that fundamentally conflicts with the national interest. The shape and power of rule implementation mechanisms will guide the behaviour of states. These will get legitimacy and strength from a transparent and fair system. Third, the intertwining of economic interests increases to such a level that any war or a threat of war hurts the aggressor as much as it damages the victims. Going by the hybrid theory, economics is now another theatre of war. Therefore, relevance or utility of kinetic tools is relegated to secondary or tertiary priority for force application. The perceived power of stakeholders at the negotiating table will gradually get delinked from military power. Lastly, and most importantly, it is about a very small group of companies that practically control the world's arms market. Rather than warmongering and lobbying, having built their expertise and a fortune in selling weapons, these companies need to switch their research and development for the welfare of humankind. This is likely to be the most difficult step.

Notes

1. A weapon of the United States Air Force MOAB– popularly called Mother of All Bombs is a 10-tonne weapon with a yield of 85GJ or 11 tonnes of TNT.
2. Amitav Malik, "High Power Lasers- directed Energy Weapons, Impact on Defence and Security", Defence Research and Development Organisation, Ministry of Defence, New Delhi, 2012, pp. 99-121.
3. Lt Col Price T. Bingham, "The Airpower Edge: Revolutionizing How the US Defeats Conventional Armies", The Mitchell Institute Policy Paper, No. 16, November 2017.
4. "The UK Ministry of Defence and The Rt Hon Mark Lancaster TD MP, British Army set to redefine warfare with joint Autonomous Warrior", June 20, 2018, available at https://www.gov.uk/government/news/british-army-set-to-redefine-warfare-with-joint-autonomous-warrior (Accessed on December 22, 2019)
5. Bill Sweetman, *Advanced Fighter Technology: The Future of Cockpit Combat*, Airlife Publishing Limited, England, 1987, p. 6.
6. Maj Gen Vera Linn "Dash" Jamieson and Lt Col Maurizio "Mo" Calabrese, "An ISR Perspective on Fusion Warfare", The Mitchell Institute Policy Paper, No. 1, October 2015.

7. Lt Gen David A. Deptula, "Interdependent Warfare: Combined Effects Power in the 21st Century", Mitchell Institute Policy Papers, Volume 10, March 23, 2018.
8. Lt Gen David A. Deptula, "Beyond Goldwater-Nichols: Roles And Missions Of The Armed Services In The 21st Century", Mitchell Institute Policy Papers, Vol. 1, March 2016.
9. Garrett Reim, "Worldwide F-35 fleet grounded temporarily for inspections related to crash", *Flight Global,* October 11, 2018, at https://www.flightglobal.com/news/articles/worldwide-f-35-fleet-grounded-temporarily-for-inspec-452617/ (Accessed on October 12, 2018).
10. Joseph Trevithick, "China Reveals Prototype Configuration Of Jam Resistant And Counter-Stealth. 'Quantum Radar'", *The Drive*, November 6, 2018 at https://www.thedrive.com/the-war-zone/24726/china-reveals-prototype-configuration-of-jam-resistant-and-counter-stealth-quantum-radar (Accessed on April 1, 2019).
11. Pranav Mukul, "Why Bio Fuel for aircraft holds out promise but isn't ready to fly yet", *The Indian Express*, August 28, 2018 at https://indianexpress.com/article/explained/why-biofuel-for-aircraft-holds-out-promise-but-isnt-ready-to-fly-yet-5327864/ (Accessed on April 1, 2019).
12. Rich Haridy, "Battery-powered electric plane quietly takes to Australian skies for the first time", *New Atlas*, January 8, 2018 at https://newatlas.com/electric-aircraft-test-flight-australia/52846/ (Accessed on April 1, 2019).
13. "China launches twin BeiDou navigation satellites", *People's Daily Online*, November 19, 2018, at https://www.globalsecurity.org/space/library/news/2018/space-181119-pdo01.htm?_m=3n%252e002a%252e2429%252eju0ao0d60s%252e28i6 (Accessed on November 19, 2018).
14. Ibid.
15. "How India joined space 'super league'", *Times of India*, March 28, 2019 at https://timesofindia.indiatimes.com/home/science/mission-shakti-all-you-want-to-know/articleshow/68608200.cms (Accessed on March 29, 2019).
16. Jan M. Olsen and Jari Tanner, "Norway says Russia jammed GPS signal during NATO drill", ABC News, November 13, 2018, at https://abcnews.go.com/Technology/wireStory/norway-russia-jammed-gps-signal-nato-drill-59173663 (Accessed on November 14, 2018).
17. Garrett Reim, "USAF Reserve and Air National Guard F-16s to be upgraded with anti-jam GPS", *Flight Global,* November 12, 2018 at https://www.flightglobal.com/news/articles/usaf-reserve-and-air-national-guard-f-16s-to-be-upgr-453564/ (Accessed on November 14, 2018).
18. Lt Col Thomas Schilling, Charles Miller, Lt Col Peter Garretson, and Hoyt Davidson, "Introducing 'Fast Space': Rethinking Access to Space", Mitchell Institute Policy Papers No. 12, May 2017.

19. Robert Burns, "US considers new ways to detect and track enemy missiles", *Military Times*, January 15, 2019, at https://www.militarytimes.com/news/pentagon-congress/2019/01/16/us-considers-new-ways-to-detect-and-track-enemy-missiles/?utm_source=Sailthru&utm_medium=email&utm_campaign=Space%201.23.19&utm_term=Editorial%20-%20Military%20Space%20Report (Accessed on January 25, 2019).

20. David Vergun, " Talks Dollars, Fiscal Sense and Space", *Global Security,* November 15, 2018 at https://www.globalsecurity.org/space/library/news/2018/space-181115-afps01.htm?_m=3n%252e002a%252e2428%252eju0ao0d60s%252e28he (Accessed on November 19, 2018).

21. PIB Press Release, Prime Minister Office, March 27, 2019 at http://pib.nic.in/PressReleseDetail.aspx?PMO=3&PRID=1569547 (Accessed on March 28, 2019).

22. Lt Gen David A. Deptula, no. 7.

23. Brig Gen Alex Grynkewich, "An Operational Imperative: The Future of Air Superiority", Mitchell Institute Policy Papers, Vol. 7, July 2017.

24. Defense Advanced Research Projects Agency "CODE Demonstrates Autonomy and Collaboration with Minimal Human Commands", November 19, 2018, press release at https://www.darpa.mil/news-events/2018-11-19 (Accessed on November 27, 2018).

25. Ibid.

26. "British Army to launch Autonomous Warrior (Land) experiment", June 21, 2018 at https://www.army-technology.com/news/british-army-launch-autonomous-warrior-land-experiment/ (Accessed on March 12, 2019).

27. The UK Ministry of Defence and The Rt Hon Mark Lancaster TD MP, no. 4

28. "China tests its first waverider hypersonic aircraft", *The Financial Express,* August 6, 2018 at https://www.financialexpress.com/world-news/china-tests-its-first-waverider-hypersonic-aircraft/1270628/ (Accessed on March 12, 2019).

29. Valeria Insinna, "Lockheed nabs another big hypersonic weapons contract", *Defence News,* August 14, 2018 at https://www.defensenews.com/air/2018/08/14/lockheed-nabs-another-big-hypersonic-weapons-contract/ (Accessed on March 12, 2019).

30. Secretary of the Air Force Public Affairs USAF, "Air Force awards hypersonic weapon contract", August 13, 2018, at https://www.af.mil/News/Article-Display/Article/1600963/air-force-awards-hypersonic-weapon-contract/ (Accessed on March 12, 2019).

31. "Putin announces Russia possesses hypersonic weapons", TASS News Report, March 1, 2018 at http://tass.com/defense/992214 (Accessed on March 12, 2019).

32. "Russia's top-notch Avangard hypersonic glider can travel at whopping

30,000km/h – deputy PM", RT News, December 27, 2018 at https://www.rt.com/russia/447533-avangard-glider-speed-russia/ (Accessed on January 10, 2019).

33. Ibid.
34. Garrett Reim, "DARPA asks for counter-hypersonic weapons proposals", *Flight Global*. November 9, 2018 at https://www.flightglobal.com/news/articles/darpa-asks-for-counter-hypersonic-weapons-proposals-453522/ (Accessed on November 14, 2018).
35. Greg Waldron, "Tokyo contemplates its future fighter plans", *Flight Global*, November 19, 2018 at https://www.flightglobal.com/news/articles/analysis-tokyo-contemplates-its-future-fighter-pla-453253/ (Accessed on November 20, 2018).
36. Robert Jackson, "Future Military Aircraft", in Phillip Jarret (ed.), *The Modern War Machine: Military Aviation Since 1945*, Putnam Aeronautical Books, London, 2000, pp. 223-236.

PART IV

Combat Aviation Trajectory in India

12. Close Quarters: Combat Aviation Trajectory in India

India does not have a defined, documented and declared National Security Strategy; however, its intent, policies and actions are in coherence with a non-expansionist strategy directed at protection of geographical integrity, development of human resources, sustainable economic growth, and preservation of a rule-based order. Accordingly, the prime focus of the Indian Armed Forces is to ensure peace through deterrence.

Since independence, India has had four conventional wars of which three were with Pakistan (1948,1965 and 1971) and one with China (1962) with mixed results. The results of 1962 and 1971 wars were at two ends of the spectrum from a comprehensive defeat to a resounding victory. In the last three decades, the situation with China on various boundary disputes has been non-violent. There have been multiple standoffs between India and China primarily based on different perceptions about the exact location of the boundary between the two states. Several meetings have been held to resolve this issue but both sides are yet to reach a consensus and the boundary between the two states is still not fully marked to the satisfaction of both sides. The last standoff on this issue was in 2017 at Doklam near the tri-junction of the Bhutan-India- China border. This standoff lasted 73 days before de-escalation.[1] However, such standoffs have not resulted in the use of kinetic weapons in the last five decades – a result of political and diplomatic engagements and multiple Confidence-Building Measures (CBMs) between the two states including the annual military exercise 'Hand in Hand'.[2]

The State of Jammu and Kashmir was the central theme of Indo-Pak conflict in 1948. And the issue is not yet resolved with Pakistan still occupying over 78,000 square kilometres of Indian territory.[3] The war in 1965 did not alter the status quo but the 1971 Indo-Pak war resulted in the creation of Bangladesh. Thereafter, to avenge, Pakistan has been using multiple hybrid war tools, specifically after the nuclear tests of 1998. The state of Jammu and Kashmir is the prime target and mountainous and inhospitable terrain at the Line of Control (LOC) favours the intruder and makes the defenders' job difficult. The terrain does impose restrictions on launching an outright offensive operation. In 1999, the aggressive usage of Pakistan's military to occupy Indian territory in the Kargil sector in Jammu and Kashmir required India to use military power to force eviction.[4] The strength of conventional forces is seen as a deterrent in the interplay between nuclear-powered China, India and Pakistan. By adding a time dimension, Thomas C. has redefined deterrence that is particularly relevant for the Indian armed forces:

> "... Deterrence involves setting the state – by an announcement, by rigging the trip-wire, by incurring the obligation – and waiting. The overt act is up to the opponent. The stage setting can often be nonintrusive, non-hostile, non-provocative. The act that is intrusive, hostile, or provocative is usually the one to be deterred; the deterrent threat only changes the consequences *if* the act in question – the one to be deterred – is then taken. To deter, one digs in, or lays a minefield, and waits – in the interest of inaction. Deterrence tends to be indefinite in its timing...."[5]

To deter, the Government of India has authorized the Indian Air Force (IAF) to hold 42 combat aircraft squadrons and equip Indian Naval aircraft carriers with over two squadrons of combat aircraft (See Annexure 8).[6] However, the current strength of combat aircraft with India is much lower than this authorization. Further, a drawdown from phasing out of ageing MiG-21 and MiG-27 is partially planned to be offset by the acquisition of already contracted Su-30MKI, Tejas – Light Combat Aircraft (LCA), and Rafale. This chapter covers some critical factors that have thus far defined the Indian combat aircraft inventory. In the first section, the combat aircraft authorization history is covered. It is followed by factors that play a role in determining the combat aircraft inventory.

Governmental Authorizations

The combat aircraft are normally organized in a group called squadron (British Model) or a regiment (Soviet Model). In the IAF, a squadron of combat aircraft comprises 18 aircraft. *Ab initio*, the IAF was the only organization authorized to hold combat aircraft in India. However, with the acquisition of an aircraft carrier—the *INS Vikrant* in 1957—the Indian Navy too was authorized to hold and operate combat aircraft. The *INS Vikrant* was commissioned in 1961.[7] The strength of aircraft carriers with the Indian Navy has fluctuated between zero and two since then. The capacity of various aircraft carriers to hold combat aircraft has been similar. Accordingly, the numbers for the Indian Navy have always been small and in the region of two squadron's worth of combat aircraft.

Combat Aircraft Squadrons/Units of the IAF

The IAF was officially established on October 8, 1932. Its first aircraft flight came into being on April 1, 1933. The IAF started with a strength of six Royal Air Force (RAF), UK-trained officers and 19 *Havai Sepoys* (literally, air soldiers).[8] Problems concerning the defence of India were reassessed in 1939 by the Chatfield Committee. It proposed the re-equipment of the RAF squadrons based in India. Accordingly, five Coastal Defence Flights (CDFs) were raised voluntarily to assist in the defence of the principal ports. An IAF Volunteer Reserve was thus authorized. The CDFs were established at Madras (now Chennai), Bombay (now Mumbai), Calcutta (now Kolkata), Karachi (now in Pakistan) and Cochin (now Kochi). One more CDF was later established at Vishakapatnam.

After Independence, gradually the authorization for combat aircraft in the IAF moved at a fast pace. This was primarily a result of re-appreciation of the threat matrix[9] and the capability that was required to meet the security challenges. By 1986, the IAF was authorized for 42 combat aircraft squadrons (Figure 12.1).

Figure 12.1: Government Authorisation of Combat Squadrons for Indian Air Force

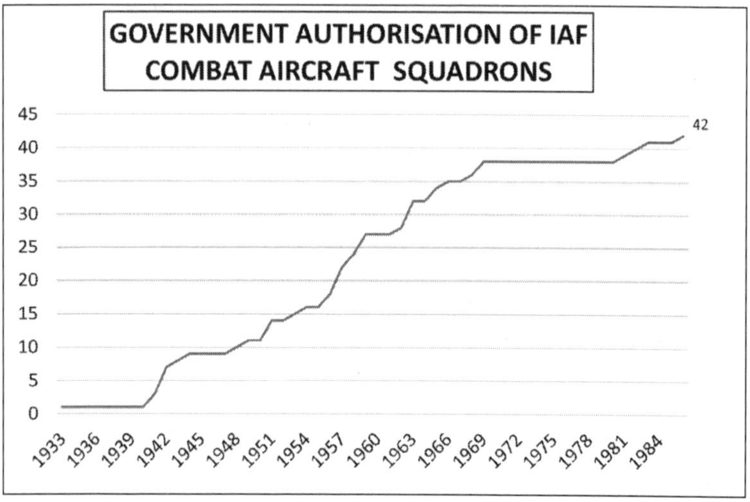

Source: Based on data in *Air Power and National Security: Indian Air Force: Evolution, Growth and Future.*[10]

Figure 12.2: Government Authorisation of Combat Squadrons for Indian Air Force

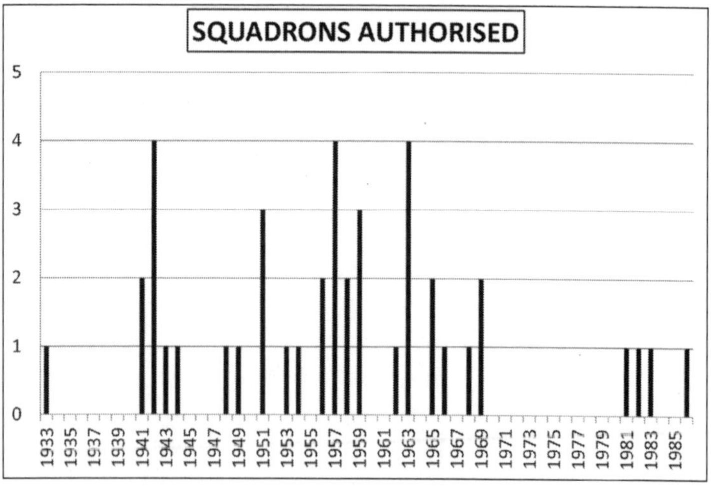

Source: Based on data in *Air Power and National Security: Indian Air Force: Evolution, Growth and Future.*[11]

Figure 12.2 gives a bird's eye-view of the phases of expansion of combat aircraft squadron authorization. The squadron authorization, stuck at one since inception in 1933, rapidly grew between 1941 and 1944. In this phase, the period before Indian independence, the Second World War was the main driver for growth. The IAF had nine combat squadrons by 1945. In October 1946, the British authorities had made their assessment of India's post-war defence needs and envisaged the expansion of the existing ten squadrons (including a transport aircraft squadron) into a balanced force of twenty fighters, bomber and transport squadrons. Owing to the partition of assets in 1947, actually, the numbers were only 6.5 squadrons that came to the IAF and the rest went to Pakistan Air Force (PAF).[12] Immediately after the Partition, India had its first war with Pakistan in the Jammu and Kashmir sector in 1948. However, the then-existing combat aircraft had a negligible role in that war. During this phase, the IAF, as well as the PAF, were headed by the officers seconded from the Royal Air Force. Possibly, that is why, there was no combat engagement in the skies over Jammu and Kashmir.[13]

After independence in 1947, the initial build-up was to make up for assets that were given away to the PAF. Thereafter, it was to grow to meet the security requirements of a newly-independent India. By 1953, the combat aircraft squadron strength had increased to 15. The next phase of growth commenced in 1954. On April 1, 1954, Air Chief Marshal Subroto Mukherjee took over the reins of the IAF. He was the first Indian to head the organization. The IAF's outlook towards operational capability changed. The IAF's expansion programme aimed at more than doubling its strength from a 15-squadron force to 33 squadrons. The IAF added another 11 combat aircraft squadrons during his tenure at the helm, till 1960. The goal was to have a 33- squadron force, including transport and helicopter units.[14]

The 1962 war with China again saw little action from the IAF combat fleet. But this led to reassessing the combat aviation capability and its role.[15] The Vampire FBMk.52s, "mothballed" since 1961, was restored to service to equip newly-raised squadrons. In October 1962, the Government of India reassessed the security requirement and sanctioned the IAF to be a 45-squadron force including transport and helicopter squadrons.[16] Five more squadrons were added to the arsenal in 1962-63. A war with Pakistan in 1965 resulted in the loss of many combat aircraft for the IAF. To build up the capability after replacing the losses, the strength of the IAF combat aircraft squadron was build up to 38 by 1970. After victory in the 1971 war that resulted in the creation of Bangladesh and 93,000 prisoners of war from the Pakistani armed forces, the Indian armed forces redeemed themselves. All three branches of the Indian armed forces had a well-coordinated campaign. The combat aircraft of the IAF played a pivotal role in this war by supporting the surface forces.

The last spurt of growth for the combat aircraft fleet was only after the major geopolitical upheaval in South Asia. The erstwhile USSR had entered Afghanistan in 1979 and the US used Pakistan as the launch pad to counter the move. This led to a flow of military hardware, including combat aircraft – the F-16 – into Pakistan from the US. To retain the balance of power, the Indian government authorized four more squadrons of combat aircraft in the aftermath of this change in the subcontinent. By 1986, the Government of India had authorized the IAF to hold 42 combat aircraft squadrons. There has been no change in the authorization since then, although the requirement projected by the IAF has been of 45 squadrons to tackle a two-front war.[17]

Besides the combat aircraft squadrons authorized by the Government of India, combat aircraft are also authorized for units for training, testing and development roles. Major units in this category are Tactics and Combat Development Establishment (TACDE), Air Defence Flight (AD Flt), Operational Conversion Units (OCU), Target Towing Flights (TTF) and Aircraft and Systems Testing Establishment (ASTE). [18]

TACDE was established as Tactics and Combat Development and Training Squadron (T&CD&TS) at Adampur, Punjab on February 1, 1971. The T&CD&TS got re-designated as TACDE in December 1972. Its prime task is to study and evolve tactical procedures for various aircraft, implementation of standard operating procedures and training of pilots in operational doctrines and tactics. Besides training, it has an operational role too. In its very first year, the unit saw action in the Indo-Pak conflict of 1971. TACDE was awarded 'Battle Honours' by the President of India in 1995 for its role in that war.[19]

Air Defence Flight (AD Flt) is equipped with combat aircraft and has trained air crew for providing realistic training to Fighter Controller for combat controlling. The Air Defence College (ADC), the institution for the training of fighter controllers, coordinates the activities of AD Flt. These aircraft too can be operationally utilized as and when required.

Operational Conversion Units (OCU) are established to provide initial fighter flying training to pilots. Its first incarnation was in 1966.[20] These units are equipped with combat aircraft. The fighter air crew learn the basics of combat aviation in these units before graduating to combat squadrons. The MiG Operational Flying Training Unit (MOFTU), the Hunter Operational Flying Training Unit (HOFTU), the Hawks Operational Training Squadron (HOTS), are some of the variants of OCU at different stages in the life of the IAF. Combat training aircraft and trained air crew from these units can be operationally deployed.

Target-Towing Units (TTU) are flying units of the IAF to tow a dummy target.[21] This towed target is then used by combat air crew for practising their gun-firing skills. For realistic training, the aircraft used for towing target needs flight characteristics similar to a combat aircraft. Therefore, TTUs are invariably equipped with combat aircraft. The Canberra, the Hunters and the MiG-23 have performed this role in the IAF. These aircraft are modified for the target-towing role. However, in case the situation demands, these aircraft can be deployed for an operational role.

In 1948, the IAF acquired its first jet fighter, the Vampire, and the Aircraft Testing Unit (ATU) was raised to accept and test these aircraft. To launch flight testing in India on a formal footing, the IAF deputed two pilots for the No. 8 Test Pilots' Course at the Empire Test Pilots' School in the UK in October 1949. These pilots were followed by several others in succeeding years and they formed the core group in the establishment of the Aircraft and Armament Testing Unit (A&ATU) at Kanpur. On August 23, 1972, the A&ATU was reorganized as the

Aircraft and Systems Testing Establishment (ASTE).[22] For its training and testing activities, many combat aircraft are held by ASTE. With ASTE's trained air crew, these aircraft can be operationally deployed.

Maintenance Reserves (MR)

Every aircraft has a maintenance servicing schedule. This may be based on the utilization rate, or the calendar life or flying event (take-offs, landings, or engine starts, etc.) or a combination of these two factors. Owing to aircraft accidents, the aircraft may also have to undergo major unscheduled repairs. These are time-consuming processes. During these repairs and servicing, the combat aircraft is not available for operational deployment. Therefore, for each fleet, several aircraft are authorized as maintenance reserves (MR) over and above the Unit Establishment (UE).

The MR is computed based on the periodicity of scheduled maintenance and the time taken for completion of these activities. As an example, take a case of an aircraft that requires to be serviced after every 1000 hours of flying and this servicing takes six months. In case the nominal utilization rate of the aircraft is 200 hours every year, this will mean that after every five years the aircraft will not be available for operations for six months. The MR for this type of aircraft will be computed by dividing the serving time by the servicing cycle; that is to say, six months divided by 66 months (60 months of utilization and six months of servicing). Simply stated, in a time cycle of 66 months, the aircraft will be on maintenance for six months. This will necessitate an additional inventory of 9.09 per cent as MR.

Strike-Off Wastage

Flying a combat aircraft has its inherent risks. Material failures, design deficiencies, servicing errors or flying errors along with difficult environmental conditions are major challenges to flight safety. However, with experience gained over time, some of the technical challenges have been partially overcome. But the human factor in maintenance and operations continues to be a key factor in flight safety. Some aircraft will be lost in accidents. This trend for the IAF has been declining in the last five decades as the quality of equipment and training has gradually improved. Figure 12.3 indicates the number of Category I accidents (aircraft lost) per 10,000 hours of flying. With over 2,50,000 hours flown by the IAF every year, the current rate of 0.22 indicates an annual loss of five to six aircraft.[23] Besides the combat aircraft, the flying effort and the aircraft losses are inclusive of all platforms including transport aircraft and helicopters.

Figure 12.3: Aircraft Accident Rate per 10,000 Flying hours for the Indian Air Force

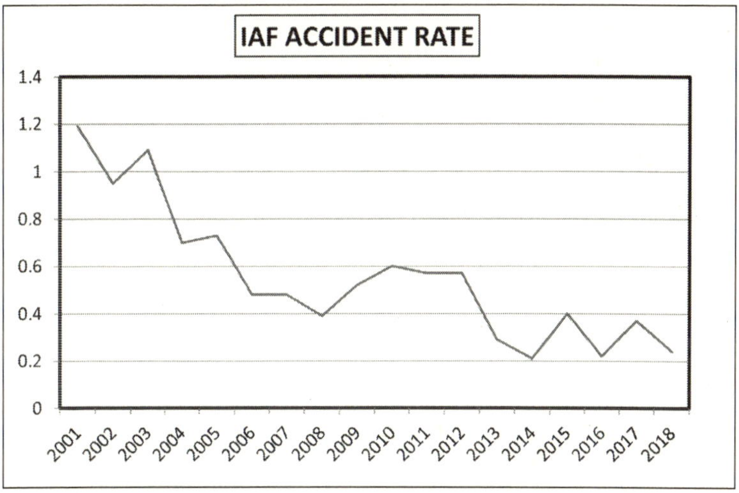

Source: Government of India, Ministry of Defence, Year-End Review – 2018.[24]

The acquisition of aircraft has to account for such losses as Strike-Off Wastage (SOW). These are losses during peacetime training and maintenance activities. The aircraft lost in accidents are replaced by acquiring more aircraft to meet the established requirements. However, as the fleet ages, losses are not replaced. The units operating that type of aircraft are gradually reduced till the fleet is phased out. On average, modern combat aircraft can have an SOW of 1-2 per cent of the fleet strength.

Adding the maintenance reserve figures and Strike-Off Wastage to the unit authorization of combat aircraft squadrons and units authorized to hold combat aircraft of the IAF and the Indian Navy (IN), the total authorization of combat aircraft for India will be approximately 1000 combat aircraft.[25]

The Current Situation

The combat aircraft situation in India is best summarized in Paragraphs 29 and 30 of the Thirty-Fifth Report of the Standing Committee On Defence (2017-18) (Sixteenth Lok Sabha) Ministry of Defence [Action Taken by the Government on the Observations/ Recommendations contained in the Twenty-Ninth Report (Sixteenth Lok Sabha) on 'Demands for Grants of the Ministry of Defence for the year 2017-18 on Army, Navy and Air Force (Demand No. 20)'] and presented to the Lok Sabha on December 19, 2017:[26]

> The Committee has been informed that the present requirement of IAF is at least 45 fighter squadrons to counter a two-front collusive threat. However, IAF as on date has 33 active fighter squadrons as against Government authorised strength of 42 squadrons. Further, the Committee is given to understand that this gap in the Force level is due to the rate at which fighter aircraft are retiring after completion of their total technical life which exceeds the rate at which their replacements are being inducted into the IAF. That as 14 squadrons of MiG 21, 27 and 29 are due for de-induction in next 10 years, the present level of 33 squadrons will further go down to 19 by 2027, and may further reduce to 16 by 2032. To arrest the drawdown, the Committee has been informed by the representatives of Air Force that induction of [the] Su-30, *Tejas* and Rafale Aircraft would help in addressing the problem.

From the time this observation by made by the Parliamentarians, the total number of combat aircraft squadrons of IAF has come down further to 31.[27] The rate of Induction of LCA is slower than expected and losses owing to accidents, operations and on account of completion of TTL are continuing unabated.

Expected Combat Aircraft Inventory in India

An appropriate selection of the time-frame to devise capability goals is of utmost significance. In the case of airpower and specifically for combat aircraft, it is dictated by the combat platform's lifespan, the rate of capability build-up, the rate of technological innovations in the operational environment and financial support visibility. Going by the trend of these factors, a period of twenty years is considered relevant in the Indian context. So what will be the combat aircraft scenario in India after two decades? This question has various facets but for an objective assessment, these have been clubbed into three verticals – Global, Regional and Internal factors. Global and Regional factors are covered in this section and Internal factors are deliberated upon in the next chapter.

Global Signs

The trend in defence expenditure worldwide, in general, and for the top 19 countries with more than 200 combat aircraft in particular, is indicative of the resources being earmarked for the defence sector. The share of the defence budget earmarked for acquisition and operation of combat aircraft indicates that the world combat aircraft inventory is expected to go down below 10,000 in the next two decades (Figure 11.2). In case this projection comes true within a reasonable error margin of 10 per cent, the Indian combat aircraft inventory, following the global trend, is likely to shrink further from its current strength. In the last three decades, the share of the Indian combat aircraft inventory has been synchronous with the share of the top 19 countries. The same trend is expected to continue (Figure 12.4).

Figure 12.4: Share of Top 19 Countries and India in World Combat Aircraft Inventory

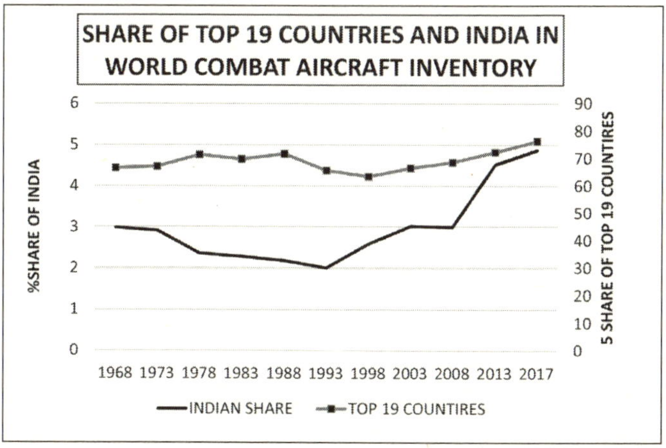

Source: CAIDB.

Currently, the Indian share in the world combat aircraft inventory is 5.1 per cent. In case the same share is retained, owing to an expected shrinking of world combat aircraft inventory, India is expected to have 540 combat aircraft in 2032 and around 350 aircraft by the time, independent India celebrates its centenary in 2047. However, in case, the trend of a rising Indian share in the world combat aircraft inventory that started in 1993 continues, it is expected to cross 7.5 per cent and is numerically expected to be around 520 by 2047 (Figure 12.5).

Figure 12.5: Projected Indian Combat Aircraft Strength 2018-2047

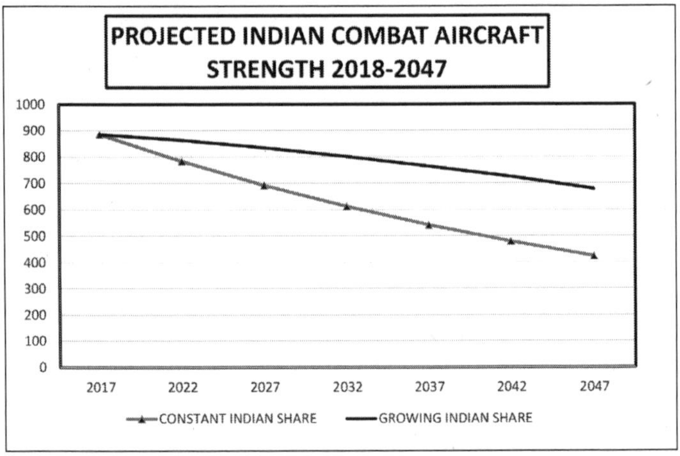

Source: Extrapolated from data extracted from CAIDB.

It is indeed difficult to predict the numbers accurately but going by the current trends, geostrategic environment, technological changes, capability expansions, emerging alternatives and financial outlays, by 2047, the Indian combat aircraft inventory is expected to be between 350 and 520, and most probably closer to 425, much lower than the authorized number of around 1000 combat aircraft with 42 combat squadrons for the IAF and the rest for the Indian Navy. Heading towards that force structure, the IAF combat aircraft inventory will be around 500 aircraft, with the Indian Navy having fifty aircraft in two decades from now. However, the actual inventory will be a reflection of the geopolitics and geo-economics in the intervening period.

Regional Dynamics

What India needs is to have relevant airpower for the security of her national interests. It will primarily depend on the expansion of the national interests and the capabilities of the competing entities in that region. China and Pakistan are of prime interest in this sector. The IAF's current capability is higher than that of Pakistan and lower than that of China. Looking at the broader parameters with respect to Pakistan, Rodney W. Jones in his research paper titled "Conventional Military Imbalance and Strategic Stability in South Asia", indicated a widening of gap in conventional capability between India and Pakistan as:[28]

> India enjoys a large and growing conventional military superiority over Pakistan.....
> .... India's ability to fight offensively with combined arms techniques has significantly outpaced Pakistan's: between 1990 and 2003 India attained and maintained a 3:1 high-performance aircraft numerical advantage over Pakistan...
> .... Overall asymmetry of economic resources and limitations on Pakistan's ability to acquire modern systems has slowed its conventional modernization by comparison with India so that the capability gap continues to widen.

However, concerning Pakistan, as far as the relative strength of airpower is concerned, an assessment by Walter C. Ladwig in the *Journal of Strategic Studies* indicates a narrowing of the gap.[29]

To make a better assessment between these two views, it will be pertinent to look at the combat airpower matrix of these three regional majors tabulated in Table 12.1. A clear picture emerges about the relative position of these three players in the region. While the numerical strength of various fleets has been taken from the *Military Balance, 2019*, classification of the fleets in various categories and the relative value of the combat potential is based on a personal assessment and is subjective.[30] While deliberating on the issue, several experienced combat aviators were consulted but as in combat, even in this aspect, views were diverse. Therefore, at best, this assessment can be used as a benchmark. In this Table, the value of the combat potential is computed by the summation of the product obtained after multiplying the number of platforms with the combat potential value.

Table 12.1: Combat Aviation Fleet in the Region

Combat Potential		China		India		Pakistan	
Potential	Value	Type	Quantity	Type	Quantity	Type	Quantity
High	1	J20	12	-	-	-	-
		SU35	24	-	-	-	-
Sub Total			36	-	-	-	-
Medium	0.75	SU30	97	SU30	242	JF17	85
		J10	426	MIG29	107	F16	75
		J11	297	TEJAS	9	-	-
		J15	20	M2000	50	-	-
		J16	60	-	-	-	-
		SU27	52	-	-	-	-
Sub Total			952		408		160
Low	0.5	H6	203	Jaguar	115	Mirage V	51
		J7	712	MIG21	153	F7	93
		J8	172	MIG27	80	Mirage III	75
		JH7	260	-	-	-	-
		JL10	24	-	-	-	-
		JL9	73	-	-	-	-
Sub Total			1444		348		219
Marginal	0.1	K8	366	Hawk	120	K8	38
Sub Total			366		120		38
Grand Total			2798		876		417
Combat Value			1508.6		492		233.3

Source: Author.[31]

The relative combat potential of combat aircraft fleets of China, India and Pakistan as it stands today is 6:2:1 respectively.

The addition of 36 Rafale aircraft by 2022 in the IAF inventory is unlikely to change this relation significantly owing to phasing out of several IAF aircraft in the interim. The terrain is an additional factor that plays a role in the India-China airpower matrix. In the likely conflict zone of North and Northeast India, Chinese airpower does not enjoy 3:1 capability superiority owing to terrain and infrastructure imperatives. Given this, where does IAF head in the next two decades? To make an assessment, it is pertinent to look at the strategic aim of capability development that, though not enunciated, can be classified at three different levels:

A. To retain matching capability with Pakistan;
B. To retain the current level of relative capability concerning Pakistan and China; and
C. To enhance the capability to match developing Chinese capability in the contest zone.

From current force levels in terms of quality and quantity, the three above- mentioned strategic goals can be achieved by the IAF combat squadron strength of 25, 35 and 45 squadrons, quantitatively. Also, the Indian Navy will have combat aircraft for its aircraft carrier(s) and the numbers could be worth two to three squadrons. Overall, Indian combat aircraft inventory based on strategic goals could be between 550 and 1000 in 2039. Expected force levels in Pakistan and China have been factored-in into this assessment. Both these countries are expected to have smaller combat aircraft inventories in 2039 as compared to their current levels and it may shrink further by 2047. Based on the available trends, Pakistan's inventory is likely to be around 300 to 350 and China's will have over 1,500 to 1,600 combat aircraft in 2039. This is because of the phasing out of almost all third-generation combat aircraft in their inventory today and a lower rate of replacement in keeping with global trends.

The role defined for combat airpower, as a subset of the overall combat capability of the nation, will provide a pivotal input in decision-making. As per the current assessment, combat airpower is a critical component and will influence the outcome of a deterrent strategy or a military conflict with China and/or Pakistan in the coming decades. Therefore, a reduction in combat airpower must be offset by adding certain combat capabilities in other domains (kinetic/non-kinetic) to retain an overall balance. With a force level of 550 combat aircraft, India's combat capability concerning China will go down drastically and may lead to loss of strategic space and thereafter, strategic freedom. For Pakistan, the current edge in combat potential will be denuded and the options available to the government of the day will be severely limited. Owing to a long gestation period of acquisition and operationalization of combat aircraft, the decision taken now about investment in combat aviation will govern the combat airpower in the next two decades. That may define the strategic choices that India will have till 2039.

Notes

1. Josy Joseph, "What is the Doklam issue all about?" *The Hindu*, January 27, 2018 at https://www.thehindu.com/news/national/what-is-the-doklam-issue-all-about/article22536937.ece, accessed on April 1, 2019.
2. Rajat Pandit, "India, China to resume annual 'Hand-in-Hand' military drill", *The Times of India*, October 17, 2018 at https://timesofindia.indiatimes.com/india/india-china-to-resume-annual-military-drill/articleshow/66264565.cms, accessed on April 1, 2019.
3. The Ministry of External Affairs Brief, "The Jammu and Kashmir Issue", April 1, 2003 at https://mea.gov.in/in-focus-article.htm?18971/The+Jammu+and+Kashmir+Issue, accessed on April 1, 2019.
4. General V. P. Malik, "The Kargil War: Some Reflections", *CLAWS Journal*, Summer 2009 at http://www.claws.in/images/journals_doc/1400824315V%20P%20Malik%20%20CJ%20SSummer%202009.pdf, accessed on April 1, 2019.
5. Thomas C. Schelling, *Arms and Influence,* Yale University Press, New Haven CT, 1966, pp. 70-72.
6. *12th Report of the Standing Committee on Defence (2015-2016),* Sixteenth Lok Sabha, Ministry of Defence, p. 18.
7. Indian Navy, " 'Vikrant'– Navy's First Indigenous Aircraft Carrier Launched" at https://www.indiannavy.nic.in/content/vikrant-navys-first-indigenous-aircraft-carrier-launched, accessed on April 1, 2019.
8. "History of Indian Air Force" at http://indianairforce.nic.in/content/history-iaf-0, accessed on December 28, 2018.
9. After independence in 1947, the security environment concerning an external threat to India gradually changed. The significance of settling border issues with India's neighbours namely Pakistan and China,

increased. The option of the use of force for deliberations from a position of strength and militarily with both Pakistan and China, grew. To mitigate these threats, the capability of a non-aligned India had to be increased.

10. Air Commodore Ramesh V. Phadke (Retd.), *Air Power and National Security – Indian Air Force: Evolution, Growth and Future,* Pentagon Press, New Delhi, 2015, pp. 263-267.
11. Ibid.
12. Ibid., p. 155.
13. Pakistan Air Force, "History of PAF" at http://paf.gov.pk/history.html, accessed on April 1, 2019.
14. "History of Indian Air Force", no. 8.
15. As per the "History of Indian Air Force" at http://indianairforce.nic.in/content/history-iaf-0, accessed on December 28, 2018, the state of emergency declared as a result of the fighting between China and India resulted in the disbandment of the Auxillary Air Force and absorption of its personnel and equipment by the regular IAF. An emergency training scheme was instituted in which the services of five flying clubs at Madras, Kanpur, New Delhi, Nagpur and Patiala were enlisted, with more than 1,000 cadets receiving primary flying instruction by the end of 1964. The IAF was expanding rapidly, its personnel strength of 28,000 officers and men at the time of the Sino-Indian conflict increasing by some two-thirds by the end of 1964.
16. "History of Indian Air Force", no. 8.
17. *12th Report of the Standing Committee on Defence (2015-2016),* no. 6, p. 18.
18. Air Commodore Ramesh V. Phadke (Retd.), no. 10, p. 266.
19. Press Release, Ministry of Defence, Government of India, November 9, 2009 at http://www.pib.nic.in/newsite/erelcontent.aspx?relid=53944, accessed on December 27, 2018.
20. Air Commodore Ramesh V. Phadke (Retd.), no. 10, p. 206.
21. Ibid., p. 300.
22. Based on details on the Indian Air Force website at http://indianairforce.nic.in/content/aircraft-systems-testing-establishment, accessed on December 27, 2018.
23. Press Release, Ministry of Defence, Government of India, December 31, 2018 at http://pib.nic.in/PressReleseDetail.aspx?PRID=1557937, accessed on January 11, 2018.
24. "Year End Review – 2018", Ministry of Defence at http://pib.nic.in/PressReleseDetail.aspx?PRID=1557937, accessed on January 11, 2018.
25. 42 combat aircraft squadrons of IAF and three of the IN with 18 aircraft each, about 100 combat aircraft with other units of IAF authorised to hold

combat aircraft and about 10 per cent as MR.

26. 164.100.47.193/lsscommittee/Defence/16_Defence_35.pdf, accessed on May 2, 2018.
27. Air Chief Marshal B.S. Dhanoa, Chief of the Air Staff, IAF during a seminar on "IAF Force Structure: 2035" at India Habitat Centre on September 12, 2018.
28. Rodney W. Jones, "Conventional Military Imbalance and Strategic Stability in South Asia", SASSU Research Paper No. 1, March 2005 at http://www.policyarchitects.org/pdf/Conventional_imbalance_RJones.pdf, accessed on February 25, 2019.
29. Walter C. Ladwig III "Indian Military Modernization and Conventional Deterrence in South Asia", *Journal of Strategic Studies*, 2015, (DOI: 10.1080/01402390.2015.1014473) states. "On an aggregate basis, the Indian Air Force has a 1.9:1 advantage over the Pakistan Air Force, possessing 881 combat aircraft to its smaller neighbour's 450. However, the capability gap between the two fleets is best understood by looking not at the total number of aircraft, but the number of high-performance aircraft in the fleet. If we define modern aircraft broadly to include all fighter aircraft of at least fourth generation –which are multi-role fighters of the 1970s or later design, equipped with sophisticated avionics and weapon systems – the picture looks somewhat worse for Pakistan. In early 2014, the Indian Air Force possessed 327 fighters of the fourth-generation or better in its fleet: 215 Su-30MkI 'Flankers', 62 MiG-29 'Fulcrums' and 50 Mirage-2000s. In contrast, the Pakistan Air Force has 76 F-16s of various types as well as 50 JF-17s which are a 4th generation aircraft jointly produced by Pakistan and China. The Indian Air Force's superiority in modern aircraft presently stands at 2.6:1; however, Pakistan has managed to narrow this gap from the 4:1 differential that prevailed in the early 2000s."
30. Data for the type and number of aircraft is derived from *Military Balance 2019*. Categorisation into High, Medium, Low and Marginal and the relative combat potential has been done by the author based on available technical details about the platforms in open domain and after multiple discussions with several combat aviators. As was expected, no consensus exists. So this at best can be a rough estimate and is subjective.
31. Ibid.

13. Wings and Wheels: India's Internal Factors

Combat aircraft are required for both Air Defence (AD) and Ground Attack (GA) roles and multi-role aircraft, capable of performing either of the roles as per requirement, offer an ideal solution. That is why the replacement of ageing fleet of MiG-21, MiG-27, MiG-29 and Jaguar was sought as a multi-role aircraft. The process started much earlier in the year 2000. The IAF, in August 2000, proposed to acquire 126 Mirage 2000 II (an upgraded version of Mirage 2000) for induction from 2004-05 onwards. The plan was to procure two squadrons from the manufacturer, Dassault Aviation, France and the remaining aircraft license-produced by Hindustan Aeronautics Limited (HAL) under Transfer of Technology (TOT).[1] This was based on available performance parameters and these matched the operational requirement. Since then, IAF has inducted more Su-30, LCA and Rafale. Before proceeding further, it is essential to look at the history of the acquisition of combat aircraft in the IAF. Two facts that emerge are:

- Besides indigenous HF24 in the 1960s and now LCA, historically the IAF combat fleet has been sourced from only three countries, i.e., the UK, France and Russia (erstwhile USSR).
- No combat aircraft has been procured through a competitive bidding process.

These two factors are critical in assessing as to why the IAF identified the Mirage 2000 II as a platform to further augment the combat fleet. Another factor that would have tilted the balance in favour of Mirage 2000 is that its safety record is much better than other combat aircraft fleets in the IAF. In fact, for Mirage 2000, after induction in the mid-1980s, only four aircraft were lost in first ten years of its operations including one in a very high risk Downward Charlie manoeuvre at the Air Force Day Parade in 1988.[2] Additionally, relatively high availability and its performance during the 1999 Kargil conflict proved its versatility for operation at high altitudes. However, one factor that goes against this fleet is its very high cost in the acquisition, operation and maintenance including upgradation. In 2011, the contract signed with Dassault Aviation for upgradation of 52 Mirage 2000s was for Rs 10,947 crores,[3] averaging an expenditure of over Rs 204 crores per aircraft. This amount was then sufficient to buy a new Su-30.[4] The expenditure related to the weapons for the upgraded Mirage 2000 was not included in this cost of upgradation and a separate contract was signed for another Rs 6,600 crores.[5]

After multiple interactions for almost five years between the IAF, Ministry of Defence (MoD) and the aircraft manufacturer Dassault Aviation, the entire process was shelved in favour of a multi-vendor competitive bidding process for acquisition of combat aircraft for the IAF. Never in the history of the IAF, had any combat aircraft been procured on a competitive basis. A new chapter was about to begin. The final quantitative requirement was retained as 126 aircraft. This scheme was referred to as the acquisition of 126 MMRCA (Medium Multi-Role Combat Aircraft). This then, became the most significant capital acquisition scheme for IAF owing to its size and the financial outlays required. There were six contenders for that contract: Rafale, F-18, F-16, Gripen, Eurofighter and MiG-35. Only Rafale and Eurofighter cleared the technical evaluation phase and Rafale emerged as L1 contestant based on LCC. Non-agreement on cost, transfer of technology and responsibility for 108 of the 126 combat aircraft to be produced by HAL in India led to the cancellation of the entire decade-long process. However, to tide over an emergent condition, a contract was signed to procure 36 Rafale along with weapons in 2016 to bolster the IAF combat aircraft fleet. A similar induction of two squadrons of new combat aircraft was executed in the aftermath of F-16's induction in the Pakistan Air Force. The combat aircraft inducted were MiG-23MF (USSR), Mirage 2000

(France) and later MiG-29 (USSR). These inductions were in the 1980s.

In 2017, another attempt was made to bolster the falling combat aircraft inventory of the IAF. A Request for Information (RFI) was issued for 100 combat aircraft. The defined parameters included the single-engine criteria so the shortlist of contenders had only Lockheed Martin's F-16 Block 70 and SAAB's Gripen. A year later, this scheme was shelved, being too restrictive. The qualitative requirements for single-engine were changed. Another RFI was issued in 2018 for 114 combat aircraft. The floor is wide open. This deal with projected numbers at best will be able to sustain the current level of the combat aircraft inventory in India. However, in case the combat aircraft that is procured finally commences its production in India, it will be a long-term gain. Such a venture will not only ease the procurement process but help in generating an aviation ecosystem that will help in modifying and upgrading various facets of combat aircraft already in the inventory of the Indian armed forces. Lockheed Martin and SAAB have already forged a partnership with Indian companies for the project in anticipation to meet the aspiration of "Make in India". After receipt of the response for this RFI in 2018, no tangible progress has been made as yet. This illustrates the byzantine character of defence acquisition in India.

A brief overview and conceptual gaps are discussed here to objectively understand this entire process of military capability build-up in India. Besides import dependency, one of the aspects that stands out in analyzing the defence capability enhancement in India, is a lengthy and very intricate procurement process with certain areas that lack objectivity as brought out by the Directorate General of Audit in their report in 2019.[6] Therefore, even though the requirement projected is very large, the vendor response has rarely been very encouraging.

> The complexities and delays in the acquisition system, narrow, over defined ASQRs and selection on basis of L1 (Lowest Bidder amongst Technically Acceptable vendors) rather than quantitative

> methods of the best value for money seem to be some of the reasons for a poor response from vendors.[7]

On account of uncertainty and delays, such a complicated process often ties down crucial resources of the vendors. This fact too has been well documented by the CAG in his report in 2019:

> ... the committee recommended in March 2015 that the RFP for the procurement of MMRCA may be withdrawn. As a result, the procurement which started in 2000 had made no progress even after the lapse of 15 years.[8]

Framing the Construct – Faulty Foundation

The Indian security matrix depended heavily on Threat-Based Planning (TBP) for development of military capability and Pakistan as the focal threat. However, it gradually shifted to Capability-Based Planning (CBP) to have a force capable of undertaking defined military missions. A huge gap exists in the conceptual construct of CBP and the capability development process. This is evident from the way capital acquisition schemes are fielded. A typical example is of the acquisition of combat aircraft for the IAF. The CBP entails that in an offensive role, the force is capable of striking a target of a defined vulnerability index at a nominal distance from the launch base with a pre-defined accuracy, reliability and preservation in the prevailing or envisaged operational environment. In a defensive role, the force can stall an air offensive of a pre-defined qualitative and quantitative strength. Key parameters for these are combat performance, range, sensors, network integration, weapon load carrying and delivery capability, ease of maintenance and operations and interoperability with other systems and weapons already in the inventory. To translate these criticalities into objective action points for acquisition, the first and the most significant step is defining the Operational Requirements (ORs). This practically defines the operational role that the new platform is expected to perform and is based on a broad operational strategy in the requisite time-frame. These are later suitably modified and converted to Air Staff Qualitative Requirements (ASQRs). While the ageing combat aircraft fleet of the IAF commenced its downward journey, a search was on for a replacement aircraft. As of 2000, the IAF together with its plan to replenish its combat aircraft fleet was also planning to reduce the types of fighter aircraft in its inventory from 15 variants to three or four.[9] Broadly, to assess the operational requirements, the IAF combat aircraft were trifurcated in three distinct classes:[10]

- Long-range and heavyweight fighters
- Medium range, medium capacity and medium-weight multi-role fighters
- Lightweight, limited capacity, low-cost fighter aircraft

The way the IAF combat aircraft fleet was classified indicated a conceptual ambiguity. For better clarity, the parameters defined in the trifurcation of the combat aircraft fleet are tabulated in Table 13.1.

Table 13.1: Classification of IAF Combat Aircraft

Classification	Range	All up Weight	Load Carrying Capacity	Role	Cost
A	Long	Heavy	-	-	-
B	Medium	Medium	Medium	Multi-Role	-
C	-	Light	Limited	-	Low

Source: Based on Comptroller and Auditor General's Report March 2019.[11]

It is evident from Table 13.1 that the All-Up Weight of the aircraft was the only criteria applicable to all three categories of combat aircraft of the IAF. Range, load-carrying capacity, role and cost were secondary and not relevant as these did not figure in the classification matrix for all combat aircraft.

Having classified the combat aircraft fleet, the IAF zeroed-in on the combat aircraft in the medium-range, medium-weight and multi-role category with the same basic performance as that of the Mirage 2000 which was already in service.[12] While defining the ORs, it was peculiar that a term related to AUW of the platform was included. In this acquisition scheme, named the Medium Multi-Role Combat Aircraft (MMRCA) scheme, the term *Medium* was to signify the AUW category of the aircraft between heavy Su-30 and the light *Tejas* LCA. The inclusion of the AUW of a combat platform as primary criteria was perplexing. The scheme was shelved and partially fulfilled by direct acquisition of 36 Rafale, contracted in 2016.

In 2017, another gap in the conceptual construct appeared in the Request for Information (RFI) issued for acquisition of combat aircraft. This time, it shifted from the AUW to the number of engines in combat aircraft. To fulfill the requirement of the balance combat aircraft after signing a contract for 36 Rafale, the plan was to acquire single-engine combat aircraft. Even this scheme was shelved –primarily to accommodate more contenders. A right decision – as the number of engines cannot be a primary criterion for the acquisition of a combat aircraft. Somehow this anomaly found its way in other capital equipment procurement plans of the Indian armed forces as well. A similar quest for an aerial refueller with two engines by the IAF and the addition of the requirement of twin-engines for combat aircraft for the Indian Navy indicates gaping holes in the conceptual construct in defining the ORs and SQRs. It needs to be understood that the number of engines does not qualify as the primary criteria that define the combat capability of a platform. The focus of the forces has to be on the intended capability only and not on the AUW or the number of engines. These parameters have relevance but of secondary or tertiary nature and cannot be primary defining parameters. Rather the ability to refuel various platforms and the refuelling rate for a refueller or defining the operational parameters that are required to be met, making the number of engines as prime criteria, indicate lack of basic operational understanding and orientation.

While the aspect of enhancing combat power with quantity was being dealt with, another key parameter defined as early as 2001 about reducing the inventory mix to three to four types was ignored completely. Had that been taken cognizance of, the emphasis would have been on the induction of a type already in the inventory like

Su-30 or Mirage 2000 or LCA that was planned for induction in any case. Amongst the three, by adding the *Medium* category in the classification, the Su-30 and LCA were thrown out of the consideration zone before the race began.

Constructing the Case – Faulty Architecture

The Air Staff Qualitative Requirements (ASQR) for MMRCA contained 660 parameters.[13] The ASQRs were made very exhaustive and detailed by including technical and design specifications, apparently putting together product specifications of various vendors and this practically obviates the possibility of any product perfectly meeting all the ASQR parameters.[14] This actually led to not even a single vendor being able to provide all the different functionalities provided by various vendors. A 'wishlist' has to be realistic.[15] The CAG's Performance Audit Report of 2007 on "Defence Capital Acquisition" recommended that ASQRs should be stated in terms of functional parameters[16] that are verifiable and measurable.[17] However, the products were selected or rejected based on ASQR parameters for which there were no objective and verifiable evaluation criteria in the Request for Proposal (RFP).[18] The ASQR parameters of the "Growth Potential" and "Design Maturity" in MMRCA's RFP had no objective, verifiable or measurable criteria prescribed for evaluation.[19] Additionally, the design or technologies stipulated in the ASQRs were found to be inconsistent with the technology offered by the world market. The vendors had sometimes offered better technology or alternative designs to meet the same functions desired by the IAF. In these cases, the ASQRs became so unique that vendors could and did claim that they had to customise their standard products to meet the unique Indian ASQRs, which entailed additional cost.[20] In the entire process, what came out starkly was that the Ministry of Defence, in addition to the IAF, lacks exposure in the formulation of ASQRs and this aspect needs recognition, acceptance and rectification.[21]The foundation of acquisition, the ASQR were faulty and this process was adversely commented on by the CAG in its report:

Audit, therefore recommends that IAF should improve its process of formulation of ASQRs to ensure that they correctly reflect the user's functional parameters. Exhaustive ASQRs with detailed technical or design specifications should be avoided unless they are functionally necessary. In the process of acquisition, the involvement of academic experts, in relevant fields, such as aerospace engineering is advisable in the view of the fact that latest and most complex technologies, evolving rapidly, are being used in almost all defence systems and weapons. [22]

Execution – Long Acquisition Process

Transparency and well-defined procedures are the hallmarks of any acquisition process. The Defence Procurement Procedures[23] are well-articulated but the outcome depends on the individuals who have to implement the procedures as defined. Some critical failures in acquisitions are covered here bringing out the gap between laid down procedure and execution. This gap in certain schemes was too wide and the procurement process often lacked transparency. The ASQRs were modified without any recorded reason after submission of the bids,[24] some ASQRs waived; and some ASQRs were shifted to Contract Negotiations Committee (CNC) to negotiate, though these were technical issues[25] And also, the MoD was ready to accept products based on presentations/commitments made by the vendor or based on lab tests/certification/documentation without practically testing and undertaking field trials of the product against required ASQRs.[26] Moreover, in a complicated acquisition process, the Ministry of Defence's stand that rejection or acceptance of the technical bid is based on several factors other than mere ASQRs, makes matters worse.[27] Consequently, the objectivity, equity and consistency of the technical evaluation process are affected[28] and was evident in the Technical Evaluation Reports.[29] Additionally, an opportunity was provided to the vendors to significantly modify their technical bid.[30] It is very clear that in the entire process for MMRCA acquisition, Dassault Aviation was treated preferentially.[31] This created difficulties during technical and price evaluation and affects the integrity of competitive tendering, and also became one of the main reasons for delays in the acquisition process.[32] The lack of objectivity brings opacity to the entire process.

The RFP for MMRCA stated that the vendor shall guarantee the performance of the product as per design specification, at the production agency or customer locations. During contract negotiations, Dassault Aviation took the position that the firm was only responsible for delivery of 18 direct flyway aircraft, CKD, SKD and IM kits and weapons and associated supply and services. HAL, as the production agency, was responsible for the quality of the 108 aircraft to be manufactured by it under ToT. The Contract Negotiation Committee insisted that Dassault Aviation should take full responsibility for the quality and performance of all 126 aircraft as required under the RFP. This led to a deadlock. Five years after the bid and after three years of evaluation and negotiations, there was no finalisation.[33] The entire process was cancelled in 2015 and instead, a contract was signed with Dassault Aviation in 2016 for procurement of 36 Rafale in a fly-away condition. Once again, India procured combat aircraft without a competitive bidding process and sourced from one of the three – the UK, France and Russia.

In broader terms, the entire execution of acquisition process needs a review. From the initiation of the case to the signing of the contract, each procurement case has to sequentially go through eleven stages. At each stage, approval of a competent authority (approval point) is obtained before moving to the next stage. Each of these approval points has about five submission points at which different subordinate officers process the file before putting it up to the approving authority. The number of points gets multiplied each time a query or objection is raised by someone, as the file has to travel right down the chain to respond to the queries. For example, before obtaining the approval of CFA for signing the contract for the procurement, MoD (Finance) and Ministry of Finance make queries five times and the file has to go through another 75 submissions between the various desks in Air Headquarters, Ministry of Defence, MoD (Finance) and the

Ministry of Finance. This multiple layers of control and oversight only reduces the efficiency of the system without adding much to the effectiveness.[34] The procurement case has to pass the scrutiny of eight committees besides being approved by the Cabinet Committee on Security in case of high-value contract. These committees on average have ten members. The Staff Equipment Policy Committee (SEPC), responsible for approving the ASQR has twelve members. The Contract Negotiation Committee has twelve members. Such an organisation has resulted in diffused accountability. [35] Despite such scrutiny and oversight, external audit detected several irregularities and improprieties.[36] The fault is not in the defined process as that allows collegiate vetting for faster decision making at every stage. Individuals holding key positions in the acquisition chain need adequate training and thereafter be held accountable for their decisions.

Hunt for a Solution

Revisiting the IAF inventory of combat aircraft for the next decade, the options are simple. Two types of combat aircraft – MiG-21 and MiG-27 – are scheduled to be phased out on completion of their Calendar Life/total technical Life (Cl/TTL) by 2022. The Mirage 2000, Jaguars and MiG-29, under upgradation, will continue until completion of their CL/TTL, which may stretch till 2030 or beyond, based on their utilization rate. This leaves the IAF with the Su-30, the indigenous LCA, and Rafale. Rather than induct a new type with considerable System Induction Cost (SIC)[37], the option ought to be enhancing the quality and quantity of these three types—the Su-30, LCA, and Rafale—to achieve requisite combat capability. The IAF may also be looking at bolstering inventory of the MiG-29, already in service, from Russia.[38] The Su-30 are available in large numbers and would need to be upgraded to retain operational relevance. Another option open to the IAF will be to enhance numbers of the Rafale and the LCA. In case the exorbitant cost of the Rafale makes it an unviable option, then the LCA remains the only practical option.

During his address to the Air Force Commanders' Conference in October 2018, the Raksha Rajya Mantri (Minister of State for Defence) Dr Subhash Bhamre said: "I commend the IAF leadership in promoting indigenisation in multiple ways. IAF's resolve to wholeheartedly support the indigenous LCA programme by committing to procure 18 squadrons of LCA and its variants endorsing its capability is notable and praiseworthy."[39] The IAF's plan to induct 18 squadrons of the LCA is rather ambitious. However, the capability of the LCA and its production, both need a comprehensive review in case it has to be the mainstay of IAF along with Su-30 for the next two decades.

Qualitatively, the Indian combat aircraft inventory needs to have an equitable distribution between high, mid- and low-end technology. This, translated in terms of generation of combat aircraft, will mean a mix of fourth to fifth-generation aircraft two decades from now. The IAF will have the Su-30, the LCA and the Rafale combat aircraft in 2039 (20 years on) from the existing inventory with all other current types phasing out on completion of their Calendar Life/Total Technical Life/ Obsolescence. From the existing inventory and the planned induction of aircraft, the number of operational Su-30 and LCA (including a likely order of 83, making the total order of 123 LCA) are expected to be between 100-120 each, and approximately 32 Rafale. Therefore, in 2039, the IAF will have about 250 combat aircraft, in case no new orders are placed. To match up the strategic capability goals A, B and C mentioned earlier in Chapter 12, in the next 20 years, IAF would need an additional 300, 550 and 750 combat aircraft respectively. This broadly will translate in the induction of one, two and three combat aircraft respectively every month for the next 20 years! (Table 13.2). For ease, this can be referred to as Plan-123. Based on the strategic capability goal for India, the induction of one/two/three combat aircraft every month for the next two decades is a necessity. Broadly, there are only two options—either procure combat aircraft from a foreign vendor or establish at least one more production line in India.

Table 13.2: Combat Aircraft Requirement Matrix until 2039

Strategic Goal	Condition	Numbers of Combat Aircraft Required	Expected Number of Existing/ contracted combat aircraft in 2039	Number of aircraft required in the next 20 years (240 months)	Average Induction of combat aircraft required per month till 2039
		(a)	(b)	(c)=(a)-(b)	(d)=(c)/240
A	Parity with Pakistan	550	250	300	1.25
B	Existing Level of Quantitative Match for China and Pakistan	800	250	550	2.29
C	Parity with Chinese deployable force on Indian Borders	1000	250	750	3.12

Source: Author-tabulated based on expected requirement and expected inventory in the next two decades.

Path Ahead

Focussing only on Scenario A, at this juncture, India will need to have a minimum of 550 combat aircraft by 2039. Three types of aircraft existing will be Rafale, Su-30 and LCA and total around 250 platforms. The basic problem statement, at this juncture, for India's combat aircraft fleet, is about the induction of a minimum of 300 new combat aircraft in the next two decades. Primarily, that could happen in two distinct ways – one by an increasing number of aircraft of an existing type and other by inducing a new type of combat aircraft in its fleet.

In 2019, with the induction of Rafale, the IAF combat aircraft fleet has its eighth type of combat aircraft: the MiG-21 with multiple variants, the MiG-27 and the twin-seater MiG-23UB (Phased out in December 2019), the MiG29, the Su-30, the Jaguar, the Mirage 2000 and the *Tejas* LCA. While specialised roles are performed by specifically designed aircraft, the trend has changed with each combat aircraft now capable of performing multiple roles. The Su-30, the Mirage 2000 and the LCA are multi-role aircraft while the Jaguar and the MiG-27 are for GA and the MiG-29 is a primarily Air Defence (AD) aircraft with limited Ground Attack (GA) capability. Various variants of the MiG-21 in today's context have limited AD and GA capability.

To achieve congruence with the larger objective of reducing the number of types of combat aircraft from eight to three/four, the ideal solution will be to accumulate inventory in one of the types of combat aircraft planned to be operating in 2039. This is also mandatory, as the fourth type will be an FGFA. The choice, therefore, is between Rafale, Su-30MKI and LCA. Licensed production of the Su-30 is approaching the last phase of scheduled production and may terminate in 2020 unless more orders are placed.[40] The LCA production line at HAL is gradually building up capacity to produce eight aircraft per year.[41] The Rafale's Transfer of Technology and production in India was stalled as part of 126 MMRCA deal and is unlikely to be set up unless accompanied by a major order and large payment. So practically, the choice facing the IAF is between the Su-30 and LCA. Amongst the two, the LCA is more relevant in the expected operational environment owing to its lower observability, indigenous design allowing unrestricted modifications and availability of all protocols for efficient integration of new avionics and weapons in future.

The economy of scale is a principle that ought not to be ignored in logistical planning for the sustenance of combat aircraft. Multiple types of combat aircraft sourced from different countries and companies need multiple logistical lines and large-scale stocking owing to lack of commonality. The average cost of spare inventory to sustain the requisite level of serviceability of the fleet as compared to the platform cost decreases with an increase in the number of platforms. Along with inventory costs, the costs associated with setting up maintenance infrastructure, number of personnel to be trained and employed for maintenance activities, size and scale of training establishments for training do not increase proportionally with the increase in the number of platforms. This difference in cost forms a significant portion of the System Induction Cost (SIC- explained in detail in Chapter 10).

To understand the concept clearly, let us paint two extreme and distinct scenarios. In the scenario I, the IAF operates only one type of multi-role combat aircraft for all 42 squadrons; and in scenario II, it operates 42 types of multi-role combat aircraft (one squadron per type). Although neither is a practical solution, all operational, maintenance, logistical and human resource experts will choose scenario I over scenario II. There is no clear mathematical formula to work out ideal numbers of platform per type to reach an optimum cost matrix. Therefore, there is a need to keep inventory diversity low. The US and China currently have an average of over 240 combat aircraft per type.[42] Going by that standard, the IAF needs to reduce its combat aircraft inventory diversity from eight to four types. Incidentally, this was the goal with which the IAF combat aircraft procurement process started in the year 2000.[43]As combat aircraft remain on the inventory for nearly three decades, it is important the decision regarding induction of new types of combat aircraft be taken in this perspective.

In case a decision is taken at present to establish a line for manufacturing combat aircraft in India, it will start production in three years, and till 2039 it will have to produce one/two/three aircraft every month for Plan-123. While the availability and acquisition of fifth-generation combat aircraft are some distance away for the IAF, what needs to be done now is to fill the capability void of the fourth-generation combat aircraft (Aspect of various generations of combat aircraft is explained in detail in Chapter 5). For cost imperatives, the same strategy of a mix of fourth and fifth generation combat aircraft is planned for the USAF.[44] Aircraft like the Su-30 fall in fourth-generation category of combat aircraft. A pragmatic and practical approach will be to commence a process of acquiring 150 combat aircraft of the 300 needed to achieve goal A. The balance 150 aircraft are to be acquired post the availability of the FGFA (Fifth-Generation Fighter Aircraft) by 2027 or earlier. In the meantime, the force matrix will have Jaguars, Mirage 2000s and MiG-29s along with the Rafale, Su-30 and LCA. This plan will give India a minimum of 400 combat aircraft in 2039, quantitatively a reduction of 45 per cent from the existing inventory. Qualitatively, it will have only 15 per cent aircraft with high technology and the balance in the mid- and low technology category, a scaled-down version of the current technology matrix. Once the FGFA is declared operational, it needs to be produced and inducted at a rate of over one aircraft/month to reach an inventory of over 150 platforms by 2039. This will give Indian armed forces adequate might to close into strategic goal B.

The choice for a planned induction of 300 combat aircraft is critical as the aircraft selected needs to be operationally relevant in 2039 and beyond until possibly 2050. The criticality in the choice is of the basic aircraft design. It needs to have low observability as the key criteria. The operational systems, including avionics, sensors and weapons, have to be modular that can be replaced with the upgraded version as and when available. These are primarily dependent on computational power and electronic arrays. While super cruise, that is, the ability to cruise at supersonic speeds without the use of an afterburner, like in the F-22 is gradually gaining ground as an operational attribute it is unlikely to surpass the impact of the combination of observability/sensor/weapon in the relevant period.

Should other platforms be considered for this order? Of course, all options must be explored. All seven contenders, Rafale, Eurofighter, MiG-35, Su-35, Grippen, F-18 and F-21, are relevant today.[45] However, based on the basic design differential, some older platforms will gradually slip lower faster with the progression of time as compared to new-generation combat aircraft. Therefore, amongst the contenders, platform selection needs to be based purely on operational relevance.

Zeroing down on the choices to bridge the capability gap

till induction of the FGFA, it is the LCA or the other type or a combination of the two. There is already a planned induction of the 123 LCA. With an additional order of 150, thus taking the total strength to 273; the economies of scale and uniformity of platforms will lead to major savings in revenue costs owing to the cutting down of operational, maintenance and training costs.[46] This, in other words, can be termed as additional SIC (System Induction Cost) should a platform other than the LCA be inducted.

The manufacturing cost will be another area where the economies of scale will have an impact. The reduced cost will lower the already stretched capital expenditure by amortisation over a larger inventory. It is difficult to assess the exact impact of a large-scale order on the production cost of combat aircraft but is expected to be in the region of 5-10 per cent. Such saving is evident from the F-35 manufacturing costs. The September 2018 contract between the US Government with the Lockheed Martin lowered the price of F-35As procured in low rate initial production (LRIP) lot 11 to $89.2 million, dropping below $90 million for the first time, and 5.4 per cent better than the previous production lot. The unit prices of the short-take-off vertical-landing (STOVL) F-35B dropped by 5.7 per cent to $116 million, and the carrier-capable F-35C's 11.1 per cent to $108 million.[47] The commonality of the platform has inherent advantages and gradually more players will come on board to exploit this attribute. In case, the LCA manages to meet the requirements of the Indian Navy, it will be a bonus. For this commonality, the current estimate for the F-35's total procurement quantity is gradually increasing from 2443 to 2456.[48] In fact, the Selected Acquisition Report of the US Department of Defense lays out the Mission and Description of the F-35 Joint Strike Fighter Program emphasising on operational and cost efficiencies of a common platform:[49]

> The planned DoD F-35 Fleet will replace the joint services' legacy fleets. The transition from multiple types/model/series to a common platform will result in smaller total force overtime and operational and overall cost efficiencies.

The Initial Operational Clearance (IOC) of the LCA took place in 2013.[50]The focus to get the Final Operational Clearance (FOC) resulted in the integration of the Derby, a Beyond Visual Range Air-to-Air Missile, one of the major objectives of FOC for the LCA. The LCA successfully fired Derby on April 27, 2018, from the firing range off the Goa coast.[51]. Additionally, the efficacy and integration of indigenous LCA aircraft in the operational matrix of the IAF were also checked out in the IAF's Exercise *Gagan Shakti 2018* along with the capabilities of the upgraded Mirage 2000 and the MiG-29 aircraft.[52] Finally, on February 20, 2019, the LCA achieved the FOC. The FOC has the addition of key capabilities to the IOC aircraft including Beyond- Visual-Range Missile capabilities, Air-to-Air Refuelling, Air-to-Ground earmarked weapons and general flight envelope expansion. The FOC standard aircraft drawings have already been handed over to HAL to start production after incorporating key changes over the IOC standard aircraft. The achievement of the FOC is the culmination of a process that started in 1983 with the involvement of multiple agencies in the design, development and production of the aircraft.[53]This additional order would entail the production of 273 LCA till 2039. The current rate of production at HAL is four per year and is expected to go up to eight per year. The production capacity will have to more than triple to around twenty-five per year. Additionally, qualitatively, the platform will have to improve to be relevant in the operational scenario in the next two decades. The LCA project is moving in the right direction, albeit at a very slow pace.

Looking at the production capacity, there are major challenges as far as HAL is concerned. In 2018-19, of the planned nine LCA, in the first ten months only one was delivered. HAL has invested in enhancing capabilities and plans to deliver sixteen aircraft in FOC configuration in 2019-20[54] ; such a target, if met, will defy the norms of low productivity that HAL has been demonstrating over the years. Several questions have been raised on efficiency and quality control of HAL products over time. Major issues in this regard are discussed in the next chapter.

Notes

1. *Performance Audit Report of the Comptroller and Auditor General of India on Capital Acquisition in Indian Air Force for the Union Government (Defence Services),* Air Force Report No. 3 of 2019 tabled on the floor of the Parliament on February 13, 2019, p 111.
2. "Mirage-2000 crashes in Gwalior, pilot safe", *Outlook*, September 23, 2004 at https://www.outlookindia.com/newswire/story/mirage-2000-crashes-in-gwalior-pilot-safe/251251 (Accessed on April 2, 2019).
3. "Government okays $2.4 bn Mirage-2000 upgrade", NDTV News, July 13, 2011 at https://www.ndtv.com/india-news/government-okays-2-4-bn-mirage-2000-upgrade-461390 (Accessed on April 2, 2019).
4. Rajat Pandit, "High cost of Mirage-2000 upgrade raises eyebrows", *TheTimes of India*, March 5, 2013 at https://timesofindia.indiatimes.com/india/High-cost-of-Mirage-2000-upgrade-raises-eyebrows/articleshow/18804336.cms (Accessed on April 2, 2019).
5. Ibid.
6. *Performance Audit Report of the Comptroller and Auditor General of India on Capital Acquisition in Indian Air Force for the Union Government (Defence Services)*, no. 1, p. v.
7. Ibid.
8. Ibid., p. 125.
9. Ibid., p. 111.
10. Ibid.
11. Ibid.
12. Ibid.
13. Ibid., p. 11.
14. Ibid., pp. 11-12.
15. Ibid., p. 13.
16. As per *Performance Audit Report of the Comptroller and Auditor General of India on Capital Acquisition in Indian Air Force for the Union Government (Defence Services)*, Ibid., p. 10, functional specification means the basic function or duty to be fulfilled by the product. For example, "Gun capable of firing targets at a minimum distance of 5 km", "Vehicle capable of carrying a load of 10 Tons". Technical specifications detail the physical description of the item including size, tolerances, materials, design or technology.
17. *Performance Audit Report of the Comptroller and Auditor General of India on Capital Acquisition in Indian Air Force for the Union Government (Defence Services),* no. 1., p.10.
18. Ibid., p. 18.
19. Ibid., p. 117.

20. Ibid., pp. 11-12.
21. Ibid., p. 114.
22. Ibid., p. vi.
23. The capital procurement for the Indian Armed Forces is covered by the Defence Procurement Procedure that is available on the Ministry of Defence website https://mod.gov.in/defence-procurement-procedure.
24. *Performance Audit Report of the Comptroller and Auditor General of India on Capital Acquisition in Indian Air Force for the Union Government (Defence Services),* no. 1, p. 11.
25. Ibid., p v.
26. Ibid., p. 18.
27. Ibid., p. 17.
28. Ibid.
29. Ibid., p. 18.
30. Ibid.
31. Ibid., p.116.
32. Ibid.
33. Ibid., pp. 123-124.
34. Ibid., pp. 31-32.
35. Ibid., pp.31-35.
36. Ibid., pp.31-32.
37. For details of System Induction Cost, see Chapter 9.
38. Manu Pubby, "IAF in talks with Russia for urgent MiG 29 purchase", *The Economic Times*, February 13, 2019 at https://economictimes.indiatimes.com/news/defence/iaf-in-talks-with-russia-for-urgent-mig-29-purchase/articleshow/67968978.cms (Accessed on April 2, 2019).
39. "Raksha Rajya Mantri, Dr Subhash Bhamre inaugurates Air force commanders' conference", Press Release, PIB, October 11, 2018 at http://pib.nic.in/newsite/pmreleases.aspx?mincode=33 (Accessed on October 12, 2018).
40. Ajai Shukla, "As Sukhoi-30MKI production nears an end, HAL worries about future", *Business Standard*, August 23, 2017 at https://www.business-standard.com/article/economy-policy/as-sukhoi-30mki-production-nears-end-hal-worries-about-future-117082000475_1.html (Accessed on February 27, 2019).
41. Gulshan Luthara, "HAL to Triple LCA Production to 24 Per Year", *India Strategic*, August 2018 at https://www.indiastrategic.in/2018/08/20/hal-to-triple-lca-production-to-24-per-year/ (Accessed on February 27, 2019).
42. Sourced from Author's Combat Aircraft Inventory Database.

43. *Performance Audit Report of the Comptroller and Auditor General of India on Capital Acquisition in Indian Air Force for the Union Government (Defence Services)*, no. 1, p. 111.
44. US Department Of Defense, "Press Briefing on the Fiscal Year 2020 Air Force Budget", at https://dod.defense.gov/News/Transcripts/Transcript-View/Article/1784354/department-of-defense-press-briefing-on-the-fiscal-year-2020-air-force-budget/ (Accessed on April 2, 2019).
45. "Lockheed Martin unveils new F-21 fighter jet to be made in India", *Business Today,* February 20, 2019 at https://www.businesstoday.in/current/corporate/lockheed-martin-unveils-new-f21-fighter-jet-to-be-made-make-in-india/story/320634.html (Accessed on March 19, 2019).
46. Based on discussion with IAF personnel involved in managing Human Resource functions for combat aircraft operations and maintenance, it is assessed that Human Resource savings are expected to be in the region of 10-12 per cent of manpower deployed in combat aircraft operation and maintenance. Taking average personnel strength in a combat aircraft squadron in the IAF and associated revenue expenditure, a savings of 1.03 per cent of IAF Revenue Expenditure on Pay and Allowances can be achieved. This is computed based on the overall strength of IAF personnel and expected the strength of personnel supporting maintenance activities in combat aircraft unit. Combining likely operational and maintenance costs with this, IAF overall revenue expenditure can be curtailed by up to 0.76 per cent.
47. Greg Waldron. "Massive F-35 deal covers production into 2023", *Flight Global*, November 15, 2018 at https://www.flightglobal.com/news/articles/massive-f-35-deal-covers-production-into-2023-453656/ (Accessed on November 18, 2018).
48. *Selected Acquisition Reports, F-35 Lightning II Joint Strike Fighter (JSF) Program (F-35) as of FY 2018 President's Budget Defense Acquisition Management Information Retrieval (DAMIR)* US DoD, December 2016, p 28.
49. *Selected Acquisition Report (SAR),RCS: DD-A&T(Q&A)823-198 F-35 Joint Strike Fighter Aircraft as of FY 2017 President's Budget Defense Acquisition Management Information Retrieval(DAMIR)* March 21, 2016, at www.esd.whs.mil/.../54/...Reports/16-F-0402_DOC_42_F-35_DEC_2015_SAR.pdf accessed on May 2, 2018.
50. "Government of India, Final Operational Clearance of LCA *Tejas* MK I for Indian Air Force", Press Release, Ministry of Defence,February 20, 2019, at https://pib.nic.in/newsite/pmreleases.aspx?mincode=33 (Accessed on February 21, 2019).
51. "LCA Tejas Achieves Yet Another Milestone Towards FOC Certification", PIB, Press release, April 28, 2018 at http://pib.nic.in/newsite/pmreleases.aspx?mincode=33 (Accessed on May 2, 2018).

52. "Conclusion of Exercise Gaganshakti-2018", PIB, Press release, April 24, 2018 at http://pib.nic.in/newsite/pmreleases.aspx?mincode=33 (Accessed on May 2, 2018).
53. Press Release, Ministry of Defence, Government of India, no. 50.
54. "HAL plans to give 16 *Tejas* fighter aircraft by year-end", *The Economics Times*, February 21, 2019 at https://economictimes.indiatimes.com/news/defence/hal-plans-to-give-16-tejas-fighter-aircraft-by-year-end/articleshow/68093547.cms (Accessed on April 2, 2019).

14. Dry Cranking Engine: Indian Indigenous Defence Industry[1]

All major economic and military powers, with the exception of India, have a robust indigenous arms and aircraft industry. The dismal state has led to India heading the list of the largest arms importers of the world. A list of major contracts in this century for aerial warfare and training with foreign vendors tabulated in Table 14.1 narrates the story. This list includes not only combat aircraft but also transport aircraft, helicopters, force multipliers AWACS, targeting pods, radars, weapons and even basic trainer aircraft and simulators. Seventy years after Independence, it is time to analyze as to who has failed India in this aspect – the policymakers or the policy implementers. To assess that, it is essential to look at various aspects of the indigenous aircraft industry. The Indian aviation industry and HAL remained synonymous for a very long time, with both struggling over the years.[2]

Table 14.1: Major Contracts for Aerial Warfare and Training Assets Imported by India since 2000

Year	Major Air Warfare Assets	Quantity	Cost (Billion $)	Source
2000	Su30	140	6.48	Russia
2001	IL38	5	0.15	Russia
2004	Hawk	66	1.42	UK
2004	MiG29	16	0.79	Russia
2004	AWACS IL76	3	1.10	Russia, Israel
2007	Su30	40	1.55	Russia

2008	C130J30	6	0.96	USA
2008	MI17V5	80	1.35	Russia
2009	P8	8	2.10	USA
2010	MIG29	29	1.47	Russia
2010	Hawk	57	1.42	UK
2011	C17	11	4.70	USA
2012	SU30	42	2.97	Russia
2012	MI17V5	71	1.35	Russia
2012	Pilatus PC7	75	0.57	Switzerland
2012	Weapons	-	0.12	Israel
2012	Doppler Weather Radar	11	0.02	Germany
2013	C130J30	6	1.01	USA
2014	Air Missiles and Equipment	-	0.36	UK
2015	AH64E	22	0.19	USA
2015	CH47E	15	1.04	USA
2016	P8	4	1.00	USA
2016	Rafale	36	8.81	France
2016	C130J30	1	0.10	USA
2016	Targeting Pods	-	0.29	Israel
2016	Full Mission Simulator for Su30	5	0.05	Russia
2017	Recce System	-	0.20	Israel
2018	C17	1	0.26	USA
2018	S400	80	5.40	Russia
		Total	47.24	

Source: Author[3]

Sound Start Weak Finish

The aircraft industry in India germinated when Seth Walchand Hirachand conceptualized the idea of Hindustan Aircraft Limited (later named Hindustan Aeronautics Limited or HAL). Taking off in 1940 with the establishment of HAL, the Indian aviation industry has grown in spurts over the past seven decades and more.[4] During the initial phase, HAL provided maintenance support to various combat aircraft of the allied forces in the Second World War and subsequently, commenced licensed production of combat aircraft. After Independence in 1947 and its nationalization, HAL grew in strength to design combat aircraft. After Independence, an attempt was also made through HAL to "re-construct" a force of B-24 Liberators from the mouldering remains of nearly 100 ex-USAF bombers of this type at the Care and Maintenance Unit Depot at Kanpur. Three IAF squadrons were equipped with B-24 bombers. But this force could not be sustained. In the last 70 years, the IAF has inducted HAL-designed and built fighter aircraft HF-24 *Marut* and trainer aircraft HT2, HJT16 and HPT32 into its fleet. Several HAL license-produced fighters (MiG-21, MiG-27, Jaguar, Su-30), trainers (Hawk), transport aircraft (Dornier 228), and helicopters (Chetak, Cheetah) were inducted in the Indian armed forces as well.[5] The largest production project for HAL so far has been for delivery of some 580 MiG-21s. The next big project is with Su-30, which is reaching its terminal stage unless more orders are placed. The hope for getting an order to build 108 Rafale as a part of 126 MMRCA deal evaporated because of manpower costs and non-guarantee for aircraft to be manufactured by HAL.[6] This is indicative of efficiency and quality control processes prevalent at HAL.

Technical Knowhow

One more critical factor in this regard is the availability of technological skills. The inability to manufacture a suitable engine or generate and develop an indigenous engine technology saw the downfall of HF-24 after limited production to equip three IAF squadrons.[7] India's low technological base and isolation meant that the high Air Staff Qualitative Requirements (ASQRs) defined by the IAF for the HF-24 could not be met.[8] Therefore, instead of maturing with age to meet the growing national demand for aviation, HAL gradually lost steam. From being a designer, it slipped back to the lowly status of a license production facility to primarily meet IAF requirements. Eco-systems required to design, develop and produce aircraft sprouted many a time at the organization, only to be quelled. After HF-24, practically, the current under-production Advanced Light Helicopter (ALH) and Light Combat Aircraft (LCA) are two stars of HAL, albeit trying to shine. Thus India, with the fourth largest air force in the world, retains the dubious distinction of operating the largest fleet of foreign-designed aircraft. The picture is bleaker in the civil aviation domain.

Policy Paradigm

Like any other industry, the Indian aviation industry is based on four pillars—policy, technology, manufacturing, and the end-user. The abysmal state of the Indian aviation industry is a result of incoherence and disconnect amongst these four verticals. The necessity of developing an indigenous aviation industry was realized as early as 1940, but it was not backed by a realistic long-term policy. Although HAL's nationalization did give it an initial impetus, the failure to allow competitors in the field, in effect ensuring a monopoly, resulted in a monolith that moved at a glacial pace. On the policy front, some movement has been made by the concept of the Strategic Partnership (SP) in Defence Procurement Procedure (DPP). But, if not modulated properly, the model could remain in assembly-line mode and unable to scale up beyond it. The assembly-line model has limited implications as has been witnessed in the last six decades. Therefore, disruptive innovation is the answer and should be the approach of the government. Competing social sector priorities, the lack of industrial development, and short-sighted vision and policies allowed the Indian aviation industry to just about exist.

Research and Development

The aviation sector has high R&D costs and the risks are extraordinary. As the largest consumer is the government itself, unless a part of the risk is covered by it, private ventures will remain skeptical. At the same time, denying entry to private players with a level playing field would make it difficult to reinvigorate the dormant aviation industry. The second factor is that in this industry the successes are rare and the successful products have to fund the cost of failures as well. Lastly, unless, the production scale of successful articles is high or a firm commitment is available, amortization of R&D costs has to take place on the first order itself. This makes the cost of equipment prohibitive. Strategic direction and appetite for higher risk and investment in research and development (R&D) were missing after the HF-24 experiment. Thus, efficiency and creativity became causalities and what should have been an organic growth of both the organization and indigenous aviation industry, stalled. Unaccounted government support, a captive market in terms of the Indian Armed Forces, and reliance on foreign vendors to supply technology reduced HAL to a mere assembly-line functionary. It is true that India went through phases of technological isolation owing to various political and diplomatic reasons. However, the intervening periods were not utilized efficiently to build a core of technical expertise. Contrast this with the development of India's indigenous space and nuclear programmes. The model followed by the Indian Space Research Organization (ISRO) focused on quality expansion rather than quantity expansion. Yet we find that this was not applied to the aviation sector. What eventually followed was the supremacy of mediocracy.[9] Even today, India is far from developing a suitable engine technology for aviation. The LCA project bore the brunt of this shortcoming. All is not bleak, however. The growth of the indigenous software industry has ensured that we are self-sufficient in some technological aspects.

Innovation

Every industry needs to innovate to survive and be relevant to the changing operational and technical environment. Those who fail to innovate are destined to stagnate and perish in this competitive world. HAL has had 28 major projects till date.[10] Lessons learnt after each project are nearly identical. The inability to learn from the past experiences and global trends is evident. Innovation is missing. Unfortunately, it is this inability that shines throughout the narration of HAL.[11]

Organisational Structure

The industry too has to be ready to keep pace in terms of technology and manufacturing even in case of a robust demand. Assured quality control and adherence to delivery timelines are two parameters on which the end-user will judge the industry and decide on supporting it further or discarding it entirely. Today, private sector entities such as Tata Aero Space Limited—in a joint venture with Lockheed Martin, and aiming to manufacture of the fuselage section of the C130—are appearing on the horizon, albeit at the lower end of the spectrum and limited scales. For the domestic aviation manufacturing industry to grow, these private ventures need to expand manufacturing processes to include high-technology aviation equipment. For that, the order book will have to initially depend on the Government of India (GoI). Even the GoI needs to move aggressively to form joint ventures with technologically relevant aviation manufacturers. The BrahMos model (GOI's share is 50.5 per cent, just short of 51 per cent so it is not classified as DPSU) has yielded results and needs replication.[12] In the aviation space, the manufacturing of the Kamov helicopter, whenever it commences, may provide the requisite boost to this sector and test new structures.

Additionally, the HAL going public is a step in the right direction to enhance its accountability. But HAL would need a strategic partner to meet the production targets. Indian private sector companies have already joined hands with Lockheed Martin and SAAB for the anticipated order of about 100 combat aircraft. The same concept can be exploited by the Indian private sector collaborating with ADA for transfer of technology and thereafter production of the LCA. This will be a game changer for enhancing HAL efficiency as a competitor and creating an ecosystem for the aviation industry in India. Reduction in the profit of HAL is a very small price to pay for developing this national capability.

End User Interface

While it is natural for the combat forces to seek the best combat equipment, their desires need to be realistic too. The HAL-designed HF-24 *Marut* became the first indigenous aircraft in the IAF. This was expected to change the complexion of the IAF's combat aircraft fleet. But HF-24 did not meet the high performance criteria set by the IAF. The Air Staff Qualitative Requirements (ASQR) for HF-24 in the 1950s[13] cannot be met by most of the combat aircraft in the IAF inventory even today! Although the end-user cannot be held accountable for the failure of the industry to grow, a pragmatic hand-holding approach is also required. Expansion of scale with greater visibility can assist the industry to cut production costs and lead to economies of scale.

Financial Prudence

Fear of defeat forces a soldier to train. If victory is assured before a conflict, it is unlikely that soldiers would sweat it out during peacetime. Same is the story with the corporate world. Any company that has profits assured fails to innovate. This is exactly what happened with HAL. Till the late 1990s, the Cost Plus bases[14] of costing ensured that the company would always be profitable no matter how inefficient it remains. Can a company running on cost plus basis ever become efficient?[15] Fortunately, this practice was stopped in 1996 but the culture has not changed much. That is why for a job with same machinery and tools, a Russian in Russia or a French technician in France takes 100 man hours but HAL takes 270 man hours! For the MMRCA deal in June 2011, HAL had stated that the French man hours had to be converted to Indian man hours by multiplying Dassault Aviation quoted man hours by a factor of 2.7.[16] It will take a while for HAL to reinvent itself to meet industry standards.

Production Capability

One of the critical factors for assessing the requirement of combat aircraft in an operational scenario is the nation's capability to replenish the battle losses. Owing to the enhanced complexity of combat aircraft, each manufacturing line averages one aircraft per month. The F-35 production line is the latest example and confirming to this norm. However, the Indian DPSU HAL has rarely met such production targets. The IAF's combat potential will continue to deplete over the next decade as the rate of phase-out is faster than the production/ acquisition rate of one combat aircraft a month. Moreover, HAL being the prime agency for repair and maintenance, that capability needs to be suitably enhanced. Low level of maintenance and reparability will demand that the basic aircraft inventory be enhanced. The new generation aircraft indeed need specialised repair and maintenance facilities as is evident in the case of the F-22 that has had only 60 per cent as the Mission Capable Rate (MCR), one measure of an aircraft's reliability and maintainability.[17] The Indian combat aircraft fleet has had periods of very low availability too with some fleets dipping below 50 per cent mark. Looking objectively at the production value versus the manpower cost since 2003-04, the trend indicates a slide (Figure 14.1).Unless this trend is stemmed and then reversed, the HAL will go into oblivion.

Figure: 14.1 HAL-Value of Production/Manpower Cost

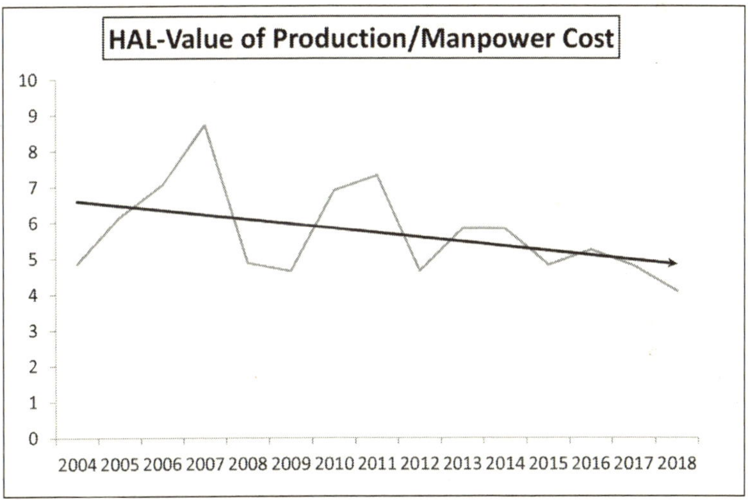

Source: Based on data in HAL Annual Report 2017-18.[18]

International Models and Comparisons

An analysis of different models for the aviation industry that have been developed and followed across the world and the lessons learnt during their application, are relevant.[19] The aviation industry in China, Russia and the US are relevant examples but Embraer (Brazil) is the most notable one. About half a century ago, HAL had a fighter jet design and production to its credit and Embraer was in its infancy looking for expert support from a fellow developing country, India. Apparently, HAL rebuffed Embraer and refused any collaboration with a minnow. Today, Embraer is the third largest manufacturer of aircraft in the world! Lessons need to be learnt and implemented for a growth strategy.

A detailed comparison of the US and the Chinese aviation industry with the HAL is already covered in Chapter 4.

The Way Forward

Models across the world underscore the following critical facets: sustained support by the governments; development of the integrator model; interface with the end-user; and logical production scales. Various models have been advised to reinvigorate HAL and are based on varying degrees of government control, ranging from complete to zero, and on the economics of R&D. A visionary policy and support by the government; efficiency and creativity by the industry; an investment in knowledge and focus on research and development to bridge the technological gap; and a practical and pragmatic end-user to assist in generating the requisite ecosystem. The need of the hour is to strike a balance between these four pillars. Unless a holistic review is carried out with all stakeholders, and an impetus given on all four fronts simultaneously, it will take a long time before Indian aviation industry can be counted among the best.[20]

The Indian Armed Forces are the prime end-users of aviation assets in India and are looking for over 500 platforms in various categories in the next decade alone! The demand in the civil aviation sector is also rising. This boom in demand could trigger an expansion of the domestic aviation industry and lead it to maturity. The indigenous aircraft industry has a pivotal role. The production capacity and efficiency of HAL have a lot of scope of improvement to match the world's industrial standards. Generating competition for HAL may be the correct driver for transformation. Transferring technology to an Indian industrial entity to manufacture Light Combat Aircraft (LCA) may be just the impetus that is required.

The Indian Defence Minister's statement at the inauguration of Aero India 2019 on February 20, 2019 sums up the various factors in the Indian defence sector.[21]

> "…. during the last four years, 150 contracts worth Rs 1,27,500 Cr had been signed with Indian vendors for procurement of defence equipment for the Armed forces.
> …. the Government had accorded AoN to 164 proposals worth Rs 2,79,950 Cr under 'Buy and Make' categories only to the Indian vendors.
> ….several policy initiatives of the Government under the 'Make in India' viz. 100% FDI in Defence Manufacturing, Defence Offset Policy 2016, Delicensing of Defence items, iDEX and the Defence Investor's cell."

Hopefully, these events and directions will set in motion a process that will pull the Indian arms industry out of the abyss and start contributing towards building tangible indigenous national power.

While charting the long-term course in this direction, India needs to have realistic goals for the medium and short term as well. Quantitatively, the combat aircraft fleet in India will continue to go down in the next two decades. This decline has to be offset by creating supporting and alternative capabilities. First among these has to be battle space transparency. Tools, methodology and processes need to be enhanced so that threat zones are continuously under surveillance. An early detection of abnormality will minimise the probability of recurrence of events like the Kargil conflict, the Mumbai attacks or the Doklam standoff. The surveillance systems need to integrate the entire electromagnetic spectrum and their tools of analysis with embedded Artificial Intelligence platforms for such tasks, to include sub-surface, surface, aerial and space-based assets. A thrust on research and development in these areas ought to be a key priority. This capability will reduce the impact of the dwindling strength of combat aircraft.

The second thrust should be on developing alternatives to minimize dependence on combat aircraft. UAV and UCAVs are relevant but have limited utility in the presence of potent air defence systems. Augmentation of surface-to-air weapons systems like the S-400 is the best thing that has happened and this needs to be further enhanced by the home-grown Akash and other systems like QRSAM and MRSAM systems developed in large numbers to provide defence to critical points. Another indigenous system that needs large-scale induction is BrahMos. This is the best weapon in its class and is of very high tactical value. The furtherance of the Nirbhaya project[22] and the development of long-range anti-shipping ballistic missiles will ensure availability of requisite deterrence in the maritime domain. With a successful anti-satellite test, India has moved up the ladder towards achieving a potent anti-ballistic missile system. This technology needs to be harnessed to achieve indigenous ABM capability.

Third, for immediate needs, India needs to fast-track integration and then operationalise long-range weapons like the BrahMos Air-Launched Cruise Missile[23] and specialist weapons like Astra – the Beyond Visual Range Air-to- Air Missile (BVRAAM)[24] and SAAW (Smart Anti-Airfield Weapon)[25] developed indigenously. This will not only reduce the dependence on imports, but allow greater inventory of weapons for force application.

Summing Up

India needs to holistically review its strategic goals and accordingly, plan military capability enhancement. Combat aircraft form a credible part of the military capability but have high associated costs. The strength of the IAF combat aircraft squadrons has come down to 31 against an authorisation of 42 squadrons. With the scheduled phase-out of existing combat aircraft fleets on completion of their calendar life/total technical life, the combat aircraft inventory is depleting at a fast pace. The rate of new inductions like the Su-30, LCA and Rafale is far slower. The net result is that this capability will further go down in case no additional procurements are initiated.

Furthermore, the Indian combat aircraft inventory is very diverse and therefore, is a logistical nightmare. Along with that, maintaining and deploying a diverse inventory has very high costs not necessarily supported by proportionate capability enhancement. On the one hand, there is a need to stem the slide in the Indian combat aircraft inventory, and on the other, to make it more homogenous. Therefore, the choice of combat aircraft to add to the existing fleet needs to be carefully considered taking into account not just the life-cycle cost of the platform but also the system induction cost. Adding to platforms that are already operational is a good option to follow and the three platforms that need consideration in this category are the LCA, the Su-30 and the Rafale.

Amongst these three, the LCA is least capable at present; however, being indigenous, it has distinct advantages. In this regard, the indigenous aircraft industry has a pivotal role. As an interim measure, the Su-30 production line can be given an extension with a fresh order. This will help tide over the crisis till production of the LCA matures and reaches requisite efficiency.

Should a type other than the existing platforms be selected for induction in the IAF, then these will have to be ordered in large numbers in the region of 240 platforms. This is to offset the high system-induction costs that may be associated with the new platform. Large orders not only offset cost-per platform but are better managed from the operational, maintenance, training and logistical viewpoints.

Notes

1. Kishore Kumar Khera, "Review of Indian Aircraft Industry: Possible Innovations for Success in the Twenty-First Century by Vivek Kapur", *Journal of Defence Studies*, 12 (3), July-September 2018 at https://idsa.in/jds/jds-12-3-2018-kk.khera, accessed on April 2, 2019.
2. Ibid.
3. Data collated from the Comptroller and Auditor General's Report 3/2019 tabled in Parliament in February 2019; *Military Balance 2019*; Press Release, PIB, Ministry of Defence, Government of India; and Press Releases by equipment manufacturers along with reports in aviation magazines. Conversion of contracted value to US $ is based on Reserve Bank of India exchange rate for the year of contract available at https://www.rbi.org.in/scripts/ReferenceRateArchive.aspx.
4. For more see Vivek Kapur, *Indian Aircraft Industry: Possible Innovations for Success in the Twenty-First Century,* Centre for Air Power Studies and KW Publishers Pvt Ltd., New Delhi, 2018.
5. Ibid.
6. *Performance Audit Report of the Comptroller and Auditor General of India on Capital Acquisition in Indian Air Force for the Union Government*

(Defence Services), Air Force Report No. 3 of 2019, February 13, 2019, p.125.

7. Kishore Kumar Khera, no. 1.
8. For more see Vivek Kapur, no. 4.
9. Kishore Kumar Khera, no. 1.
10. For more see Vivek Kapur, no. 4.
11. Ibid.
12. Kishore Kumar Khera, no. 1.
13. Vivek Kapur, no.4, p. 41.
14. Cost Plus bases means that the sale price will be guided by the actual cost of production and an assured profit over that cost.
15. There is an anecdote which may not be true, about a meeting between the Chairman of HAL with the CEOs of Dassault (France) and BAe (UK) during the Paris Air Show. The BAe CEO proposed a dinner at Eiffel Tower restaurant (one of the most expensive in Paris). The three met and had a wonderful dinner. When the time to pay the bill came, the BAe CEO offered to pay stating that it was his idea so he must pay. The Dassault CEO objected that they were in his country and he was the host so he should foot the bill. The HAL Chairman said both of them had a valid and emotional reason for paying the bill but he must pay because it made business sense. The other two were perplexed. Then the HAL Chairman explained that HAL operates on Cost-Plus basis. That means, whatever the cost of production; he gets to add 10 per cent as profit for his company to fix the sale price. By footing the bill, the cost of production goes up and so does the HAL's profit. So it made business sense for him to pay the bill and increase the profit of his company.
16. *Performance Audit Report of the Comptroller and Auditor General of India on Capital Acquisition in Indian Air Force for the Union Government (Defence Services)*, no. 6, pp. 121-124.
17. Jeremiah Gertler, "Air Force F-22 Fighter Program, *Congressional Research Service Report 7-5700, L31673*, July 11, 2013.
18. *HAL Annual Report 2017-18* at https://hal-india.co.in/Common/Uploads/Finance/Annual-2017-18.pdf, accessed on January 11, 2019.
19. For more see Vivek Kapur, no. 4.
20. Kishore Kumar Khera, no. 1.
21. "Runway to a Billion Opportunities – Raksha Mantri Inaugurates Aero India 2019", Press Release, Ministry of Defence, Government of India, February 20, 2019 at http://pib.nic.in/newsite/pmreleases.aspx?mincode=33, accessed on February 21, 2019.
22. "Press Release, Press Information Bureau, Ministry of Defence, Government of India, November 7, 2017" at http://pib.nic.in/newsite/pmreleases.aspx?mincode=33, accessed on November 23, 2017.

23. "Press Release, Press Information Bureau, Ministry of Defence, Government of India, November 22, 2017", at http://pib.nic.in/newsite/pmreleases.aspx?mincode=33, accessed on November 23, 2017.
24. "Press Release, Press Information Bureau, Ministry of Defence, Government of India, September 15, 2017", at http://pib.nic.in/newsite/pmreleases.aspx?mincode=33, accessed on November 23, 2017.
25. "Press Release, Press Information Bureau, Ministry of Defence, Government of India, November 3, 2017", at http://pib.nic.in/newsite/pmreleases.aspx?mincode=33, accessed on November 23, 2017.

15. Touch Down

Combat aviation plays a significant role in shaping the battle space and combat aircraft define the way nations orchestrate their battles or project power. Combat aircraft do not exist for their ends, but to serve as tools that empower national security leaders with a range of effective policy options[1] owing to their ability to transcend the physical barriers and deliver kinetic weapons accurately over a long-range in quick time. An Indian Air Force strike on Balakot terrorist training camps in Pakistan on February 26, 2019, is one such example. That is why combat aircraft are one of the most sought-after weapon systems. The number of countries that deploy combat aircraft has doubled in the last fifty years.

The Cold War era of a bipolar world and similar inter-state contests in various regions set the ball rolling for the proliferation of combat aircraft in large numbers. The Cold War triggered an arms race in all domains and combat aircraft were a subset of this competition. Within two decades, in the 1970s and 1980s, the world combat aircraft inventory doubled to a peak of over 38,000 in 1988. However, in the last three decades, it is the geopolitics that has triggered a slide in the combat aircraft inventory. With the breakup of erstwhile USSR and the end of the Cold War, threat dynamics changed and so did the defence budgets. This resulted in a steep fall in high-cost combat assets like combat aircraft, especially in Europe. The world combat aircraft inventory has shrunk by over 50 per cent to reach a level that existed five decades ago. Other factors that have contributed to this decline in the last three decades include the changing character of warfare, technological advancements and the development of alternatives.

Conflicts in the 21st century are markedly different from the last century. Capabilities, in both the real and the virtual domains, can challenge a state considerably. While cyber and communication tools in the virtual domain can subjugate individuals, institutions and significant parts of a state, and military capability acts in the real domain to inflict physical damage. The present century is witnessing a greater amalgamation of virtual and real tools in the form of hybrid threats to states. The current conflicts include the use of kinetic and non-kinetic means with the use of state forces and non-state actors. With changing threat matrices, the character of warfare has changed. The hybridization of war is a reality and clear definitions of the enemy, tools and timelines are elusive. The operational environment has transformed in the last thirty years. Besides nuclear-powered states, threats today include non-state and transnational actors and a dynamic web of terrorism and illicit networks.[2] Consequently, the defence strategies are changing to contend with a range of varied threats and challenges and resultant transformation of the capability development models for defence. The capacities and capabilities of various domains are being reassessed and redefined. It is a fact that the national resources are finite and need to be utilised judiciously and efficiently to develop capabilities that will protect the nation in these times of multi-domain conflicts. A balanced approach towards capability development in relevant domains is essential and a failure in this regard may prove disastrous. Accordingly, resources are gradually being diverted from kinetic tools like combat aircraft to cheaper and more effective non-kinetic tools. This has resulted in declining combat aircraft inventory.

Military aviation has come a long way since airpower was first employed on the battlefield over a hundred years ago. An analysis of conflicts and application of airpower over the last five decades is indicative of the changing force application methodology and the impact of combat aviation on battle outcomes. Asset ratios between opposing forces have limited implications on the result of air battles; rather, the quality of technology and its understanding in force applications have greater relevance than mere numerical strength. Moreover, it cannot be denied that technological superiority plays a decisive role in the outcome of combat air operations. The Arab-Israel war of 1973 and the Falklands War in 1982 are a testimony to these factors. In both these conflicts, the sides with lower numbers prevailed. A decisive role played by combat airpower in Gulf War I in 1991 re-emphasized the power of technology as a lynchpin in combat aviation. The prime missions of combat aviation to attain and sustain air superiority retain relevance for any kinetic conflict, be it between states or non-state actors. But the changing character of warfare with the induction of non-state actors without large-sized military targets over time, has redefined the role of combat aircraft in conflicts with low intensity. In conventional conflicts, combat aviation played a decisive role, but the dynamics of a hybrid conflict are different. Combat aircraft continue to play a role in the prevailing 'no war no peace' conditions; although, in both Afghanistan and Syria, combat airpower was reduced to a minor and supporting player. Aerial warfare in the future will by necessity become more disaggregated than in the past.[3]

Derived from overall objectives, force planning and operational planning processes play a vital role in defining the equipment profile and resource allocation to various verticals of military capability. Like a balanced diet essential for human growth, a balanced approach in the development of transparency, offensive, defensive, and requisite support structures is essential for optimizing resource employment. Combat aircraft remains a significant tool in battle space as it can be easily employed in both offensive and defensive roles. To sustain combat aircraft operations, several support systems are also required in terms of logistics, maintenance and infrastructure. Three critical factors that define the combat aviation capability are battle space transparency, range and accuracy of air-launched weapons and the effort-generation rate.

Conflict hybridization and enhanced range of its tools, has led to battle space expansion. Therefore, in the current context, to fully exploit the potential of a combat platform as offensive or defensive vectors, a high degree of battle space transparency is essential. Battle space transparency practically is a race to out-detect the adversary's combat and combat support elements. In the aerospace domain, the main instruments for achieving this transparency were ground/ship-based radars. With the miniaturisation of components, radars found their application on aerial platforms. This assisted in creating a situational awareness model beyond the line of sight limitation of surface-based radar platforms. Additionally, space-based assets augmented the capability to locate various surface target systems. Additionally, numerous sensors found their way on aerial and space-based platforms using optical, infra-red and electromagnetic bands. Enhanced battle space transparency, thus has changed the way combat elements, and more specifically, combat aircraft are deployed and employed. Moreover, greater engine efficiencies allowed longer flight duration for combat aircraft and longer ranges for propelled weapons. Increase in availability of Airborne Warning and Control Systems (AWACS) and Flight Refuelling Aircraft (FRA) in combination with an increased range of aircraft and weapons, allowed an increase in the area that can be targeted by a combat aircraft. Overall, the size of the battle space is expanding and thus enhancing the salience of its transparency. Availability and integration of radars, AWACS, data links and surface mapping electronic systems, backed up by robust EW systems, have become as significant as kinetic tools like combat aircraft. Better sensor and communication technology has allowed high-fidelity battle space transparency and therefore, the ability to accurately select the targets in a system of targets. This reduces the number of targets to be engaged to achieve the desired outcome in a sector, thus reducing the number of combat aircraft required.

Changes in designs and material have enhanced chances of the physical survival of a combat platform with adequate redundancies. As is the case for F-15 that can be recovered even in case one of the two fins or one of the three wing spars is severed.[4] Additionally, low observability has enhanced the survival rate of the combat aircraft against air defence systems. Today combat aircraft can achieve mission objectives far more efficiently than was possible earlier.

Weapons capability is an integral part of an air power matrix and a critical component of combat aircraft and a measure of their combat potency. Weapons are the deliverables and are responsible for tactical, operational and strategic implications by damaging the target system. Significant developments in the air-to- surface and air-to-air weapons in the last five decades have played a major role in redefining the role of combat aircraft. Specifically, in the last thirty years, improving the power of computation and communication along with sensor technology, effective ranges and accuracies of air-launched weapons have shown marked improvement. Weapons, with their increased effective range and accuracy, have transformed battle orchestration and improved the combat potential per platform across the spectrum. Combat aircraft, now, are capable of carrying out multiple-precision attacks with small weapons from long standoff ranges, thus reducing the number of combat aircraft required for a mission. The ability to launch a missile to shoot an enemy aircraft before entering the lethal envelope of missiles on board the intended target aircraft, gives an unprecedented advantage. With all other aspects being equal, aircraft with longer range weapons will invariably win the battle. While effective range is one criterion defining weapon efficacy, the other is the ability of the missile to home on to the target aircraft. This is dependent on the type of tracking system and terminal guidance used. The side that exploits these two advantages of aerial weapons tactically can win the combat even with a quantitative and qualitative disadvantage.

The air-effort generation rate plays a crucial role in defining the outcome of the war. It is based on maintenance philosophy of the platform, the availability of trained human resources and an efficient logistics chain. The ability of a force to quickly re-arm and re-launch the aircraft can negate the numerical inferiority by a greater rate of effort generation in the 24-hour cycle. Additionally, offensive operations in quick succession can unhinge the defender. A greater force application impulse with a better rate of effort can also negate the operational or technological disadvantage.

The success of combat aviation in shaping battle space is based on the availability of suitable target systems. In a force-on-force military conflict, concentrated force application is desirable to overcome a weak point of the enemy. This, in turn, leads to a conglomeration of various combat assets in a confined space. Such a high density of combat assets presents an ideal target system for airpower. The 1991 Gulf War is a classic case wherein the collation forces utilized airpower to successfully target many surface-based combat units concentrated in small areas. This helped in a facile ground operation and victory. However, in Afghanistan and Syria, the absence of such concentrated combat elements diluted the impact of combat airpower and stretched the timelines for a conclusive victory.

In the last five decades, combat aircraft have significantly enhanced their combat power not only in terms of platform performance but also by their weapon mix. With a large number of new technologies, new materials, and new manufacturing processes, aircraft and weapon performance has improved rapidly. The technology-driven enhanced combat potential per platform results in a reduction of combat aircraft for achieving the same goal. At the same time, new technologies increase the aircraft's structural complexity and the need for precision. Notwithstanding the changing dynamics, this niche market has been tightly controlled by the same set of countries in the last fifty years and the status quo is reinforced year after year. The area that can be dominated by a combat aircraft has increased and led to the reduction in the number of platforms required for a specified sector. Furthermore, there are alternatives in terms of the long-range surface-to-surface missiles, unmanned combat aerial vehicles and surface-to-air missiles that complement the combat aircraft in force application. Development of computing power and communication technology has assisted in the UAV emerging as an effective supporter in combat operations and relieving combat aircraft of many repetitive tasks. However, the UAV's growing potency, a presage for manned combat aircraft, with developments in the field of artificial intelligence and hypersonic weapons will redefine the conflict and thereby combat aviation. Combined with emerging potent alternatives and support elements of combat aviation, the networking of various sensors will hold the key in future battle space. With the development of these three credible alternatives, the prime dependence on combat aircraft for rapid force projection has reduced. A combination of these factors has changed the way combat forces are equipped which is evident in the reduction of combat aircraft inventory the world over.

Going by the trend that the world's combat aircraft inventory has followed in the last fifty years, in general, and in the last three decades in particular, a downward trend is expected over the next three decades. The expected combat aircraft inventory from current level of 18,000, will go below 10,000 by 2037 and shrink further to about 7000 by 2047. This forecast is based on a current assessment of future geopolitics, the operational environment, technological advances, emerging alternatives, expanding capabilities of platforms and weapons.

The technology has redefined the way a combat aircraft is designed and alongside has changed the skillsets that pilots need. Practically, in the last five decades, the combat aviator, the cutting edge, has transformed from being a knight to a scientist. With hybridisation of the conflict, their role is likely to further transform. Combat aviators must train to fight effectively in a much more decentralized and degraded set of conditions. Irrespective of how advanced the aircraft is, the man-machine interface will still dictate terms of combat outcome in the coming decades. The gradual induction of Artificial Intelligence in the cockpit will further transform the way combat aviator is trained.

India, with two nuclear-powered neighbours, needs to retain the adequate conventional capability to deter, and combat aircraft are a significant tool in this matrix. While the number of combat aircraft have fallen the world over, this has not happened at the same rate in our neighbourhood. The IAF with 31 combat aircraft squadrons is well below the authorised strength of 42 combat squadrons. So as things stand today, the combat aircraft strength will continue to go down as the planned inductions of Su 30, LCA and Rafael are at a rate lower than the fleets being phased out. At what juncture will the dwindling combat aircraft strength fail as a deterrent? Unless steps are taken to stem this fall, we as a nation may be surprised by the answer to this very expensive question.

Governments all over the world can allocate only finite resources to their armed forces. It is incumbent on the armed forces to assess the operational environment realistically and then draw out an appropriate equipment procurement strategy. Assets to tackle the existing security challenges must be provided for and only thereafter should the capabilities for tackling future threats be built up. Unless re-prioritized, the defence budget, in general, and the allocation for combat aircraft, in particular, will come under severe strain in the next three decades.

The internal processes within the Ministry of Defence and the IAF will have to be streamlined for capability development, preferably through the development of the indigenous aviation industry. Equipment acquisition is a small but critical subset of this process. The capital acquisition system, as it exists, is unlikely to effectively support the IAF in its operational preparedness and modernization.[5] Specifically for combat aviation, the IAF, defining the Air Staff Qualitative Requirements in terms of functional parameters instead of detailed technical or design specifications, will go a long way in correcting the faulty processes.[6] Additionally, the IAF needs to refocus on a goal of reducing the number of types of combat aircraft from the existing eight to three or four. This will assist in enhancing maintenance-logistics efficiency and result in greater operational capability within existing budgetary parameters. Moreover, because of dwindling numbers, developing capabilities in various domains, like battle space transparency, electronic warfare and weapons capability to support combat aviation, is an operational necessity and needs requisite attention.

Notes

1. Douglas Birkey, Lt. Gen. David Deptula, and Maj. Gen. Lawrence Stutzriem, "Manned-Unmanned Aircraft Teaming: Taking Combat Airpower to the Next Level", The Mitchell Institute Policy Papers, (15), July 2018.
2. Lt. Gen. David A. Deptula, "Beyond Goldwater-Nichols: Roles And Missions Of The Armed Services In The 21st Century", Mitchell Institute Policy Papers, (1), March 2016.
3. Lt. Gen. David A. Deptula, "Interdependent Warfare: Combined Effects Power in the 21st Century", Mitchell Institute Policy Papers, (10), March 2018.
4. Robert Jackson, "The Modern Defensive Fighter", in Phillip Jarret (ed.), *The Modern War Machine, Military Aviation Since 1945,* Putnam

Aeronautical Books, London, 2000, p. 167.

5. *Performance Audit Report of the Comptroller and Auditor General of India on Capital Acquisition in Indian Air Force for the Union Government (Defence Services)*, Air Force Report No. 3 of 2019, February 13, 2019, p. vi.

6. Ibid., p. v.

Annexure 1

Team Concept

To evaluate the effectiveness of any institution or organisation, four significant strands that need consideration are Thoughts, Equipment, Application, and Management (TEAM). Certain attributes of these specific strands for the armed forces are covered here.

Thoughts: Concepts, Strategies and Doctrines to Stay Ahead of the Curve

Thoughts encompass concepts, strategy, and doctrine. These essentially have to be based on the national aims and objectives. The national aim for all countries invariably resonates and includes preservation of possessions and acquisition of new capabilities. The scales and methods may vary but the intent of all states essentially remains the same. The National Military Objectives (NMO) are derived from the national aim, based on current capability and intent.

To achieve NMO, the identification of applicable concepts and dovetailing them into military strategy is essential. Our strategic, operational and tactical environment is changing with developments in our area of concern, specifically concerning China and Pakistan. Anticipating the nature and character of future conflicts and creating suitable capabilities will thus be the key to success. The situation will remain dynamic as force structures and capabilities on both sides of the border continue to evolve. The winner of future conflict will be the side with a flexible approach to operating in an evolving and changing environment and with focussed goals. Surprise and succeed is likely to be the simplest *mantra.* Surprise at strategic, operational, tactical and technological levels and ability to respond to such surprises will define the outcome of any future conflict.

Equipment: Synergising Technology and Resources

Equipment refers to military hardware primarily in the kinetic domain. The individual capabilities of the systems are increasing in terms of range, reliability and precision. The proliferation of high capability systems poses another problem. The most significant change in the quality of the military hardware is that now a multitude of systems can be used to create an identical effect on a target system. A target can be attacked by an aerial platform, a surface-based system on land or on/in water, and even from a subsurface platform. Such an option was not available to the military strategist earlier. How does one prioritise, synergise or categorise capabilities for different arms of the armed forces? Should every arm be capable of waging a war in all domains or should specific expertise be developed and synthesised? Once these questions are answered, there will be no debate on the type of equipment to be inducted in the armed forces. Technology and resources will define the quality and quantity of equipment.

Application: Synergising Capabilities and Intent

Application of kinetic force denotes the process of employing available military capability. It is a function of thoughts, equipment and training. Most military equipment is capable of undertaking multiple tasks like offensive action, defensive action or supportive action. Similarly, several systems can be identified as targets but cannot be engaged owing to quantity restrictions. Therefore, identifying the sequence, areas and means of force application has a great bearing on the outcome of the war. A focussed application strategy with fewer resources can outwit a competitor with large resources and more capable equipment. Therefore, it is necessary to identify key areas for developing capabilities that will shape the outcome commensurate with intent.

Management: Continuous Optimisation

Management includes managing key attributes required for battle. Human resource, communication, infrastructure, logistics, information, defence research and development (R&D), defence industry, finances, defence diplomacy, and the decision-making processes are some of the key areas that require effective management for building war capability. An efficient and effective management system ensures the achievement of objectives before even a single bullet is fired. However, in case such deterrence fails, the system ought to have adequate resilience and redundancy for effective use of all available tools till the achievement of defined objectives.

Annexure 2

Battle Space Transparency Spectrum and Techniques

The first step of any strategic/operational/tactical analysis deals with the availability of information of the enemy to get the Plan, Intentions, Capabilities and Plan. This includes Order of Battle (ORBAT) (Who/what is where?), likely intentions and probable plans for force application. Own ORBAT before the commencement of operations is modified to suit the operational plans. However, with enhanced mobility, operational appreciation is based on frequent updating of own ORBAT and tactical appreciation is based on near real-time availability of all combat elements. Tools to create battlespace transparency can be classified into three broad categories - Sensors, Communication Systems and Analysers.

Sensors

Human beings with their sense organs become the most basic tool for battlespace transparency. Taste and touch sensations need rather a close contact, smell and acoustic signatures can give a range of few meters and visual signatures can be picked up at a distance up to a few kilometres. Use of sensitive smell capabilities of dogs has been used for a few centuries to forewarn intrusion by a likely enemy. Primarily, it is the visual and audio signature that formed the basis of capability development to enhance battlespace transparency initially.

The invention of binoculars increased the ability to capture the visual signature a little farther than was possible with naked eyes. The line of sight limitations was further overcome by the use of balloons to enhance the height of the observer and the advent of aircraft further increased the range and rate of visual observations. With an increase in speed and range of the aircraft and limited capability of an observer to accurately narrate the observations, imaging was utilised as a new tool to capture information about the enemy. Gradually, the spectrum utilised for capturing images expanded from the visual spectrum to Infrared to overcome barriers to visual spectrum through camouflage.[1]Acoustics analysis had severe limitations for enhancing battlespace transparency on the ground as compared to the visual signature. However, in the maritime domain, it plays a significant role. Sensors utilising acoustics signatures assisted in assessing and locating maritime combat assets.

Discovery of properties of electromagnetic waves and the ability to make their controlled use changed the landscape for battlespace transparency. RADAR deployment in battlespace increased the range well beyond visual signature to assess the battlespace.[2] Increase in the range of observation and accurate assessment of the distance of a combat element changed the battlespace transparency matrix. The line of sight limitations was initially overcome by mounting radar antennas on high grounds and masts and later on aerial platforms and satellites. Use of lower frequencies allowed to look beyond the horizons.[3] To overcome various impediments in the traversing medium, like clouds, water vapour and dust, various bands in the electromagnetic spectrum are being utilised to maintain 24x7 all-weather vigil. The accuracy of the geographic location of combat assets has been enhanced with shorter wavelength carriers and LASER/LiDAR. Receivers of various bands in the electromagnetic spectrum assist in intercepting communication between various components of enemy national power and thus enable enhanced battlespace transparency.

Communication Systems

Information flow from observation post to the decision-maker and from decision-maker to the executor is the essence of a communication system in making battlespace transparency a tangible force application system. Information from observer flowed through audio messaging by beating of the drums or carried on horsebacks or by visual signatures like smoke/flags. Use of pigeons to communicate information was an upgradation of older systems. Radio and telegraphy changed that and significance of physical distance between the observer and decision-maker shrunk virtually. Various modulation techniques invented for electromagnetic spectrum allowed multiple users to exploit the same bandwidth. Optical fibre and data flow through it ensured availability of combat assets data to the decision-maker in near real-time. Communication relay systems through a network of antennas, ground-based/airborne have helped overcome the line of sight limitations. Communication satellites and data links between combat assets have made battlespace communication an effective tool in battlespace transparency.

Analysers

A variety of sensors collect battlespace information and transmit to the nodal decision maker using a plethora of communication systems. All inputs need to be fused to generate a comprehensive battle picture for taking a holistic view of the battlespace. An analyser system undertakes this activity. Advanced systems can assist the decision-maker by not only throwing up different options in the prevailing combat situation to take tactical or operational decisions but also helps in a comparative analysis between the options with likely outcomes of the decisions.

Key Parameters to Assess Battlespace Transparency

Space. The volume of space of relevance for orchestrating combat operations that can be monitored.

Depth. The depth of penetration of various sensors determines the depth to which the battlespace transparency can be generated.

Fidelity. Resolution of sensors employed defines the fidelity of the input and therefore the quality of emerging scenario.

Time. Time of travel of information about combat assets from the observer to the decision-maker.

Frequency. The frequency of monitoring the same asset/location/attribute is a key component in generating high-quality transparency.

Sensors and Platforms

Owing to high attenuation rate, acoustic sensors have limited range as compared to Electromagnetic (EM) wave-based sensors. The EM Waves can be divided based on their frequency into various categories to be used as battlespace sensors.[4] Atmospheric attenuation, antenna size, power available, the range required, target dimensions and radar reflectivity, accuracy required are some of the parameters that determine the portion of EM spectrum to be utilised in the sensor.[5]. Broad parameters and characteristics of various segments of the EM spectrum for sensors are tabulated in Table AN 4.1.[6]

Table An 4.1: Electromagnetic Spectrum

Band	Frequency	Main Usage
ELF	3-30Hz	Communication and navigation
SLF	30-300Hz	
ULF	300-3000Hz	
VLF	3-30KHz	
LF	30-300KHz	
MF	300-3000KHz	Navigational Aids
HF	3-30MHz	Communication
VHF	30-300MHz	Communication and Radars
UHF	300-3000MHz	Communication and Radars
SHF	3GHz-30GHz	Weapon system radars

EHF	30GHz-300GHz	Weapons
THF	300GHz-3000GHz	Detection of thermal variations
VISIBLE	430-770THz	Detection of visual signatures, LASER
UV	770THz-30 PHz	UV light
X-Rays	30PHz-30 EHz	Detection of an opaque material

Source: Author.

Based on the size of the sensor and power required, they are either deployed on the ground or mounted on vehicles, ships, submarines, aircraft, helicopters, balloons and unmanned aerial vehicles and satellites. Typical deployment pattern of mounted sensors is tabulated in Table An 4.2.[7]

Table An 4.2: Deployment Pattern of Electromagnetic Spectrum Sensors

Platform	Criteria	Basic Limitation	Primary Purposes	Remarks
Vehicle	Mobility	Power supply	Surveillance and tracking associated with weapon systems	For redeployment in the battlespace
Ships, Submarines, Aircraft, Helicopters	Combat Elements	Power and size of the antenna	Situational Awareness and weapon employment	Target engagement
Balloons	Line of Sight	Weather	The line of sight enhancement	Long-range Surveillance
UAV	Quick repositioning	Power and size of the antenna	Surveillance, recce and targeting	Long duration missions
Satellites	Large footprint	Distance, power	Surveillance, recce and targeting	Multispectral vertical/slant imagery

Source: Author.

Counter Transparency Operations

A tactical and technological differential between two warring combat forces defines the degree of battlespace transparency for these entities. The scope of technological adaption in a combat force defines its ability to undertake battlespace transparency operations in terms of space, depth and fidelity, however, the output of these operations is dependent on the ability of the other side to undertake Counter Transparency Operations (CTO). The CTO would normally consist of operations that deny the enemy information about the location of own combat elements, elements of national power and intent through safeguarding communications. While the effectiveness of sensors using the acoustic signature is minimised in CTO by suppressing acoustic signature and creating acoustical distractions. Beating the sensors using EM is more intricate but the best solution is to operate behind an EM opaque wall or beyond EM line of sight.[8] Passive and active methods employed in CTO are- Camouflage, Concealment, Deception, Jamming (Noise and Deception)[9]. Locating, degrading and destroying transparency sensors, communicators or analysers is also part of CTO to deny battlespace transparency to the other side. [10]

Notes

1. For more on imaging using Infrared with LASER radar see VV Rampal, Photonics in Warfare, Defence Research and Development Organisation, Ministry of Defence, New Delhi, 2002, pp95-100.
2. JPR Browne and MT Thurbon, Electronic Warfare, Brassy's UK limited, UK, 1998, pp p109
3. Ibid., pp 163-169
4. Ibid. pp 43-52
5. MV Maksimov et al, Radar Anti Jamming Techniques, Artech House books, Dedham, USA, 1979, pp 29-76
6. JPR Browne, no 2, pp 53-72
7. Ibid., and MV Maksimov, No 5.
8. JPR Browne, no 2, pp 235-280
9. MV Maksimov, no 5, pp 29-76
10. JPR Browne, no 2,p109

Annexure 3

Threat And Capability - Definitions and Dimensions

Threat Zones

Geographical space and systems that can be targeted by a potential hostile element to disrupt components of national power can be classified as threat zones. Defined threat zones would keep varying based on the offensive capability of the enemy. An enemy with only foot soldiers and small arms will lead to the creation of threat zones only along the border but enemy's air power enhances the threat zones within the Radius of Action of aerial platforms from the possible airbases. In case of a coastal state, threat zone covers maritime routes as well that can be interdicted by sea power. The depth of critical components of the enemy's power defines the range required for the offensive reach. Additionally, the maximum distance in the adversary territory that an offensive tool can penetrate while operating from a secure launch base/platform states the available range. Combinations of these two factors define the threat range and threat zone. The availability or absence of infrastructure at various embarkation/ disembarkation/ launch points for force mobilisation and force application plays a pivotal role in defining threat zones. For example, for sustained operations, combat aircraft can be launched only from a place with requisite infrastructural, operational, maintenance and logistical support. These, thus far, have been the physical dimension of the threat zones and now have expanded to space as several players have demonstrated anti-satellite technology capability. With increasing dependency of societies and states on the virtual world, the virtual world too has become a part of the threat zone. Cyber-attacks and information war have become an integral part of all conflicts.

Threat Quantum

The aggregate of offensive capability that can be brought to bear on an adversary defines the threat quantum. It is a total of the impact of all offensive weapons. Reusable offensive tools like combat aircraft can continue to systematically enhance the threat quantum. Timeline for repeat use of offensive tools, its frequency and attrition become parts of calculations. A minimum number of target systems that need to be engaged to ensure breach of threshold level defines the quantum of offensive tools required. Reusable tools, their turnaround time and timelines to breach the threshold are factors to compute the quantum. Assessment of threat quantum is based on the types of weapons, the quantum of weapons and concentration of force that can be achieved on a single target system and several systems that can be targeted within a pre-defined period. As an example, a force of 10 combat aircraft, each with a capability of carrying 2000 kg weapon load, can deliver 20 tonnes of weapons in a single wave. The same strike repeated five times a day will be able to generate an effect of 100 tonnes of weapon delivery. Alternatively, the attack with 50 aircraft can deliver 100 tonnes of weapons on the intended target in one wave.

Threat Duration

The overall capacity of an entity to pursue the offensive policy that can cause tangible disruption of national power defines the threat duration. Timeline to breach the threshold of the enemy defines the quantum of offensive capability or rate of the effort of offensive tools. Besides, logistical functions, it is a function of sustainability of combat power and ability to absorb attractional losses for the offensive force. As the conflict progresses along the timeline, the ability of the defender too will be denuding. Therefore, invariably the tempo of operation will continue to slide till one side caves in or futility of continuous conflict is realised. Continuing with the example of 10 combat aircraft in the previous section, to generate an effect of 100 tonnes of weapon in a single day, the prerequisite will be the availability of these weapons and maintenance and sustainability of the entire fleet, without any attrition. The utilisation rate of effort has to be closely linked to the rate of supply of consumables (weapons, spares, equipment) at the force application area. The supply chain dictates the pace of operations. Practical commencement of threat duration is only after completion of mobilisation of force from dispersed locations to force application area. In the Gulf War I, this mobilisation time for the US-led forces in the region was from August 1990 to January 1991.

Threat Impulse

Threat Impulse is a combination of Threat Quantum and Threat Duration and can be defined as the multiplication of maximum threat quantum that can be applied for the longest period. Threat impulse will invariably define the requirement of a defensive capability needed. A lower threshold for the defensive capability in any domain could result in a dominos effect for other elements of national power. This aspect plays a significant role in the identification of the selection of a target system. Based on the ability of an offensive entity, the defender will be required to create adequate hardening of critical systems to withstand the assessed threat impulse. Continuing with the example of 10 combat aircraft force, the maximum impulse this force can create is of 20 tonnes of weapon in a short duration of fewer than five minutes and 100 tonnes in a day. Therefore, the critical systems need to be able to absorb this impact of 20 tonnes in one go and be able to recuperate and regain strength to withstand a similar attack after another five hours.

Battlespace

Land battles were confined to the defined physical ground in two dimensions for force on force attrition conflicts. Maritime forces expanded this zone over waters and the advent of airpower expanded it to the third dimension in the early 20th century. With technology enabling powerful tools in space and cyber domains, practically, the battlespace has become a convex set enclosing all elements capable of contributing, directly or indirectly, to war-waging potential. Essentially, in the last 100 years, battlespace has transformed from being a physical area on land/sea to a notional space with three-dimensional space as its subset. A similar transformation has taken place in the human aspects and share of uniformed regular combat soldiers for war-waging has systematically and steadily declined. Accordingly, vulnerabilities have also been spread in every dimension of the new battlespace and so have the offensive tools. Therefore, battlespace can be assessed as a union of the entire threat zone concerning offensive tools of the enemy and zone covering own offensive reach. The classic distinction between strategic and tactical battlespace is blurred.[1]

Notes

1. Robert Jackson, Offensive Aircraft in a New Age, in Phillip Jarret (Ed), The Modern War Machine, Military Aviation Since 1945, Putnam Aeronautical Books, London, 2000, pp125.

Annexure 4

Force Structure Planning Process

The Armed Forces are developed to be an effective instrument of political will. Equipment, weapons, infrastructure and human resources in requisite strength with relevant skills are essential to achieve kinetic capability with all pertinent elements for the operational planning process to meet the objectives. In essence, objectives define the level of capability that is required and existing capabilities delineate the achievable objectives. This capability planning cannot be in a vacuum and is an iterative process. The capability planning processes themselves have undergone many changes. With a well-defined enemy and a good assessment of enemy capability and intent, Threat Based Planning (TBP) is an effective tool. In this process, the strengths and weakness of the enemy and requirement of protection of own vulnerable areas and points filled up all the boxes in the matrices to give an output that defined the development model of the armed forces. After the Cold War era, there has been a noticeable shift in the way the political will is being attempted to be imposed on other states. Non-state actors supported by states have been playing a major role in this. In two decades after the Cold War, the binary definition of war or peace has blurred and many activities other than kinetic means included as tools in the coercion process. To counter the foreseeable and certain unforeseeable aspects, limitations of TBP were exposed and the development of armed forces focussed on Capability Based Planning (CBP). In this model, the central theme was developing capabilities that may be required in the scenarios in the future. Many assumptions, scenario building and consequent capability attributes for the armed forces were derived and thereafter developed. A large amount of literature is already available on TBP and CBP for the armed forces.[1]

However, in the last decade, an exponential increase in communication technology and the dependence of states and societies on this has transformed the definition of the battlespace. Now the battlespace is not restricted to a geographical holding of the conflicting sides but also covers virtual space along with all possible approaches in the physical domain including space. Role and power of non-state actors in conflicts have increased and all conflicts have turned into a hybrid of kinetic and non-kinetic tools. The changing character of conflict calls for changing methodology to develop capabilities to tackle the existing and emerging threats.

Battlespace expansion is the biggest change that has happened in the last decade. Now the attacker could be located anywhere in the world and operate with little physical threat and use kinetic and non-kinetic tools to hamper the victim's capability and resources. With an increase in the range of kinetic weapons, the physical dimensions of the battlespace have increased too. This expansion needs to be tackled and the resources required to cover this envelope will be humungous. So we are forced into a situation to either devote a large number of resources or accept enhanced threat and probability of damage. Both TBP and CBP have limitations in this aspect. Assumption-Based Planning (ABP) is another methodology but is based on a large number of assumptions and fails in case one of the critical assumptions falters. There are methods embedded in ABP for course correction as and when the developing situation deviates from the assumptions and the entire process is reviewed and recast. In TBP, CBP and ABP, the focus has been to develop kinetic means and its supporting tools. Broadly, the three-pronged development strategy is witnessed- to develop Offensive Capability, Defensive Capability and their Supporting Structures that includes organisation, logistics, infrastructure, communication and information and ability to move resources/people.

There is a need to redefine the basis of capability that a nation needs by bringing a method in capital acquisitions and resultant capability. Several states are too focussed on an acquisition of offensive capabilities as a method of conventional deterrence. Without requisite battlespace transparency, states may not be in a position to employ this offensive capability efficiently. On the other hand, a smaller offensive capability with requisite battlespace transparency may be a suitable solution at a lower resource cost.

Military Capabilities

In most cases, a majority of national interests are confined within the geographical boundaries of the state. Therefore, the prime role for the Armed Forces is to protect the territorial integrity and access routes. Accordingly, the major threat matrix is built around geographical neighbours and the nations located in areas dominating access routes. All three elements of Armed Forces viz Army, Navy and Air Force build capabilities - coherently or individually, in their specific domains to meet the challenges to the national interests. Simplistically stated, armed forces role in a conflict situation is like a warrior entering a dark room with a hostile element inside. To come out as a victor, the warrior needs to locate the hostile element, have greater offensive reach than the enemy and be ready with a defensive shield to protect against an enemy strike and also have adequate support for the sustenance of these capabilities. Using this example, capabilities for armed forces can be classified into four basic domains Transparency, Offensive, Defensive and Support system (TODS).

Battlespace Transparency

Expansion of battlespace beyond the XYZ plane and dispersion of capability building and force application assets, well beyond the borders, has enhanced the complexities of the decision-making process. Besides a clear understanding of the location and capability of each component contributing to war, an interplay between various subsystems needs to be assessed for own as well as the opposing side. Ability to identify and locate with requisite precision, the geographical location of critical components of static and mobile elements of the enemy's national power is critical. Identification is based on the criticality of the component in the national power matrix and associated vulnerability analysis. High-resolution satellite images analysed over a prolonged time can assist in localising static elements. However, several sensors are required to achieve the same transparency concerning mobile elements. Mobile elements of interest have a wide array of characteristics in terms of visual, infrared, EM wave, networks and connectivity with physical speeds ranging from a few kilometres/day to a few kilometres/sec and location vary from subsurface to space and network speed in GB/sec. Battlespace Transparency, can thus, be defined as a system to provide to a decision-maker, location, capabilities, dependencies and vulnerabilities of all components present in the battlespace. Ideally, all activities in the battlespace should be known to mitigate the impact of the fog of war. Lt Gen David Deptula, USAF has comprehensively put this aspect as[2]:-

> "Desired military effects will increasingly be generated by the interaction of systems that share information and empower one another. This phenomenon is not restricted to an individual technology, nor is it isolated to a specific service, domain or task. This concept can be envisioned as a "combat cloud". The combat cloud treats every platform as a sensor, as well as an "effector," and will require a C2 paradigm enabling automatic linking, seamless data transfer capabilities while being reliable, secure, and jam-proof."

Offensive Capability

Offensive reach is a function of the ability to strike designated target systems to reduce the enemy's national power. Weapons/Vehicles/Tools that can penetrate the enemy's defensive shield and strike at the vulnerable area is based on range, lethality, penetrative characteristics and damage mechanism. Ability to identify the impact of the offensive strike and garnering resources to repeat such actions until the desired end state is achieved largely defines the timelines of a conflict.

Defensive Capability

Creation of a defensive shield against a possible enemy strike is based on the criticality of various national power components and the assessed ability of the enemy to strike. In an ideal scenario, the defensive shield should be able to neutralise the incoming weapons/tools before their impact and interaction with the intended target systems. With no system assurance of effectiveness at perfect one, the defensive shield should have physical barriers to mitigate the impact of an incoming strike.

Support Systems

All three verticals of military capability in terms of battlespace transparency, offensive reach and defensive shield mentioned above have a common necessity of support systems. Support systems can be clubbed in various sub-verticals as - Mobility systems, Infrastructure and Processes. Mobility systems permit the transfer of military capability tools and equipment from one location to another for force application. These systems include surface, subsurface and aerial mobility in terms of vehicles, ships, submarines, aircraft and helicopters. These systems could be manned or unmanned and/or combat-capable or combat supporters. Invariably, most of the mobility systems need some infrastructure of functioning. Roads, railways, ports, airfields, heli fields, logistical hubs, communications systems are all part of the infrastructure that is required for operations. The operational planning process then takes into account all sub-processes associated with the management of each of these subsystems to create an operational mosaic. Streamlined operational process for force application is based on efficient integration of all sub-processes for various elements.

Overlaps

TODS domains are not mutually exclusive. Resources available for defence can often be utilised for offence and vice versa. Similarly, subsets of defensive and offensive tools contribute towards battlespace transparency. The categorisation of combat equipment in TODS matrix will primarily depend on its intended employment. Strike aircraft are offensive tools but multirole aircraft can undertake both offensive and defensive roles and if configured with radar, electro-optical systems and data link can contribute to battlespace transparency. In case the aircraft is utilised with refuelling pods for buddy refuelling other combat aircraft then these form part of the support systems. A single system can be employed in various roles based on operational requirement.[3]

Resources

The combat capability of any combat element categorised in TODS is defined with three predominant attributes - Human Resource, Technological Resource and Equipment. Each resource is associated with a finite financial cost and has to be met from the earmarked financial resource for the purpose. National resources that can be committed to capability development of the armed forces are finite and this is where the optimisation process commences between four basic tenets of capability development as each development has an associated cost. To examine the inter se priority between these four domains of capability development of the armed forces, it will be pertinent to examine the impact of each vertical on the likely outcome of a conflict. A simplistic resource allocation methodology is to equitably distribute available resources between all TODS components and a similar distribution of financial resources between three resource verticals viz. human, technology and equipment. Such an approach will be suboptimal. Logically, the resources required for each vertical need to be based on the gap between the existing capability and the required capability. However, to reach a consensus on the level of required capability in each domain has always been the most difficult task. There are very strong arguments that support capability expansion in each of the four domains but a balance needs to be achieved to optimise overall capability in sync with national military objectives. Basic tenets of the operational planning process are covered here to outline the framework for rationalisation of intra military resource allocation and understand the role of combat aviation and battlespace transparency in the entire process.

Notes

1. John Christianson, The Search for Suitable Strategy: Threat-Based and Capabilities-Based Strategies in a Complex World, United StatesArmy, 2016 available on https://apps.dtic.mil/dtic/tr/fulltext/u2/1021927.pdf (Accessed on March 26, 2019) and Tony Balasevicius, Is It Time To Bring Back Threat-Based Planning? The Mackenzie Institute Security Matters, April 7, 2016, available on http://mackenzieinstitute.com/is-it-time-to-bring-back-threat-based-planning/ (Accessed on March 26, 2019).

2. Lt Gen David Deptula, USAF (Ret.), *Evolving Technologies and Warfare in the 21st Century: Introducing the Combat Cloud*, (Arlington, Virginia: Mitchell Institute for Aerospace Studies), September 2016.
3. Robert Jackson, The Modern defensive Fighter, in Phillip Jarret (Ed), The Modern War Machine, Military Aviation Since 1945, Putnam Aeronautical Books, London, 2000, pp165-186.

Annexure 5

Geopolitics and Military Expenditure

Geopolitics defines the need for military capability. The Cold War was a major security challenge to the two superpowers and the rest of the world. The competition between the erstwhile USSR and the USA led blocs was fierce and in all fields including the weapons of mass destruction. Both sides could annihilate the other. Although mutual destruction was assured apparent advantage was with the first mover. This led to a lack of trust and risk of tripping the wire with a minor miscalculation or misunderstanding - a major security challenge. However, the immediate post-Cold War security scenario was different but no less dangerous. Technology proliferation led to military capability building by many players that included weapons of mass destruction. While the Cold War era had a binary threat definition, post-Cold War era saw a transition to multilateral threat and on varying scales but primarily from states. Even that phase is over. The cold war era had two prominent blocs and all major military powers were backed by one of these two. With the gradual integration of global economic, environmental and ecological systems, operating in isolation is passé. Interdependencies are common. Therefore, across the world, security concerns have transformed.[1] Simultaneously, the world order is reshaping with economics taking the lead. Technology has allowed the emergence of potent non-state actors with diffused presence reducing the relevance of state boundaries. This has led to greater security interdependency given that a large chunk of the Eurasian landmass has a commonality in facing non-state terrorism. This appeared on the horizon in the 1990s and took firm roots at the beginning of the 21st Century with multiple wars in West Asia as a trigger.

The USA continues to be the sole superpower with unmatched economic, technology and military might. But second-placed China is fast reducing this gap. At present, the competition between the USA and China is in the economic and technological sphere and leading to a trade war. But it will not be long before the conflict of interest leads to tacit use or threat of use of force abinitio indirectly leading to direct military competition between the two. The USA intends retaining numero uno position while the Chinese aim to attain the pole position by 2049, their centenary year. Rising China is gradually leading to a bipolar world but there are several other players with considerable regional clout. This may lead to a multipolar world with many players trying to enhance their influence by expanding their economic and military capabilities. Regional groupings are also being formed to protect regional interests. In case this aspect develops further, the world hierarchy will appear flatter.

After the Second World War, the P5 dominated.[2] While China maintained a low profile, a contest between erstwhile USSR with USA supported by UK and France was instrumental in all-around growth in military expenditure. Geopolitical reality has changed and as put in by the Indian Prime Minister during Inaugural Address at Second Raisina Dialogue, New Delhi on January 17, 2017:[3]

> ......For multiple reasons and at multiple levels, the world is going through profound changes. Globally connected societies, digital opportunities, technology shifts, knowledge boom and innovation are leading the march of humanity. Instability, violence, extremism, exclusion and transnational threats continue to proliferate in dangerous directions. And, non-state actors are significant contributors to the spread of such challenges. As the world begins to re-order itself a quarter-century after the strategic clarity of the Cold War, the dust has not yet settled on what has replaced it. But, a couple of things are clear. The political and military power is diffused and distributed. The multi-polarity of the world and an increasingly multi-polar Asia is a dominant fact today. Because it captures the reality of the rise of many nations.

A new geopolitical reality is also that power – that was West/Atlantic centric in the aftermath of the Second World War, -- has since then shifted eastwards to Asia. While the roots of that are economic, but it is economics that is the foundation for any security capabilities that a nation builds up and capitalises on.

Changing the character of warfare and emerging new world order has redefined the role of conventional military power. Speed, tools and means of the conduct of warfare have increased. These trends have yielded an exceedingly challenging set of circumstances. Key is to synthesize combinations of kinetic/ non-kinetic, lethal/non-lethal, direct/indirect, and permanent/reversible effects to effectively and defiantly strike targets in hours, minutes, or seconds.[4] To manage these changed security circumstances, an evolution of processes, organizations, tasks, and doctrines is a necessity.[5] Gradually, the armed forces the world over are redefining their roles. With changing roles, the equipment profile is transforming too.

As of 2018, the USA and China are the biggest spenders on military capabilities (Figure An 6.1). Together, they account for half of the military expenditure in the world. China is looking to exploit its economic strength for enhancing its global stature and its Belt and Road Initiative (BRI) is a step in that direction.[6] Role expansion will be contested by smaller regional players but that can be steamrolled or appropriately hedged by the Chinese economic might.[7] Sooner rather than later, a conflict will appear in interests of the USA and China, and military potency will play a role in settling the issue. In all probability, as was the case during the Cold War, rather than direct conflict, the issues will be settled via proxies. Arming the proxies will be a priority for both sides. An era of Cold War 2.0 has begun. Focus has shifted from USA-Russia rivalry in Europe to the USA – China in East Asia. Korean peninsula as a theatre suits the USA with two powerful allies in South Korea and Japan on its side and Taiwan as an irritant to China. This area is much closer to both China and Russia than any other area for flexing military muscles. North Korea or Taiwan may be the central theme. American talk of strengthening the Indian armed forces by supplying military hardware and fostering Quad (USA, Japan, Australia and India) may just be another hedging strategy for this theme.[8] China, on the other hand, is strategising differently. It is cooperating with a large number of states on various bilateral and multilateral fora to build a better understanding.[9] This appears to be a long-term plan to garner support for its plans to be a leader. No large-scale military encounter is envisaged by either side in the near term. However, both sides will continue to invest in upgrading their military capability to retain/ reach the top slot. This may lead to a quantitative and qualitative change in the military equipment inventory.

Figure An 6.1: Military Expenditure 2017 in US Dollars

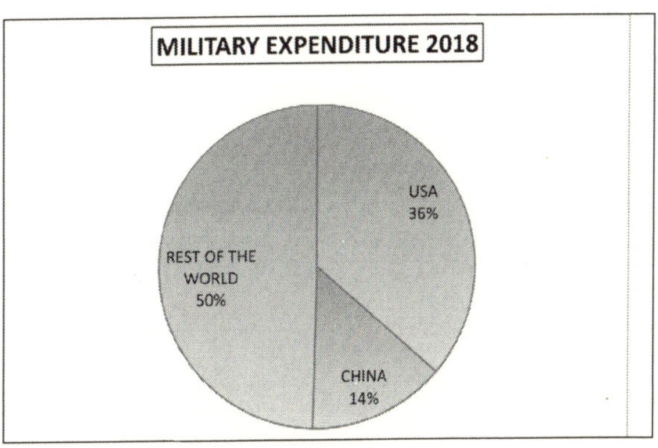

Source: SIPRI database.[10]

Ongoing conflicts in Syria and Afghanistan may continue for a while until a situation of equilibrium is reached between various stakeholders in these regions. However, the type of conflicts in West Asia and its neighbourhood is unlikely to flare up further into a conventional war with large scale force mobilisation. Therefore, the application of combat aircraft in this region will remain at low key with low rate of effort. However, regionally, there are two hot spots with a high density of combat aircraft and a relatively high probability of interstate military conflicts. Both are in Asia and with Chinese centrality. China-DPRK-ROK-Japan-Taiwan on eastern borders of China and on its southwestern border China-Pakistan-India. These two sub-regions have over 6200 combat aircraft constituting 34 per cent combat aircraft of the world. Moreover, all six countries along with Taiwan figure in the top ten countries as far as combat aircraft inventory holding is concerned. Geopolitical stability in these two regions could trigger a major decline in the number of combat aircraft in the world. It is, therefore, of great interest to the combat aircraft manufacturer, to see or seek the pot simmering around China.

Australia Oceania, Africa and South America, with hitherto low penetration, are seen as a potential market for combat aircraft. But the momentum can pick up only after an increase in or a threat of large interstate conflicts. A contest between major powers for increasing their influence in Africa could be the trigger, more so given the continent's rich deposits of commodities that make them of interest to outside powers. A conflict of interest or a threat to investments of major powers may force some of the African states to develop their military capabilities at the behest of their investors. With most African countries embroiled in internal security conundrums, this possibility is low under current circumstances. The probability of large scale interstate conflicts in Australia Oceania and South America with high intensity of combat aircraft usage is even lower. However, greater economic growth and possible conflict of interests in the coming decades could see a rise in the number of combat aircraft in Africa and possibly overtake Asia.

Notes

1. Lt Gen David A. Deptula, Beyond Goldwater-Nichols: Roles And Missions Of The Armed Services In The 21st Century, Mitchell Institute Policy Papers, Vol. 1, March 2016
2. Five permanent members of the United Nations Security Council – China, France, Russia, UK and USA.
3. Inaugural Address by Prime Minister at Second Raisina Dialogue, New Delhi (January 17, 2017) available at https://mea.gov.in/Speeches-Statements.htm?dtl/27948/Inaugural_Address_by_Prime_Minister_at_

Second_Raisina_Dialogue_New_Delhi_January_17_2017 (Accessed on March 31, 2019).

4. Lt Gen David A. Deptula, Interdependent Warfare: Combined Effects Power in the 21st Century, Mitchell Institute Policy Papers, Vol. 10, March 2018.
5. Lt Gen David A. Deptula, No 1.
6. China Power Project, How will the Belt and Road Initiative advance China's interests? Centre for Strategic and International Studies, available onhttps://chinapower.csis.org/china-belt-and-road-initiative/ (Accessed on March 31, 2019).
7. For details please see Wu Chicun, Solving Disputes for Regional Cooperation and Development in the South China Sea, A Chinese Perspective, Chandos Publishing, UK, 2013, p 149.
8. Remarks by US Secretary of Defence James N Mattis at Plenary Session of the 2018 Shangri-La Dialogue, June 2, 2018, available on https://dod.defense.gov/News/Transcripts/Transcript-View/Article/1538599/remarks-by-secretary-mattis-at-plenary-session-of-the-2018-shangri-la-dialogue/ (Accessed on March 31, 2019).
9. ZhongFeiteng, China's grand strategy in a new era, East Asia Forum, June 5, 2018, available on https://www.eastasiaforum.org/2018/03/05/chinas-grand-strategy-in-a-new-era/ (Accessed on March 31, 2018).
10. SIPRI Database available on https://www.sipri.org/databases/milex (Accessed on January 28, 2019).

Annexure 6

Development of UK Combat Air Strategy[1]

On July 16, 2018, the opening day of the Farnborough Air Show, UK Secretary of State for Defence unveiled the UK Combat Air Strategy (CAS). Alongside, in a significant move, a plan to develop a new combat aircraft, 'Tempest', was announced. The United Kingdom, a pioneer in airpower, was the first to establish an independent air arm. In 2018, the Royal Air Force completed 100 years of its existence. The UK led and shaped the field of military aviation with several innovations. Of late, rising research and development costs have forced the UK to collaborate with other partners in combat aviation. The Tornado, the Typhoon and the F-35 are its notable outcomes. However, the UK's share in these collaborations has systematically declined, and for the F 35, it is a paltry 15 per cent.[2] With a new look CAS and a pilot project "Team Tempest", the UK is seeking to fly its way back into the space of combat aviation.

The CAS is guided by the 2015 Strategic Defence and Security Review (SDSR) and the 2018 National Security Capability Review (NSCR). The SDRS outlined an intensifying and evolving threat picture, thus necessitating a well-defined strategy for generation and employment of combat airpower.[3] The UK National Security Council (NSC) has placed domestic and overseas risks into three tiers, based on a judgement of the combination of both the likelihood and impact of such risks.[4] Accordingly, the 2015 National Security Risk Assessment (NRSA) placed terrorism and cyber threat at the top of the Tier I category. The category also includes scenarios relating to international military crises which draw in the UK through treaty obligations. Tier II includes a conventional or hybrid attack on allies and a threat of use of Chemical, Biological, Radiological or Nuclear (CBRN) weapons. A military attack on the UK is in the Tier III category.[5] The new CAS needs to be seen in this context.

Interestingly, after the release of the SDSR, the UK Ministry of Defence put out a series of policy papers outlining strategies in various areas. These include Innovation Strategy (March 24, 2017), Shipbuilding Strategy (September 6, 2017), MOD Science and Technology Strategy (November

30, 2017), Commercial Strategy (Jan 10, 2018) and Defence Knowledge Strategy (April 3, 2018).[6] These policy papers outline plans for specific fields. However, the CAS is different as it carefully intertwines combat equipment and industry considerations at the strategic level.

Divided into six chapters, the CAS begins with the Strategic Context. It emphasises the significance of combat airpower for national objectives. Strangely, in this domain, the focus is only on three combat aircraft, namely, the Tornado, the Typhoon and the F35. All other facets of military aviation are not touched upon. Acknowledging diminishing technological differential concerning prospective adversaries, the CAS assesses integrated air defence systems and electronic warfare as major concerns. Thereon, the focus shifts to the UK's military aviation industry, with the document eulogising the technological prowess of the industry and the role it has played in the generation of employment and revenue through exports. The CAS pitches for the upgradation of the Typhoon for sustaining its operational relevance and garnering contracts for maintenance and upgrade of the F35. Both these proposals are designed to keep the combat aircraft industry going. Practically, the document can be termed as a Combat Aircraft Industry Strategy.

With the Tornado scheduled to be phased out in 2019, the onus of combat aviation will be on the Typhoon and the F35. The UK has a total commitment to acquiring 138 F-35s over the life of the programme.[7]Early models of the Typhoon will start phasing out in the 2030s and their replacement by a sixth-generation combat aircraft will be necessary. [8] Looking at the development time and cost of the F35, it indeed is prudent to commence work now for a relevant combat aircraft capable of operating in the 2040s. The CAS brings out the gradual decline of the UK Combat Aircraft Industry. From the BE 2 in 1912 till the Tornado in 1979, 12 different types of combat aircraft were produced and in very large numbers to meet the demands of the domestic and international market.[9]

However, in the last 40 years, the only notable contribution is a collaborative effort to produce the Typhoon (2003) and a minor role in the manufacture of the F35.[10] With the Typhoon production ceasing in 2020, barring minor support to the F35, the UK combat aircraft industry would lose relevance. So, the revival of the combat aircraft industry seems to be the lynchpin of the CAS and the pilot project called 'Team Tempest' the tool to help achieve the revival.

Team Tempest is part of the Future Combat Air System Technology Initiative programme announced in the SDSR. It is a government-industry partnership and planned to be used as a catalyst and testbed for industry revival. It comprises Ministry of Defence personnel from the Royal Air Force Rapid Capabilities Office, the Defence Science and Technology Laboratory, Defence Equipment & Support and industry partners (BAE Systems, Leonardo, MBDA and Rolls-Royce).[11]

The Team has a clearly defined roadmap. The plan starts with outlining the business case including military requirements by the end of 2018. This is followed by an initial assessment of the international collaboration by mid-2019 and finalising operational requirements and partners by end 2019. 2020 is the year for final decisions on these issues and final investment decisions are expected to be taken by 2025 to have the initial operating capability by 2035.

The outline plan is to have an open architecture design in Tempest. This will allow easy integration of various subsystems. Additionally, to keep the development cost and time under check, the project will keep an option to retain many existing systems, albeit upgraded to suit the operational environment. The significance and relevance of this approach can be assessed from the fact at a team from the USA rushed to meet UK MOD officials a day after its declaration.

The European aviation industry is looking to revive its glorious past. Although in the last two decades three notable and similar products the Rafale, the Eurofighter and the Gripen have proved their technical competence. But the failure of a synergised and synchronised approach spiralled up the cost of development and manufacture. The result was that the American combat aircraft quickly filled up the vacuum created by the decline of the erstwhile USSR market. The arms trade, including combat aircraft for the USA, increased by 19.2 per cent from 1989 to 1996 while the Russian exports plummeted by 73.2 per cent (Figure 8.1). It appears that the same story will be repeated in Europe. Although the head of Airbus Defence & Space, Dirk Hoke, has cautioned that Europe cannot afford a scenario where its aerospace industry again develops three competing combat aircraft. In this regard, France and Germany are moving together for a joint future fighter to find a replacement for Eurofighter and Rafale. The work has commenced on this joint project as indicated by the Tweet of French Defence Minister Florence Parly "*Ca avance*!"("It's moving!")[12]. The project has moved from a tentative pact in 2017 to a concrete agreement between the two nations, with clear timelines and industrial partners Dassault, Airbus Defence & Space, Safran and MTU. Spain - another member of the Eurofighter consortium - may join too. On the other hand, the UK's pursuit of its Tempest programme via BAE Systems may have Italy and/or Sweden joining in. To again end up with two competing programmes would be sub-optimal, to say the least, but the political winds appear to be blowing in that direction.[13]

Notes

1. Based on authors IDSA commentary titled Unpacking UK Combat Air Strategy dated July 23, 2018, available at https://idsa.in/idsacomments/unpacking-uk-combat-air-strategy-kkkhera-230718
2. 'The Combat Air Strategy: An ambitious Vision for the Future', Ministry of Defence, UK, 2018, p 13 available on https://www.gov.uk/government/publications/combat-air-strategy-an-ambitious-vision-for-the-future (Accessed on July 19, 2018).
3. 'National Security Strategy and Strategic Defence and Security Review 2015', presented to the UK Parliament on November 21, 2015, available at https://assets.publishing.service.gov.uk/government/uploads/system/uploads/attachment_data/file/555607/2015_Strategic_Defence_and_Security_Review.pdf(Accessed on July 20, 2018).
4. Ibid. p 85.
5. Ibid.p 87.
6. ListofPublications, Ministry of Defence, the UK available on https://www.gov.uk/government/publications?keywords=strategy&publication_filter_option=policy-papers&topics%5B%5D=defence-and-armed-forces&departments%5B%5D=ministry-of-defence&official_document_status=all&world_locations%5B%5D=all&from_date=21%2F11%2F2015&to_date(Accessed on July 20, 2018).
7. Craig Hoyle, UK confirms new deal for 17 F-35Bs, Flight Global, November 15, 2018 available on https://www.flightglobal.com/news/articles/uk-confirms-new-deal-for-17-f-35bs-453689/ (Accessed on November 18, 2018).
8. No2, p 29.
9. Ibid. pp 9-10.
10. Ibid. p10.
11. Ibid.p18.
12. Flight International, November 23, 2018, Franco-German future fighter still has many hurdles to overcome, available on https://www.flightglobal.com/news/articles/opinion-franco-german-future-fighter-still-has-many-453871/ (Accessed on November 29, 2018).
13. Ibid.

Annexure 7

Trends in Military Expenditure in Africa[1]

Africa aspires. In 1963, 33 independent African states gathered in Addis Ababa, Ethiopia to form the Organization of African Union, now the African Union (AU). On the occasion, its Golden Jubilee in May 2013, Africa's political leadership rededicated itself to the Pan African vision of an integrated, prosperous and peaceful Africa. The continental aspirations are well documented in 'Agenda 2063'.[2]With a laid out implementation plan for well-articulated goals to meet the aspirations, Africa is moving in the right direction.[3] Albeit a little slowly. The main reasons are intertwined and interrelated - conflicts and slow economic growth. To top this, the governments are splurging on building their military capabilities. Three reasons for analysing military expenditure in Africa make it relevant and applicable to almost all states. First, Africa, though not a monolithic entity as far as defence expenditure is concerned, represents a large variety of states covering the entire spectrum of economic, military, industrial, geographical and societal strength. Almost all constituent countries have different definitions and perceptions of national interest and/or threats and therefore define individually their military budget and the capabilities required. This is the continent with all major players of the world are entrenched in different pockets for different goals. Second, there exists a common vision and a defined goal - Agenda 2063. This primarily means that all states individually and collectively are heading in the same direction. This is unique. Although groupings like the European Union and the ASEAN fall in a similar bracket but with much lower membership. Lastly, the threats that individual states face cover entire spectrum from internal strife to conventional military conflicts from organised piracy to terrorism. Therefore, trends, logics and orientation from this case can be of use to many states and different regions.

Agreed that military capabilities are essential to ensure security and thus economic activities. But these need to be developed following the envisaged threat scenario. The capability development programmes need to meet essential targets first before looking at desirable characteristics.

Secondly, the expansion of military capabilities needs to be in harmony with the national strategy and within the means available. Expenditure on non-essential military capability development not only impacts on other governmental schemes internally but also sets off a chain reaction in the region leading to an arms race. Gradually and systematically, the regional military expenditure increases and developmental goal relegated. Therefore, it is essential that the AU monitors developments in this respect and keeps 'Agenda 2063' within reach.

Stockholm International Peace Research Institute (SIPRI) database on military-related expenditure up to the year 2017 indicates that Africa, on an average, is spending more than the world average on its military (Figure An 7.1).[4] The Governments in Africa spend 100 percentile points more than the world average on their armed forces. That has been the trend for the last 30 years. After the end of the Cold War, the world over, government expenditure has been declining steadily. The same is not true for Africa. After peaking of over 12.5 per cent of government expenditure in 1999, it has come down but continues to stay higher than the world average.

Figure An 7.1: Military Expenditure as the Share of Government Expenditure

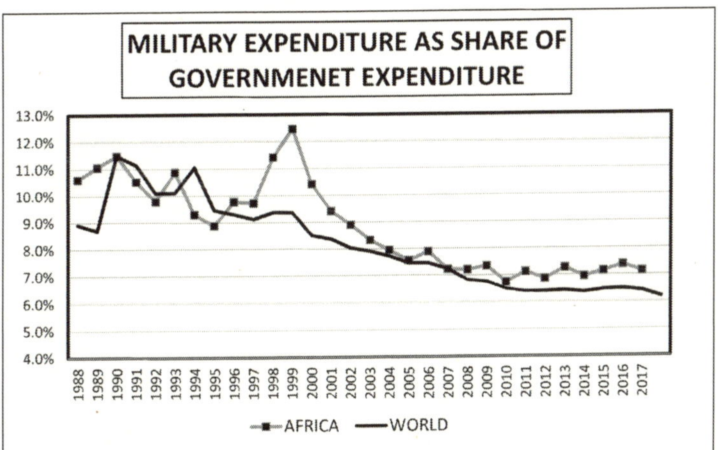

Source: Graphics based on data collated from SIPRI Database.[5]

In absolute terms, the military expenditure in Africa is much lower than the world average. However, in the last 30 years, Africa share of world military expenditure has increased from 1.9 per cent to 2.3 per cent. Today, per capita military expenditure in Africa is around one-sixth of the world average (Figure An 7.2). Trend analysis of the last 30 years indicates that the per capita military expenditure in the world has increased by 26.8 per cent and in Africa, it has grown three times faster. Low base and inflation can be cited as contributory factors yet the growth rate is alarming. This accelerated growth in military expenditure in Africa has socio-economic costs. The development growth has been stunted and goals of Agenda 2063 pushed a little further.

Figure An 7.2: Average Per Capita Military Expenditure (at current US $ rate)

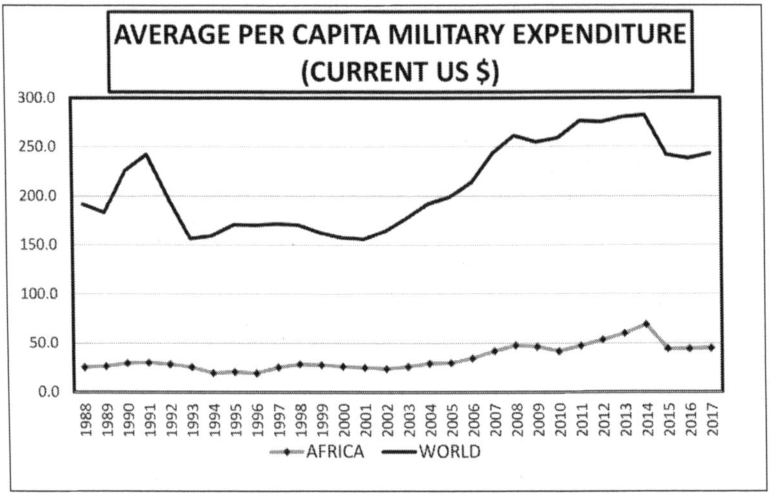

Source: Graphics based on data collated from SIPRI Database.[6]

Military expenditure as the share of GDP is an important parameter and often utilised as a benchmark in assessing international military spending. On this account, Africa is spending a lower share of its GDP than the world average (Figure An 7.3). In the last three decades, the share of GDP, the world spent on the military, has come down from over 3.7 per cent to current levels. Africa military expenditure nearly matches the world trend reaching 1.5 per cent of its GDP in 2017. For developing and underdeveloped countries, this still is a huge financial burden and needs to be further corrected.

In the last 30 years, seven countries account for three fourth of the total military expenditure in Africa (Figure An 7.4). The scenario has not changed much and Algeria continues to be at the pole position with a greater lead over other nations in military spending in Africa (Figure An 7.5). The big spenders in this arena need to relook and reassess their threat perceptions and synchronise it with the military capabilities that need to be developed. While countries in North Africa need preparations to deter any expansion of conflict from war-torn West Asia, the same is not true for the central and southern part of Africa. Induction of frontline combat aircraft like SU30and Gripen in countries with no military threat to its borders is perplexing. The driver for building such a military capability has to be either an existential threat or a plan to expand the area of influence. Neither appears to be the case. The only plausible reason could be a desire of the military hardware sellers to enhance their market size and exploiting the not so transparent system of governance in these countries.

Figure An 7.3: Military Expenditure as Share of GDP

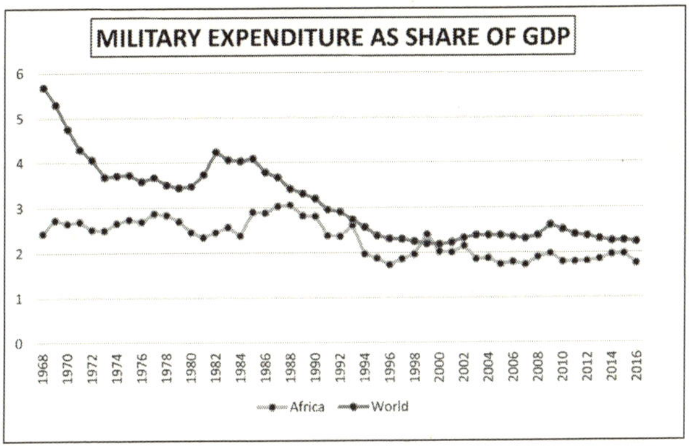

Source: Graphics based on data collated from SIPRI Database.[7]

Figure An 7.4: Military Expenditure in Africa from 1988-2017

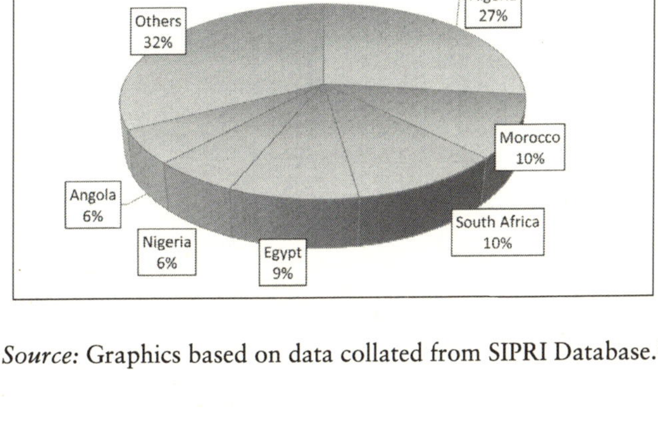

Source: Graphics based on data collated from SIPRI Database.[8]

Figure An 7.5: Military Expenditure in Africa in 2018

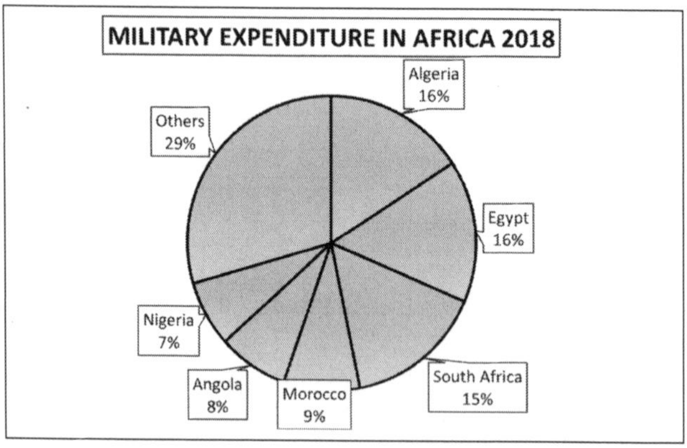

Source: Graphics based on data collated from SIPRI Database[9].

The Africa Union (AU), since inception, has done a reasonable job of reducing number and intensity of interstate conflicts in the continent. Is there a sense of insecurity among states in Africa? Possibly, yes.[10] That appears to be the main reason for the development of military capabilities in certain countries. The perception seems to prevail that the developed military capability allows negotiations from a position of strength. This possibly has resulted in large spending on militaries. The AU needs to take initiative to build and evolve robust and transparent conflict-resolving mechanisms. That will allow states to cut back on their military expenditure. Secondly, democracy is still taking roots in Africa. Militaries, being loyal to the state, tend to be pampered by the ruling class who intend to retain control of the state.[11] For internal dynamics and extension of control, states exercise little direct control over military expenditure. This mechanism suits the political class and the military but the state suffers. Lastly, in most parts of the world, military expenditure skips professional scrutiny and hides behind the garb of national security. A fertile ground for corruption. Agenda 2063 unambiguously lists corruption as a major risk.[12] Procurement of high value desirable military hardware instead of low-value necessary equipment is a common folly. Several high-value deals for military equipment in Africa may not meet the essentiality criteria. With communication improving, democracies will mature and so will transparency. This will allow the growth of apolitical militaries with enhanced professionalism. The result will be a rationalisation of military expenditure.

Africa, despite plenty of natural resources, remains low in the

Human Development Index.[13] It needs to develop its infrastructure. However, with finite financial resources, investments need to be prioritised and the government expenditure on military needs to be rationalised. Operationally, the possibility of large interstate conflicts is low and diminishing further. Credit for this goes to the visionary leadership of the African Union. However, intrastate conflicts and non-state actors continue to threaten Africa. These have the potential to derail Agenda 2063. The threats that most of the African states face today, do not need strong and large conventional military forces. Rather, the need of the hour is small and potent groups that can move quickly to thwart potential threats. To implement this strategy, the most critical tool is battlespace transparency. A synergetic pan Africa approach can ensure a high level of transparency with a large number of sensors monitoring the critical areas. Broadly, the focus needs to be on trimming the conventional military capabilities and building smart forces that can handle the security challenges of tomorrow. Infusion of technology in intelligence and decision-making loop along with the development of rapid deployment capabilities will hold the key. It will lead to significant resource conservation and achievement of "Silencing the Guns by 2020'.[14] An audit of required military capabilities and therefore, military expenditure in Africa is essential. Efforts need to focus on scaling down on conventional military capabilities. An appropriate step taken in this direction at this juncture will assist Africa in achieving its visionary goal of Agenda 2063. The following paragraphs discuss specific models followed by two African countries- Botswana and Nigeria- towards combat aviation to further amplify the approaches that states follow. These two states have different levels of resources and types of threats. Analysing these gives two distinct approaches to tackle a similar problem.

Botswana[15]

Landlocked Botswana, located in the heart of Southern Africa, shares her borders with Namibia, Zambia, Zimbabwe and South Africa. A stable democratic set up since independence in 1966 has allowed Botswana to grow systematically to be one of the most affluent countries in the region. Botswana has had no major military threat to its borders. In past, during the apartheid era in the second half of the last century, the country had often got caught in the crossfire between two regional military powerhouses - South Africa and Angola. However, relations between South Africa and Angola are peaceful at the moment. A real and practical threat is from small insurgent groups that may disrupt the economic and development activities. To safeguard national borders, the Botswana Defence Force (BDF) was established in 1977. The BDF is small, with only 9,000 personnel.[16] Operationally, its outlook is primarily defensive, aimed at protecting the country from infiltration. Its doctrine appears to be heavily influenced by its officers who have been trained in the USA.[17]

The BDF Air Wing is very small but efficient as a contingent of only 500 personnel manages 63 aircraft including 14 F5, five O-2 aircraft along with 19 transport aircraft, five training aircraft, 16 helicopters[18] and four Unmanned Aerial Vehicles (UAV).[19] With the induction of Gripen (in South Africa)[20] and Su30 (in Angola)[21] in the region, BDF F5 will have limited capability to stop airspace violations. To ensure that the sovereignty of airspace is not infringed, Botswana is boosting its air defence network. Creation of a comprehensive air picture in real-time is the first step in air defence activity. This is also essential to employ combat power effectively through combat aircraft or surface-based weapons because of the enhanced situational awareness. To achieve this, the BDF, in Phase I, in 2005, tasked Indra of Spain to develop and implement a full air defence command and control system for an amount of 7.1 million euros within two years.[22] The system planned for entire Botswana airspace was with one operational control centre, nine air traffic tracking and control posts to process the information from air surveillance radars. Such airspace transparency allows for active monitoring and is a key element for the initiation of action against any hostile intent.

BDF ground-based air defence system is equipped with Javelin[23], Igla-1 (SA-16), Strela-2 (SA-7) and 20mm Vulcan towed guns.[24] These air defence weapons have severe limitations in terms of range and environmental conditions. These weapons needed clear weather and daylight for efficient functioning and could not provide air defence cover beyond three kilometres. In the next phase, to bolster the air defence, better surface to air missiles were contracted for. In 2012, Botswana bought 100 Strela-3/SA-14 surface-to-air missiles from Ukraine.[25] This system can engage targets up to 4.1 km range and over 7000 feet altitude. But most importantly, its seeker head is more sensitive than SA-7 and gives the missile an all-aspect engagement envelope. Its modified warhead with an additional secondary charge enhances the probability of damaging the target.

A Government of France, Parliamentary Report on Weapon Exports for 2017 indicated that Botswana is a recipient of MBDA air defence systems and missiles.[26] France delivered 14 missile launchers in 2016 and the total value of French defence exports to Botswana is estimated at 304.2 million including MICA-VL and Mistral missiles. This most recent acquisition from France of MICA VL air defence system with 50 MICA missiles and 50 Mistral portable air defence systems, on induction, will further strengthen the air defence.[27] The MICA-VL is a short-range, ground-based air defence system using MICA missile, capable of being fitted with either an infra-red homing head or with an active radar seeker head. With an active seeker, major environmental limitations are overcome and a higher Single Shot Kill Probability (SSKP) achieved. Its interception range of 20 km gives BDF a ground-based area defence weapon for the first time. With such a large engagement envelope covering 1,242 square kilometres, a large number of short-range air defence weapons, earlier deployed to protect the vital areas, can be redeployed to cover a larger number of vital points. Its Vertical Launch (VL) capability gives it 360-degree coverage without any restriction on the grazing angle and allows it to be deployed in constricted spaces. On the other hand, Mistral man-portable air defence system (MANPADS) is a short-range weapon with an infra-red seeker head and an effective range of 6 km. This range is also greater than the range of earlier held SA-7 and SA-16 systems. Overall, Botswana's area under active air defence has increased substantially with these acquisitions.

While operationally, this is good for BDF as it is difficult to maintain and operate ageing F5 especially for air defence duties. To enhance the self-defence capability, the Air Wing of BDF is looking to replace its F-5 fighter aircraft, with the Swedish Gripenor South Korean FA-50.[28] As a precursor, reportedly, in January 2017, Botswana and South Korea signed a military-cooperation umbrella agreement and simultaneously negotiations are on for eight to 12 Gripen at an estimated price of $1.7 billion.[29]The combat aircraft acquisition for self-defence capability is a long drawn and expensive process, Botswana has moved systematically to enhance its low-cost variation - by improving ground-based air defence system.

Boosting ground-based air defence capabilities may also help in instances of the use of Unmanned Aerial Vehicles (UAV) by other states and non-state actors. With the proliferation of UAV technology and the relatively low cost of its acquisition, coupled with minimal training required for its operation, it has become a prime threat to defence establishments worldwide. UAVs can be used as a terror tool. These can be fitted with cameras to give bird's eye view of the intended target to the terrorists. In desperate situations, these low-cost flying machines can be fitted with explosives to create havoc at key locations or public places. Several ready-to-make kits for UAVs are commercially available and within Africa, several agencies are already manufacturing UAVs. Therefore, availability of UAVs to groups with hostile intent is highly probable. To protect against UAV attacks, several methodologies are being employed like jamming or blinding the UAV. However, shooting it down remains the most effective method. Fighter aircraft have a low probability of intercepting low-speed UAVs because of the large speed differential. Small arms have severe limitations against UAVs flying above 1000m and in such a scenario, air defence systems with larger engagement envelope play a pivotal role. This is where the new acquisitions of BDF will be able to provide an effective cover against UAV threat.

Nigeria[30]

Nigeria is one of the most affluent and powerful West African countries, with the highest GDP in the continent. It shares land boundaries with four countries — Niger, Benin, Chad and Cameroon. The cumulative combat power and national power of these four neighbours is less than that of Nigeria by a large margin. The differential in combat airpower between Nigeria and these four countries is even more glaring.[31] Consequently, the prime focus of Nigeria's creation and employment of airpower has been to manage internal conflicts and insurgency, besides ensuring the protection of the coastline and Exclusive Economic Zone (EEZ). The country is nearly square-shaped (1100 km long and 1000 km broad). The three military airbases are strategically located and over 30 airstrips evenly spread across the country allow an efficient application of airpower.

Insurgency is the main threat that Nigeria faces. The Islamic State in West Africa or Islamic State's West Africa Province formerly known as Jam 'at Ahl as-Sunnah lid-Da'wahwa'l-Jih d and commonly known as Boko Haram (BH) is the chief perpetrator. The BHisbased in Northeastern Nigeria, also active in Chad, Niger and northern Cameroon and intends establishing Islamic rule. In the last five years, many attacks carried out by BH have led to thousands of deaths. Nigeria has been trying to contain the insurgency confronting it with all possible means. Although the army has had a dominant role in containing the insurgency, the Nigerian Air Force (NAF) has started playing a major role in this mission and has intensified air operations in North-Eastern Nigeria. NAF operations from December 20-22, 2017 neutralized scores of Boko

Haram Terrorists (BHT) in Tumbun Rago, a settlement in the northern fringes of Borno state, bordering Lake Chad. The operations started with an intelligence, surveillance and reconnaissance (ISR) mission. This was followed by air interdiction to strike the identified targets. Then came Battle Damage Assessment (BDA) missions after the strikes to assess the nature and extent of damage to the targets. Finally, follow on mop-up operations by helicopter gunships at multiple locations enhanced the degree of target neutralisation.[32] A similar operation was carried out by NAF in conjunction with the Nigerian Army (NA) on January 3-4, 2018 in Sambisa, Njimia and Camp Zairo.[33] These operations constitute a classical example of airpower employment in anti-insurgency operations.

The only combat aircraft in the NAF inventory at present are 14 Chinese built F7 procured in 2005-08. MiG-21s and Jaguars have been phased out. For counter-insurgency (COIN) operations, it has 13 Alpha Jets, 23 L-39 and 12 MB-339 aircraft, besides 11 attack helicopters made up of Mi 24/Mi 35.[34] The further growth trajectory of Nigerian airpower can be assessed by analysing its defence budget and likely procurements. The proposed defence budget for 2018 with an allocation of the US $1.5 billion amounting to 4.1% of the GDP, one of the highest in the world as a share of GDP. A major share of the budget (77 per cent) is earmarked for salaries and overheads. This limits the funds available for modernisation and up-gradation. Out of this limited modernisation budget, an allocation of $66.32 million is planned for aviation assets, including payment for three light utility helicopters for the army, two helicopters for the air force, one UAV for the navy, and the maintenance of two Alpha Jet aircraft and one C-130 transport aircraft. Nearly 53 per cent of the money earmarked for aviation assets is for part payment for the acquisition of three JF-17s from Pakistan.[35]

A significant event took place on December 27, 2017, when the US Ambassador to Nigeria, Stuart Symington, presented the Letters of Offer and Acceptance (LOA) in respect of 12 A-29 Super Tucano Aircraft to the NAF.[36] This will no doubt boost the NAF's air power potential. The Trump administration's offer reverses the Obama administration's decision to block the sale of military hardware to Nigeria. The LOA represents the official US Government offer to sell defence articles and services to the Nigerian Government.[37] It is expected that the LOA would be signed and necessary payments made before February 20, 2018, to ensure the commencement of the production of these aircraft.[38]

The US $ 593 million deal includes aircraft, weapons, training, spare parts, aviation and ground support equipment, hangar, facilities, and infrastructure. These aircraft will augment the NAF effort in operations against the Boko Haram, as well as Nigerian efforts to counter illicit trafficking both within the country and in the Gulf of Guinea.[39] The deal also includes $29 million worth of weapons including 200 GBU-12/58 Pave Way II tail kits, 400 laser-guided rockets, 2,000 MK-81 (250lb) bombs, 6,000 unguided rockets, 20,000 rounds of .50 calibre machine gun ammunition, seven AN/AAQ-22F electro-optical/infrared (EO/IR) sensor and laser designators. Besides, all aircraft sold will include weapons software to support forward-looking infra-red (FLIR).[40] It would thus appear that Nigeria's defence budget of 2018 will have to provide for this deal at the expense of some other equipment.

This deal, on fructification, will permit sustained and effective round the clock COIN operations by the NAF. The combination of sensors and precision weapons will be difficult for the insurgents to beat. Precision strikes by the proposed low-calibre guided weapons will also reduce the probability of collateral damage. However, the mission can be effective only when it is supported by adequate ISR and suitable communication grids. NAF is presently not very well equipped in this regard. With the available ISR resources, it will not be possible to fully exploit the offensive assets on its inventory. NAF has a large area to cover for surveillance and monitor activities in specific sectors on a round-the-clock basis. The time lag between the initial ISR mission and follow-on mop-up attacks in December 2017 and January 2018 is of the order of 24 hours. With the kind of mobility available to insurgents, this time is adequate to relocate safely, thus staying ahead of the ISR cycle. Operational necessity is to shrink the sensor-to-shooter time.

To upgrade its ISR capabilities, NAF is looking intently at UAVs.[41] These provide an optimal low cost and safe solution for a long duration, repetitive missions. A benign air defence environment makes a perfect backdrop for UAV operations. The issue, however, is of the availability of resources to fund this need. And the answer lies in a re-look of the operational environment and reassessing the combat equipment requirement. One deal that stands out in this regard relates to the JF17. Is there a conventional threat on its borders, that NAF is equipping itself with the high-cost JF17s at this juncture? Its existing fleet of F7 is barely a decade old and adequate, along with ground-based radars, to ensure air superiority in its neighbourhood against known threats for another decade. The financial resources earmarked for the three JF17s could optimally be utilised to upgrade the surveillance and communication network and reduce the sensor-to-shooter time for COIN operations.

Building up the capability to douse the current insurgency should ideally take precedence over the necessity to tackle a hypothetical conventional threat. Additionally, the procurement of just three JF17s will not stand professional scrutiny concerning its maintenance. A fighter platform like the JF17 will necessitate the setting up of first and second lines of maintenance facilities for unhindered operations. This will tantamount to sub-optimal utilisation of the investment in the project for just three platforms. In the absence of these facilities, the aircraft will be non-operational for a prolonged duration owing to the scheduled maintenance servicing. Either way, the cost of operation of the three JF17s will further bloat the already burgeoning revenue expenditure. That will prevent further modernisation. Unless reprioritised, the Nigerian defence budget will come under severe strain in the next three years.

Notes

1. Based on Kishore Kumar Khera, Military Expenditure in Africa, Africa Trends, Jan –Jun 2018 available at https://idsa.in/africatrends/military-expenditure-in-africa, Botswana Spruces Air Defence, Africa Trends, Jan- Jun 2017 available on https://idsa.in/africatrends/botswana-spruces-air-defence-kkkhera and Nigerian Air Force and COIN Operations dated January 16, 2018, available on https://idsa.in/idsacomments/nigerian-air-force-and-coin-operations_kkkhera_160118.
2. The African Union Commission, Agenda 2063, Frame Work Document, September 2015 available on www.un.org/en/africa/osaa/pdf/au/agenda2063.pdf (Aaccessed on July 17, 2018).
3. The African Union Commission, FIRST TEN-YEAR IMPLEMENTATION PLAN 2014 – 2023, September 2015 available on www.un.org/en/africa/osaa/pdf/au/agenda2063-first10yearimplementation.pdf (Accessed on July 17, 2018).
4. SIPRI Databases available on https://www.sipri.org/databases/milex (Accessed on July 17, 2018).
5. Ibid.
6. Ibid.
7. Ibid.
8. Ibid.
9. Ibid.

10. The African Union Commission, Agenda 2063, No 2. p 102.
11. Ibid.p 62.
12. Ibid. p 64 states that modest progress is being made in fighting corruption, however according to Transparency International, four out of five African countries are below the world average and p 102 mentions about corruption in the military.
13. AsperthеHumanDevelopmentReportofUNDP,2015availableonhttps://ipfs.io/ipfs/QmXoypizjW3WknFiJnKLwHCnL72vedxjQkDDP1mXWo6uco/wiki/Human_Development_Report.html and (Accessed on July 17, 2018).
14. No 2, p 119 states Silencing the Guns by 2020: aims to fulfil the pledge of the AU Heads of State and Government meeting on the occasion of the Golden Jubilee Anniversary of the founding of the OAU, "not to bequeath the burden of conflicts to the next generation of Africans, "to end all wars in Africa by 2020" and "make peace a reality for all African people and rid the continent free of wars, end inter- and intra-community conflicts, violations of human rights, humanitarian disasters and violent conflicts, and prevent genocide."
15. Based on Kishore Kumar Khera, Botswana Spruces Air Defence, Africa Trends, Jan- Jun 2017 available on https://idsa.in/africatrends/botswana-spruces-air-defence-kkkhera.
16. International Institute for Strategic Studies (IISS), *Military Balance 2017*, London: Routledge, Chapman & Hall, 2017, pp 497-498.
17. Ibid.
18. Ibid.
19. IHS, *Jane's World Air Forces*, Edition 44, 2016, pp 71-73.
20. No 16,p. 498.
21. Ibid.
22. Press Release, "Indra is Awarded Botswana's Air Defence Control System", *Defence Aerospace*, January 2, 2005, at http://www.defense-aerospace.com/articles-view/release/3/51663/indra-wins-botswana-air-defense-contract-%28jan.-18%29.html (Accessed May 10, 2017).
23. IHS, Jane's World Armies, Edition 40, 2016, pp. 81-82.
24. No 16, pp 497-498.
25. Stockholm International Peace Research Institute, *Arms Transfers Database*, athttp://armstrade.sipri.org/armstrade/page/trade_register.php (Accessed May 10, 2017).
26. Government of France, *Rapport au Parlement 2017 sur les exportations d'armement de la France, Annexure IX*, athttps://www.defense.gouv.fr/content/download/.../2016-FranceControlArmTrade.pdf (Accessed May 10, 2017).
27. Ibid.

28. No 16, pp 497-498.
29. "Botswana, South Korea agree to collaborate on defence", *Defence Web*, January 19, 2017, at http://www.defenceweb.co.za/index.php?option=com_content&view=article&id=46504:botswana-south-korea-agree-to-collaborate-on-defence&catid=56:diplomacy-a-peace&Itemid=111 (Accessed on May 10, 2017).
30. Based on Kishore Kumar Khera, Nigerian Air Force and COIN Operations dated January 16, 2018, available on https://idsa.in/idsacomments/nigerian-air-force-and-coin-operations_kkkhera_160118.
31. No 16,pp. 498-537.
32. Nigerian Air Force, "Press Release: Nigerian Air Force Intensifies Air Operations In Northeast, Neutralizes Scores of Boko Haram Terrorists in TumbumRago, Bogumeri," January 9, 2018, available at http://www.airforce.mil.ng/post-nigerian_air_force_intensifies_air_opera..., (Accessed on January 11, 2018).
33. Nigerian Air Force, Press Release: Nigerian Army Elements Combine to Inflict Heavy Casualties on Boko Haram Terrorists, January 6, 2018, available at http://www.airforce.mil.ng/post-nigerian_air_force__nigerian_army_elemen..., (Accessed on January 12, 2018).
34. No 16, p. 529.
35. Guy Martin, "New Acquisitions Proposed in Nigeria's 2018 Defence Budget," *Defence Web*, January 4, 2018, available at http://www.defenceweb.co.za/index.php?option=com_content&view=article&id... Itemid=30 (Accessed on January 11, 2018).
36. SegunOlaniyi (Abuja) and Isa Abdulsalami Ahovi (Jos), United States to sell A29 Super Tucano aircraft to Nigeria, The Guardian, December 28, 2017, available on https://guardian.ng/news/united-states-to-sell-a29-super-tucano-aircraft-to-nigeria/ (Accessed on March 9, 2019).
37. News Release by Nigerian Air Force on January 9, 2018, available at http://www.airforce.mil.ng/post-united_states_ambassador_presents_letter..., (Accessed on January 11, 2018).
38. Guy Martin, "Nigeria Proceeding with Super Tucano Purchase," *Defence Web*, January 2, 2018, available at http://www.defenceweb.co.za/index.php?option=com_content&view=article&id..., (Accessed on January 11, 2018).
39. Defense Security Cooperation Agency, USA, press release on August 3, 2017, available at http://www.dsca.mil/major-arms-sales/government-nigeria-29-super-tucano-..., (Accessed on January 11, 2018).
40. Office of the Federal Register (US), notification on August 28, 2017, available at https://www.federalregister.gov/documents/2017/08/28/2017-18201/arms-sal..., (Accessed on January 11, 2018).

41. Nigerian Ministry of Defence, "Press Release: Nigeria Air Force UAV unveiled," available at http://defence.gov.ng/index.php/78-featured/169-nigerian-air-force-uav-u..., (Accessed on January 12, 2018).

Annexure 8

India's Combat Aircraft Fleet

The first squadron of the Indian Air Force was equipped with four Westland Wapiti IIA army co-operation biplanes at Drigh Road, Karachi (now in Pakistan) on April 1, 1933. In April 1936, more aircraft were added. But, it was not until June 1938 that No. 1 Squadron ostensibly reached its full strength, and this remained the sole IAF formation when World War II began. The Hawker Hart was the next aircraft inducted. The next types of combat aircraft inducted were Lysanders followed Hurricane IIB.[1] The first non-British aircraft-the US-built Vengeance 1 dive bomber was inducted in mid-February 1943. By 1944, the Spitfire came into the IAF and other than the Hurricane all types were phased out. Gradually, the Hurricane was phased out and by mid-1946 the entire fighter force was Spitfire-equipped. A couple of months later, Tempest II started replacing Spitfires. On August 15, 1947, and with the division of both India and her armed forces, the principal combat aircraft of the IAF was the Tempest and the Spitfires.

To make up for splitting of forces and attrition suffered in Kashmir, more Spitfires and Tempest were procured. An attempt was made through HAL to "re-construct" a force of B24 Liberators from the mouldering remains of nearly 100 ex USAF bombers of this type at the Care and Maintenance Unit Depot at Kanpur. Three IAF squadrons were equipped with B24 bombers. On November 4, 1948, three Vampire F.Mk.3 jet fighters reached India making the IAF first Asian air arm to operate jets. More than 400 Vampires of various types were procured by the IAF with HAL commencing licensed manufacture.

After the Indian independence, the entire IAF combat aircraft inventory was of British origin barring resurrected B24 bombers. The Government of India began to seek non-traditional and alternative sources of combat aircraft procurement. Selection of the DassaultOuragan fighter from France at this time reflected the decision to initiate diversification of supply sources. The first four of over 100 Ouragans, or Toofanis as they were to become known in the IAF, reached Palam from France on 24 October 1953. This was followed by induction of another French aircraft the Mystere IVA. Particularly significant in IAF was the year 1957, which witnessed true beginnings of the major re-equipment programme. Deliveries began of

110 DassaultMystere IVAs, carrying the service into the realms of transonic flight for the first time, and two aircraft of British origin Hawker Hunters and English Electric Canberras began to enter the IAF inventory.

By the early fifties, the ageing fleet of Vampires, Toofanis and Mysteres were required to be upgraded and eventually replaced, to meet fresh challenges.[2]Several new squadrons were raised or reequipped with Vampire FB Mk. 52s, Canberra B(I) Mk. 58s, Canberra PR Mk. 57s and the Hunter. The early sixties were accompanied by the IAF's induction of yet more new aircraft types, the most interesting of these arguably being the Folland Gnat lightweight fighter. With its startling agility, the Gnat proffered outstanding cost-effectiveness and during the mid-fifties, a license agreement was concluded for its manufacture by HAL following delivery of 23 complete aircraft and 20 sets of components by the parent company. The first IAF unit converted to the Gnat in March 1960. Two more squadrons were re-equipped with the Gnat in 1962. After its success in the 1965 war, four more Gnat squadrons were formed during 1966-68.

The HAL-designed HF24 Marut became the first indigenous aircraft in the IAF. This was expected to change the complexion of the IAF combat aircraft fleet. But HF24 did not meet the high-performance criteria set by the IAF. So the IAF combat aircraft inventory remained dominated by the British and French designed aircraft. A protocol signed by the Government of India with the Soviet Union in August 1962 changed that. The protocol was for a purchase IAF's first combat aircraft of non-western origin MiG21 fighters from the Soviet Union along with Soviet technical assistance for setting up its production facilities in India. Additionally, the supply of Sukhoi Su-7BM from the Soviet Union started coming in March 1968. With some 580 MiG21s delivered by HAL and nearly 250 MiG21s (including the two-seat operational trainers) imported as "fly-aways", the type remained the mainstay for the Indian Air Force for over a quarter-century and is still part of the IAF.

By the mid-'70s, re-equipment decisions led to about twenty new aircraft types and sub-types entering the IAFbetween 1978-1988. To replace the Canberra and the Hunter, after many years of evaluation and negotiation, the Anglo-French Jaguars came to India in July 1979. With the various development programmes to enhance the operational performance of the HF-24 Marut by HAL abandoned for one reason or the other, the Government of India concluded an agreement with the Soviet Union for the MiG23 variable-sweep fighter. The MiG23BN followed by the MiG27 was inducted in the mid-1980s. Induction of the new generation F16 fighter by the PAF in 1981-82 led to induction of the MiG23MF air superiority version of the swing-wing fighter. However, these were considered only an interim solution and, in the absence of suitable, known, Soviet equivalents,

India turned to Western sources for an advanced technology interceptor. In 1982, a contract was finalised with France for the Mirage 2000 and inducted in 1985. Induction of air superiority fighter, MiG29 known as the Fulcrum, was a result of the Governments of India and the Soviet Union formalised the agreement.

The next combat aircraft to be inducted was Su30 from Russia in 1997. Additionally, for training role, British Hawks as Advanced Jet Trainers (AJT) came in after a very long procurement process stretching nearly two decades. Indigenous Light Combat Aircraft started rolling out of HAL into IAF operational squadrons in 2016.[3] Induction of Rafale from France is expected in 2019 after an Inter-Governmental Agreement was signed in 2016.

The rise and decline in the number of combat aircraft squadrons of the IAF are given along with historic landmarks in Figure An 8.1. With a peak achieved in 1986 with 42 combat aircraft squadrons, there has been a gradual decline as brought out in the Standing Committee On Defence (2017-2018)(Sixteenth *Lok Sabha*) Ministry of Defence Demands for Grants (2018-19) Army, Navy and Air Force (Demand no. 20) presented to *Lok Sabha* on March 13, 2018:[4]

> 3.9 At present, the Indian Air Force (IAF) has 31 active fighter squadrons. Concerning the sanctioned requirement of force level, the Committee was apprised that the said information is sensitive. However, there is a gap in the force level since induction and de-induction is not commensurate.

Figure An 8.1: IAF Combat Aircraft Squadrons

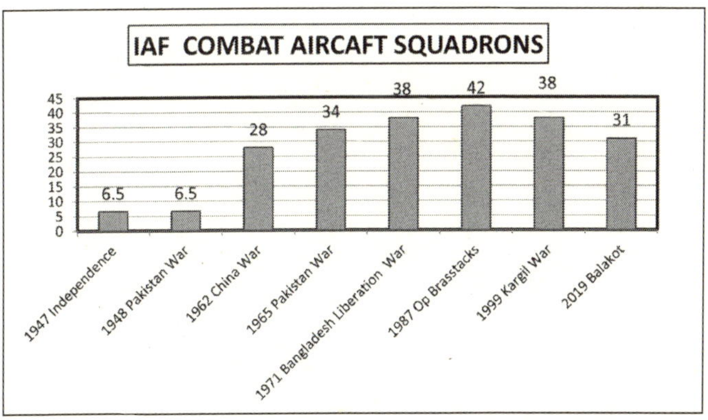

Source: Based on data in Air Power and National Security, *Indian Air Force: Evolution, Growth and Future*[5] and IISS, Military Balance 2000 and Report of the Standing Committee On Defence (2017-2018)(Sixteenth *Lok Sabha*)

The Indian Navy combat aircraft started with Alize and Sea-Hawks later converting to Sea Harriers and followed by the current fleet of MiG29K. Additionally, Hawks are employed for basic flying training. For the under construction aircraft carrier, a new fleet of combat aircraft is likely to be selected.

Notes

1. The History of Indian Air Force available on http://indianairforce.nic.in/content/history-iaf-0 (Accessed on December 29, 2018).
2. Indian Air Force website available on http://indianairforce.nic.in/content/aircraft-systems-testing-establishment (Accessed on December 27, 2018).
3. Sanjay BadriMaharaj, The Tejas One Year After Induction – HAL must take ownership of the project, IDSA Commentary, July 12, 2017, available on https://idsa.in/idsacomments/tejas-one-year-after-induction-hal_sbmaharaj_120717 (Accessed on April 1, 2019).
4. Report of Standing Committee On Defence (2017-2018)(Sixteenth *Lok Sabha*) Ministry of Defence Demands for Grants (2018-19) Army, Navy and Air Force (Demand no. 20) presented to *Lok Sabha* on March 13, 2018.
5. Air Commodore Ramesh V. Phadke (Retd.), Air Power and National Security, *Indian Air Force: Evolution, Growth and Future,* Pentagon Press, New Delhi, 2015, pp 263-267.

Index

Afghanistan, 11, 17, 18, 25, 26, 29, 30, 81, 95, 122, 158, 244, 294, 297

Africa, 55, 61, 153, 216

Airborne Warning and Control Systems (AWACS), 37, 88, 113, 117, 118, 131, 132, 145, 185, 278, 295

Alexandre, Jacques, 9

Al-Qaeda, 26

Arab, 17, 18, 20, 127, 294

Argentina, 20, 21, 22

Asia, 55, 59, 61, 79, 152, 153, 154, 158, 159, 194, 224, 244, 251

Australia, 55, 61, 63, 67, 153

BAE Systems, 83

Bahrain, 67, 79

Balakot, 12, 181, 292

Bangladesh, 240, 244

Belgium, 84

Bengaluru, 66, 78

Bhamre, Subhash (Dr), 267

Bhutan, 239

Birkey, Douglas, 87

Bofors, 204

Borisov, Yuri, 229

Botswana, 216

Brazil, 285

Buck, Michael, 12, 44, 75

Canada, 174,

Charles, Cesar, 9

Changing Mission Profile, Technological Innovations in Combat Aviation, 71-89

- life of a combat aircraft, 77-80
- material and structure, 72-74
- rising combat power, 80-87
- shifting core capability, 74-77
- sum up, 87-89

China, 13, 56, 57, 58, 59, 63, 69, 105, 111, 117, 127, 138, 141, 145, 224, 228, 239, 240, 243, 251, 252, 253, 254, 268, 270, 285

Close Quarters, Combat Aviation Trajectory In India, 239-254

- current situation, 248
- expected combat aircraft inventory in india, 248-254
  - global signs, 249-251
  - regional dynamics, 251-254
- governmental authorizations, 241-247
  - combat aircraft squadrons/units of IAF, 241-246
  - maintenance reserves, 246
  - strike-off wastage, 246-247

Cockpit View, Human-Technology Interface and Training, 167-189

- conclusion, 188-189
- pilot-cockpit ratio, 173-175

- shifting core skillsets, 168-171
- single-twin-single transition, 171-173
- what matters in aerial combat, balakot strike and aftermath; case study, 181-188
- women in combat aviation, 175-181
  - capability, 176-177
  - compatibility, 177-178
  - economics, 179-181

Cold War, 60, 142, 152, 153, 158, 159, 194, 202, 221, 292

Cone, Robert (General), 71

Cruise Climb Range Descent: Combat Aircraft Inventory (1968-2018), 51-69

Czechoslovakia, 78

Davis, Malcolm, 229

Defence Research and Development Organisation (DRDO), 130

de Gusmao, Bartolomeu, 9

Denmark, 67

Deptula, David, 83, 146, 313

Doklam, 239, 287

Dry Cranking Engine, Indian Indigenous Defence Industry, 278-289
- end user interface, 283-284
- financial prudence, 284
- innovation, 282
- international models and comparisons, 285-286
- organisational structure, 282-283
- policy paradigm, 281
- production capability, 284-285
- research and development, 281-282
- sound start weak finish, 279-280
- summing up, 288-289
- technical knowhow, 280-281
- way forward, 286-288

Egypt, 19, 59, 127, 209

Electronic Warfare (EW), 97, 113, 131, 145, 183, 295

England, 204

Eritrea, 175

Europe, 55, 59, 60, 61, 62, 152, 153, 154, 159, 194, 199, 292

F-16, 40, 67, 75, 78, 79, 84, 107, 112, 126, 143, 182, 183, 184, 186, 187, 188, 244, 258, 259

F-18, 67, 75, 258, 271

F-21, 271

F-22, 40, 71, 72, 77, 84, 85, 86, 87, 112, 172, 209, 223, 271, 285

F-35, 41, 67, 77, 80, 83, 93, 94, 112, 143, 209, 222, 272, 284

Falklands, 17, 20, 21, 22, 100, 153, 294

First World War, 55, 193

France, 9, 27, 58, 59, 77, 105, 111, 199, 205, 207, 257, 259, 265, 279, 284, 290

Frontal Scan, Emerging Contours in the Field of Combat Aviation, 220-232
- artificial intelligence, 226-228
- future combat aircraft inventory, 229-232
- hypersonics, 228-229
- space, 223-226

Gafoor, Asif (Major General), 182

Gokhale, Vijay, 181

Gravy Check, Economics of Combat Aviation, 193-217
- big picture, 194-207
- costing model, 207-210
- determination of total life cycle

cost- MMRCA project, 210-216
gestalt, 216-217
Greece, 59
Greenwood, John T, 154
Grynkewich, Alex (Brig Gen), 11
Gulf War, 17, 22, 30, 151, 158, 221, 294, 297, 309

Harward, Robert, 79
Hindustan Aeronautics Limited (HAL), 66, 257, 258, 265, 269, 273, 278, 279, 280, 281, 282, 283, 284, 285, 286
Hiroshima and Nagasaki, 193
Houthi Movement, 160
Hussein, Saddam, 25

India, 4, 5, 12, 13, 14, 56, 58, 59, 63, 66, 78, 79, 84, 87, 129, 177, 180, 181, 183, 184, 187, 194, 203, 204, 206, 207, 208, 212, 215, 226, 239-254, 258, 259, 265, 267, 268, 269, 270, 271, 278, 279, 281, 282, 283, 286, 287, 288, 298
Indian Air Force (IAF), 4, 12, 13, 14, 97, 181, 182, 184, 186, 187, 188, 199, 204, 213, 214, 215, 240, 241, 243, 244, 245, 246, 247, 248, 250, 253, 257, 258, 259, 260, 261, 262, 263, 264, 266, 267, 269, 270, 273, 280, 283, 284, 288, 289, 298, 299
Indian Space Research Organization (ISRO), 282
Iran, 23, 59
Iraq, 19, 23, 24, 25, 81, 158
Israel, 17, 18, 19, 20, 27, 59, 67, 79, 127, 175, 207, 278, 279, 294
Italy, 59, 67, 83

Jaguar, 171, 172, 204, 252, 257, 269, 280
Jaish-e-Mohammed, 181
Jammu and Kashmir, 12, 181, 182, 239, 240, 243
Japan, 59, 67, 83, 94, 318, 319
Jones, Rodney W, 251
Jordan, 27, 127

Kanpur, 245, 280
Kargil, 240, 258, 287
Khan, Imran, 182
Kuwait, 11

Ladwig, Walter C, 13, 251
Lancaster, Mark, 71
Lebanon, 20, 160
Light Combat Aircraft (LCA), 13, 54, 63, 78, 80, 87, 94, 240, 248, 257, 262, 263, 266, 267, 268, 269, 271, 272, 273, 280, 282, 283, 286, 288, 289, 298
Lockheed Martin, 13, 14, 67, 68, 75, 79, 83, 85, 93, 222, 259, 272, 283
London, 9

Macau, 73
McSally, Martha, 178
MiG-21, 12, 67, 74, 78, 79, 84, 137, 171, 182, 183, 184, 186, 187, 240, 257, 266, 269, 280
MiG-23, 204, 245
MiG-27, 84, 137, 204, 240, 257, 266, 269, 280
MiG-29, 204, 257, 259, 266, 269, 273
MiG-35, 258, 271
Mirage 2000, 182, 204, 257, 258, 261, 263, 266, 269, 273
Mission Buddies, Evolving Alternatives and Combat Enablers, 116-147
combat enablers, 130
gestalt, 146-147

surface-to-air missiles, 128-130
surface-to-surface missiles, 117-120
targeting, 119
maritime targeting, 119-120
unmanned aerial vehicles, 120-128
endurance and risks, 125-128
quantity and costs, 124-125
sensors and dynamic situation processing, 122-123
speed and manoeuvrability, 123
weapon carrying capacity, 123-124
USAF expansion plan, 138-146
Mission Plan, Imperatives of Combat Aviation Application, 33-46
assessing potential of combat aircraft, 39-46
environment interface, 44-46
human interface, 43
performance, 40-42
potency, 43
signature, 42-43
operational imperatives for combat aviation, 33-35
operational planning process, 35-39
summary, 46
Modi, Narendra, 13
Moscow, 27
Mukherjee, Subroto (Air Chief Marshal), 243
Mumbai Attacks, 241, 287

Netherlands, 67
Nigeria, 216
North Atlantic Treaty Organisation (NATO), 152, 153, 154, 158, 159, 199
Northrop Grumman, 83

Odisha, 130
Operation Desert Storm, 23, 96
Operation Enduring Freedom, 11, 26, 128
Operation Parakaram, 204

Pakistan, 12, 13, 59, 117, 178, 181, 182, 183, 187, 239, 240, 241, 243, 244, 251, 252, 253, 254, 258, 260, 268, 292
Pakistan Air Force (PAF), 12, 181, 182, 183, 187, 188, 243
Pakistan-Occupied Kashmir (POK), 12, 182, 187
Parly, Florence, 199
Pentagon, 143
People's Liberation Army Air Force (PLAAF), 59, 126
Phadke, Ramesh V (Air Cmde), 5
Pratt & Whitney, 64, 83
Pulwama, 181
Punjab, 244
Putin, Vladimir, 71, 229

Rafale, 13, 76, 205, 212, 240, 248, 253, 257, 258, 262, 265, 266, 267, 268, 269, 271, 279, 280, 288, 289
Robert, M, 9
Russia, 27, 56, 58, 59, 61, 63, 69, 105, 111, 138, 141, 145, 153, 155, 156, 200, 207, 228, 257, 265, 266, 278, 279, 284, 285

Saudi Arabia, 59, 127, 160, 206
Scanning Rear Airspace: Historical Perspective of Combat Aviation, 17-30
afghanistan war, 2001 onwards, 25-26